THE OPENING OF TIBET

AN ACCOUNT OF LHASA AND THE COUNTRY AND PEOPLE OF CENTRAL TIBET AND OF THE PROGRESS OF THE MISSION SENT THERE BY THE ENGLISH GOVERNMENT IN THE YEAR 1903-04

THE OPENING OF TIBET

AN ACCOUNT OF LHASA AND THE COUNTRY AND PEOPLE OF CENTRAL TIBET AND OF THE PROGRESS OF THE MISSION SENT THERE BY THE ENGLISH GOVERNMENT IN THE YEAR 1903-04

PERCEVAL LANDON

INTRODUCTION BY
COLONEL YOUNGHUSBAND

ISBN : 978-93-5324-511-5 (HB)

First Published, New York, 1905

Published, 2020

Published by

Facsimile Publisher
12 Pragati Market
Ashok Vihar, Ph-2
Delhi-110052
E-mail: books@facsimilepublisher.com

Printed at: G. Print Process, Delhi.

The Opening of Tibet

Author: Perceval, Landon

THE OPENING OF TIBET

AN ACCOUNT OF LHASA AND THE COUNTRY AND PEOPLE OF CENTRAL TIBET AND OF THE PROGRESS OF THE MISSION SENT THERE BY THE ENGLISH GOVERNMENT IN THE YEAR 1903–4

WRITTEN, WITH THE HELP OF ALL THE PRINCIPAL PERSONS OF THE MISSION, BY

PERCEVAL LANDON

SPECIAL CORRESPONDENT OF THE "TIMES"

INTRODUCTION BY

COLONEL YOUNGHUSBAND

*πὰρ δ' ἴσαν ὠκεανοῦ τε ῥοὰς καὶ λευκάδα πέτρην
ἠδὲ παρ' 'ηελίοιο πύλας καὶ δῆμον ὀνείρων
ἤισαν.*

NEW YORK
DOUBLEDAY, PAGE & CO.
1905

THE AMERICAN EDITION OF THIS BOOK

IS DEDICATED TO

W. W. ROCKHILL, ESQ.,

HIS COUNTRY'S FOREMOST REPRESENTATIVE IN

THE FIELD OF TIBETAN EXPLORATION

CONTENTS

LIST OF ILLUSTRATIONS

INTRODUCTORY NOTE

We of the Tibet Mission and its escort were honored with the conduct of a task which for fascination of interest could hardly be surpassed. Few, if any, of us doubted the wisdom of the great and far-seeing statesman who initiated the enterprise and inspired it throughout. But, whether the policy was wise or unwise, we determined that it should not suffer in the execution. On us, we felt, were fixed the eyes of many millions, not in India alone, nor in England alone, but all over Europe and America also, and in many an Asiatic country besides.

We who work in India know what prestige means. Throughout the expedition we felt that our national honor was at stake, and down to the latest-joined sepoy we bent ourselves to uphold and raise higher the dignity of our Sovereign and the good name of our country: to show that not even the rigors of a Tibetan winter nor the obstinacy and procrastination of the two most stolid nations in the world could deter us from our purpose; above all, to try to effect that purpose without resorting to force. If, as unfortunately proved to be the case, fighting were inevitable, we were determined still to show moderation in the hour of victory, and to let the ignorant Tibetan leaders see that we would respect them as we demanded they should respect us, and, in place of distrust, to establish a confidence between us which would prove the surest foundation for future relations.

A loss of life was indeed necessitated which every one of us regretted; yet I for one believe that at any rate some good will come to the Tibetans as the result of our work. War does not always mean oppression. Nor does the breaking of the power of a despotic Government mean the down-treading of the people.

From the first the Tibetan peasantry showed good-will toward us. They were especially anxious to trade—no keener traders could be found. We have, as one result, partially freed the people from the terrible incubus of priestly control, and there are unmistakable signs that we left them better disposed toward us after our advance to Lhasa than they were before. Owing to the magnificent behavior of the troops, the confidence of the people was entirely gained. Villagers and traders thronged to our camps. Soldiers went about unmolested in every part of the Lhasa bazaar. Officers were admitted to the most sacred shrines. Captain O'Connor, my right-hand man in dealing with the Tibetans, was received not only with real ceremony, but with real warmth, by the Tashi Lama at Shigatse. And, last but by no means least, Tibetan wool-merchants are already making arrangements for trading with India.

How all this was effected none can tell better than Mr. Landon. He reveled in the mysteries of Tibet, and appreciated to the full the wonderful scenery which to my mind was infinitely the most fascinating of all our experiences. I have not had the advantage of reading the proofs of his book, and I cannot be responsible for any political views which he may have expressed. But I feel confident that no more competent chronicler of what the Tibet Mission saw and did could be found, and we were indeed fortunate in having with us one of his enthusiasm and powers of description.

F. E. Younghusband.

London,
December, 1904.

TO FRANK YOUNGHUSBAND

My dear Colonel:

It was into the mouth of a British chieftain in the first century that Tacitus put a criticism which has become famous. "Men," protested Calgacus, "are apt to be impressed chiefly by the unknown." In a sense, somewhat different from that in which it was originally intended, this estimate has remained just to the present day. Spread out the map of the world and there before you is proof enough of one of the most marked, most persistent—perhaps also one of the best—characteristics of an Englishman. You are but the latest of a succession of explorers which has no rival in the history of another race. The sturdy trampings of Sir John Mandeville, perhaps also his even more robust imaginings—be it remembered, that without the latter we should not have had the former—have had their successors in unbroken line to the present day. Other nations have had their home-keeping centuries—years in which the needs of commerce or high politics have demanded that they should for a time develop and not explore. But, decade after decade, the English have always had their representatives creeping on a little beyond the margin of the traveled world—men to whom beaten tracks were a burden, men for whom the "free air astir to windward" was inevitably more than the new-found territory, however rich, upon which they were just turning their backs.

Century after century it is the same old story. The instinctive tracks of voyagers in Elizabethan years; the restlessness ashore of merchant 'venturers the moment Blake had won for them and for us the peaceful occupation of the seas; the lonely dotted lines that drive a thin furrow of knowledge across the blank salt wastes of Australia; the quick evaporation of the mists of African ignorance; above all, the prosaic English place-names of arctic peak and tropical island and anchorage, unrevisited and unknown, except by a shore-line on an Admiralty chart no longer dotted as conjectural—all these have carried on an unconscious tradition; and there is no apology needed for the present story of another English expedition which won its way where all other living men have failed to go.

For us the door was opened, and though it has now again been locked as grimly as before, at least for many months we have lived in the very heart of the real Tibet. The course of our expedition lay through no deserted wastes of sand, through which a stealthy or disguised European creeps painfully from water-hole to water-hole, avoiding the least sign of man or human habitation, learning little and caring to learn less of the people from whose notice he is shrinking. We have moved through the only populous and politically important districts of the country, we have made our stay in the centers of Tibetan life, and of necessity we were brought into immediate contact with that mysterious government and religion upon which no other European transgressor into the forbidden land has been able to throw the light of personal knowledge. It has been but a passing chance, but perhaps for that very reason the more interest attaches to the simplest account of men and places upon which the curtain has again impenetrably fallen.

Yes, the chance has been a great one, but there is a touch of regret in our ability to use it. One cannot forget that the network of baffled explorers' routes which circumnavigate and sheer painfully off from Lhasa, represents the last of the greater explorations possible on this earth. The barriers that guard the pole are of nature's making only. It is not endurance only, or even chiefly, that has attracted us in the past, but for the future there will be little else for our explorer to fight. The hostility of man, which has added a spice of interest to all exploration hitherto, will never again whet the ambition of a voyager to an undiscovered land.

That the last country to be discovered by the civilized world should be one which has few rivals in its religious interests and importance, fewer still in the isolated development of its national characteristics, and none in its unique government and policy is a fitting close to the pioneer work of civilization; and that the English, who have long been faithful servants of that restlessness on which all progress is based, should have done the work, is not unjust; and that you, my dear Younghusband, should have been chosen to lead this rear-guard of exploration was for all concerned a good deal more than fortunate. In these pages I do not intend to praise, or indeed lay greater stress upon your work, or that of others, than such as the bare narrative may of itself suggest from time to time, but I am none the less aware of the debt which this country owes to your quiet constancy and determination.

I am,

My dear Younghusband,

Sincerely yours,

PERCEVAL LANDON.

5 PALL MALL PLACE, LONDON,
January 1st, 1905.

AN ACKNOWLEDGMENT

WRITERS on Tibet have acquired an unenviable reputation for concealing their indebtedness to other workers in the same field; I take this opportunity of saying that it would be difficult for me to set down the full number of those to whom I am indebted for help in the writing of this work. Besides the authors of all books on the subject, I am glad to think that there is hardly a man on the expedition who, consciously or not, has not added his tale of help to the book, and will not recognize lurking in some phrase or footnote a fact which could only have been given me by himself. Some, however, I must single out for my especial thanks, and in mentioning these I trust that I may not be regarded as ungrateful by those whose names I am compelled to omit. The actual writer of such a book as this is among the last to whom a reader should feel gratitude.

To Sir Francis Younghusband, to Lord Curzon, and to Captain W. F. T. O'Connor, to Captain H. J. Walton, Lord Ampthill, and the late Major Bretherton, to Mr. Claude White, Lieutenant-Colonel L. A. Waddell, Colonel Sir James R. L. Macdonald, Captain C. H. D. Ryder, and Captain H. M. Cowie, to Mr. E. C. Wilton, Lieutenant-Colonels Iggulden and Beynon, Mr. H. H. Hayden, and to Majors Sheppard and Ottley, my obligations throughout the following pages are continual and, I hope, obvious. Less patent but almost equally indispensable for any success has been the help I have received from Mr. L. Dane, Sir Edward Maunde Thompson, Mr. Filson Young, Mr. Herbert Blackett, Mr. A. W. Paul, and Mr. Valentine Chirol. I should be glad to receive any additional information, notes, or criticisms, as I hope to make of "The Opening of Tibet" a work of Tibetan reference, and, in any future edition, shall carefully revise the book up to date.

THE OPENING OF TIBET

THE OPENING OF TIBET

CHAPTER I

FORMER EXPLORATIONS OF TIBET

THE earliest historical relic of the Tibetans—like that of many, perhaps of most, other races—is a weather-beaten stone, the Do-ring. It stands in the center of Lhasa, across the courtyard in front of the western doors of the Cathedral or Jo-kang, beneath the famous willow-tree. Like Asoka's pillars on the one hand or the Black Stone of Mukden on the other, it both records a treaty and is the outward symbol of the prosperity of Tibet. One might also add that, like the Omphalos at Delphi or London Stone, it is to the Tibetans not only the center of their strange shoulder-blade-shaped earth, but, more practical, the goal from which their journeys and stages are reckoned. But the Do-ring is even more than this. The terms of the treaty of 783 A.D., now barely decipherable upon its cup-marked surface, corroborate, in some degree, the legendary history of Tibet so far as it can be found in Chinese chronicles.

This history is not one of great interest, and may be chiefly dismissed as one of continued hostility with China, but of hostility on equal terms. That the result of these border skirmishings was by no means as uniformly satisfactory to China as one might imagine from her version of the events, is clear, for about the year 640 A.D. the King of Tibet, Srong-tsan-gambo, succeeded in obtaining the hand of a princess of the imperial house of Tang against the will of the emperor and after some years' fighting.

The story of this Srong-tsan-gambo is incrusted with inconsistent legend. He appears to have been a devout Buddhist, to have married also a Nepalese princess, to have led an army into India, where, about the year 648, he inflicted a defeat upon the King of Magadha, from which place he carried off the famous image which is to this day the chief and central treasure of the Jokang. Another story says that it was presented as a free gift from the Buddhists of Magadha by the hand of the returning Tonmi-Sambhota, a minister whom Srong-tsan-gambo had despatched to India to inquire more perfectly about the Buddhist religion. The legend that this man introduced writing, and his Chinese wife several of the best-known arts of her own country, merely reflects the impetus given to foreign influences in Lhasa by the origin and travels of the two.

Srong-tsan-gambo's grandson, Ti-srong-de-tsan, resumed hostilities with China, and in 763 actually sacked the capital, Changan, or Hsia-Fu. Before that he also had given proof of his Buddhist zeal by inviting the famous Buddhist saint Padma Sambhava to visit his country. This was a more important matter than it then appeared, and was destined to mold indefinitely the future of Tibet; for, apart from his personal influence at the time, this man, known also as Padma Pani or the Guru Rinpoche, founded the Samye monasteries and the Red Cap school in 749, and eventually reappears as the central figure of Lamaism—actually more important than the Buddha himself in its tradition and ritual. And it is his soul, itself a re-incarnation of that of Amitabha, the Bodisat, which is born again both in the person of the Grand Lama of Tashi-lhunpo, and, vicariously, as Avalokiteswara, in the body of the Dalai Lama or Grand Lama of Lhasa also. To this king Ti-srong-de-tsan must be credited more than military skill or religious fervor. It is clear that the position of Tibet as a sacrosanct center of religion is due to his recognition of the vast importance of Tibet as offering a permanent home to the faith which was being slowly but completely expelled from India at this time. War after war followed his death, and in or about 783 his successor, King Ralpachan, made with the Emperor Tai-tsang the Second the treaty which is engraved upon the Do-ring at Lhasa. It is to be noted that the high-sounding epithets which the contracting parties apply to themselves already reflect the semi-sacred and mystic importance of Tibet.

These dry particulars are necessary in order to understand much of later Lamaism, but the era of important legend closes with the assassination of Lang-darma, the younger brother of Ralpachan, who had ascended the throne in 899. Lang-darma, who had murdered his brother to clear the way for his own succession, is the Buddhist Julian, and the assassination of this persecutor of the faith is still annually observed in Lhasa on the threshold of the Jo-kang, where a fanatic monk achieved his purpose at the cost of his own life. From this date onward Tibet was divided into a large number of petty principalities, and its history is for many centuries obscure. Lamaism, however, flourished at the expense of the body politic, and in 1038 Atisha or Jo Ji-pal-den again reformed the religion of the country. In 1206 the country was conquered by the Tartars, and in 1270 Kublai khan recognized the supremacy of the head Lama of the Sakya monastery as titular ruler of Tibet, an arrangement which lasted until the foundation of the Yellow or Gelukpa sect by Tsong-kapa in the fifteenth century and the final establishment of the re-incarnate hierarchy of Lhasa two hundred years later. But before that momentous *coup d'état*, the first European traveler had entered Tibet, and it is the aim of this chapter rather to give a brief account of the attempts of foreign nations to enter into communication with this hermit country, than to dwell at any length upon its internal history.

Friar Odoric or Ordericus of Pordenone, a Minorite friar, appears to have visited Tibet about the year 1328. He was returning from the east coast of China, by Shensi, hoping eventually to strike the main European caravan routes through Asia. It seems clear that he never reached Lhasa. Astley dismisses him as "the prince of liars," but some of his notes are good and interesting. He reports of the capital of Tibet that its walls are black and white; that its streets are well paved; that the Buddhist prohibition against the taking of life was strictly observed there; and that the Tibetans of the country districts lived, as now, in black yak-hair tents. The title of the Grand Lama of Sakya he gives as Abassi, in which a reflection of the Latin title of the chief of a monastery may probably be seen.

But from that time there is a blank of many years, at the end of which the present régime was established by Tsong-kapa,[1] a monk from the then populous region of Koko-nor, far to the northeast of Lhasa. His reformations were sweeping in their scope, and though at this day the various sects of Lamaism are divided rather by tradition, ritual, and costume than by any vital dogmatic schism, the stricter moral code of the Gelukpas or Yellow Caps, Tsong-kapa's sect, is still to be recognized. Before the next European visited Lhasa, the Gelukpas had consolidated their rule, and in 1624 Antonio Andrada, of the Society of Jesus, found the chief power in their hands at Tashi-lhunpo. This missionary was the author of the most widely known description of Tibet until the travels of Turner were issued at the close of the eighteenth century. But it is certain that his acquaintance with the country was limited to the western and northern parts—Lhasa still remained unvisited.

The doctrine of political re-incarnation had now been fully accepted. The first re-incarnation of Amitabha or Manjusri[2]—the Indian synonyms are conveniently used for the chief personages of the Greater Vehicle of Buddhism—was Gedun-tubpa, Grand Lama of Tashi-lhunpo, in whom Tsong-kapa recognized the per-

[1] "He of the Orion Land."

[2] The Tibetan name is Chenrezig.

sonality of Padma Sambhava. Gedun-tubpa thus founded a series of re-incarnations near Shigatse, of which the successive holders made such good use that toward the middle of the seventeenth century Na-wang Lob-sang made himself master of Tibet. But he then transferred his capital to Lhasa, accepted the title of Dalai Lama from the Emperor of China,[1] built the Potala palace, and, most important of all, discovered that, besides being, as Grand Lama of Tashi-lhunpo, a re-incarnation of Amitabha, he was also a reappearance of Avalokiteswara. This produced a curious result, for Avalokiteswara was an emanation of Amitabha and, therefore, inferior to his "father" as touching his potential manhood. Thus, though the entire political power has been absorbed by the Dalai or Grand Lama of Lhasa, the Tashi Lama—as the Grand Lama of Tashi-lhunpo is commonly called—remains in theory his senior and superior in spiritual matters. A government, similar in most respects to that which is now established, was afterward inaugurated, the forcible introduction by the Chinese Emperor of two Ambans or Viceroys with a strong guard being the result of the Dzungarian raid and the occupation of Lhasa in 1717. Chinese suzerainty may be said to date from 1720.

In 1662, in the middle of Na-wang Lob-sang's revolution, the first European, Father Johann Grueber, also a Jesuit, reached Lhasa in company with Father Dorville. He left few records of his travels, but Astley's "Collection of Voyages" contains an abstract of his account of this journey. Lhasa—or, as he calls it, Barantola—is described as the capital of the country and the residence of the Buddhist Pope, whose castle "Butala" reminded Grueber of the Rhenish fortresses of his own fatherland. He remarks that the religion was essentially identical with Christianity,

[1] The title means Ocean (of learning). It has originated the perpetual "surname" of Gya-tso (expanse of water) for the successive re-incarnations of the Dalai Lama.

though, as he says, no Christian was ever in the country before. Among other remarks which are true of Tibetans to-day, he mentions the feminine habits of wearing the hair plaited tightly into a number of small cords, of bearing the "patug" or turquoise-studded head-dress, and of smearing the face with kutch.[1] In 1708 the Capuchin mission in India was pushed forward and four fathers were sent to make a settlement in Lhasa. Elsewhere I have sketched the career of this ill-fated hospice. For the moment it is only necessary to say that it was persecuted by the Jesuits and eventually abandoned in 1745. Brother Orazio della Penna of this mission acquired a perfect knowledge of the Tibetan language. He wrote an account of the country, which is a somewhat bald aggregation of facts and fancies. To him is probably due our knowledge of the mineral wealth of the country, and a certain light upon its internal dissensions during the first quarter of the eighteenth century. His summary of the chief features of Lamaism is colored by the scholasticism of his own religion.

Hippolito Desideri and Manuel Freyre, Jesuit spies, reached Lhasa in 1716, and stayed there thirteen years, until they were recalled by the Pope. The manuscripts of the former are still unpublished, but, contrary to general belief, they have been thoroughly examined, and full extracts have from time to time been made from them for private use. About this time the famous survey of China was made under the auspices of the Jesuit colony in Peking.

One Samuel Van der Putte was the next visitor. He was a shrewd, adventurous Dutchman, and twice succeeded in making his way to Lhasa. But the anti-foreign prejudices of the Tibetans

[1] Grueber drew a picture of the Potala palace in his day, which is of considerable interest. In its earlier state it must have resembled Gyangtse-jong in the disposition, character, and stability of its buildings, and it is also clear that the gigantic buttress-building which sweeps sheer up the side of the rock from the plain to the Dalai Lama's own palace covers two deep ravines which are probably converted into secret treasure chambers at this moment. See Appendix B.

were fermenting. Van der Putte was obliged to travel between China and India in disguise, and during the whole of his stay in Tibet and China—a period of about twelve years, 1724-1735—was unable to compile any connected narrative owing to the danger which surrounded him. He made his notes upon slips of paper, and ultimately, in fear lest improper or inaccurate use should be made of them, ordered them in his will to be burned. He appears also to have kept a small journal which was, it seems, destroyed at the same time. It is difficult to find a parallel to the loss which scientific exploration has suffered by the holocaust of the entire notes of a man who was equally distinguished as a traveler, a linguist, and a scientific expert.

About this time the names of three Englishmen are conspicuous among those who have explored Tibet. It is, indeed, almost entirely upon their notes that our information as to the interior of Tibet rested until the organization of the traveling Pundits by the Indian Survey Office comparatively late in the nineteenth century. Between the years 1774 and 1812 Mr. George Bogle, a young writer of the East India Company, Lieutenant Samuel Turner, and Mr. Thomas Manning—an eccentric mathematician and Oriental scholar—all penetrated with more or less success into this country of mystery. The three men represented different types: Bogle, as his diary shows, was, though a comparatively young man, a peculiarly suitable envoy for the delicate work which Warren Hastings intrusted to him. The Governor himself showed in his dealings with Tibet the same grasp and foresight that characterized his actions in every part of his huge Dependency; he realized the importance of securing friendly relations with a country which seemed at that time to be the most obvious link between Bengal and the rest of Asia. He therefore sent George Bogle, as the accredited agent of the Company, to establish communication, and, if possible, improve the commercial intercourse between the two countries. A thin current of merchandise filtered down over the passes into India, its owners exchanging the musk, wool, and turquoises of Tibet for the rice and hardware of India, but it is not likely that Warren Hastings had any very definite intention to open up a thoroughfare to India from the north and east. Many years were needed to consolidate the British rule in Bengal, and he had difficulties enough in India proper to contend with without in any way inviting the interference of outside tribes or nations. It is probable that his chief aim was to secure information. Nothing whatever was known of this particular route between India and Tibet; the very names of the towns, the nature of the country, the disposition of its inhabitants, its products, its government, all were alike unknown, and George Bogle was set a task by Hastings which might well have daunted a diplomatist more experienced than the young and unknown writer twenty-seven years of age. But from first to last he carried through his mission with unfailing tact, and, so far as it was possible, with complete success. His object was not Lhasa. The Dalai Lama was then a boy of fifteen, and the virtual government of the country lay in the hands of the Tashi Lama; this man, whose name was Jetsun Poldan Yé Shé, has remained the most distinguished figure in all the list of re-incarnate Grand Lamas. He was a man of commanding personality, of wide-minded sympathy and toleration, and remarkable, even beyond the confines of his country, for his courtesy and wisdom. To him, therefore, Bogle was sent, and making his way through Bhutan, he arrived at Tashi-lhunpo without serious delay in December, 1774. His diary and the official report which he sent to Warren Hastings, by that time appointed first Governor-General of India, contain by far the most judicious description of the life and customs of the inhabitants of this unknown country that has been written. He was received as an honored guest, and, though, indeed, he was asked not to press his request for permission to visit Lhasa, the favor of the Tashi Lama was sufficient to secure for him unique opportunities of examining the nature, habits, and peculiarities of this unknown neighbor across the Himalayas. All that could be done to promote friendly relations between the two countries was cheerfully attempted by the Tashi Lama, but it is clear from Bogle's own account that he met with considerable opposition from the representatives of Lhasa, even in the court of the actual ruler of Tibet, and the death of the Tashi Lama shortly afterward, combined with the accession to supreme power of the Dalai Lama in 1776, effectually put an end to any hope of an amicable understanding between the two countries. Bogle's narrative will be quoted in the following pages, and it would be difficult to improve on the shrewd insight and steady judgment with which many of the peculiarities of Tibet were unerringly noted down, generally with some characteristic comment, shrewd or satirical.

After the death of the Tashi Lama in 1780, followed within six months by the decease of Bogle himself at Calcutta, and the consequent failure of his intended scheme, Warren Hastings determined to make another attempt. Samuel Turner, his own cousin, was despatched at the head of a small party to Tashi-lhunpo. After some delay in Bhutan he successfully accomplished the journey, traveling over the same route as that which had been taken by Bogle, and reached Tashi-lhunpo on the 22d of September, 1783. Turner, however, found that the center of Government had been transferred to Lhasa; the new Tashi Lama was an infant, and the Dalai Lama showed no disposition whatever to allow his visitor even to discuss the object of his mission. After formally congratulating the Tashi-lhunpo hierarchy upon the speedy and successful re-incarnation of the deceased primate, he took his leave. On his return to England, Turner embodied the result of his observations in a sumptuously printed volume, illustrated with steel engravings, which for a long time remained the only English printed record of

Great Tibet, and we owe a deep debt of gratitude to Sir Clements Markham for having given to the world, in 1875, the somewhat more interesting and reliable account written by Turner's predecessor at the Tashi court.

The third, and last, name of these three, Mr. Manning, presents one of the most curious psychological studies in the whole history of travel. That he was a man eccentric in his habits and tastes throughout his life may be fairly argued from his behavior during his last years, but it is difficult to reconcile the extraordinary energy, courage, and fixity of purpose which enabled him successfully to carry through, at the utmost personal risk, the most dangerous expedition that any man in his day could attempt, with the utter vacuity of the only record which he has left of his great and successful enterprise. It is not too much to say that on no single point did the recent expedition glean a fact or an opinion of the slightest use from the record left by a man who, presumably for the purpose of observation, had traveled over a route to Lhasa which for the most part was identical with that of 1904. From the first day recorded in his journal, the 7th of September, 1811, to his return to Indian territory, in June of the following year, such notes as these constitute the main bulk of his observations:

"I came in thoroughly wet and dried my clothes on my body. Afterward, upon walking across the room, I was seized with a violent palpitation. The insects disturbed me all night.

"I saw a lad gnawing a turnip, and called to him immediately, and, showing it to my conductor, asked the name and told him to give me plenty of it. I thus got an excellent well-dressed stew with turnips."

His account of his own behavior during the crossing of the Tsang-po is one which most Englishmen would have blushed to recall, far more to incorporate in their record of travel.

"The reminiscences occasioned by the motion of the boat

brought on a fit of European activity. I could not sit still, but must climb about, seat myself in various postures on the parapet, and lean over. The master of the boat was alarmed, and sent a steady man to hold me tight. I pointed to the ornamented prow of the boat, and assured them that I could sit there with perfect safety, and to prove to them how commodiously I was seated, bent my head and body down the outside of the boat to the water's edge; but finding, by their renewed instances for me to desist, that I made them uneasy, I went back to my place and seated myself quietly. As the boat drew near shore I meditated jumping over, but was pulled back by the immense weight of my clothes and the clumsiness of my boots. I was afraid of jumping short, and having the laugh against me."

The manner in which he permitted his Chinese servant to treat him is a revelation to those who know the East. His only protest against the discourtesy, insubordination, disobedience, and, at last, openly expressed contempt of his Chinese servant, was to fill the pages of his diary day after day, and week after week, with whining complaints of the man's "unkindness." It will hardly be believed that, after he had achieved the end which he had set before him, and at last actually found himself inside the Sacred City, he still occupies himself with petty personal grievances, with long notes upon the treatment which he applied to his patients there, with the effect of his medicines, and with lengthy moral disquisitions upon the underlying influences which affect all human nature alike. Until almost the end of his visit, with the doors of the Jo-kang open to him, he does not seem to have visited a single temple, and when at last he did so he occupied a page of his diary by a petty narration of his servant's incivility and his own silly conduct; of the temples visited, he left no description whatever, and the only clear thing is that the Jo-kang was not one of them.

Manning returned to England after this great expedition and lived a life of seclusion, and, it must be confessed, of eccentricity. Sir Clements Markham has published the diary to which reference has been made, and it certainly possesses a very remarkable interest, if not as a record of observation, at least as a psychological document which has probably no parallel in the world.

With one exception, the record of Tibetan travel from that day to the present year is, so far as Europeans are concerned, a record of interesting and picturesque failure. That exception was the visit of two Jesuit Fathers, Evariste Huc and Joseph Gabet. Traveling by the southwestern route from China, through Sining, these two adventurous priests reached Lhasa in January, 1846. After a stay of less than seven weeks they were expelled by the Amban, and returned to China by the eastern route through Tachienlu. The book which Huc wrote upon his travels in Eastern Asia is graphic and vivacious, and the picture which he draws of his own experiences in Lhasa is graphic and true; but of the natural and architectural features he says almost nothing, and there was wanting in him a realization of the intense importance, as well as interest, of his travels. It is true that many of his statements, which at the time were received with undisguised incredulity, have since received corroboration from later travelers, but Huc cannot be said to have added very much to our scientific knowledge of the countries through which he passed, and, though his narrative possesses a racy charm of its own which will always make it a popular classic in the history of missionary effort, it is greatly to be regretted that he did not use his unique opportunities in a steadier and better informed record of the national and physical peculiarities of this almost virgin country.

As has been said, the record of all other travel to Lhasa has been a record of failure.[1] In the whole history of exploration,

[1] Huc gives a curious account of the supposed visit of an Englishman, Moorcroft, to Lhasa. Briefly stated, his assertion is that, though William Moor-

there is no more curious map than that which shows the tangled lines of travelers' routes toward this city, coming in from all sides, north, south, east, and west, crossing, interlocking, retracing, all with one goal, and all baffled, some soon after the journey had been begun, some when the travelers might almost believe that the next hill would give them a distant glimpse of the golden roofs of the Potala. It has often been remarked to the writer that this consistent failure to reach a known spot, barely 200 miles from our own frontier, across a thinly inhabited region, has never yet been accounted for. As a matter of fact, the reason is, I think, clear enough when that region has been visited. Roughly stated, there is in Tibet only one way of going from one place to another, whether the necessity lies in the nature of the ground or in the inability to obtain food, fuel, and fodder elsewhere, and that in itself effectually reduces the chance of traveling without attracting observation. Thanks to the extraordinary system of Chinese postal relays, it is absolutely impossible for a traveler to prevent the news of his arrival reaching Lhasa. The population of Tibet is, it is true, small, and it might be thought that therefore a traveler enjoyed greater opportunities of escaping detection. It is a fact that one may go, not for hours only, but for days, along a well-known trade route without meeting a soul more than half a mile from the nearest village. But this very scantiness of population is the undoing of the trespasser; every face is as well known to the Tibetan villager as the face of the local Chinese official, to whom, under horrible penalties, the presence of a stranger, in whatever guise, must be at once reported. The

croft is supposed to have died in 1825 at "Andkou," he really reached Lhasa in 1826, and lived there for twelve years undetected. Even his own servant believed him to be a Kashmiri. He was assassinated by brigands on his return journey, and the discovery of elaborate maps upon his person after death was the first indication to the Lhasans of his nationality. It must be remembered that Huc had this story direct from the Regent in Lhasa only eight years afterward. The authority for the fact of his death in 1825 is a letter written by Trebeck, his companion. Trebeck himself died a few days later.

merchants who pass up and down upon the road are the only new faces that the Tibetan sees from year to year. High Lama officials may hurry through, and now and then the Chinese garrison of the nearest post may be relieved, but in both these cases there is a robe or uniform readily distinguishable by the villager, and he would be a daring man indeed who would attempt to thrust himself in disguise into the company of either the actual, or the nominal, ruling class in Tibet. Excepting these two classes, every passer-by along the high road is subject to an unceasing scrutiny, which, it can readily be understood, has hitherto effectually prevented all attempts to visit the Forbidden City by stealth.

We have not space to include even the briefest summary of these plucky but doomed enterprises, but each of the tracks that contribute to the tangled skein which envelops Lhasa has its own peculiar interest. One remembers, one after another, the light-hearted and purposeless raid of Bonavalot and Prince Henri d'Orleans in 1890, the steady and scientifically invaluable progress of Bower and Thorold in 1891, the triple attempts of Rockhill—a determined American, whom every one in the column would gladly have seen accompanying us into the city he had striven to reach for so many years at such a cost of time and labor—and the debt which geography owes to Henry and Richard Strachey must not be forgotten. All of these enterprises have, unfortunately, not ended in failure alone, and the murder of Dutreuil de Rhins, in 1894, and the disappearance of Mr. Rijnhart, in 1898, remain as significant proof of the very real danger which has been in the past, and, so far as one can forecast the future, will still remain an inevitable characteristic of travel in Tibet. Of all these journeys, that of the Littledales, in 1894, was perhaps the most interesting, and those who knew either Mr. Littledale, or his nephew, Mr. Fletcher, will realize that further progress was absolutely and irrevocably prevented when even these two determined men acquiesced in the inevitable and gave up the attempt when within 70 miles of their long-desired goal.

The work of Russians in Tibet has been watched with some interest from India, and the names of Przhevalsky, Roborovsky, Kozlov, and Pevtsov honorably recall a series of explorations, extended over many years, of which the pursuit and ultimate object were none the less admirable in themselves because they did not happen to commend it to the policy of the British Government.

These men were, of course, all Europeans. Of the secret surveys undertaken by the Indian Government I shall speak later.

Of Sven Hedin, it is not necessary to remind the reader. His own gallant attempt to reach Lhasa, which occupied over two years, is sufficiently recent to need no further description at this moment. His own record—unostentatious, and bearing the stamp of accurate observation in every line—is still wet from the press, and, though his adverse opinion as to the justice of our expedition had been freely expressed, the regret felt by every member of the Mission that Sven Hedin was not with us in Lhasa was genuine and deep.

CHAPTER II

THE REASONS FOR THE EXPEDITION

FOR many years there were almost no relations between the English conquerors of India and Tibet; but so far as any might be said to exist, they were, if anything, friendly. The policy of isolation which the authorities of Lhasa adopted had been formulated first in the early years of the eighteenth century, and we must not suppose that even previous to that date the lamas would have been willing to allow strangers to come to their capital in any numbers. But, as a matter of fact, the incredible remoteness of Lhasa, and the extreme difficulty of the road thither, had always prevented any but the hardiest from even attempting the grim journey. When, therefore, it became obvious that European trade and European traders were going to flourish in the Far East, it made no great difference that the Lhasan authorities decided once for all that strangers were not welcome there. This decree, however, they did not put into force with extreme rigor for a long time, and it is possible that Bogle, so late as 1774, might after all have succeeded in overcoming the opposition of the Regent.

Chinese supremacy over Tibet nominally dates from the year 1720, and as about that time the policy of isolation was adopted, it is not unreasonable to suppose that the Chinese pressed it upon the Tibetans with the idea of making a "buffer state" of the most impenetrable description between their western province and the unknown but growing power of the foreigners in India. Perhaps it was not the white foreigners alone that they dreaded; Nadir Shah's invasion of India in 1727 must have been the cause of some anxiety to the Middle Kingdom. In any case we may fairly accept the definite statement of many travelers that the isolation of Tibet was in its origin a Chinese device. But they taught willing pupils, and the tables are now so far reversed that the Chinese are unable to secure admittance into the province even for the strangers to whom they have given official permission. Mr. W. W. Rockhill, than whom no man has earned more deservedly a reputation for Tibetan erudition, has of course long wished to visit Lhasa. The American Government, on three occasions, has sent in a request to the Chinese that he should be permitted to make the journey, and that the Tibetan authorities should be compelled to receive him. The first promise was readily granted; the second, that which presupposed a real suzerainty over the Tibetans, they were frankly unable to make. They did their best: three times, as the suzerain power, they sent an order to Lhasa. Three times the Dalai Lama flatly and unconditionally refused even to consider Mr. Rockhill's admission.[1] The main responsibility, therefore, for the exclusion of foreigners from Tibet rests now with the Lamaic hierarchy. But the great game of exchanging responsibilities is as well known to those Oriental hermits as it was to the firm of Spenlow and Jorkins. At one time the Chinese said that they were willing enough to allow strangers to travel freely in Tibet, but they deplored their inability to coerce the Lhasan Government; the Lhasan Government, on the other hand, stated that they would be glad to see foreigners within their borders, but unfortunately the orders of China were imperative. Latterly, however, the Tibetans abandoned this pretense, and at a great meeting of the Tsong-du, which was attended by representatives from all parts of the country, they made a national vow that no stranger, under any circumstances whatever, should

[1] This we discovered after our arrival in Lhasa.

henceforth be permitted to enter the country. This vow they made doubly sure by annexing it as an article of faith to the Buddhist creed! One of Colonel Younghusband's earliest diplomatic successes was the silencing of this plea. He asked them whether it were indeed part of the Buddhist faith or not? They answered that it was; he replied, that he knew the Buddhist scriptures well, and that nowhere from end to end of them was there one word which could justify this assertion. Retreating a little from their position, the Tibetans then said, "Well, it is not perhaps really an article of faith, but we have decided that so it must be." To this Colonel Younghusband naturally answered that those who could make could also unmake, and that if their religion were not concerned there was no reason that they should not at once reconsider what was a mere matter of policy.

Had the Tibetans confined themselves to this assertion of their inviolability, our relations with the country would have remained as satisfactory as could have been wished. The loss of trade was after all a small matter, and, in any case, it was one which the Tibetans had every right to decide. But the presence in Lhasa of a single man began the trouble which eventually made the expedition necessary. The history of Dorjieff may as well be told at once.

About twenty-five years ago there arrived in Lhasa a young lama from the Siberian steppes to the east of Lake Baikal. He was by birth a Mongolian Buriat, but by nationality a Russian subject. He was born at a place called Azochozki, and was destined from his youth to holy orders. He came to Lhasa and was received into that hot-bed of sedition, the Debung monastery, where, displaying unusual ability, he ultimately became professor of metaphysics. In no way did he dabble in political affairs, and he seemed destined to spend the autumn of his life as a teacher. He had reached the age of fifty-two when, more by chance than by design, he found himself involved in high international politics, and entered upon the adventurous career of intrigue which has made his name notorious in the chancelleries of Calcutta, London, and St. Petersburg. His first journey from Lhasa to Russia was innocent enough; he was sent in 1898 to collect contributions from the faithful, of whom there are many communities in the southeastern provinces of Russia in Europe. He traveled in the country from town to town, and at last the Russian ministers seemed to have awakened to the opportunity which lay before them.

Throughout this book I do not wish to suggest that Russia, in attempting to gain influence in Lhasa, was guilty of anything which reflects the least discredit upon her statesmen. On the other hand, it was a far-sighted and, from many points of view, an entirely laudable attempt to consolidate the Central Asian Empire which she believes to be her rightful heritage. The only reason why the British found it necessary to intervene was that the equally justifiable policy which they had themselves deliberately adopted, and their own vastly greater interests in Tibet, clashed all along the line with those of the Muscovite. Except that we have no wish to make ourselves responsible for the protection and good government of this huge and unwieldy province, the aims of the government of the Tzar are no doubt those of ourselves also. On either side it has been a mere measure of self-protection; we happen to have been the better placed to achieve our end. What the Russians did in allowing Dorjieff to represent them unofficially in Lhasa we should have been glad to be able to do, and it is a deplorable thing that the millions of northern Buddhists under our sway do not produce men of the capacity which is exhibited by a Dorjieff or a Norzunoff; if these men were to be found I fancy we should have used them willingly long ago. For these quick-witted adventurers are often the most effective screen which can be interposed between two advancing nationalities, so long, of course, as they are officially recognized by neither. But there was no one whom we could oppose to the dexterity of this Buriat lama.

He was originally best known by his Tibetan name, Ghomang Lobzang, but after his adoption of the position in which he has become famous, he is known to Western nations by his Russian title of Dorjieff—a name, by the way, which is merely a Russianized form of the typical Tibetan word, which means a "thunder-bolt," a "diamond," or, more important than all, the ultimate symbol of Lamaic authority, a small brass ornament, shaped somewhat like two royal crowns joined together by an inch of molded brass. Other names, too, he has; Kawaguchi, the Japanese traveler, refers to him as Ngaku-wang-dorje; the commonest name in Lhasa itself for this man was that of his official position, or Khende-chega, and his name appears also as Akohwan Darjilikoff. This list does not exhaust the number of his aliases, but it may indicate why the Government of India took some time to realize that one and the same man lay behind these different personalities which had, it was clear enough, at least one bond of union—that of hostility to British influence.

Precisely what took place in Russia has not been made public, but in these days of indiscreet memoirs it is not likely that the true inner history of Dorjieff's mission to Russia will long remain a secret. All that is known is that when he returned to Tibet, Ghomang Lobzang found himself in the unofficial position of Russian agent in Lhasa. He brought with him a large number of exceedingly valuable presents, and he lost no time in trying to persuade the Lhasan hierarchy that it was to their interest to secure the informal protection of the Tzar of Russia. Briefly stated, his arguments were these: You have no strength in the country to resist invaders; your natural protector and suzerain, China, is a broken reed; even at this moment she is entirely under the domination of the British. If you remain any longer trusting to her support, you will find that she has thrown you as a sop to the Indian Government. The English are a rapacious and heretical nation; they will not respect your religion; they will bring you into servitude, and the ancient and honorable rule of the priests in this country will be surely put an end to. On the other hand, if you will ask the aid of Russia you will secure the most powerful protector in the world. You will have gained on your side the only military power which is able to crush the English nation. More than that, you may be able to induce the great monarch of that nation to embrace your faith. Another emperor, as great as he, has in past ages been converted to our great faith, and if you can convince Nicholas, whose sympathies with Buddhism are universally admitted, it will not be long before the whole Russian race are obedient servants and loyal disciples of your Holiness.

Such, in rough outline, was Dorjieff's policy. It produced an almost immediate effect upon the Dalai Lama himself. Impetuously, without consulting his national council, he accepted the suggestion, and even proposed to visit St. Petersburg in person. The sacred cushion on which his Holiness should sit in audience with the Tzar, and a beautiful *codex aureus* from his own library, were sent at once, and will probably remain in the Imperial museum on the banks of the Neva as a curious and significant reminiscence of the great and daring policy which so nearly succeeded in Russianizing, at a stroke, the most autocratic and far-reaching religious empire of Asia. But the Dalai Lama had reckoned too hastily; the Tsong-du had still to be consulted, and here the Dalai Lama received a check which was the beginning of all the internal troubles which have hampered the proper management of Tibetan diplomacy ever since. The Tsong-dü replied diplomatically that it was very nice of the Russian Emperor, but that they required no protection, and that the Dalai Lama had exceeded his authority in committing the country even to a consideration of Dorjieff's offer. The Grand Lama did all in his power to induce them to accept his scheme, but without avail, and the next year another ruse was adopted by Dorjieff to further the interests of his patrons.

He went again to St. Petersburg, and there was received in audience by the Emperor himself; he returned after a short stay, the bearer of two interesting things.[1] One was a letter, asking that the Dalai Lama should despatch an envoy to Russia to discuss the matter more fully. The other was a complete set of vestments appertaining to a Bishop of the Russian Church. Later on in this book their importance and significance will be referred to; for the moment, the political fruits of this embassy to St. Petersburg claim our attention. In spite of the recent declarations of the Tsong-du, the Dalai Lama, on his own responsibility, sent in response Tsan-nyid, an abbot of high rank, to accompany Dorjieff, who, a month after his arrival at Lhasa, was again on the road to Europe. The two men made their way through Nepal and India to Colombo, where they embarked on a Russian vessel for Odessa. Upon their arrival in Russia they were received with the highest consideration, and a second audience with the Tzar was granted them. Ultimately they set off on their return journey and reached Lhasa about December, 1901. They there laid before the Dalai Lama a proposal from the Russian Government, that a Prince of the royal house should take up his residence in Lhasa for the purpose of promoting friendly relations between the two countries. It may well be imagined, whether it were so expressed or not in the message, that the Russians would have considered it necessary that a small armed guard should accompany his Imperial Highness. The other document which the returning abbot laid before his master was the hotly discussed agreement between Russia and Tibet. Those who deny that a treaty was

[1] It is of some interest to note that he made the record journey between Urga and Lhasa; he covered the distance in ninety days.

A TIBETAN MONK WITH HIS PRAYER-WHEEL

ever formally made between Tibet and Russia are perfectly correct. It requires no great perspicacity to see that under the relations then existing between Tibet and China no such treaty could have been valid, even if it had been made. But it was not made; the treaty, the terms of which were definite enough, remained rather as a pledge than as an assurance; it represented, in a permanent form, the kindly feelings of the Russians toward Tibet; it was there to encourage the Tibetans should any difficulty arise with their southern neighbors; it was a comfortable guarantee that the Russians would encourage Buddhism in their extending empire of Central Asia. In return, the Russians asked for facilities which the poor people of Lhasa may be pardoned for having misunderstood. Concessions to construct railways must seem insignificant enough to a country which has not a wheel within its borders except a prayer-wheel; but to the eye of the uncharitable European diplomatist the very mention of railways in connection with Russia calls up a wide field of reminiscence and implication. That treaty was an informal reduction to terms of an unratified and an unratifiable arrangement with Tibet. It was none the less dangerous. The Chinese officials in Lhasa were from the first aware of it, and at once attributed to this understanding with Russia the sudden insolence and insubordination with which Tibet continued to treat the advice and even the orders of their suzerain.

So far as the Dalai Lama was concerned, the treaty would have been signed at once, but the other authorities were immovable. On behalf of the suzerain's power, the Chinese Viceroy denounced it as treason to his Imperial master; as to the proposed residence of a Russian Grand Duke, the objections of the high officials to the intrusion of a European among them, be he prince or peasant, were loud and universal. The Tsong-du refused to be drawn into the discussion again, or to allow the Chinese Emperor's position as suzerain of Tibet to be ousted by the Tzar, or by any one else!

The Dalai Lama, in bitter anger, then adopted other tactics; if he could not persuade the Tsong-du to accept Russian protection by fair means, he was not averse to use others. From this date onward he was without question riding for a fall with the English. To provoke aggression with India would, in his opinion, bring the whole matter to a crisis. The Chinese were neither willing nor able to interfere effectually to protect Tibet. The Russians were, as he believed, both able and willing, and he looked to compel the Tsong-du to adopt his policy by placing them in a position in which they had no other resort but to accept it. Russian rifles came into the country in camel-loads; the arsenal at Lhasa was furbished up and a new water-wheel put in, and Dorjieff, on his side, stated that the Russians would have a detachment of Cossacks in Lhasa by the spring of 1903. It occurs to one that there must have been a considerable body of opinion in Lhasa sympathetic to Dorjieff's suggestions, or he would never have ventured to make so daring a prophecy. As it was, however, he seems to have taken pains that this boast should reach Lord Curzon's ears. It did, and the fat was in the fire.

Such, then, was the position of affairs into which it became imperative for India to intervene. Excuses for interference were ready to hand. The Tibetans had encroached upon our territory in Sikkim, they had established a customs post at Giao-gong, fifteen miles inside the frontier, and had forbidden British subjects to pass their outposts there; they had thrown down the boundary pillars which had been set up along the undisputed water-shed between the Tista and the Ammo chu. They had insulted the treaty rights of the British by building a wall across the only road from Tibet to the market of Yatung, which had been thrown open to trade with India by the stipulations of the Convention of 1890–3; more than this, they returned unopened letters sent by the Viceroy to the Grand Lama in Lhasa. These insults would never have given rise to the despatch of an expedition if the Tibetans had not added injury to them by their dalliance with Russia. As it was, there was nothing else to do but intervene, and that speedily. With characteristic decision Lord Curzon made up his mind to come to an understanding with these turbulent children, and in the spring of 1903 he sent hastily to Major Bretherton and asked him to present a scheme for the immediate advance to Lhasa of 1,200 rifles. But this was found to be impracticable, and the home authorities were as yet far from understanding the urgency of the matter.

It is not unjust to say that from first to last the home Government had mistaken the real importance of the issue. The utmost that Lord Curzon could persuade them to do was to sanction the despatch of Colonel Younghusband, with a small escort, to await the Tibetan representatives in the little post of Kamba-jong, some fifteen miles north of the true Sikkim frontier. This the Government consented to do, but they added loudly and publicly that under no circumstances whatever would an advance from Kamba-jong be permitted. This intelligence was instantly communicated by a gentleman in the pay of the Chinese to the Amban in Lhasa, and from that moment, naturally enough, the ultimate necessity of an advance to Lhasa itself was insured.

The stay at Kamba-jong of the Mission was, therefore, not of the greatest political importance, but a brief account of it is here necessary. At the end of July Mr. Claude White, the Political Officer in Sikkim, and Captain W. F. T. O'Connor, the only white man who can speak Tibetan fluently, moved up the Tista Valley, and arrived at Giao-gong, where they were met by a small party of Tibetans who attempted to oppose their progress. It was pointed out to them that Kamba-jong had been chosen by the Indian Government for negotiations, and that the Chinese Government had assented and undertaken to co-operate with the Tibetans in negotiating at that place. To Kamba-jong, therefore, the members of the Mission intended to proceed. Hands were laid upon their bridle-reins, but easily brushed aside, and no further active opposition was offered. They moved on that day to the true frontier at the Kangra Lamo Pass. On the next day they actually set foot on Tibetan territory and were met by a small Chinese official named Ho, who asked them not to go on to Kamba-jong; they returned the same answer to him as to the Tibetans at Giao-gong, whereupon he ceased all further opposition and drowned his cares in opium. On the next day Kamba-jong was reached, and a small encampment was made at the foot of the hill on which the fort is built. This fort is an imposing structure, crowning, in the usual Tibetan manner, the crest of a sharp hill; the plain over which Kamba-jong dominates is a wide, flat stretch, separated only by low hills from the main Himalayan ranges. This first view of the world's backbone from the north is, from one point of view, disappointing, because of the great height, 15,000 feet and more, from which it is seen. But the distant view of Mount Everest, here clearly distinguishable from the surrounding ice-fields, is imposing, though nearly a hundred miles away. The plain of Kamba is a bare stretch of earth and wormwood, dotted with big boulders, and here and there affording a scanty pasturage of coarse grass.

The camp was pitched in two portions and earthworks were thrown up; small as it was, it would have been a difficult camp to take by storm, and here the Mission waited in patience. For the reasons I have just suggested their patience was not rewarded; emissaries did, indeed, come down from Lhasa, but after a formal visit to Colonel Younghusband, who followed Mr. White after an interval of a few days, they shut themselves up in the jong and had nothing further to do with the Mission. At times a Chinese official, more out of curiosity than anything else, would come into the camp. Always there were a few Tibetans lounging outside the earthworks in mild curiosity, but the days went on and nothing further was done than the surveying and geological work of the Mission experts. Mr. Hayden, of the Geological Survey, was intrusted with the latter work; Captain Walton, I.M.S., here began his natural history notes and collections. Mr. White roamed about the district as far as the Tibetans permitted him to go. Life was not unpleasant,[1] but no business was done, and the advent of the Abbot of Tashi-lhunpo was a welcome break in the monotony. This typical ecclesiastic appeared bringing a courteous message from the Grand Lama of Tashi-lhunpo. He was an intelligent man of a superior type, and evinced the utmost interest in all the instruments and habits of the English. The gramophone was employed to impress him; hereby a somewhat amusing tale hangs. This gramophone had been exhibited before to some Tibetan officials, who had said that it was not half as good as the gramophone in Lhasa. This statement somewhat paralyzed the Mission. They inquired the reason. "Oh," said the official, "the Lhasa machine will not only give out sounds, but it will take down and give out again our own voices!" After this there was no question but that phonographs were among the European luxuries which Dorjieff had brought from his new masters. Something had to be done to restore British credit, so by night a disk was scraped flat, and it was found that a fairly good original record could be made. On the following day, therefore, a Tibetan was asked to speak or sing into the machine; this he promptly did, and after a pause of some anxiety the gramophone rendered back his voice, to his amusement and delight. This record was triumphantly rendered on the machine to the Abbot of Tashi-lhunpo, but it was not until the interpreter explained the matter afterward that the growing stoniness of the worthy cleric's face during the performance was fully understood. Apparently our Tibetan, being in a mischie-

[1] On one occasion Mr. White and Major Iggulden rode up on ponies to a height of 21,000 feet above the sea. This must sound strange to many Alpine mountaineers.

vous mood, had recited into the gramophone a popular Tibetan song of the most unfortunate description.

One thing is worth recording: One morning the Abbot paid a visit to the camp and listened to accounts of the latest discoveries of Western science calmly and not without interest. He himself suggested no criticisms until he was directly asked by Captain O'Connor some point in connection with the Tibetan knowledge of this planet. He answered courteously, but very decidedly, that what we English believed as to the nature of the earth was interesting as showing the strides which science had begun to make in distant parts; "but," he said, "of course you are quite wrong in this matter; the earth is shaped like a shoulder of mutton bone, and so far from being only a small country, Tibet occupies nearly one-half of its extent. However, do not despair; if you will continue to read industriously and will read better books, there is no doubt that you will be learned in time." In the face of this I regret to have to record that our scientists collapsed ignominiously, and no one even attempted to justify the illusions of Europe.

Now and then the usual message was received: "Go back to Giao-gong and there we will discuss the matter; we will not discuss the matter while you are at Kamba-jong." On one occasion a small durbar was held, though Colonel Younghusband entirely demurred to the social position and the political importance of the men who represented themselves as the Tibetan delegates. He explained the whole position at full length; he set out the reasons which had induced us to attempt to come to an amicable arrangement with our neighbor; he recapitulated the events of the past few years, reproaching the Tibetans with having broken the treaty of 1890–3, and, finally, concluded by earnestly asking that the Tibetans should co-operate with ourselves in bringing matters to a satisfactory conclusion. In order that there might be no mistake his speech had been carefully written out to be handed on to the Dalai Lama. At the conclusion he presented the envelope to the chief Tibetan official, who shrank from it in horror; he utterly refused to touch it, and he as positively declined even to report in Lhasa the speech to which he had just listened; no one, in fact, would take the responsibility of having any official intercourse with us.

This was the universal attitude of the Tibetan representatives up to the last. The following story is a curious illustration of it: The Tibetans once sent in an oral protest chiefly directed against the extended ramblings of Mr. White and others of the Mission. They also protested against Hayden's chipping little pieces from the mountains; they said, and it was difficult to refute it, that we should not like them to come and chip pieces off the houses in Calcutta. Nor did they approve of the heliograph, by which they believed that we could both see through mountains and control the rain. But the wanderings of the members of the Mission were what they particularly disliked. This was, perhaps, not unreasonable, though a certain amount of reconnoitering was necessary in order to collect firewood, and even country produce, which the good people of the country were always eager to sell us, provided they could appease their superiors by the pretense that we had compelled them to trade with us. Colonel Younghusband, wishing in every way in his power to accustom the Tibetans to communicate with ourselves, asked that the request should be put into writing and signed. It was a very simple thing, and the Tibetans wrote the request without demur, but, to the Colonel's surprise, they point-blank refused to sign it. After interminable persuasion one of them snatched up a pen and made a little mark in the corner of the sheet; this, when examined, proved to be no signature at all. The thing was so ridiculous that the ponies for another excursion were saddled up and brought to the gate of the camp, and the Tibetans were told that if they could not put their names to this protest the English could not believe that they had authority to make it. Then, and then only, in despair did the Tibetan officials sign the paper. This was a most illuminating little incident, and to the very end the Tibetans were faithful to the policy of which it forms so good an illustration.

So it became evident that nothing could be done at Kamba-jong, and Colonel Younghusband suspected, as was indeed the case, that the Tibetans had got wind of his strict injunctions not to advance further into the country. It then became necessary to take stronger action, and with the concurrence of the India Office it was arranged that he should go to Gyantse, and there make a second attempt to carry through the negotiations with which he had been intrusted.

At this point a divergence of opinion occurred; it was originally suggested by Younghusband that two columns should converge upon the Kala tso; one with 2,500 yaks as transport should occupy the Chumbi Valley, and move on directly by the side of the Bam tso, under Colonel Macdonald, who had been at work for some time in Darjeeling as C.R.E., organizing the routes along which the Expedition was to travel; the other, consisting of the Mission, of which the guard was to be considerably reinforced, with 500 yaks, was to go across country by the Lango la; at the same time, 400 Nepalese troops were to occupy Kamba-jong, and cover the advance of the Mission. To this scheme Macdonald, who now appeared for the first time, demurred; he pointed out that this advance in two weak columns without means of communication gave the Tibetans the opportunity of dealing with each separately; that the rendezvous was an unknown point in the enemy's country; that the roads to it were also unknown, and that it was, therefore, difficult to effect a meeting at a given moment. He further pointed out that the Mission, which would be the weaker of the two columns, would have to march with its flank exposed to the enemy and without communications in its rear. On the 16th of October, Colonel Younghusband, who had returned from Kamba-jong, seeing the uselessness of any further residence, met Colonel (now Brigadier-General) Macdonald at Darjeeling. By this time the matter was further complicated by the question of yak transport. The Nepalese made a present of 500 yaks to the Mission; these were intended to act as transport for the Mission in their cross-country journey; the other yaks were to be bought in Nepal and taken across Sikkim. Macdonald pointed out the dangers of attempting to take the yaks through the Tista Valley, and his forebodings ultimately proved to be well justified. But the 500 yaks which were to cross into Tibet by the Tipta la were turned back by the Tibetans; whereupon the Nepalese asserted that, in spite of anything urged to the contrary, the yaks could safely be taken down to the level of the Tista Valley, and the military authorities, accepting their statement, committed themselves to this course.

The official estimate of the distribution of the Tibetan force at this date is interesting; they were supposed to have 500 men at Kamba-jong, where a night attack was imminent, 2000 men at Shigatse, 500 between Shigatse and Kamba-jong, 1000 at Gyantse, and a few in the Chumbi Valley. On the 8th of November the Tibetans were reported to be moving 3000 men toward Chumbi, and a week later it was said that nearly 3000 more soldiers were advancing upon Kamba-jong, a somewhat significant action: foot-and-mouth disease was at the same time reported to have made terrible ravages among the Nepalese yaks.[1] For these accumulated reasons the advance in two columns was abandoned, and it was decided to advance in a single strong column through the Chumbi Valley.

The question then arose, first, as to the route by which the Chumbi Valley should be reached, and, secondly, as to the date at which the retirement from Kamba-jong should be carried out.

[1] This was afterward discovered to be anthrax.

Colonel Younghusband was naturally anxious, under the circumstances, that no retreat should be made from Kamba-jong until a footing had been effected in Tibetan territory in the Chumbi Valley. It was, therefore, decided to make the two movements coincident in point of time. As to the route to be adopted, Mr. Claude White was of opinion that the Jelep Pass in October was preferable. There was this to be said in its favor that it was already well known to us, and had been used in the 1888 expedition. It was arranged that the original advance was to be made over the Jelep, but it was also decided to improve and utilize the Natu la route through Gangtok, and this eventually became the sole line of communication. By the 10th of December there were concentrated at Gnathong two guns of No. 7 Mountain Battery, the machine gun of the 2d Battalion Norfolk regiment, two seven-pounders, half a company of the 2d Sappers, eight companies of the 23d Sikh Pioneers, and six companies of the 8th Gurkhas, with the necessary hospital, ammunition, and postal columns. On the 11th a short march was made to Ku-pup, and on the 12th the Jelep was crossed in bitter weather. On the 13th the column reached Yatung, and after a formal protest made its way through the gateway in the Tibetan wall, where a not unfriendly welcome was extended by the officials. On the 16th Chumbi was reached, and two days later a column of 800 men set out to Phari, which was reached on the 21st; the jong at this place was at once occupied by our troops. This gave rise to a difference of opinion between the Commissioner and Macdonald. The former had, for diplomatic reasons, undertaken to the Tibetans that the fort should not be occupied unless it were defended; the General, for overbalancing military considerations, decided that it would be dangerous to leave it unoccupied, and it was consequently taken.

The behavior of the Tibetans now became more threatening.

Representatives of the Three Monasteries [1] arrived at Phari, and forbade the people round to supply us with any of the necessaries of life; the Chinese Colonel Chao was willing to do all he could, but he evidently had little authority, and his successor, Major Li said that nothing could be done in Lhasa at this moment, as the Grand Lama was relying upon Russian support and would pay no respect to the Chinese demands. Colonel Younghusband noticed about this time the despondency even of our own followers at the thought of invading Tibet. They believed that we were doomed men; the whole of the drivers of the Tibetan Pony Corps had bolted at Gnathong, and the desertions of followers and even private servants were innumerable. He summed the position up tersely: "We have not one ounce of prestige on this frontier." From political motives, he determined to winter at Tuna, a small village about nineteen miles from Phari, across the Tang la. He adopted this course because of the unwillingness of the Tibetans to admit that entrance into the Chumbi Valley was really entrance into Tibet itself; and he felt it necessary to occupy a position at least as far advanced into Tibet as Kamba-jong had been. General Macdonald found the position inconvenient from the point of view of transport, but the political reasons were important enough to decide the question.

At Tuna, therefore, three months of weary waiting ensued while Major G. H. Bretherton, a man of experience and great capacity, was organizing supply and transport along the lines of communication. It was felt that a very large amount of stores must be accumulated in the Chumbi Valley before any advance to Gyantse was possible. Life at Tuna was uninteresting and bitterly cold. The Tibetans had gathered in considerable strength

[1] The three monasteries of Sera, Debung, and Gaden, near Lhasa, are the ultimate political authorities in Tibet. In very important matters they are able to overrule even the Grand Lama.

at Guru, a place about nine miles away on the road to Gyantse. Here for the first time the Commissioner was able to deliver his message to thoroughly representative men. But its reception was unsatisfactory. After a fruitless attempt to make the delegates pay him an official visit, Colonel Younghusband determined to ride over in person to their camp informally; it was a characteristically audacious action, and if it had failed—if, that is to say, Colonel Younghusband and the two or three officers with him had been killed or kidnapped, as was not unlikely—the responsibility for the outbreak of war which would have inevitably followed must have rested upon the Commissioner. But Younghusband is a shrewd judge of Orientals, and, besides, he is not one of those men with whom an Oriental takes a liberty; and, though, as will be seen, the visit was not entirely successful, it seemed at the time to be almost the last chance of coming to terms with our opponents upon a perfectly friendly basis. The Tibetan general was the senior Dépen of Lhasa, one of the Lheding family, and he received Colonel Younghusband with great politeness. But upon the Commissioner's introduction to the room in which the representatives of the three monasteries were seated, the atmosphere became electric at once. They neither rose nor returned his salutation, but after an informal discussion had been initiated they took command of the conversation, maintaining throughout an unfriendly attitude, and insisting that no European could be allowed in Tibet on any account, and that if any settlement was to be carried through we must return to Ya-tung.[1] As Younghusband was taking his leave and expressing a hope that the Tibetans would visit him at Tuna their tempers changed; in a threatening way they clamored for the instant retirement of the British; they demanded insolently to know the exact

[1] This place was sometimes confounded by the Tibetans themselves with Gna-thong. It is spelled "Sna-mdong," and the "*s*" and the "*m*" are of course not sounded. I do not know how the English pronunciation was originated.

date on which the British would evacuate Tibetan territory, trumpets were blown outside, and the attendants closed round the small party. Younghusband betrayed not the slightest uneasiness, and O'Connor helped to save the situation by the almost superhuman suavity which he can assume when he wishes. A messenger accompanied Colonel Younghusband back to Tuna to receive his answer, which was, of course, to the effect that he was obliged to carry out the orders of his Government.

The Lheding Dépen subsequently called at Tuna; he was a pleasant man, but, in the words of the Commissioner, he was not clever; he had little strength of character, and he was entirely in the hands of his three monk colleagues. Nothing, therefore, had been done, and Colonel Younghusband was obliged to wait in the cold everlasting wind of the Tuna plateau for the first advance of the troops. Meanwhile the Tibetans gathered strength in his immediate neighborhood, and from time to time there were disquieting rumors of their intention to make a night attack. Colonel Hogge, with four companies of the 23d Pioneers and the Norfolk Maxim detachment, was, however, thoroughly able to hold Tuna against any conceivable concentration of Tibetan forces. The telegraph wire was not put up to Tuna till March, so a heliograph on the summit of the Tang la was in daily use.

Meanwhile, the General took up his quarters at Chumbi, in a not uncomfortable house at Bakcham, about three-quarters of a mile from the encampment at New Chumbi. The Coolie Corps, which Mr. White had undertaken to organize, was in working order by the middle of January, and under the able superintendence of Captain Souter contributed greatly to the accumulations of stores, which were steadily passing over the Jelep route, and creating tarpaulin-covered hillocks at Chumbi. The choice of the Natu la was accepted by Mr. White after the alternative road over the Yak la [1] had been tried. The Yak la is the shortest road between Chumbi and Gangtok, to which place a good cart-road runs from Siliguri in the plains of India, but to the best of my belief only one party ever crossed it. It was my fortune to be one of them. Bad as all these passes are, the eastern descent of the Yak la is beyond comparison the worst—a mere semi-perpendicular scramble four miles deep, down which one could only go by jumping from one boulder to another; many of these were coated with ice, and some crashed down the *khud* upon the lightest pressure. I do not think I have ever been so cold in my life as when I was helping Mr. White to put up a valuable self-registering thermometer upon the extreme summit of the Yak la. I do not remember what the temperature exactly was; I remember that when we took it out of the box it was 4° below freezing-point, but in the five minutes which it took us to set up strongly the pole to which it was to be attached, it had fallen over 30°; there was a wind like a knife edge the whole time, against which thick clothing and poshteens were as gauze. To illustrate the difficulty and hardship of that crossing, it is, I think, only necessary to say that that thermometer still stands at the summit of the pass; no one has ever summoned up enough courage to go and take it away. The idea of using the Yak la was abandoned, and the lines of supply were thenceforward the Jelep and the Natu la. Over these no burdened beast can pass. Only on the backs of coolies could the precious stores be carried across, slowly and painfully. It was a tremendous task, and it was difficult to believe that day after day, week after week, month after month, obstacles so appalling could be overcome by the small men of Sikkim who composed the corps.

Still, forty thousand pounds' weight of stores was daily delivered in Chumbi, and Major Bretherton and Captain Souter are

[1] The yak pass—pronounced Ya la. The Jelep is the "beautiful flat pass" and is spelled "Tges-lep-la."

alike to be congratulated indeed upon so brilliant an achievement. The road from India that these stores had traveled is worth a chapter to itself. Beyond all question the track that leads from Siliguri through Sikkim to Phari is the most wonderful and beautiful on earth.

CHAPTER III

CROSSING THE HIMALAYAS

SILIGURI itself was of no greater interest than the rail-head of any expedition usually is. It is true that it had become transformed from an idle little junction, whence the toy train started daily for Darjeeling, into a bustling warehouse of military supplies. New tents sprang up in rows, tarpaulin-covered heaps rose like great boulders from the plain, loaded trucks crammed the sidings of the station, long droves of mules detrained and were sent off—too soon in many cases—on their long journey to the front. Officers reported themselves and went on, but the village itself remained the same dull, mosquito-ridden spot, which has always been avoided like the plague by any one whose business or duty brings him into this part of the world. There is an English club at Jalpaiguri, an hour's run away, and the inadequacy of the dak bungalow at Siliguri is chiefly due to the fact that no one used it. A man can get a good dinner at seven o'clock in the railway refreshment rooms, take the Calcutta express an hour later, and sleep at Jalpaiguri. Travelers who have looked out from the train at the scattered patch of low houses that spot the burnt brown grass of the plain have seen all that there is of interest in Siliguri. The tiny track of the Darjeeling railway runs in timidly beside the broad gauge of the Bengal line, and the place is only remembered by most travelers as the point at which they climbed into the little char-à-banc cars that suggest rather a child's playing at traveling than a serious railway which is going to deposit them and their luggage in

Darjeeling 7,000 feet up in the clouds to the north. Then Siliguri passes into the limbo of forgotten things, even while the train is making its violent little scamper across the flat to the foot of the hills, or leaping, catlike, from side to side of the slowly up-winding cart-road, pouncing upon it only to let it crawl out again from under the wheels of its little engine for another two hundred yards on the other side.

But there is another journey to be made from Siliguri, a different journey indeed. It promises little enough at the beginning. One rides out from the station, threading one's way at first through the little houses of the town, and then dodging across the irrigation channels of the fields until the North road is gained. As you climb the slope of the low embankment and kick up the first hoofful of the deep dust you are on the road to Lhasa. The opening stage is common and dreary enough, but four hundred miles away this road, which you see slowly slipping below you, ends in a loop insnaring the golden roofs of the Potala and of the Cathedral, and round that loop the sad-eyed lamas, muttering their unchanging prayer, creep solemnly all day, turning ever to the right.

Here all round is the wide flat plain, north, south, east, and west; the grass is burned, the fields are dusty, and the white ribbon of the road swerves and straightens between the heavy-scented, white-flowered siris trees, like any other road in the peninsula. To the northward the clouds conceal the rampart of the Himalayas with a deep gray and indigo veil; elsewhere the sun shines crudely from the hard white sky. Napil-para slowly heaves in sight, just where a belt of trees slants inward to the track; a mile further on the road plunges into the great Baikuntpur sal forest. A country bullock cart, with whining wheels, jolts very slowly in front, haloed in a cloud of dust. The driver is asleep, and the flies settle spectacle-wise around the sore eyelids of the sedate beasts. In after days, the moaning, dusty cart, redolent of all the heat of

Indian plains, just entering the shade of the tall straight sal trees with their wide, crimsoning leaves, was a curious memory in which the "ching-chik, ching-chik" of the spear-bells of the mail runners, bringing their letters over the last stage of their long journey, rang continually in very different scenes. Under the shade of the sal forest the white dust heaps itself on either side of the track, powdering the glossy vegetation and reducing every bush and plant alike to the nameless insignificance of the undergrowth which is common to all countries in all dry seasons. For sheer folly the idiotic energy of a sweeper sweeping in mid-jungle was equaled by the inspiration of the English engineer, who had wasted hundreds of precious iron telegraph posts beside the road where nature was offering him a pole every six yards gratuitous and perfect.

Half-way through the wood the crossing of the Phulbari Ghat path attracts two or three huts. At last there is a dip and the road drops at the eleventh mile to cross the stream into Sevoke. The sight of a Himalayan river reaching the plain is worth looking at. The Tista, pent up between narrow and precipitous hills for eighty miles, here bursts fan-wise over the Terai, marked and parceled by long smooth banks of sand, through which in twenty channels the suddenly contented water drifts slowly and at peace.

The Himalayas' southern front ends with an abruptness which is almost startling, and five or six miles away it would have been difficult to point out a fissure in the great wall of mountains which stands untopped across the wide flat waste of northern Bengal. Through this curtain there is this one narrow channel and India ends at its jaws. The towering cliffs, clothed suddenly with vegetation wherever root-hold can be found, spring sharply upward and the first turn in the track by the river hides the plain, with their blue lines of trees fifteen miles away beside the leveled water. Sevoke, planted at the water-side just where the sticks of the fan diverge, is a little street of grubby huts. Dust hangs heavy in the

A ROAD IN THE HIMALAYAS

air, and dryness dulls the leaves. The only wet thing at Sevoke is the water itself, as it slackens way and gently swerves outward at the foot of its long stair. Even the rough dug-out boats, moored to the pebbly bank, are coated with dust, and the lumps of camphor are almost indistinguishable in the boxes in the shops from the inevitable Pedro cigarettes beside them. From Sevoke onward the beauty of the road begins to grow. The track runs on the westward bank of the Tista, fifteen or twenty feet above the snow-green water. Almost from the first mile-post it is a gradually increasing riot of foliage such as Hooker himself admitted to be unparalleled in the world. There is no color on God's palette which he has not used along this road. There is no variety of vegetation which he has not permitted to find its own place somewhere beside the slowly chilling path. Sal and gurjun lead on through teak to kapok and bamboo, then on through tree fern and rhododendron to the pine. Beyond these last, birch-trees alone survive among the frozen rocks of the upper snows. At their roots, or from the hill-side above their tops, round their stems, or springing from their wood is almost every flower known to man, here wasting its luxuriance along the loneliest and loveliest two hundred miles on earth. Pepper ferns, with their dark green glossy foliage, vines and bind-weeds, begonias and asphodel tangle themselves about the undergrowth of gorgeous shrubs, or stumps gay with scarlet fungus and dripping moss. Overhead the bald scarp of the rock, orange and ocher and cinnamon, rarely broke through the trailing glories of smilax and other creepers. Once or twice down on the road itself, where a passage had been blasted years ago, the deep crystalline garnet rang not only with the echoes of the sweeping water below, but with the tiny persistence of the drip-well from its roof. Ferns lurk in every cleft, and, higher up, the majesty of some great osmunda thrusts itself clear of the green confusion round its roots. Of greens, indeed, from the dark moss myrtle of some varnished leaf that ought to have been a magnolia, but probably was not, to the aquamarine of the young and dusted bamboo grass, from the feathery emerald of some patch of giant moss to the rich olive of a crown-vallary of orchid, none is unrepresented.

Where the valley vegetation lies in the ugliest putrefaction, there you will find the living jewels of this long fillet—a flash of emerald and chrome glazed with chocolate; a patch of brown, shot through and through with sapphire in the sun; a swallow-tail with olivine and black velvet where we may rarely see, beside some Norfolk broad, the dun and cream of his poor English cousin. Strong in the wing, zigzagging unballasted in ten-foot swoops of pure color, the butterflies lace the sunlight. And underfoot in the deep soft white dust the kidney footmark of the brown ox or the kukri-like print of the high-instepped native are the only reminders in that hot world of color that there are other things as graceless as oneself.

At Riang, where the road falls into the river every year with a regularity worthy of something better, a stream breaks through from the west, and for a moment the dingy picturesqueness of a semi-Indian settlement beneath its trees drives back the beauties of the road. But in half a mile the path turns again beneath close matted branches overhead and winds, deep rutted, beside the rank dark vegetation which is characteristic of just this place—flowerless, amorphous, and heavy. The Tista bridge swings out its curve from behind a rock, and one crosses the narrow span, realizing from its scanty width that one has left behind the normal limits of wheeled cart traffic. The road, still ascending, keeps on the left bank of the Tista river, passing Mali-ghat among its trees three miles on. Slowly the character of the vegetation changes, though the fact of its being still tropical is clear enough from a tiger trap half-way between Mali-ghat and Tar Kola. Beside this latter place the road runs along tirelessly, curving and recurving beside the shallow stream. At the junction of the Tista with the

ENCAMPED UNDER THE SHADOW OF THE HIMALAYAS

Rang-po the creaming white crests over the rock points below valiantly hold their own all day against the down sweep of the green turquoise flood. Sometimes for a mile one does but hear the stream of the Rang-po murmuring invisibly through the trees; again over its very waters the track clings scantily round the bare red scarp of some intruding spur, hand-railed most rottenly. A warm breath of guimauve-like scent pants out at one here: there is the sweet acrid perfume of wild geranium, more taste than smell. The fierce glare of the day sinks imperceptibly into a cooler and a steadier light; there is no sign of sunset yet awhile; only the high crowned ridges of the western heights break his force. And presently the dust on the patient road-side foliage seems half shaken off, and tints and shades creep out on surfaces which the blatant heat of midday had frightened into an insignificant blur of neutral colors.

Here the cactus stops for a while, why, I do not know: there are many puzzles in this Himalayan botany. Why does the rhododendron grow to the very highest spot on the south and refuse to put forth a leaf at any elevation to the north? Why does the blue poppy of Tibet despise utterly the identical rocks and ledges offered at the same height south of the Tang la? Why does the bamboo stop with a certainty and cleanness at a height of 9,500 feet on the south, which enables the Bhutanese to use it as their frontier mark, while two hundred miles away on a hillside at Lhasa a flourishing twenty-five-foot hedge keeps the cold from the Chief Wizard's house, nearly 13,000 feet above the sea?

You will cross the bridge at Rang-po; and there you will stay the night, sleeping under mosquito nets for the last time. The stream you have just crossed you will meet again under very different circumstances, but some suggestion of the clear emerald of its ice-bound pools at Lagyap still lingers as it joins the snow-stained waters of the Rang-po. Still going on, your path lies on the left bank of the latter river, chiefly bound up against the side of the river cliff. Six miles will take you to the last river that you will have to follow till Tibet is reached. The Rong-ni is, after all, the most beautiful stream that you will have tramped beside. Here the two vegetations mingle, and the orange groves of Dowgago mark the transfusion of the two. Here the maples and the violets begin, the geraniums and the daphnes, the lobelias and the honeysuckles, the ivies and the elder-trees—the first outposts of the European zone. But we have not yet lost the creepers and hydrangeas of the south before the first azalea-like rhododendrons bear promise of the shrub that, towering at the 7,000-foot line to eighty feet in height and dwindling again to three or four inches on the pass, will remain with us till the frontier line is crossed. Here the bamboos insinuate themselves at last, and as the road sweeps up and up, the undergrowth rising here and there into the magnificence of the tree fern, every corner betrays a fresh scene of luxuriance and grace. Sometimes the bank opposite rises steep as a precipice and red as an old English garden wall, veiled with overhanging creepers and rich with green moss in every crevice and on every ledge: elsewhere the bank breaks away into a wide slope of tangled jungle, clothed with small ponds of greenery where the need of the dotted white huts has cleared, leveled and sown. Here the first tender rice tips peep above the mud. Round the echoing, waterworn curves of rock overhung by trees and screw-pines, hanging on, God knows how, to the bare face of the rock, crossing some small stream rustling under its canopy of shade, still mounting every mile, the track goes on, until the last bridge is crossed and the long splendid zigzags of the new road to Gangtok, which no one uses, seam the hill in front. The barest novice knows the short cuts, and with your ears cracking every twenty minutes, you clamber up the old stony road, which saves two miles in six. At last the Residency, or rather the foliage which conceals it, seems less hopelessly distant than it did, and coming out again upon the white, well-made road, one climbs at an easy gradient to the capital of Sikkim. On the left is the deep green cutting of the river we have crossed, a league in width and lost behind a ten-mile distant corner. The double Residency gates open and shut behind one, and through the tree ferns and the dying bamboos of the drive [1] one emerges into the English roses and clean, short turf of Mrs. Claude White's home-made Paradise.

The Residency brings a whiff of England into this far distant country. It is a substantial and handsome little building of stone, roofed in red of such a well-remembered tint, that it is some time before one realizes that tiles are impossible at Gangtok. Hitherto it has been the end of all northern travel in India, and it must have been curious for the rare travelers who made demands on Claude White's famous hospitality, to find this dainty gem of a house, furnished from Oxford Street within, and without encircled with the tree ferns and orchids of this exquisite valley. It is a perfect spot. Far off to the west rise the pinnacles of Nursing and Pan-dim; to the north there hangs in heaven that most exquisite of all peaks of earth, Siniolchu.

Beyond Gangtok, before the Expedition came, there was no road. Indeed, a road wide enough for carts was finished only eighteen months ago up to the gates of the Residency. Further on, it is still a bridle track hugging the side of the hill, barely thrusting its way through the dense wall of bamboo which rises on either side like the green walls through which Moses led his flying countrymen.[2] Overhead the giant rhododendrons branch upward to the sky, high as a London house. No one who knows the rhododendron of England can form the faintest conception of what these monsters of the upper hills are like. The trees at Haigh Hall and at Cobham are regarded by their own-

[1] All the bamboos of the Gangtok district fertilized and died in 1904.

[2] The color, too, contributes to the fantasy, for here the blue-leaved Hooker's bamboo grows more freely among its commoner brethren than anywhere else in the Himalayas.

ers with some complacency. But in size they are mere shrubs compared with their brothers of Sikkim, and in beauty they are left far behind. "I know nothing of the kind," says Hooker, "which exceeds in beauty the flowering branch of *rhododendron argenteum,* with its wide-spreading foliage and glorious mass of flowers." This variety, though it does not grow to the height of its brethren, is the finest of them all. The enormous glossy leaves, powdered with white underneath, are thrown with a careless grace around the splendid blossoms, arranged with all the delicate looseness and lightness which none but the Master Gardener could give to this royal and massive foliage. The actual florets of the commoner kinds are undoubtedly poorer than those of the English variety, and there is an ineffective conical arrangement of their azalea-like blossoms which the Englishman notices at once. But in their masses, crimson, lemon, and white, they star the dark green steamy recesses of the path, and, excepting only the magnolia, are the most striking flowers upon the road.

These magnolias are strange plants. They seem to turn color as they reach the limit of their growth, and the pure white is lost in a tinge of purple. Unlike the magnolias which occasionally overpower the scents of an entire rectory garden in England, the waxen flowers grow on naked lilac stickery. The wide, enameled leaves, which seem so indispensable at home, are gone. I do not know whether they appear later, but the magnolia seems to be outside ordinary rules of plant life. One species has even the depressing habit of dropping its flowers unopened on the ground below. Oaks grow here, though in a chastened way. An English tree which takes fuller advantage of the rank vegetable mold and steamy hothouse climate of Sikkim is the juniper. This, which is best known to the inhabitants of towns in the shape of "cedar" pencils, grows to a height of forty or fifty feet, and Mr. White has, on two occasions, made an attempt to develop a regular trade with the manufacturers. They admitted that the wood sent was as good as any they could buy, but the contracts they had entered into for the supply of this wood bound them for some years to come. Another industrial product of this jungle is madder, and the dark crimson robes of both Tibetan churches, Red and Yellow alike —for the distinction is shown only in the cap—owe their richness to the hill-sides of Sikkim. Elephant creeper winds up the forest trees, the huge leaves nuzzling into the bark all round like a swarm of gigantic bees. The common white orchid, which is wired to make a two-guinea spray in London, is a weed at Gangtok. Its quaintly writhen blossoms of snow hang overhead in such profusion that one welcomes a shyer blossom, trumpet shaped, and of the color and coolness of a lemon-ice. The orchids are not the only epiphytes; other parasites than they crown the living branch with their coronals of leaves, more lovely than the trees they feed upon.

The game here is very scanty: the reason is not uninteresting. For, dormant or active, visible or invisible, the curse of Sikkim waits for its warm-blooded visitor. The leeches of these lovely valleys have been described again and again by travelers. Unfortunately the description, however true in every particular, has, as a rule, but wrecked the reputation of the chronicler. Englishmen cannot understand these pests of the hot mountain-side, which appear in March, and exist like black threads fringing every leaf till September kills them in myriad millions.[1] Spruce grows here under a Latin name, and the writer enters thereupon a layman's protest. It takes away half the interest of new and tropical vegetation if the only names that one can

[1] It is worth a passing note that these unwelcome visitors can be driven from the nostrils of the cattle exactly as MacComglinney enticed the "lawless beast" from the throat of King Cathal. A bowl of warm milk at the cow's nose, a little slip-knot, and a quick hand are all that is required. Fourteen or fifteen have been successively thus taken from the nostrils of one unfortunate heifer.

be told for some magnificent or graceful thing are Latin atrocities, generally embedding some uncouth Teutonic surname. In a country like Sikkim one's resentment is doubled; when a good English word lies ready to hand, why should it be necessary to call the spruce tree *abies excelsa*, or, worse still, *Smithiana?*

Leaving Gangtok, the last reminder of the West, one strikes out east by north to make the final climb which takes us out of the Empire. For five miles the road is—or rather, until the rains came, was—a good one. Beyond that, in spite of much hard work of pioneers and sappers, the track is bad indeed. Karponang,[1] when I returned through it for the last time, is a far-stretched hamlet, lying in long tiered sheds against the mountain wall, and the last pretense of a road along which a wheel can go is here frankly abandoned. Beyond it is a section of the road which for months was the despair of the engineers. "The tenth to the thirteenth mile" passed into proverbial use as a standard of utter badness and instability. When the road was cut out of the rock it was too narrow for the easy passage of a loaded beast; where it was cut out of the hill soil, a night's rain sent it down the khud. Where it crossed a cataract, the bridge gave more trouble than a quarter of a mile of honest rock. Where, as it too often did, it jutted straight out on bamboo brackets from the side of the cliff, 800 feet above the whispering stream below, the bamboos used to rot with a rapidity unknown elsewhere. Landslips were the rule rather than the exception. The whole length was sprayed with continual rivulets through the rank vegetation which overhung the track;

[1] The name Karponang was suggested for the ten-mile stage by the writer. From a perilously insufficient knowledge of Tibetan, *karpo* seemed to mean "white" and *nang* was clearly a "house"; and as some shorter title was needed for the political officer's bantling, Karponang stuck, though it is not, perhaps, a particularly idiomatic rendering of what it was intended to mean.

all afternoon these washed away the mold with which the bald sharp rock-points of the blasted road were covered; all night they formed a coat of ice which made it impossible for man or beast to stand or go upon it. Accidents upon this stretch were painfully common; two men were killed by a dynamite explosion, though in common fairness to even this unfortunate exhibition of nature, she can hardly be held responsible for the folly of men who dry their dynamite at a fire. Four men were overwhelmed here by a gush of liquid mud, just when three weeks' hard work upon the road at that point was finished. One man slipped down, or maybe he was kicked—for the mules disliked this "trang" with almost reasonable intuition—and the loss of mules near Karponang was heavier than anywhere else upon the road. On a winter afternoon a mile an hour was good going along this stage. Any attempt to ride was out of the question; painfully prodding one's way with a khud-stick, one scrambled up or glissaded down over the unfenced ice-slides thinly veiled with dirt. One's beast was led behind one with mincing steps and starting eyes. It was a bad road; and the noise of waters many hundred feet sheer below was always painfully present in the ears. Lagyap was the next halting-place, hanging over the gulf like an eagle's nest.

Beyond Lagyap, the road, as a road, did not exist. The ascent was tolerably steep, and one either strode from boulder to boulder, or trod, at the risk of one's ankles, between the stones. This, after five miles, is wearisome work. And even the sight of Lagyap Pool, the most beautiful basin of ice-bound emerald water that I have ever seen, fails to cheer one up. Up under the pine-trees, slipping and staggering, where no road pretended to have been ever cleared, we reached Changu Lake at last. Here we were clear of trees; the dwarf rhododendrons ran along the ground in acre patches, a foot in height, but the last tree barely showed its head over the great natural dam which shuts in the waters of the lake. One leaves a land of timber; one comes to a land of rock, and the dividing-line is as clean as if it had been the work of man. Behind us, also, we left one of the most magnificent views in the world, for the deep green valleys of Sikkim, like some loosely thrown length of myrtle-green velvet, lie out for the last time many thousands of feet below, stretching on till the gray gauze of sheer distance overtook the tint, and only the pure, clean argent of those Himalayan snows, which have no rival on this planet, lifted themselves into the blue.

It is an austere country into which we are now moving. The lake is a mile long and perhaps 600 yards in width; nearly all the year round it is frozen, though in the bitterest days of mid-winter, when the thermometer is nightly going down to 5° or 10° below zero, there is always on the southern side of the lake an unfrozen pool. The cliffs sweep down into the basin, bare and unlovely. To the east, whither our road still is to run, the nakedness of a steep ascent of wearisome boulders is barely qualified by the stunted rhododendron growth. At Changu there is now a comfortable bungalow, and only those in dire necessity will fail to stop the night. The hardest work of all the road to Lhasa lies before us on the morrow, and though I have more than once passed through from Chumbi without a halt, there is no doubt that the exertion can only be justified by real urgency. Leaving Changu in the morning, the traveler, considering the very short way he knows he has to go, will demur at the earliness of his start. But there will be no mercy shown him. He will be allowed, perhaps, to ride for 500 yards; after that he will prefer to trust to his own feet until all except the last three miles of the stage have been covered. Climbing over these boulder-strewn surfaces would be bad at the sea-level; here, where the air is so thin, it soon becomes a burden to pull one's solid body over the heartless obstacles. If the ascent be at all steep, the newcomer will sit down every twenty or thirty yards. His muscles are not tired, and he regains his strength in a surprisingly short time, but at the moment he sinks upon some friendly stone he thinks that another step forward would be his last. This is a peculiarity which it is impossible to describe to those who have never been more than a thousand feet or so above sea-level. The lungs seem foolishly inadequate to the task imposed upon them; the pluckiness of one's own heart is an unmistakable, but somewhat terrifying, symptom, for it goes on beating with increasing strokes till it shakes the walls of the body; and not the written testimony of the leading heart expert in London will convince you that it is not on the point of bursting its envelope. Then you may be thankful indeed if you escape mountain sickness. If that should come upon you, your bitterest enemy will lead your horse for you. I have seen cases of mountain sickness in which amazement overwhelmed even one's sympathy. I have seen men in such a state, that they seem to have every symptom of habitual drunkenness; all the limbs shiver, and in the bloodless face the eyes have that extraordinary look of insanity which is, I think, caused by an inability to focus them. The speech comes with difficulty, and in one case that I saw the mental coherence was as obviously at fault as the physical. But, strange though the appearance is to the outsider, for the sufferer himself I do not suppose that there can well be condensed into three or four hours such an agony of aching. The brain seems cleft into two, and the wedge, all blunt and splintery, is hammered into it as by mallet strokes at every pulsation of the heart. Partial relief is secured by a violent fit of sickness (which, however, is not always forthcoming), and through all this you have still to go on, to go on, to go on.

Here, too, the wind exacts its toll, and drives a cold, aching shaft into your liver. This is no slight matter, for the toil of climbing is excessive, and the exertion of covering half a mile will drench a man with perspiration. He then sits down, and this strong wind plays upon him to his own enjoyment, and to the destruction of his lungs.[1]

Up one still goes till the lake lies a mile behind one, still untouched by the first rays of the dawn. Often a steep descent as treacherous to the foot as the ascent has to be made. One of the most tedious and tiresome things about this track is the wearisome necessity, which awaits you round every corner, of losing at a stroke two-thirds of the advantage that you have just won by an hour's hard work. It appeals to the mind, and shortens the temper at a time when any friction in the human microcosm is waste of strength. One resents the man who first pointed out the track. One is inclined to think, that had one only a few hours more, one could oneself find a far more economical path than that by which one is now obliged to go. This, a very common failing, as I have noticed myself, perhaps indicates that one's common sense also is a little affected in these high altitudes. Two miles from Changu is the only level portion of the day's march. One goes across the little plain, and makes for exactly the one point which a stranger would decide to be the most impossible in all the amphitheater.

The Sebu la is beyond question the most difficult point of all the road from Siliguri to the end, a sheer wall of precipitous rock, springing up from the level plain. On looking closely one can see some symptoms of a zigzagging road climbing upward, and by those zigzags you have to go, for the rock itself allows no other path. This is the most heart-breaking climb of all the day. You may, perhaps, here overtake the slow, painful tramp of the coolies sent on, even before your own rising, from the last stage; pack animals are impossible on a road like this. The strange thick-calved, patient men, carrying bur-

[1] Pneumonia caused more deaths than any other disease.

dens which no Englishman would shoulder, move steadily onward over their six-mile stage.[1]

One climbs at last to the crest of the Sebu la. One goes thirty yards round a projecting rock, and at once one is obliged to scramble as best one can down a declivity which lands one 400 feet below the level of the little plain from which one has climbed to the top of the Sebu la. It all seems so unnecessary, so wanton. At the bottom, one crosses the bed of a river closely packed with rough and heavy water-worn rock, but no stonier than the road leading down to it on either side. There is still another steady rise to the heights of the Natu la. One seems to have wandered in a vast amphitheater of rock and stone for days. The homely bungalow at Changu has faded among the recollections of another year, and you are wise if you do not ask how long it will still take to climb to the summit of these weary hills. Just about this time, you begin to realize why Tibet has remained a shut-up country for so long. The transportation of an army and, what is far more wonderful, its daily supply across the water-shed between the Tista and the Ammo chu will probably remain an unrivaled feat of transport and supply in the history of warfare. In old days, marches, which would to-day be regarded as impossible, were somehow carried out. But we have never been told the loss of life that

[1] The weight that these Central Asian coolies can carry is astounding; the ordinary load is from 80 to 100 pounds, nearly double a man's pack on the level plains of India. But these Bhutias, when paid by the job, do not hesitate to double and even treble the load. I have myself seen a man carry into camp three telegraph poles on his back, each weighing a trifle under 90 pounds. Further east the tea porters of Se-chuan are notorious and loads of 350 pounds are not unknown. Setting aside the story of a Bhutia lady who carried a piano on her head up to Darjeeling from the plains as too well known to be likely to be exact, the record seems to be held by a certain Chinese coolie who undertook, in his own time, to transport a certain casting, needed for heavy machinery, inland to its owner. The casting weighed 570 pounds, and the carriage was slowly but successfully accomplished.

An English bricklayer is forbidden, by the rules of his union, to carry more than 14 pounds.

accompanied the ultimate arrival in India of Genghiz Khan, Alexander, or Nadir Shah. But the road dips downward for the last time at the half-way stage, and we are free to make the best of the remaining clamber which lies now uninterruptedly before us to the pass.

Much has been made of the added horrors of ice and snow. As a matter of fact, bare-footed though the coolies are, it was a merciful relief for them when the snow lay packed into a kindly carpet blanketing the boulders under foot. The only difficulty then was said to be that of losing the road. Only those who have been over the Natu la can quite understand the grim foolishness of speaking of losing the road over it. It is true that there is a track. Probably that track, so far as it can be distinguished from the hill-side, above and below, represents as good a means of getting to the top as any other. But so far as the ground is concerned there is almost nothing to choose; and not the least remarkable thing is the steady persistent refusal of the coolies to use the easy zigzag path which has been made for them over the last 200 yards to the top. It is roughly true to say that no hill coolie will deign to use an easier path than that which goes straight to his journey's end, though one might have expected that after a long and wearying climb over this heart-breaking mountain-side, the chance of an easy and steady climb for even so short a distance would have been eagerly accepted.

We have now reached 14,300 feet, and before we climb the last remaining steps, it is worth while to turn back and watch for the last time the scenes through which we have come so painfully. Away to the left a gigantic bastion of rock carries the sister road over the Jelep la, and away to the southwest Ling-tu, on the crest of the 6,000 feet precipice up which the road is zigzagged, can be seen in the clear air. The Jelep Pass itself is hidden by the bulk of the range, though only three miles away. A little lake lies frozen in the stony bowl up the sides of which we have just come. Far below its edge falls another mighty hollow, and yet we do not see a blade or leaf. Only beyond and below, peering through one of the little crevasses in the ringed hills, there is the dark mantle of the Sikkim woods. One turns one's back upon it for the last time, and gains the summit, where three heaps of stones, piled by pious travelers, support a flagged bush, the usual ornament of every pass in the country. One takes another step, and one is in the Chumbi Valley.

The first sight of Tibet, thus seen, is not without a somber interest of its own. It is at once obvious that the general level of the country is very much higher than that of Sikkim. The mass of Chumolhari fills in the end of the valley. Glittering in the bitter air, it rises thirty-five miles away, though the richer aquamarine of its crevasses can be seen from where we stand. The ridges and ranges swarm between, intersected with the courses of rivers invisible. All is bare and dull, but a thousand feet below us the dripping pines send their single spies up toward the barren and unlovely path.

There is something fascinating about the very sight of this long, slow line of burdened men, in spite of the miserable cold that almost prevents your watching anything. Up there, high above the most venturesome pines, where only the dwarf rhododendron, two or three inches high, survives here and there beneath the shelter of a friendly rock just piercing the two-inch snow that fell last night, the laden team crawls slowly to the top. The green and golden lichen spreads over the dull and bitter crags of gneiss, and under foot the tense stiff bents of frozen grass prick themselves scantily through the dirty ice. Up hither the coolies thrust their way painfully, and the thick, duffle-clad figures in a long line zigzag up the side of the pass, swaying from side to side under their burdens as they gain a bare foothold on the blunt rocks; the sky is overcast and this vivid cold searches through everything, in spite of the thick winter clothing which has been liberally supplied. Butterflies, birds, and beasts are alike fled. Only a lammergeier floats still in the air some 300 feet below, wheeling slowly with motionless wings, and far down in the gulf there is a scurry of lavender snow pigeons. The pass itself is nothing but elemental rock, and the Indian file of men drops down again as quickly as it can into the stiller cold of the sheltered side of the peak. One goes down. At first lichen and stunted moss alone mask the coarseness of the huge boulders; lower down the scarlets and reds of the barberry and a few stunted bushes of feathery juniper, as high as one's hand, come up as forerunners of the fast-thickening vegetation of the gorge. Two thousand feet below the pass, while one is still sliding and scrambling over frozen washes of curving ice across the track, the silver firs and stunted junipers crowd beside the zigzag path that still leaps from rock to rock. Of undergrowth there is but little, even when the mountain-ash and silver fir have given place to the *Pinus excelsa* and a silver-gray variety of the deodora, and the air is heavy with warm resin. Behind, fifteen miles away on the Sikkim side of the pass, the dull roar of blasting may perhaps remind one of the wide ten-foot road which the Government are still intending to throw across this terrible sierra.

The coolies still crawl upward and over. Compared with the western face, the descent of the Natu la on the Tibetan side is a comparatively easy thing. The road soon runs at a gentle gradient over the spurs which buttress the precipices that frown over Sikkim, and after a mile you may, if you come in winter, get thankfully upon your pony once again. The track runs straight and level along the mountain-side, and you may wonder why the engineers have corduroyed the road. There seems so little reason for this fearful waste of time and timber. But if it is your luck to retrace your steps when the rains are in full swing, you will wonder no longer.

There is no end to the devilish ingenuity with which Nature has strewn this path with obstacles. That one which hitherto we had hardly found was waiting us after all. And you may have to get wearily off your pony once again to pick your way unsteadily from rock to rock, in a sea of mud which defies description. Two feet deep, black, stinking, slippery, your pony has to make the best of it. And once in every ten paces you too will sound it to the knee. Not a mere stretch of a quarter of a mile is this disheartening morass; before the transverse logs were laid there were five miles of this unending slide and slip and splash to be overcome. Corduroy itself is no luxurious floor. Your beast will like it only a little better than the quagmire he has scrambled through. The wood is slippery, and though the ribbing of the road prevents a long slide it insures a short one at almost every step.

The path on the bare mountain-side, bad as it was, is better than that which threads the close pine trunks of Champi-tang. Torrential rain may wash a path away, but nothing so entirely ruins a made track as the drip from trees. There is something about the slow persistence that does harm which even a waterspout could not compass. And if by this time you have any spirit of curiosity left in you, you may notice that the corduroy work upon the road coincides with those very parts, which at the first blush you might consider most protected by foliage overhead. It is getting late now in the afternoon, and you will thank your good fortune in having as companions unfeeling men who made you rise at five. The worst is over, and you can stumble along at more than two miles an hour. The hill-sides opposite become clothed with forestry, and after an hour or two you will find yourself before the blazing hearth of the luxurious bungalow at Champi-tang.

On the following day, you go down to Chumbi. You make your way along a greasy path, now passing underneath a lonely little shrine, half hidden by the trees, now emerging among the bared, charred trunks of the pine army which was burned three years ago. Doubling the spurs again and again, you make your way at a fairly level altitude, until a Bhutia-tent marks the division between the official main road by the Kag-ué monastery, and the short cut over the hills to Chema. Down the first you elect to go. The road is longer, but the road is easier, and you have not yet acquired either the mental attitude or, what is more important, the muscles of a hill man. Through junipers and birch you pass out to the bare hill-side, and descend sharply to the monastery.

This is a curious place. It is the most important religious community in the valley. It is a special favorite with the Dalai Lama, and when, some years ago, owing to certain scandals which were, unfortunately, too well known in the valley to be disregarded, the older monastery in these parts was broken up, the lamas were permitted to build a far more magnificent temple within a mile of the scene of their misdoings. Service is going on as you enter the courtyard. They will pay no attention to you if you go into the shrine itself—that is, the monks will not. Only the acolyte children will gaze, round-eyed, at the unknown white men, while their mouths still move with the shrill and simple cadence of the chanted office. Now and again a bell is rung, or a drum beaten with the sickle-shaped stick. Once in a while the long, eight-foot trumpets emit a ponderous blast of discordance. Tea is handed round continually, and the chant pauses now and again to allow the presiding lama to monotone a passage from the Buddhist scriptures. At the further end, in the darkness, lighted by the pale beads of butter-lamps, sits the gilded image of Gautama, half-hidden by "katags" or scarfs.

Leaving the monastery, the track flings itself down the steep sides of a hollow, and at last comes out upon the good and welcome level of the Chumbi road. We have almost reached the end of the first stage of the long journey.

CHAPTER IV

THE TIBETANS OF THE CHUMBI VALLEY

BEFORE the coming of this Mission, no white man had ever seen the Chumbi Valley.

The women of Chumbi think a good deal of themselves, though to the eye of the stranger there seems very little distinction between the stunted and dirty little people of one part of Tibet and those of another. The head-dress used by them is the usual turquoise-studded aureole of the province of Tsang. The outer and possibly only garment [1] is of the same very thick crimson dun cloth, tied round the waist with a string and fastened at the throat with a plain yoke-like hasp of silver. This dress is generally patched, until it is difficult to say with certainty which part of it is the original garment, and it is of course open to more objections than the presence of inanimate dirt alone presents. The shoes worn reach up to the knee, and are made of the same dark red cloth, variegated over the instep by a streak of scarlet extending down to the toes. Here the plain tanned yak hide incases it. These shoes are not uncomfortable, though the entire absence of any heel makes it necessary that a little practice in them should precede a long or a difficult tramp, otherwise the Achilles tendon is apt to make a violent protest. In face, the men and women are strangely alike. Neither here nor elsewhere in Tibet do the men grow mustaches or beards; the utmost that one ever sees is a thin fringe of scanty hair marking the lips or pointing the chin of a

[1] These ladies seem to use their outer dress as their *dessous* when torn and worn beyond decent use. A girl at Bolka had apparently two such undergarments.

high official. It cannot be claimed that Tibetan ladies look beautiful. It is, of course, difficult to say what the effect would be if some of them were thoroughly washed. As it is, they exist from the cradle, or what corresponds to it, to the stone slab on which their dead bodies are hacked to pieces, without a bath or even a partial cleansing of any kind. One could imagine that they were of a tint almost as dark as a Gurkha, but this is by no means the case. In spite of the dirt, wherever the bodies are protected by clothes the skin remains of an ivory whiteness, which is indistinguishable from that of the so-called white races. At times also accident, perhaps in the shape of rain, has the effect of removing an outer film of dirtiness, and then it is quite clear that Tibetan girls, until they are two or three and twenty, have a complexion. Of course the habit of the race, of besmearing the forehead, cheeks, and nose with dark crimson kutch, which blackens as it dries, militates against any display of beauty. The origin of this strange custom is, like most facts and theories about Tibet, the subject of hot dispute. Some contend that it originally marked the married women only: some will have it, and there seems some evidence in their favor, that this disfigurement was intentionally introduced in order to save the ladies of Tibet from the sin of vanity, and incidentally, also, to reduce the chances of young men's infatuation. The third and more prosaic explanation is that it is done to mitigate the glare of the sun from rock and snow.[1] This would be a more convincing reason, if the kutch was actually worked into the hollow of the eye, and on the eyelid; but these are left unstained. Two other reasons, also of a flatly contradictory nature, have been suggested to explain this custom of Tibetan women, but there does not seem any necessity to accept either view. One thing must in common fairness

[1] Mr. Talbot Kelly recommends essentially the same thing for use against the glare of Egypt. The Sikkim coolies pull their hair over their eyes in a curtain for the same purpose.

be said, and that is, that nowhere in the world will you find such exquisite teeth in men, women, and children alike as in Tibet, though it is beyond dispute certain that no tooth-brush, or any form of cleansing them, has ever been practised, or indeed known, from one end of the country to the other.

Prayer flags in Tibet are the commonest possible means of invocation. The "airy horses" printed upon long perpendicular strips of limp tarlatan, or rather butter muslin, about twelve inches wide, are nailed to the pole, from twenty to thirty feet in height. These fringes stand out in the wind, till they are frayed back to the very nails, or tear themselves loose in ragged streamers.[1]

Among the private convictions of Sir Isaac Newton was the singular belief that prayers went to Heaven by vibration. It was not, perhaps, one of the most demonstrable theories of that great man, and very little stress has ever been laid upon this curious idea, though I believe it underlies the almost universal use of incense as a symbol of prayer. But your pious Tibetan would have understood Sir Isaac in a moment; to him, movement is prayer, and no inert petition finds its way to the ear of the gods. The turning of a prayer-wheel, whether in the hand, or by the agency of water, wind, or fire, is the best illustration of this. The peregrinations round the Ling-kor or the Jo-kang at Lhasa are other examples of an acted prayer. Attention is not necessary; merit is acquired, whether the mind be fixed or not, and Claudius' truism, "Words without thoughts never to Heaven go," would be scouted as foolishness by the piety of this land. Nor would the Lamas be inclined to agree with the counsel which deprecates repetition, for some of the larger prayer-wheels contain the sacred mantra, "Om mani padme hum," repeated to an extent that almost defies calculation. Very thin sheets of paper made from the

[1] In Lhasa itself a peculiarity is noticeable. The prayer flags there are tightly bound in to the pole.

Daphne Cannabina, as thin as Oxford India paper, are printed with symbols of this invocation as closely as the space permits. Many hundreds of sheets of this paper are compressed into every inch within the great revolving tub. The contents remain in a tight, hard block, even if the outer covering is broken. A prayer-wheel eight feet in height may contain this same mantra about a hundred million times. Every revolution of a wheel like this adds considerably, therefore, to the credit side of the Tibetan's account in Heaven. So easy is it to add a thousand billion or so of these ejaculations to one's account in a five minutes' visit to the nearest gompa, that the plain mind of the Occidental wonders why, if all this is really necessary, the Tibetan does not accumulate his merit in this easy fashion, instead of wandering all day long, uneconomically twisting in his hand the comparatively inefficacious hand wheel, or moving the still less expeditious lips. But here we soon learn to leave behind us all the logic of the West. A thing is so in Tibet because it has always been so; research is not encouraged; progress is a form of heresy.

Galinka lies at the foot of the great dam which once fell across the waters of the Ammo chu and made a lake where now the plain of Lingma-tang stretches itself. This is a curious feature of the valley. One climbs 200 feet up from Galinka by the side of the sprawling torrent and at last reaches a piece of turf about a mile and a half long, a quarter of a mile wide, and as flat as Lord's. In the rainless months the turf grows here short and thick, and provides the best grazing of all the valley. It would be easy to make some arrangement for the draining of the plain in the rains, but, as it is, from the end of July onward, Lingma-tang is a mere swamp, overgrown indeed with luxuriant vegetation and bright flowers, but, from a more practical point of view, a useless nuisance. Through this plain, in the curves of a tortured worm, the Ammo chu winds and rewinds itself. When the expedition first crossed the plain the rocky sides of the containing hills were bare of all but the seemingly dead trunks of birch, and the hardly more lifelike blackish-green of the pines. A scanty and thorny brush filled in the interstices among the boulders just where the steep hills stood knee-deep in the plain, but that was all. The "vleis" of South Africa, which have been formed in a similar manner, will offer the best suggestion of the exactly perfect surface—then covered with brown, burnt grass, cropped short by sheep, and, as we once discovered, by shao also. At the southern end of the valley the forest comes down close to the plain, and one leaves behind the treeless level to be engaged at once among the junipers and pines of the last stage of vegetation which at this great altitude the valley of the Ammo chu can show. The thorny shrubs cease as if by magic when the road has reached the upper part of the rocky slope which has to be scaled before the road begins again an even ascent by the side of the stream. The silver firs come down thickly to the very edge of the water, and under their shade the track runs between moss-covered rocks some twenty feet above the water, which here falls in a torrent from boulder to boulder, pausing only when delayed by the frost, which hangs great combs of ice from every gray dead fir athwart the stream. Junipers and a few twenty-foot rhododendron trees take advantage of the shelter of a turn in the range of hills just where the stone breast-work of Tong-shong crosses the road. The heavy, resinous smell of the pines harmonizes well with the carpet of dark-green moss which sprawls at will over the seamed rocks of Indian red and sienna. The mountains, 2,000 feet over our heads, barely allow the road to squeeze between their gigantic Symplegades. Five miles beyond the end of Lingma-tang the road crosses the torrent twice and one comes out over a stony patch and a carpet of brown pine needles into a little clearing, where a heavy fall of grayish-black granite warns the traveler of the strange characteristics of the road for the next two or three miles.

Some years ago—ninety or a hundred, perhaps, if one may judge by the size of the largest of the trees growing among the débris—a Himalayan convulsion shattered vertically the eastern side of the hills which hem in the tumbling river on the west. They now stand stark, austere, and perpendicular a thousand feet above the roadway and the stream. No trees crown their summits, not a bush can find root-hold on their granite faces. But at their feet a long, continuous buttress of granite, torn rawly from its matrix by the shock, forms a ramp 200 feet in height below the crannies and clefts of the gigantic curtain overhead. This ramp is composed of boulders varying in size from mere splinters of granite, which have been used wherewith to metal the bridle-path, to one great giant at Ta-karpo or "White Rock." This is one of the most prominent features of the Chumbi Valley. There are in it over 70,000 cubic feet of stone above the level of the débris over which the road goes, and on which the Chinese post has been built.[1]

The name of this rock must have been given years ago. When this granite is newly exposed to the air it is of a vivid, crystalline whiteness. Such granite is not, perhaps, to be found elsewhere in the world. For not only is it incomparable in color, but its hardness almost defies dynamite; the explosion of the charge does not cleave the boulders, it merely breaks out great craters from the stone. The stone darkens rapidly on exposure to the air, and the sparkling purity is soon hidden under a film of dull grayish-black. Beside this sloping terrace, crowned only with birch and juniper, the river rushed between frozen banks. Sometimes there was only a narrow channel left in the middle, and one could see the three-foot balks of

[1] The use by the Tibetans of the stored warmth of the sun in these vast blocks of stone is quite intentional. The vegetation immediately surrounding this great rock showed the stimulating power of the accumulated heat, slowly surrendered all the frosty night by the fallen monster. To this may also be due the constant use by wayfarers of the natural shelters formed by hollows under projecting rocks.

ice which hedged the water in, and listen to the quiet "seethe" with which, now and again, a thin detached layer of ice begotten of last night and astray upon the current mounted and came to rest upon the thickening, greenish mass below. It was just like the prickling crackle of a glazier's diamond. Sometimes the ice extended from shore to shore, broken here and there by some whirlpool which had defied the cold, or some spirt of water where the stream flowed too viciously over a rounded stone to be entirely caught by the closing-in grip of the frost. It was a wild scene, and very soon the limit of vegetation, which is here about 13,300 feet, was apparent a little way up the hill-sides. Birches are the last to go.

Another sharp climb brings one to the last phase of the Chumbi Valley. This, indeed, is different from all the scenes through which we have passed. A promontory, now being avoided by the work of pioneers, gave us a view of the bare plain of Dota ahead. To the east a frozen waterfall, nearly a hundred feet in height, was the rallying-point of our attention. It was a gigantic, irregular pillar of ribbed ice, through which the evening sun played with the colors of a Pacific shallow. But this was the last example of abruptness. From that point till the Tang la rises gently beneath the ice-bound crags of Chumolhari, on all sides the hills sweep down gently to the stream or valley, bellying, brown, grassy slopes—for all the world like Sussex downs tilted together at an angle. There was not on all that waste of formless and almost naked rock a stick of vegetation a foot high. Only little dead bents of aconite prick up still brown and innocent. Nothing else breaks the monotony of the finger-long blades of coarse low-lying grass. I do not suppose that in all the world you could find a contrast so great as that which meets the eye at Dota during your stage from Gautso to the plain below the pass. From Dota to the Tang la, and indeed on northward for three thousand miles, ex-

A MEMBER OF THE EXPEDITION

Outfitted to cross the high passes of the Himalayas in July

cept for the fertile alluvial flats which hem in the rivers of southern Tibet, this scenery remains monotonous, waterless, heartbreaking. One has said good-by to the Himalayan landscape with a suddenness that can hardly be conceived, and from this point onward the track winds round the easy curves of hills or picks its way along the flat, stubbly plains till, as one turns the last corner beyond Kamparab, Phari Jong comes out from behind the last spur on the left and dominates the distance, a square, grayish block of keep and bastion and parapet commanding the converging highways of three States, and itself humiliated by the overhanging 10,000 feet of Chumolhari's rock and ice.

The town of Phari deserves more than a passing notice. The name—which in Tibetan is spelled "Phag-ri," or the "pig-hill"—has been explained in many ways. The small mound on which it is built may, or may not, have been shaped like a pig, as the inhabitants say. The name may or may not have some reference to the pig goddess who is re-incarnated by the shores of the Lake of Palti as the Dorje Phagmo—the Abbess of Samding. There is a third explanation, which the lamas of the monastery of Chat-sa, four miles away to the north, say is self-evident, but of that later. The Jong itself is clearly of Chinese-plus-European construction. Its date, as ascertained by papers at Lhasa, was said by the two Jong-pens, or fort commandants, to be about 1500 A.D.; it is, indeed, impossible to assign it to a date later than 1600, and the assertion of the custodians may well be true. A well-constructed stone parapet eighteen feet high, with corner bastions, surmounts a low hill about twenty feet in height. Above this, occupying the center of the hill, stands the keep, about fifty feet in height and a hundred and twenty wide, of several stories, and irregularly bastioned, or rather buttressed. The fort lies square to the points of the compass, each side of the parapet being about 110 yards in length. The peculiar features in its construction conclusively prove that the place was built in unreasoning imitation of some European model, for the little machicolated galleries which bestraddle the corners of the outer bastions are entirely useless. Nothing could be dropped from them, as they dominate precisely the points at which no sane commander would deliver an attack. Moreover, they are of the flimsiest construction, and, at present at any rate, do not even possess floors. Inside, the Jong is dark, badly constructed, and, to some extent, positively dangerous, as the seeming solid walls are actually thin skins of granite masonry filled with rubble. In many places one skin has fallen and the interior beams are supported wholly upon the other. Quite recently a large part of the northern wall has completely fallen. A certain amount of armor, both of iron and bamboo, was found in the Jong, but every weapon of modern construction had been carefully removed to the north or buried.

It is, however, the town of Phari which will remain longest in the memory of those who have seen it but once. The headquarters mess of the escort to the Mission included several men whose experience of the outlying places of the world it would be difficult to equal round another table. But by common consent Phari was the filthiest town on earth. This is a charge not infrequently made against other towns, so it may be worth while to justify the right of Phari to that bad eminence. First, let it be said in fairness that there are more than a few reasons why the inhabitants of this town are of necessity dwellers in dirt. To begin with, Phari, at a height of 15,000 feet, is the highest town worthy of the name in the world. The cold is consequently fearful, a nightly temperature ranging in February rather downward than upward from —3° F., being often joined with a merciless grit-laden cold wind from the north. Cold is admittedly an excuse for dirt, but it is not cold only that palliates the filth of Phari. At this altitude the least exertion brings on breathlessness and apathy. To put on a pair of boots and gaiters is often a serious exertion for the new-comer, and it is not, perhaps, to be expected that the good people of Phari should go out of their way to secure by unwelcome activity a sanitation and cleanliness which appeal to them as little as to other Tibetans. Indeed, any others of that uncleanly race would, under similar circumstances, attain an equal degree of dirt. The absence of trees, compelling the wretched people here to use argol or dried yak-dung as their only fuel, is another contributory cause. The heavy, greasy blue fumes of these fires coat the interior of the squat houses with a layer of soot which it would be useless labor to remove. Unfrozen water is almost non-existent, except during the summer, and, so far at least as the women are concerned, the dirt which seams their faces is not perhaps unwelcome, for, as we know, custom compels the disfigurement with kutch (or raddle resembling dried blood) of the brows and cheeks of women in Tibet.

Having thus pleaded the cause, I have now to explain the results of this want of cleanliness upon the town of Phari. The collection of sod-built hovels, one or, at most, two stories in height, cowers under the southern wall of the Jong for protection against the wind from the bitterest quarter. The houses prop each other up. Rotten and misplaced beams project at intervals through the black layers of peat, and a few small windows lined with crazy black match-boarding sometimes distinguish an upper from a lower floor. The door stands open; it is but three black planks, a couple of traverses, and a padlock. Inside, the black glue of argol smoke coats everything. A brass cooking-pot or an iron hammer, cleaned of necessity by use, catches the eye as the only thing in the room of which one sees the real color. A blue haze fills the room with acrid and penetrating virulence. In the room beyond, the meal is being cooked, and a dark object stands aside as one enters. It is a woman, barely visible in the dark. Everything in the place is coated and grimed with filth. At last one distinguishes in a rude cradle and a blanket, both as black as everything else, an ivory-faced baby. How the children survive is a mystery. It is the same in every house. Nothing has been cleaned since it was made, and the square hole in the flat roof, which serves at once to admit light and air, and to emit smoke, looks down upon practically the same interior in five hundred hovels.

But it is in the streets that the dirt strikes one most. Let it be said at once that in the best quarter of the town, that in which the houses are two-storied, the heaped-up filth—dejecta and rejecta alike—rises to the first-floor windows, and a hole in the mess has to be kept open for access to the door. It must be seen to be believed. In the middle of the street, between the two banks of filth and offal, runs a stinking channel, which thaws daily. In it horns and bones and skulls of every beast eaten or not eaten by the Tibetans—there are few of the latter—lie till the dogs and ravens have picked them clean enough to be used in the mortared walls and thresholds. The stench is fearful. Half-decayed corpses of dogs lie cuddled up with their mangy but surviving brothers and sisters, who do not resent the scavenging ravens. Here and there a stagnant pool of filth has partially defied the warmth, and carrion, verminous rags, and fur-wrapped bones are set round it in broken yellowish ice. In the middle the brown patch is iridescent. A curdled and foul torrent flows in the day-time through the market-place, and half-bred yaks shove the sore-eyed and mouth-ulcered children aside to drink it. The men and women, clothes and faces alike, are as black as the peat walls that form a background to every scene. They have never washed themselves. They never intend to wash themselves. Ingrained dirt to an extent that it is impossible to describe reduces what would otherwise be a clear, sallow-skinned, but good-complexioned race to a collection of foul and grotesque negroes.

THE TWO ABBOTS OF A TIBETAN MONASTERY

"Dirt, dirt, grease, smoke." Thomas Manning's concise description of Phari as he knew it on the 21st of October, 1811, holds to this day, and the cleaning up which went on inside the walls of the great buttressed fort after our arrival provoked no imitation in the foul streets and grimed turf-built hovels at its foot.

And the disgust of all this is heightened by an ever-present contrast, for, at the end of every street, hanging in mid-air above this nest of mephitic filth, the cold and almost saint-like purity of the everlasting snows of Chumolhari—a huge wedge of argent a mile high—puts to perpetual shame the dirt of Phari.

The Jong-pens, or twin commandants of the fortress, had trimmed their sails with some dexterity under the stress of this breeze of foreign influence. They had served us not unfaithfully, a fact which they had doubtless kept from the knowledge of those far Lhasan authorities with whom their correspondence was neither confessed nor unknown to us. For their reception of the English into the fort—an occupation which every succeeding week more fully justified—the two Jong-pens were ceremonially degraded at Peking. This, however, is the East. At the request of the very Power whose reception had caused their disgrace, they were at once, with equal formality, reinstated in their dignities of the crystal button and the backward-slanting peacock feather—avowedly for services rendered to the English. What wonder if these two worthy men were a little bewildered as to their duty! Nor was it clear to them on which side their bread would ultimately prove to be buttered. With gratitude they accepted the offer of a monthly salary of 50 rupees apiece during our occupation of Phari; with foresight they declined to accept any money from us until after the expedition was over. Asked whether they believed that we should be unsuccessful, they smilingly put the question by. But, they said, there were many and powerful forts lying between us and Gyantse, and though the Pilings—they ought not to have used the word to us—were beyond question a mighty race, who could foresee the future? They accepted the invidious position with a good grace, and, on the whole, after a preliminary attempt to smuggle cattle over the near Bhutanese frontier, they acted with apparent integrity.

Such was the road along which the toilsome preparations for the advance crept slowly to the storehouses of Chumbi and Phari from the plains of India. Through all the tedious months necessitated by this provision for the future, Brigadier-General Macdonald, with the exception of one or two expeditions up and down along the line of communication, remained at Chumbi. Meanwhile, Colonel Younghusband, with the members of the Mission, remained pent up in the wretched little houses which cower beneath the hills of Tuna from the eternal blast which drives the grit under foot along the open frozen wastes of Tuna.

CHAPTER V

THE FIGHT AT THE WALL

ALL preparations were ready by the last week in March, and on the 26th Brigadier-General Macdonald started from Chumbi. His first march brought him to the small wooded plain of Gautso, where a strong little camp had been maintained for some time. It was the last halt below the upper limit of trees, and for the last time we enjoyed here an unlimited supply of fuel. The next day the force pushed on to Phari, where a day's halt was made to compose the column finally for the advance. On the following day a short march was made to a camping-place on the bare plains one mile short of the Tang la. It was a bitterly cold spot, utterly unprotected in any way, and the two slight valleys which meet here acted as funnels for the wind that blows everlastingly across these frozen plains. On the 29th of March,[1] the camp was struck early. Chumolhari rose overhead, veiling its vast icy slopes with thin, half-frozen cloud. From behind it the sun rose coldly, forming, by some curious series of accidents, the most beautiful and complete white rainbow that any of us had ever seen. There is something about a white rainbow which is not entirely different from the plumage of a white peacock. If you look closely you will find that the structure of the missing bands of color remains almost unchanged, and in this perfect half-circle of the purest white one could almost imagine the ghostly lines of division between the customary tints. For twenty minutes it arched over the

[1] Nel mezzo del cammin di nostra vita.

valley running up westward toward Pahamri, and vanished slowly as the long line of the expedition moved out of camp.

It was a bitter morning; the promise of the sun was betrayed, and, as we ascended the last furlongs of the southern slope, the cold came down upon us again with bitter intensity. Crossing the Tang la into Tibet proper was a terrible experience. The frozen mist, laced with stinging splinters of ice, was blown horizontally into our faces by the wind which never sleeps over this terrible pass. Men and animals alike were stiff with an armor of ice, and beards and even eyelashes were powdered and hoary with the fine particles of frozen mist. It was difficult to see fifty yards away, and it would be difficult to form a just idea of the hardships which no human activity can ever hope to remove from the highway leading on to Lhasa.

Slowly creeping on against the blizzard, the long line of animals and men moved into and out of the narrow radius of one's sight, demi-cloaked with ice. About eight o'clock the sun gathered enough power to melt the frost in the air, and an hour later, looking up from the mist which rose like steam from the plain, one could see the clear white top of Chumolhari sailing against the thin light clouds of the upper air. We had crossed the frontier. Half an hour later the plain was clear to the horizon, and we trudged on against the wind and over as forbidding a floor as exists on earth. It was grit and pebbles all the way. There was not the slightest hint of even the dead brittle shrubs of wormwood that gave promise of greenery on the plain of Phari: Two streams, hard bound with ice, lay across our path, and Tuna was not to be seen till we were almost upon it. When it at last came in sight it seemed a strange place, indeed, for the residence of a British Commissioner for the whole winter. Backed by arid sand-stone dunes 600 or 700 feet high, its only outlook is toward the snow-fields, peaks, and glaciers of the dividing range between Bhutan and Tibet, culminating to the west in the gigantic mass of Chumolhari. There had been nothing to do all the winter. There was little game to shoot, and the only walk, unless one climbed the hills at the back of the post, was "there and back again" across the accursed frozen waste. As we came near, the houses which the Mission had originally occupied appeared. They are squalid in the extreme, and one could well understand that Colonel Younghusband and his men had early preferred to brave the cold of the winter in their tents.

On our arrival we had luncheon with the Mission—these were the days before the stores began to run low—and a surprisingly good luncheon it was. We heard the latest news. The Tibetans had been watched for some days; they had built a wall across the road at a point between six and seven miles to the north, and there was no doubt that, besides the force (then estimated at about a thousand men) who were manning this defense, large bodies of Tibetans were also busy on the other side of the Bam tso. From the old narratives of the eighteenth century, one had expected to find this lake within sight of Tuna, and it is quite clear that at no very remote period Tuna itself was almost washed by its waters. But not a sign of them was now to be seen, though the short cut to Lhasa through the La-tse Karo la, just visible across the plain, proved how recently the ground had at any rate been a swamp by the wide curve which it took before it started northeast, from the posting-station and village of Hram.[1]

A typical day followed. From the earliest dawn till after sunset, a piercing wind swept the camp from end to end with a hurricane of tingling grit, and the discomfort of the men was increased by the device which Brigadier-General Macdonald adopted to deceive any Tibetan scouts who might be lurking

[1] This village is supposed to give an alternative name to this sheet of water. It appears as the Hramtso on many maps, but without any real justification.

among the hills which hemmed in the plain to the west. All tents were struck and the men received strict orders to conceal themselves. Captain Ottley, after a reconnaissance with his mounted infantry, reported that the Tibetans had temporarily retired from their wall, and from the string of sangars which led upward from its western end over the spurs of the neighboring hills. But as they had returned in full force by the morning of the 31st, it is more probable that they were driven away, not in any belief that the Mission had retreated, but simply because even the Tibetans found the discomfort of the day unbearable.

At twenty minutes past eight on the 31st the column moved out. About a mile and a quarter of the road ran eastward immediately under the high spur to which I have referred. Then, turning sharply to the north, it makes its way five miles to the little promontory and ruined house between which the road runs. Here, as we could see two miles away, the Tibetans had built their defenses. On the plain itself, the wall ran from the spur to the house, constructed in the shape of four redans with narrow openings between them. On the left hand the hills, grassless and stony, rose steadily until the saddle joined the two-thousand-foot ridge three miles away to the west. Here there were seven or eight sangars. But to our right a clear space of three thousand yards of level plain stretched between the end of their poor little defenses and the nearest swamp bordering the far but just visible waters of the lake. The fatuity of the Tibetan scheme of defense would, one thinks, have been manifest to a child. No attempt whatever to block this space was made. The truth is that the whole project had been conceived in Lhasa. The authorities there were guided by an obsolete map, or possibly by a mistaken remembrance of the locality, and the general who came to conduct operations had no authority to select another field for his defense. The fact that the lake had retreated about two miles from its ancient shore was a matter of which the lamas in the capital were either ignorant or careless.

We tramped steadily across the plain—a mere continuation of the Tuna plateau, frozen deep, and barely supporting the scanty growth of thistles that pricked up here and there through the patches of still lying snow. Everything under foot or in the distance was gray and colorless. You will understand more clearly the scene of the coming incident if you will remember the bitter frost-laden south wind blowing all day with increasing strength beneath a hard ash-gray sky.

Just when the Tibetan wall had become clearly visible in the distance, a messenger, riding forward in haste, announced the coming of the leading men of the defending force. The Lheding Dépen himself was in the field, and he, accompanied by his brother general from Shigatse, the late Commandant of Phari, and Gesur Yeshe Wang-gyuk (the representative of the great Ga-den monastery), ambled quickly across the plain, and an informal conference was held between the military and political chiefs on either side. It was merely a repetition of the same old story. Coached from Lhasa, the delegates had no power, if, indeed, they had the wish or saw the necessity, to say anything but the old parrot-cry, "Go back to Yatung." As Colonel Younghusband himself reminded them, this obstinacy had served the Tibetans in good stead for fifteen years. Hitherto it had always succeeded; how then were they to realize that at last the British Government was in earnest? After twenty minutes of excited but fruitless discussion, carried on through the interpretation of Captain O'Connor—at such times the most immovably patient of men—the small durbar was broken up and the more important of the Tibetans cantered back to their defenses in a cloud of dust. One or two only endeavored, by violent gesticulation and shouting all together, to secure the retreat of the English commissioner. O'Connor, though he was being jostled and ridden off ten times a minute, retained his composure, explaining again and again that the advance must now continue, and that Colonel Younghusband could listen to nothing before Gyantse was reached. At last they were made to understand, and shouting excitedly to each other they, too, scampered away on their stout little ponies. It was a curious incident—the impassive *non possumus* which Younghusband returned to the heated declamations of the two senior delegates; the gay yellow and green coats of the generals from Lhasa and Shigatse; the various head-dresses; the purple and blue of the robes; the strange forked guns embossed with turquoise and coral; the richly worked sword hilts; the little gray and bay ponies, saddle-clothed with swastika-patterned stuffs and gay with filigree brass headbands and wide molded iron stirrups—all these things straight from the sacred and forbidden city possessed a new and intense interest for all of us.

There was no doubt about it; the Tibetans intended to defend their walls, and this created a most unpleasant predicament. Acting upon Colonel Younghusband's instructions, the General ordered that not a shot was to be fired until the enemy had begun. This, in other words, meant that our men were to forego every advantage which discipline and modern weapons conferred upon them. At the worst, it meant that they were obliged to march straight up to sangars, held by men equipped with firearms of unknown strength, and that, not only were they to suffer a possibly destructive volley before opening fire, but that they might even be compelled to carry on the combat at a range so short and from ground so coverless that the Tibetans would enjoy other advantages besides that of sheer numbers, which they already possessed. Still, the thing was done. It was such a policy as has probably had no parallel since the days of the Old Guard at Fontenoy, and it is more to the credit of Indian discipline than English readers may realize that not a man, Gurkha or Sikh, disobeyed the order all the day.

AWAITING AN ATTACK BY THE TIBETANS

The scene was a strange one. Out toward the lake a thin extended line was pushed forward, far outflanking the wall and entirely commanding the line of the Tibetans' retreat. Meanwhile, the 23d Pioneers and the 8th Gurkhas were slowly clearing the hills on the left, making each sangar disgorge its holders one after the other. It was done in silence, and almost with good-humor; but there was a hush of suspense among the two staffs out in the plain who were watching with straining eyes the slow progress of the khaki dots on the hillsides two miles away. At any moment a shot might fire the powder magazine, and it was not till the last of the hundreds of gray-coated figures had slowly come down to the wall that the officers shut up their field-glasses and moved on to where the work of disarmament was just beginning. The sense of an insecurely leashed anger which might break out at any moment was suddenly replaced by an exaggerated sense of security and congratulation. The incident was regarded as practically over. The Commissioner and the General rode in together to the wall to watch the huddled group of Tibetans massed behind it, covering as much ground as a battalion in quarter column. On either side of them were our men. In front also the wall was lined with the 32d Pioneers; the line of retreat alone lay open to them. Two hundred others had been taken prisoners up the hillside and disarmed there. These remained passive and thankful spectators of what was to follow.

The main body of the Tibetans were bewildered, but not subdued. The whole thing must have been incomprehensible to these poor men. No order had been given to them to retreat, and they seemed to have acquiesced in their friendly expulsion by the Gurkhas and Sikh Pioneers in a dazed way. Gathered together in a body, their enormous superiority in numbers must have struck them. They had no idea, of course, of the advantage which we possessed, and there was a growing murmur as they discussed the matter excitedly behind the wall. Some of them then and there concocted a scheme which might have had terrible results, and the unwitting action of the Mission leaders almost put it into their power to carry it out. As we afterward found from the prisoners, they on the spot determined upon nothing less than to permit the advance guard of the expedition to go through, and then fall suddenly upon the members of the Mission themselves. The disarmament upon which the General insisted of course defeated their plans, and it was in the attempt to carry out this operation that the storm broke. When the Sikhs advanced toward the wall and began the work there was difficulty from the outset. In some cases the Tibetans actually struck the Pioneers; in others, there ensued a struggle for a weapon; but this was not immediately noticeable from where Younghusband and the General were standing, ten yards away from the house at the far end of the wall. Homer has given the explanation of what then took place: Steel of itself, says he, draws a man, and this handling of weapons was a terrible risk. It was almost exactly noonday.

The Dépen of Lhasa himself was the man who set the slumbering mine ablaze. He was seated on his horse just outside the wall, and, exempt himself from the confiscation of his arms, he shouted hysterically to his men to resist. They replied by stoning the Sikhs. Even then, though the whole affair hung in a slippery balance indeed, the latter held themselves in check. One of them advanced to the head of the Dépen's pony as the Lhasan General tried to move up toward the wall. In an evil moment for himself and his countrymen, the head of the great house of Lheding drew his pistol and fired, smashing the Sikh's jaw. There was an awful pause, that lasted for perhaps three seconds; and then another report broke the stillness. A jezail, for which a Sikh and a Tibetan were struggling, discharged itself into the air. But it was almost unnoticed in the sudden yell with which the Tibetans hurled themselves with drawn swords against the thin line of Pioneers leaning up against the wall. Such of them as had their

JUST BEFORE THE FIGHT AT THE WALL

The Gurkha scouts deployed on the hillside: the Sikhs beginning to disarm the Tibetans at the further end of the wall

pieces ready fired point-blank at the Indian guard, and then dropping them, flung themselves with their long, straight, heavy swords into the mêlée. Two Europeans were caught inside the wall, and both were wounded. One, Mr. Candler, the correspondent of the *Daily Mail,* was severely cut about before his assailants could be shot down. The other, Major Dunlop, found himself confronted by a furious Tibetan who cut his hand upon his rifle stock with a fearful thrust before Dunlop was able to kill him.

By this time the storm had broken in full intensity, and from three sides at once a withering volley of magazine fire crashed into the crowded mass of Tibetans. It was like a man fighting with a child. The issue was not in doubt, even from the first moment; and under the appalling punishment of lead, they staggered, failed, and ran. Straight down the line of fire lay their only path of escape. Moved by a common impulse, the whole mass of them jostling one against another with a curious slow thrust, they set out with strange deliberation to get away from this awful plot of death. Two hundred yards away stood a sharply squared rock behind which they thought to find refuge. But the Gurkhas from above enfiladed this position and the only hope they had lay in reaching the next spur half a mile away. Had we been armed with their weapons, another hundred yards would have brought them into safety, even in the open. It was an awful sight. One watched it with the curious sense of fascination which the display of unchecked power over life and death always exerts when exercised. Men dropped at every yard. Here and there an ugly heap of dead and wounded was concentrated, but not a space of twenty yards was without its stricken and shapeless burden. At last, the slowly moving wretches—and the slowness of their escape was horrible and loathsome to us—reached the corner, where at any rate we knew them safe from the horrible lightning storm which they had themselves challenged.

All this was necessary, but none the less it sickened those who took part in it, however well they realized the fact. This was no fighting in the usual sense of the word. As soon as their first assault had failed there was nothing for the Mission escort to fear, except, perhaps, the bullets of their own companions. This was so real a danger that the company of the 32d, which had been sent round on the right, as has been described, was obliged to retreat so as to leave a clear field for the fire of the Gurkhas on the slope of the spur. The guns had come into action on the right as soon as possible, but the extraordinary difference which these high altitudes make in the burning of a fuse[1] nullified their work to a very great extent. I do not suppose that any white man in the force was anything but sincerely glad when one more dark-coated little figure disappeared in safety behind the distant corner. But the behavior of the native troops was beyond all praise. They had kept their temper and their discipline till it was almost beyond human endurance. And when the word was given they naturally had no mercy upon an enemy whose attempt to equalize matters by the hand-to-hand use of vastly superior numbers had been tried and failed. It was a short but a terrible lesson.

An attempt was made to defend Guru itself, two miles on, but this was easily defeated; and after leaving a small garrison in the place, the column returned to Tuna against a bitter wind and a darkening sky.

The lesson which Guru should have taught was hardly learned by the Tibetans. It should have been patent to them from that moment, that until they had adopted modern weapons and, perhaps, also had adopted some of the methods of the tribes on the northwest frontier, it would be vain for them to attempt to resist by force the progress of our troops. But every one of the men

[1] At the Kara la a distance requiring a 19 half-second fuse was only properly shelled by reducing the fuse to 9.

A FEW MINUTES LATER
The British force still firing at the retreating Tibetans

whose report might have carried weight in Lhasa was dead, and all we could ever afterward learn suggested rather that this complete and utter rout of the pick of the Tibetan army was looked upon in Lhasa rather as a disgrace to the officers concerned than as a final proof of the foolishness of opposing us in the open field. We afterward found that about fifteen hundred men in all had been detailed for the defense of the Tibetan position on this side. Another force of about one thousand men was ready to defend the road to Lhasa across the lake, where twenty-four well-made sangars had been built across the road. Another body of men, estimated variously at from two hundred to one thousand, remained in Guru when their companions advanced to their position.[1] The troops returned to Tuna for the night, and before we advanced again, it had been found necessary to amputate Mr. Candler's left hand. He stayed at Tuna some time, and when he was well enough to be moved, returned to Darjeeling till the final advance began.

This incident made it imperative that the advance to Gyantse should be carried out as quickly as possible. The road was reported clear to the Kala tso. Beyond that, vague rumors reached us of a concentration of Tibetans, generally embroidered with accounts of mailed horsemen and other picturesque details, which unfortunately were never justified by the fact.

[1] Here, as elsewhere, it seems to me that the numbers of the enemy have been overrated in the official estimates.

CHAPTER VI

FORCING THE WAY TO GYANTSE

AFTER the fight at the Hot Springs the force remained at Tuna for three days. On the morning of the 4th of April the Mission and its escort moved on to Guru, passing over the scene of the sudden disaster of the previous Thursday. Everywhere, indeed, ugly traces of the tragedy were still only too visible. Everything that could possibly be done had been carried out by the medical officers, and it is only fair to record the quiet work among the Tibetan wounded which was done on their own initiative by the surgeons connected with the force. Captains Walton, Baird, and Kelly, and Dr. Franklin had worked unceasingly all day on the 1st among the wounded Tibetans, and it would be difficult to describe adequately the blank amazement with which our prisoners regarded this treatment. Mercy to prisoners is not a characteristic of the Oriental, and not one of the wretched men whose wounds had rendered it impossible for them to escape or to be carried away had the least idea that any mercy except a *coup de grâce* would be extended to them. They were tenderly treated and the resources of the expedition were lavishly used. In the end the inevitable occurred, and it was with the utmost difficulty that we could shake off from us the Tibetans whom we had restored to health and strength.

The information that was received from these men was simple and always to the same effect. They had no quarrel with us; they had been driven to the front unwillingly, partly by the superstitious hold which the Lamas had over them, partly by the threat of physical punishment which the hierarchy did not fail to wield; and they realized soon enough that any attempt to stop us was not only unnecessary but impossible. At any rate they would prefer to take up any service, however menial, with us rather than go back to the tyranny of their priests. Many wounded men came in from a distance of their own accord. Morning after morning one or two dead figures would be found a few hundred yards away from our outposts—men who had been painfully trying to drag their broken bodies in to this miraculous healing of which the fame had spread far and wide. It has often been said, and no doubt said with some truth, that the work that we then did to heal our wounded enemies, besides sorely depleting our stock of bandages and other surgical necessities, was a source of weakness rather than strength to the subsequent negotiations. The methods of a Genghiz Khan would no doubt have brought our Mission to a speedier end. But knowledge is not to be confounded with wisdom, and many of our Oriental experts have forgotten in their experience of detail that, after all, the Oriental is a man. Whatever may be the ultimate success or permanence of our diplomatic relations with the present priestly government of Tibet, the reputation for magnanimity which we have secured among the poor unlettered peoples of these uplands will as a tradition long outlive the remembrance of political success, however great. Besides, the thing had to be done.

The column halted at Guru. This is an unattractive spot, bare and wind-swept, and marked only by a few disreputable houses in two clumps, gathered in each case round a house of more respectable appearance. Here the Chinese "General" Ma appeared. But Captain Parr, of the Chinese Maritime Customs, declined to recognize his representative character. On the morning of the 5th, the Mission moved on past Dochen toward Chalu by the northern shore of the lake. It was a long march, and the narrowness of the shore made it impossible to advance in more than one column. Here we struck into the heart of the land of Bogle and Turner. What they wrote 130 years ago is true to the letter to-day. The high, naked spurs which inclose the plain upon which the Bam tso is now but a dwindling stretch, frowned upon us as we moved past the successive openings. Some grazing might perhaps be found here in the height of the summer, but in April there is no blade of vegetation except the usual wormwood. Divided from the road by a wide swamp, the waters of the lake, then partly frozen, were dotted with the innumerable wild-fowl which the previous explorers had reported. Ruddy sheldrake, pintails, bar-headed geese, pochards, terns, teal, and wild-duck were all to be seen and it was easy to approach within twenty yards of them. A curious thing was here to be seen. These birds undoubtedly migrate annually across the Himalayas from the plains of India. Lower down, they had had experience enough of the meaning and danger of a man's figure. Here in Tibet, where no bird had been shot since Bogle offended the susceptibilities of his companions, they did not show the slightest fear when the long dusty column bore down upon them. But after the evening of the 5th, when shooting was for the first time permitted after our arrival in camp, the change that came over the fowl was strange indeed. In a moment they became, and remained, as shy as ever they had been in India.

Under foot, on the cinderous slopes, the only vegetation was the hard circular sponges of saxifrage or the tiny plants of edelweiss, no larger than a florin, hiding away between the boulders and the stones. Here and there a hare scurried away before the feet of the column, but it was a rare break in the monotony. Across the lake to the east, the road to Lhasa ran visibly, and away to the south-east could be seen the deserted walls and sangars of Hram, which the enemy had deserted during the fight at Guru. Chalu was reached about three o'clock.

The village itself lies half-way between the two lakes on the borders of the stream which flows from the Bam tso into the Kala tso, a distance of about three miles. A halt was made just where this stream leaves the former lake. It was a cold, pitiless afternoon, with a horizontal sleet blowing and the promise of heavy snow that night. A few duck were shot and a welcome store of bhusa was obtained from Chalu. Lu-chea monastery was visible half-way up the hills to the east, but it was not visited, except by a foraging party. The stream joining the two lakes is traversed by a long stone causeway, about a quarter of a mile from the upper lake, and on the following morning it was crossed by the column, who were to make only a short march that day. The road between the two lakes runs at a little height above the stream in the defile. On either side there are steep hills, and Chalu occupies the only level place beside the road. It is only a short distance before the gorge ends and the waters of the Kala tso are seen. Even the most recent map makers, I notice, have insisted that this gorge is ten miles long. It is curious that they should have persisted in this mistake in spite of the far more accurate map which Turner drew in 1784.

As one goes on an extraordinary optical delusion is seen. The Kala tso stretches out, a great shield of silver gray on the left front, and the river, some thirty feet below us on the same side, appears to run up hill into it. This delusion, which is very striking, can only be accounted for by assuming that the eye is mistaken in the apparent height of the Kala tso. This lake certainly seemed to be on a level with the path along which we were marching, and the river is perhaps only seen as an accidental item in the picture. When, however, it is perceived running close under our feet, the inference that it has to make its way up hill to fall into the lake is, I suppose, irresistible. In any case, it is a curious spectacle, and one to which Manning evidently referred in his journal, though he must have misread his notes. He records this optical delusion as visible in Red Idol Gorge. The Kala tso, on the banks of which the column halted for the night of the 6th, after a short march, is the remains of a very much larger lake, which in earlier days covered the whole plain that now lies east of its shore. The scenery was the same as before, though the scanty grass bents now became a little more frequent, and thick wormwood appeared here and there in patches on the mountain-side.

The most remarkable thing here is the evidence of a very large population in earlier days which the continuous string of ruined walls and houses supplies. For a space of nearly two miles the hill-side road—which clings still to the mountains in avoidance of the now vanished lake—is marked by a wilderness of great pebbles which have dropped from the walls and houses of a lost civilization. The ground is still marked by lines of crumbling structures held together in the ground plan of their first shape by dry layers of mud-mortar. Thousands must have lived here once. As with most other things in Tibet, there are many different reasons suggested for this wholesale desertion—a small-pox, the subsidence of the lake, the Mongol invasion, the utter inability of the inhabitants to adjust themselves to so wretched and inhospitable an environment. Perhaps, also, the closing of the trade routes over the Sikkim passes may have had its effect. It is only clear to-day that the scanty duffle-clad figures who bow with protruded tongues at the entering in of their hamlets and the black-aureoled women whose heads appear inquisitively over the sordid sod-parapets of the roofs above are but the hundredth part of the population of a scattered but important trade center in the past.

The question that now exercised the General was whether the jong would be defended or not. It was apparent, even at this distance, that it would be no light matter to drive an enemy, however weakly armed, from so strong a position, and we were, as

THE EXPEDITION HALTING FOR THE NIGHT

a matter of fact, confronted by the easier slopes of the rock upon which it is built. There is no approach on the western side. Standing out as it does in the plain, joined only by a narrow saddle to the hills beside and above it, the jong is a formidable fort indeed. There was some delay about crossing the river, and then the column encamped above the river flats on the edge of the wide, fertile plain.

Emissaries came out from Gyantse—the Jong-pen and the Chinese General Ma who had first accosted us at Guru. The Jong-pen put the whole situation clearly enough. On the one hand, he said, if he were to surrender the jong to us, his throat would be cut by the Dalai Lama; on the other hand, he said, with naïve simplicity, that as all his soldiers had run away, he was not able to offer any effective opposition to our occupation of it. This was indeed true. Hundreds of Tibetan soldiers during the last halt made by us on the plain took advantage of our inaction to escape, carrying with them, it was reported, most of the available weapons from the jong and town. The Jong-pen of Gyantse is a kindly heavy old man like a saddened Falstaff; and it was with considerable regret that we were obliged to disregard his petitions. As events proved, however, it would have been a wiser thing if, instead of a temporary occupation of the fort, followed by inadequate demolitions near the two main gateways, we had boldly undertaken to occupy the place. Meanwhile it was clear that the Tibetans could not be allowed to remain undisturbed in the fort which commanded the country round. They were indeed promised that no harm should be done to any one in the place, and that the temples of the jong and of the town should remain untouched if, on their side, the Tibetans behaved with straightforwardness to us. We camped for the night beside a new and well-built house, and on the following morning moved in, prepared both for treachery and for the task, if need be, of taking the fort by storm. There was, however, no necessity for apprehension. The

Jong-pen and the Chinese General came out to meet us and surrendered the entire place. Still, precautions were not relaxed until the small party of pioneers, which we sent forward to investigate the ruined walls and towers that crowned the great rock, had climbed to the topmost pinnacle, and the Union Jack run up beside the gilt copper finial which marked the highest point. The utmost courtesy was shown to the Jong-pen, and he in his turn, though it must be feared with a heavy heart, undertook to help in the collection of necessary foodstuffs from the town and from the surrounding villages. Already a cursory examination of the storehouses and cellars of the jong had shown that the whole place was one gigantic granary. All was not, of course, discovered at first, but nearly eight thousand maunds [1] of grain and tsamba were found inside the storerooms of this fort alone. Two positions were selected by the military authorities as suitable for the residence of the Mission. One of them, Chang-lo, lay at the head of the approach across the Nyang chu, 1,350 yards from the large modern barrack round which the defenses on the jong were centered. The other lay within 500 yards of the rock, and (as the jong was not occupied by our troops) would have proved utterly untenable in the circumstances which afterward resulted in the practical investment of the Mission post. As it was, Chang-lo, the place occupied by Colonel Younghusband, was unpleasantly near and a thousand yards within the range of a Tibetan jingal. The following day the work of collecting the foodstuffs of the jong began under the able generalship of Major Bretherton, and the long convoys of mules began to go backward and forward between Chang-lo and the jong. Small bodies of mounted men went out to report upon the stores that could be supplied by the surrounding villages, and the amount far exceeded that reported as likely

[1] The maund used in the north-east of India weighs 80 pounds. This was, during the expedition, the accepted unit of measurement, and was also the normal weight carried by a single coolie.

THE HIGH PRIEST AT GYANTSE
"Who looks like a saddened Falstaff"

by the Mission. On the fourth day, Colonel Younghusband and the men moved into the smaller of the two compounds which comprise Chang-lo. It was a pretty place. A beautifully painted and columned open room opened upon a small courtyard, in the south wall of which was a gateway leading straight out on to a graveled court in which the finest poplar trees we ever saw in Tibet rose bare and branching over our heads. The other part of Chang-lo consisted of a very irregularly shaped building which probably represented the actual daily living-house of the ducal family of Chang-lo. It was very thickly built, and presented its most impregnable side toward the jong. This peculiarity, which was common enough in the houses of the plain to suggest that it was not wholly unintentional, proved afterward the salvation of the situation. The place was capable of defense, and to the south, away from the jong, a thick plantation of leafless willow-thorns was carpeted from end to end with iris. The river ran beside us sixty yards away, turning in its course toward the far distant spur upon which the scattered houses and temples of Tse-chen were built. Other white houses dotted the plain on all sides within a mile, and twelve hundred yards away to the north-east the little village of Pala, then deserted, guarded the road to Lhasa.

It is worth while to review the political situation at the time of our arrival at Gyantse. Colonel Younghusband had sent a letter to the Amban announcing to him the impending arrival of the British Mission, and requesting him to come to Gyantse to discuss the terms of the agreement, bringing with him properly qualified Tibetan representatives of sufficiently high rank. This letter was sent off during the march up, but I do not suppose that any one in the force really believed that the Tibetans were willing to treat with us. The news of their loss at Tuna was brought to the Lhasan authorities in a wholly mendacious form. It is easy to see how the incidents of that unfortunate day lent themselves to misconstruction. It was reported, and believed, in

Lhasa that the English had decoyed the Tibetan soldiers away from their defenses and had then wantonly shot them down. The truth was indeed known to the friendly States of Bhutan and Nepal, but these carry little weight in Tibetan councils. The only man in Lhasa who seems to have understood the gravity of the situation was Dorjieff himself. His action was immediate and characteristic. As soon as the news arrived of our occupation of Gyantse he suggested to the Tibetans the advisability of overwhelming the Mission by a night attack. This had been proposed by him already, while the Mission were still encamped at Kambajong, and it is likely that the retirement of the Mission from that place was rendered doubly ignominious in the eyes of the Tibetans because they believed our evacuation to be directly due to the attack for which they were preparing. Dorjieff was, however, far from confident as to the upshot of this experiment. He realized, better perhaps than any one else in Lhasa, that if the small force accompanying Colonel Younghusband were able to force their way on to the capital they would unhesitatingly do so. The name of Younghusband is unpleasantly well known in the chancelleries of St. Petersburg. He has never been associated with want of enterprise or of readiness to seize the least opportunity afforded by his opponent, but his far-sighted prudence was perhaps better recognized still. That the Colonel should have decided to remain in Gyantse with a small escort while Macdonald returned to the Chumbi Valley to organize arrangements for a further advance to Lhasa cannot, therefore, have seemed to Dorjieff to be the rashness of an over-confident man. So far Dorjieff's influence with the Dalai Lama was unimpaired; his position in the country was however weakened, not only because in spite of his assurances the English had actually been able to penetrate into the country, but also because it was now becoming known that Japan was actually at war with Russia, a disquieting suggestion of the latter's real strength. News of the Russian defeats did not reach Lhasa until

A VALLEY NEAR SAMONDA

EAST END OF THE JONG, OR FORTRESS, AT GYANTSE

Captured after a long and bitter fight

the middle of May, if information received there is to be trusted. Dorjieff, therefore, determined, after setting the fuse alight, to make the best of his way to a place of safety. If the British Mission were annihilated he could always return and claim the credit of the suggestion. If, on the other hand, the English were able to beat off the attack, Dorjieff foresaw only too clearly that his influence in Lhasa was doomed, and that even the Dalai Lama himself could not protect him.

While the Tibetans were preparing to send a fresh force for this hostile purpose they naturally refused to allow the Amban to negotiate with the Mission. The Viceroy himself repeatedly saw the Dalai Lama in person, but could get nothing from him; to his demands for transport and for responsible and accredited representatives of Tibet in the forthcoming negotiations no answer was returned. At one time he thought that when it came to the point the Tibetan government would hesitate to repudiate in any direct manner the suzerainty which he represented. He therefore bluntly reminded them that he was acting under the orders of the Chinese Emperor in demanding that they should negotiate; he added that the responsibility of acquiescing in the refusal of the Tibetans was so serious that he declined to be any party to their action. The orders had been given and signed with the vermilion pencil—those orders he intended to carry out. The immediate answer of the Dalai Lama was an assumption of all responsibility for the action of the Tibetan government. He said that he was willing to accept the onus of acting in contravention of his suzerain's commands.

Meanwhile, Colonel Younghusband found himself in a difficult position. The advance to Gyantse had been accepted as inevitable by the home government. But they did not believe that it would be necessary to make any further advance, and their policy at this time assumed the ultimate submission of the Tibetan government during this phase of our relations with the country, and Younghusband, in some way which is neither entirely clear nor entirely fair, was regarded as unduly anxious to press on to the capital. This was true in so far as that he recognized the importance, in dealing with Oriental nations, of concluding the treaty in no place short of the capital. Sound as this theory is in all cases, it is especially so in the case of Tibet. Gyantse is a place the political importance of which has been greatly over-rated; the truth is, that no city or district, except Lhasa, is of any political importance whatever. A treaty signed at Gyantse might have achieved one object. It might have given us a satisfactory basis for insisting, when we thought fit, upon the observation of its terms. But as binding the hierarchy of Lhasa it was of no more real importance than the treaty of 1890–3, which they had repudiated. Colonel Younghusband appreciated the difficulty of securing any finality in our relations with the Dalai Lama by negotiations at Gyantse, but he was throughout perfectly willing to accept the opinion of the Government and negotiate at this place. He may have regarded it as a half measure, but he recognized the necessity of carrying out his orders to the letter, if it were possible for him to do so. At the same time he also recognized the improbability of getting the Tibetans to co-operate.

Tradition and experience alike had combined to persuade the Tibetans of the truth of Disraeli's statement that delay is the secret of success. They had always succeeded in the past by a policy of abstention; why, then, even if we were able to reach a town of the political insignificance of Gyantse, should they be induced to abandon the policy which had served them in good stead for so many centuries? The Dalai Lama had perhaps good reason for his confidence. He remembered that assurances had been received long ago from a trustworthy source that the British Government were opposed to the risks involved by sending troops further into Tibet. It is true that he cannot be supposed to have understood the enormous advantage which the Parliamentary system of England put into his hands: he cannot have known that there was any serious criticism of Lord Curzon's policy in England: of the chance—which seemed to us in Tibet to be a considerable one—of a change of policy as the result of a General Election he can have known nothing. But there were many other things which may have influenced him in risking our unwillingness to proceed further into the country. In the first place, first by a long interval, Lhasa had never before been reached, and he may well have trusted to the experience of history. In the second place, he probably imagined that the advance to Lhasa would necessitate the employment of a very much larger force than that with which we had reached Gyantse, and no one knows so well as a Tibetan the impracticability of taking large bodies of men over these high uplands without long and careful preparation. Then, again, he looked forward to the evacuation of southern Tibet by the English as a matter of necessity, not so much because they were unable to withstand the climate there as because it was impossible to maintain communications during the winter over the terrible passes of the Chumbi Valley. Delay, therefore, was his obvious policy. It is an odd thought that if he had limited himself to this, his opposition might perhaps have been successful.

Of all these considerations, Colonel Younghusband was fully aware. He did not for a moment believe that negotiation at Gyantse could be carried through. His knowledge of Oriental habits and thought told him unerringly that in the capital only was there a chance of making such an impression as might secure the due observation of the treaty. But, on the other hand, his instructions from home were clear enough, and for some time, while the matter hung in the balance, it must have been difficult for him to see how any middle course was possible which would enable Lord Curzon to achieve even the most moderate triumph in the face of misconceptions in Whitehall. As we now know, the Tibetans all along were on the point of settling the matter by their own foolish action, but until the early days of May the outlook was blank indeed.

In the light of after events it was lucky that during those first three weeks after our arrival at Gyantse we did not let the grass grow under our feet. Much had to be done by the military authorities in putting Chang-lo into a proper state of defense, but for the members of the Mission, excepting Captain Ryder, R.E., and Captain Walton, I.M.S., there was little to do. Negotiation of any kind was obviously not intended by the Tibetans, and some of us spent our time in making expeditions to every point of interest in Gyantse and in the plain around.

CHAPTER VII

LIFE IN A TIBETAN TOWN

THE first view of Gyantse is imposing. Across the wide, level plain, cultivated in little irregular patches as closely as an English county, the high-walled peak from which the town gets its name[1] rises 500 feet into the air. From the first the jong fills the eye, and it is not until one is close that the low, white two-storied houses of the town are seen at its foot, nestling under the protection of the battlements and bastions of the great fort.

So huge is the mass of masonry and sun-dried brick with which the steep and isolated hill is crowned, that it is a matter of some surprise that it has received scanty or no attention from the few travelers who have passed beneath it. Manning, indeed, in 1811, refers to it as "a sort of castle on the top of a hill," a somewhat inadequate description of a pile of buildings hardly less in size than those of Mont St. Michel. Ruinous it was even in April, but that was hardly perceptible at a distance, and the apparent strength of the huge towers and curtains which overhang the almost precipitous rock would, one thinks, have impressed the most incurious of observers, among whom Manning, the only Englishman who has ever reached Lhasa, is unfortunately to be placed. Even in its existing condition, a week's siege and a couple of hundred casualties would have

[1] The name is written RGYAL-RTSE and means "Royal Peak." The "n" is merely an example of a common tendency to nasalize the close of a first syllable. "Palden Lhamo" is almost invariably pronounced "Panden Lhamo." The great monastery at Gyantse is often called the "Pan-khor Choide."

been the price of any attempt on our part to take the successive defenses by storm in the face of the slightest really well-handled opposition.

Leaving the level of the town at the south-eastern corner of the rock—which is 400 or 500 yards in length—one makes one's way up the zigzag approach hewn out of the side of the ocherous quartz-seamed sand-stone. The roadway, after running the gauntlet of a large detached bastion built against the flank of the almost perpendicular stone, leads up to the great gateway, in the deep recess of which—then partly supported by two stout wooden pillars and of no great strength—there hung from the ceiling four huge stuffed carcasses of dongs or wild yaks, with artificial eyes and tongues protruding in a fearsome way. But the beasts were falling to pieces from age, and rather resembled badly stitched leather bags than anything else. Everything that could fall from them—hair, horns, hoofs—had already fallen, and handfuls of the straw stuffing bulged out from every seam. After passing the gateway the road zigzags upward again, protected by a rough breast-work in which recent repairs and new loopholes were obvious every few yards. The latter were "splayed" on the inside, contrasting strongly with the older useless little slits which only allow a defender to fire straight in front of him. Higher up, beside some houses which are falling rapidly to pieces, was a new and well-built barrack store-room, in which thousands of pounds of powder, tons and tons of supplies, and tens of miles of matchlock fuse were found. Another hundred paces to the left brought one to the door of the most interesting series of rooms remaining in the jong. Darkened by the blocking up of their windows, one cellar-like low room leads into another—some little chapels, some living rooms, some storerooms. Out of these one came into a little court with a rotten wooden ladder and a loyal dirty gray watch-dog who exhibited more pluck than his flying masters had. At the

THE TOWN OF GYANTSE

Here the Mission made a long halt. It did not advance until the military escort, after a fierce battle with the Tibetans, captured the stronghold. The Palkhor Choide, inclosed in walls, fills the upper end of the picture.

top of the ladder a step to the left takes one into a small yard, one end of which is occupied by a little gompa or temple. Looking in from the sunlight one could just distinguish the great dull gold figure and smiling, placid countenance of the Master whose presentment no superstition or latitude can either deface or materially change. Whatever stage in art his devotees may have reached, the great teacher's own image remains the same from Japan to Java, and the gaudy "katags" or ceremonial scarfs hide in Gyantse as severely simple a design as you may find at Kamakura or Mandalay. One large turquoise supplied the ever-present bump of wisdom on Gautama's forehead, but otherwise there was no decoration. But when one entered the luxury that had been denied to the central figure was seen to be lavished on the ornaments that strew the *kyil-kor* or altar shelves beneath the Buddha. One great wrought-steel chorten with chased courses and turquoise and gold ornamentation stood out among a crowd of lesser ones of brass or silver, antique ivories from India, vases with peacock feathers, and great brass and copper lamps. These lamps are perhaps the most striking ornament of a Buddhist shrine. Sometimes single, there may be dozens and even hundreds, each composed of a wide and deep bowl of heaped-up butter, in which, floating in a little pool which its own warmth has made, burns a single wick with a small yellow flame. These are the last things that the priests will take away. If they fear looting, they will hide every other ornament, replacing them by strange, many-colored erections of butter (*torma*), which they mold with extraordinary dexterity into conventional structures, sometimes five or six feet high. But the altar lamps must, and do, remain, whatever the risk, and one of the pleas subsequently brought forward by the Abbot of Gyantse was that a fine to be paid in butter might be commuted, as they needed all the butter they could get for ceremonial use on their hundred altars—and they urged, with shrewd flattery, it was well known that the British never interfered with the religion of the countries into which they made their way.

Outside this little orange-walled gompa were five pots in which bloomed courageously well-grown plants of simple English stocks. It was a curious shock to see them. How they came there it would be useless to guess, but surely never before did stocks justify so well Maeterlinck's eulogy of those little flowers that "sing among ruined walls and cover with light the grieving stones." For up above the gompa rise the great towers and buildings which lead up to the topmost structure on the very edge of the precipice which confronts the Lamasery to the north-west; and even then, before the bombardments and explosions of later days, they were all roofless shells of stone which quivered in the light afternoon wind.

From the castle a fine view is to be had of the town of Gyantse and the great Lamasery of Pal-khor Choide, which stretches on the slope of a southerly spur facing the jong three-quarters of a mile away, protected by a long crimson wall from the assaults of the prevailing north-west wind. There are two curious things about this monastery. First, although it is subject to Lhasa, and therefore nominally a Gelukpa or Yellow Cap foundation, it contains representatives of nearly all the recognized sects in Lamaism, which are numerous and jealous, though not vitally opposed to each other in doctrine. A curious custom, however, is, that when the Nying-mas or Red Cap communities in Pal-khor Choide worship with the Gelukpas the former make the not inconsiderable concession of wearing the yellow cap instead of their own distinctive red one.

The other point, which is perhaps of little interest, is the legend that the great chorten or caitya outside the central temple was copied from the well-known temple of Buddh-Gaya long before the restorer's hand had obscured some of the characteristic features of the latter. This legend is, as a matter of

MURAL PAINTINGS IN THE LAMASERY OF PALKHOR CHOIDE

fact, wholly untrue. There is hardly any similarity between the two buildings. Chandra Das calls the architecture of the Gyantse building unique. In a way this is true, but the lower part represents fairly well on a minute scale—the whole base is only 120 feet each way—the great vihara of Boro-Bodoer in the middle of Java. There is the same number of balustraded terraces, and the sides of each contracting stage are broken by square projections in a similar way. Each projection or angle contains a small chapel. The upper part of the structure consists of a large white drum with four grotesquely ornamented doorways of a Burmese type, and a thirteen-ringed cone surmounted by a "htee" and finial, decorated with leaf-clapper bells, is also suggestive of Burma. The upper part is thickly ornamented with gold leaf, and the gilt copper plates composing the rings are each decorated with two incised figures of Buddha. The lower part of this pagoda—which is generally white—is roughly decorated here and there with color in an effective way, and the interior walls and passages are painted with microscopic finish, in some medium that produces an enamel-like surface.

As one leaves the chorten and enters the main temple, an exquisitely painted "Wheel of Life" (if we may accept the rough translation which Rudyard Kipling borrowed for "Kim" from Waddell) meets the eye to the left of the doorway leading from the vestibule to the central apartment. It is difficult to convey any idea of the minute finish of this piece of work. A few will realize it when I say that it is probably the only product of man's brush which rivals the "Book of Kells" or the "Lindisfarne Gospels." Up in the balcony above there is exquisite work, but upon this circle the artist has lavished an obvious affection and care which must be seen to be believed. In style it resembles thirteenth century illumination, but, for example, no Vision of Hell was ever drawn with such amazing delicacy and hideous ingenuity as are the quaint tortures of the damned in this representation of the Buddhist Sheol. Inside the central crimson-pillared hall the only conspicuous object is the great seated figure of Maitreya, the next Buddha to be re-incarnated. He is, as always, seated in European fashion, a tradition which is more suggestive than most modern Buddhist legends, and instinctively recalls the belief of Lamaism that the end of the present age will be marked by the surrender of Buddhism into the hands of the "Piling" or western foreigner.

In a recess of each of three sides of the central hall are great seated images of the Buddha. Sakya-muni himself is surrounded in the dark northern chapel by half-seen gigantic standing statues of Egyptian massiveness and simplicity, almost touching each other as they line the walls, and looming out of the obscurity with dignity and no small dramatic effect.[1] To the left of the vestibule is an odd chamber of horrors. It is reported to be sufficient to overawe the most insubordinate of lamas, but the decaying stuffed beasts that hung from the roof and the dingy demons painted on the walls were scarcely as horrible as the common blue and scarlet guardians of religion who protect the entrance to every gompa. A dragon's skin was pointed out to me. It was, perhaps, no bad imitation. Allowing for contraction, the python which once owned this covering must have been at least 25 feet long and 13 inches in diameter. Chain-armor, bows, quivers, flags, painted cloth, skins, a few old guns and spears, and a few little untidy altars, from which, as from every other shrine we visited in the Lamasery, every ornament, except the lamps, had been taken and hidden away in terror, and, of course, dirt everywhere, completed the furniture of this dismal chamber. But there remained many more temples and apartments, from the inspection of few of which we were excused by the talkative and, apparently, perfectly friendly

[1] A similar arrangement is to be seen in the sanctuary of the "Jo" in the cathedral of Lhasa.

IMAGES OF SOME OF THE GREAT BUDDHIST TEACHERS WORSHIPED BY THE TIBETANS

In the Palkhor Choide

lamas. After drinking tea with the Abbot under the somewhat oppressive chaperonage of four Sikhs armed to the teeth, we left the monastery with many expressions of good-will.

This was the first of many excursions to places of interest in the neighborhood. The strangest visit we ever paid was that to the Buried Monks. One day O'Connor and I rode out down the valley about twelve miles to a small village in the cleft of the mountains almost opposite Dongtse; we took with us the Shebdung Lama. Nothing could have been more peaceful and rustic than the long stretches of the plain dotted here and there with little figures engaged on their farm work. We stopped once to examine more closely the elaborate head-dress of a couple of plowing yaks, much to the pleasure and pride of the clear-eyed boy who was their driver. Everywhere the villagers were pleased enough to see us; the first prickle of green was rising from the brown squares of irrigated mud, and some of the trees were timidly putting out the purple that precedes the green of spring. The nights were still cold, though the heat in the middle of the day was excessive, and the hot dry wind that scoured the valley every afternoon still burned up the vegetation on the hill-sides and in other places where no artificial moisture could supply sap for the young foliage. We took the road on the right bank, not crossing over the bridge at Tse-chen; this road keeps a constant level following the curves of the mountain-sides ten feet above the valley flats. There was little enough to mark the journey down. Carelessly enough we ambled along with our two Mounted Infantry men, whom we had taken out of deference to Colonel Brander's wishes, rather than from any real belief that then or thenceforward we should be in actual need of them. Nothing could have been more peaceful and promising than the affairs of Gyantse at that moment; we had come through the town and—an unquestioned proof of our popularity—the beggars had become both familiar and insolent. It was a bright day and we had our luncheon with us. The good people of the valley were always willing enough to give us hospitality to the best of their ability, but after all it was as well to have a couple of sandwiches and a boiled egg. About twelve o'clock we paused opposite Dongtse, lying out sleepily in the sun with the great three-decker palace of the Pala family anchored in the trees below. Very soon after this we rode through a little hamlet with some name like Chi-lang. A sharp turn round a projecting spur brought us face to face with the little valley in which the monastery of Nyen-dé-kyi-buk hides itself. The ascent was easy between bushes of thorn and roses covered with a wealth of traveler's joy; we passed beside the usual chortens and through a gateway over which a peach-tree spangled the blue of the sky with pink and snow. There was another blossoming against the walls of the monastery half-way up the hill. A hundred yards further on we found the abbot and the "chanzi" of the community waiting to receive us.

The Shebdung Lama had lived for many years across the valley and must have seen from his master's windows above the town and gompa the rock-clinging monastery to which we had come was really responsible for our visit. With the usual inability to recognize the things which really interest a traveler in a strange country he had, while insisting upon the interests and the beauty of the Sinchen Lama's home, only incidentally spoken of a small community across the valley where, he said, extreme self-mortification was practised by a small company of the Nying-ma sect. We left our ponies in the monk's care and went inside the temple. We were glad to escape the white and dazzling sunshine. There was instantly visible a curious distinction between the monks of Nyen-dé-kyi-buk and those whom we had met elsewhere. With the exception of the officials of the monastery these recluses wear their hair long, not plaited into a pigtail, but allowed to fall almost loose over their shoul-

GAILY BEDECKED YAKS DRAWING A PLOW

ders in a matted and filthy tangle. But besides this, there was not very much to distinguish the lamasery from others in the valley. The abbot, a quiet, sad-eyed man of about forty, was shaven, as also were a dozen children playing about with wholesome bickerings in the dust of the courtyard opposite the great doorway of the temple. All were dressed in the usual sacred maroon, and they seemed cheerful and contented. Inside the chapel of the monastery, however, there was certainly an austerity which we had not seen elsewhere. This Du-kang had few of the usual silk banners and hangings which contribute so much both to the color and the darkness of an ordinary gompa. There were the usual cushions on the ground, but the rows of images and ceremonial ornaments which generally fill the sanctuary end of these chapels were replaced by precise rows of books, each lodged sedately in its own pigeon-hole. In the center, in place of the usual *kyil-kor,* with its multifarious confusion of cups and bowls and lamps, there was a narrow shelf in front of a glazed recess. I think that there were on this shelf ten or twelve little brass bowls full of water, but there were no butter lamps. The sight of glass in Tibet always attracted attention: it was rare enough to see a piece a foot square; this glass was five times as large, and one wondered how it had escaped safely across the passes to this sequestered spot. Behind it a hard-featured Buddha scowled, a very different representation of the Master from that placid and kindly countenance which sanctifies him still to many not of his own creed. Under the abbot's guidance we visited the rooms opening out from the temple. There was nothing of great interest, nothing to distinguish it from twenty other gompas. We then had tea with our host, and afterward we asked permission to see one of the immured monks. Without any hesitation the abbot led the way out into the sunshine, which lay sweltering over the spring-teeming spaces of the valley below, and venturesome little green plants were poking up under our feet between the crevices in the stone footway. We climbed about forty feet, and the abbot led us into a small courtyard which had blank walls all round it, over which a peach-tree reared its transparent pink and white against the sky. Almost on a level with the ground there was an opening closed with a flat stone from behind. In front of this window was a ledge eighteen inches in width, with two basins beside it, one at each end. The abbot was attended by an acolyte who, by his master's orders, tapped three times sharply on the stone slab; we stood in the little courtyard in the sun, and watched that wicket with cold apprehension. I think, on the whole, it was the most uncanny thing I saw in all Tibet. What on earth was going to appear when that stone slab, which even then was beginning weakly to quiver, was pushed aside, the wildest conjecture could not suggest. After half a minute's pause the stone moved, or tried to move, but it came to rest again. Then very slowly and uncertainly it was pushed back and a black chasm was revealed. There was again a pause of thirty seconds, during which imagination ran riot, but I do not think that any other thing could have been as intensely pathetic as that which we actually saw. A hand, muffled in a tightly wound piece of dirty cloth, for all the world like the stump of an arm, was painfully thrust up, and very weakly it felt along the slab. After a fruitless fumbling the hand slowly quivered back again into the darkness. A few moments later there was again one ineffectual effort, and then the stone slab moved noiselessly again across the opening. Once a day, water and an unleavened cake of flour is placed for the prisoner upon that slab, the signal is given, and he may take it in. His diversion is over for the day, and in the darkness of his cell, where night and day, moon, sunset, and the dawn, are all alike, he—poor soul!—had thought that another day of his long penance was over.

I do not know what feelings were uppermost at that moment

A LONG-HAIRED MONK AT HIS MONASTERY

in the others, but I know that a physical chill struck through me to the marrow. The awful pathos of that painful movement struggled in me with an intense shame that we had intruded ourselves upon a private misery; and that we should have added one straw to the burden borne in the darkness by that unseen and unhappy man was a curiously poignant regret. We came away, and the abbot told us the story of the sect. "These men," said the abbot, when we questioned him, "live here in this mountain of their own free will; a few of them are allowed a little light whereby reading is possible, but these are the weaker brethren; the others live in darkness in a square cell partly hewn out of the sharp slope of the rock, partly built up, with the window just within reach of their upraised hand. There are three periods of this immurement. The first is endured for six months; the second, upon which a monk may enter at any time he pleases or not at all, is for three years and ninety-three days; the third and last period is for life. Only this morning," said the abbot, "a hermit died here after having lived in darkness for twenty-five years." The thing was almost more revolting because the men entered willingly upon it. "What happens when they are ill?" O'Connor asked the abbot. The answer came concisely enough, "They never are." It is true that when pressed he qualified this statement a little, but it seemed still to have considerable truth. He himself was waiting for the moment, now not long to be delayed, when he should bid his final farewell to the world.

Voluntary this self-immolation is said to be, and perhaps technically speaking it is possible for the pluckier souls to refuse to go on with this hideous and useless form of self-sacrifice, but the grip of the lamas is omnipotent, and practically none refuse. These hermits store up such merit—for themselves—by these means as no other life insures. That may be some consolation for a Tibetan mind; it would be little enough for any one else. On our return the children in the courtyard were invested with a terrible pathos. To this life of painfully useless selfishness they are condemned, and the very difference in their coiffure is one more link which ties down their young lives. After their first immurement their hair is allowed to grow, and the sanctity which enhaloes a Nyen-dé-kyi-buk hermit, whenever recognized by his tresses, effectually prevents his turning back. He is a marked man, and, as in so many other cases in this world, he ends by doing what he is expected to do. Our horses were made ready and we said farewell to our kindly host and rode away into the warmth and life of the valley in silence.

This memory still makes a deeper impression than one thought possible even in the first shock of the moment. Even now the silver and the flowers and the white linen and the crimson-shaded lights of a dinner table are sometimes dimmed by a picture of the same hand that one shook so warmly as one left the monastery, now weakly fumbling with swathed fingers for food along the slab of the prison in which the abbot now is sealed up for life; for he was going into the darkness very soon.

At Little Gobshi (one had to distinguish it from the better known Gobshi, seventeen miles away along the Lhasa road) there was, and now probably is again, the finest rug factory in Tibet. A large two-storied house with a courtyard was filled entirely with the weaving looms of both men and women workers. The patterns used are native Tibetan, and the colors are excellently blended and rich in themselves. It is difficult for them to make a piece of stuff wider than about thirty inches, because their looms are of a primitive description, scarcely more advanced than those of the Chumbi Valley, nor do they attempt to make a pattern larger than can be contained upon a single width. The plain orange and maroon rugs are made in narrow strips and sewn together to any desired width, but this is not done with the figured cloths. The difference in quality between one rug and another is often a matter of expert knowledge only. At first one is surprised

THE WINDOW OF A HERMIT CELL AT NYEN-DÉ-KYI-BUK

and inclined to resent the great differences in the price of these rugs; two will be shown you, one slightly softer in the pile, perhaps also slightly looser in design. You will get that for three rupees. The other one, crisper to the touch and, if you will look closely, far richer in color, they will not sell you for less than twenty-five. But when the eye is once taught to recognize the difference, the cheaper rugs are easily seen to be inferior from every point of view. They are, however, more than good enough for the London market, and this is one of the industries at Gyantse which might most profitably be developed. Even now if a big London firm were willing to place an order for five hundred rugs in Gobshi, that is to say, if it were to buy up practically the entire annual output of this first factory in Tibet, it could, while it held the monopoly, charge almost any price it liked to London buyers and obtain it. It is an experiment which is, perhaps, worth the attention of Farringdon Street Without. In those halcyon days at Gyantse I wrote to Lord Curzon in London and offered to act as commercial traveler for any firm which cared to make a trial of these really beautiful things, but long before an answer could be sent, times had changed and we were prisoners in Chang-lo.

The village of Gobshi, which, like so many other villages in Tibet, is divided into two entirely distinct parts, separated by a waste of common-like land dotted with willow thorn, is not uninteresting. It lies comfortably among its trees, with a truant channel of the main river plashing lazily over hard pebbles within a few hundred yards. Overhanging it to the north is a very sharp conical rock, surmounted by an orange-colored building, which attracts the eye from afar. This is the residence of the local magician. He only resides there during such part of the year as the young crops are in danger from damage by the weather. He then takes up his residence, and is ready at any moment with due incantations to deliver a charm against lightning or hail to a timid countryman. The charms against hail are large circular sheets, adorned, not in the most delicate way, with figures of the four Winds. These figures are represented bound and shackled, to signify the supernatural power exerted by the magician; pointing at them from the inscribed center are the eight instruments of power: the *Dorje,* the bow and arrow, the sword, the double *purbu,* the flame-like knife, the scepter, and one other thing that might be anything.

These magicians occupy a very curious position. They are all now sanctioned by the Gelukpa hierarchy, but this does not mean that they have always been obedient and loyal members of the orthodox church. As a matter of fact, many of them remain disciples of the *Beun-pa,* or aboriginal devil worshipers of the country. This sect is bitterly opposed in every way to the tenets of Buddhism, and it is only on this point that a truce has been proclaimed. The reason of this is clear enough. Successful in all other ways, the Yellow lamas have never been able wholly to transfer to themselves by the exercise of wizardry the deepest awe of the plain village peasants of Tibet. These men continued to pay their tribute of terror to the old autochthonous sorcerer, whose tradition and succession were undoubted. The authorities of Lhasa were shrewd enough to recognize the one case in which the invincible ignorance, which they deliberately foster in their flock, has turned to their own harm. They accepted and indorsed the magicians of the countryside *en bloc,* making no distinction of creed. By these means the sorcerer works hand in hand with the lamas of the district, and thereout, we may be sure, they both suck no small advantage. There is in Lhasa the head of all these magicians, but it is necessary at this moment to draw a sharp line of distinction between him, a responsible and revered reincarnation—whose authority is hardly less than that of the Dalai Lama, and whose position, though different, is scarcely less venerated—and these local magicians, whose scope is very different from his.

To a small degree every great gompa in Tibet trades upon the influence of occultism upon the Tibetan peasants. Charms and written *mantras* are by no means issued by the magicians alone. The *katags,* which lie sometimes in heaped-up confusion over the shoulders of the chief Buddha of a monastery, can afterward be sold in fragments, and few relics are more potent. These little charms, to which reference has already been made, are worn round the neck, in what the Tibetans call a *gau-o.* These are little boxes, of silver as a rule, thickly set with turquoise, and suspended round the neck by necklaces of beads; in the case of the rich, they may be fronted with gold, but this metal is but rarely used for the rest of these trinkets. It is used in Tibet in a singularly pure state, and in the economical amounts with which the Tibetans are obliged to be satisfied would not be strong enough. Men, especially when going on some dangerous expedition, carry much larger *gau-os* of copper, upon which the monogrammatic symbol of the great *mantra* is embossed by repoussé work. These also are always stuffed with relics and charms of different kinds; everything, it might almost be said, in Tibet that is capable of being stuffed is full of these little luck-bringing spells or charms. The biggest idols are packed with paper and silk charms, interspersed here and there with small brass images and occasionally silver ones. To this fact unfortunately the destruction of several of the larger idols—which were afterward "taboo" to the troops—was due at Gyantse. Lieutenant-Colonel Waddell gives, in his learned and careful work upon Lamaism, a large number of instances of the cases in which these charms are used, and the ritual employed.

One odd fact came under our notice. The charms issued from Lhasa to the Tibetan soldiers opposing our advance included protection against almost every known material used in war. After Guru, some of the wounded who were being tended by us were asked whether their faith were shaken or not; they, in some surprise, entirely repudiated the idea. "We did not know in Lhasa what metals we should guard ourselves against: lead and iron, and steel and copper, and silver, none of these could have hurt us; but we did not even know that there was a metal called nickel; therefore no charm was given us to protect us against your bullets." The unwinding of a grimy little silk-covered packet from the inside of a *gau-o* is rather an interesting occupation; the contents are cleaner than might be thought. One of the oddest things I found in any was a little pebble with the thumb imprint of the Dalai Lama upon it in vermilion. Unfortunately damp had blurred the lines.

The prayers printed on the prayer-flags of Tibet are generally identical in arrangement and, perhaps, also in the words of the prayer. In Gyantse I bought one of the wood-blocks, from which these flags are printed; it is a curious piece of careful and not ineffective wood engraving. It is about sixteen inches in length and twelve inches in width. This is about the largest size that is used; the flag, being attached to the mast perpendicularly, only allows a thin upright fringe to be printed, and you will find fifteen or twenty repetitions of the same prayer, reaching one above another all the way up the mast. These "flying horses" (*lung-ta*) were probably mistaken by the traveler who originated the idea that the Tibetans sent horses to belated wayfarers by throwing to the winds pieces of paper with the figure of a horse printed upon it. It is quite possible that this may actually have been done, but continued inquiry on my part elicited no corroboration whatever.

To return to the country surrounding Gyantse. The monastery at Dongtse, twelve miles away toward Shigatse, the sacred residence of the Sinchen Lama, was visited by O'Connor, Wilton, and myself very soon after our arrival at Chang-lo.

The road to Dongtse serpentines across the wide level plain of the Nyang chu, idly acquiescing in the obstacles which villages, water-courses, field boundaries, chortens, houses, or irrigation ditches throw in its way. The patchwork of cultivated fields, some no larger than allotments, none more than an acre in area, reminds one of high farming in Berkshire, so jealously is every square foot made to serve the owners and grow its patch of barley. There are no trees, no hedges, not even a weed. The very dikes which restrain the irrigation channels are grudged from the rich, dry, gray loam, as fertile as the Darling Downs.

Agriculture is a serious business with the Tibetans. Here and there, but very rarely, the darkened garnet or dirty amber of a lama's dress adds a note of color to the thirsty stretch of alluvial soil, fenceless and flat. But generally the work is done by quiet little figures, whose patched gray dresses are blotted out among their own furrows and whose very existence is often betrayed only by the slow plod and turn of the scarlet and white head-dressed yaks in the plow-yoke. Among these people there is no shyness, scarcely even curiosity. The spring work has to be done, and there is no one but themselves to do it—perhaps the yaks can only be borrowed from friend Tsering up at the hamlet for this day; perhaps, too, the lamas will exact their corvée to-morrow. And there is much to do. Meanwhile these strange foreigners can wait to be inspected.

Always, of course, there was civility as we rode by. The Tibetan peasant's manners are perfect. The small boy jumps off the harrow upon which he has been having a ride, and, stopping his song, bows with his joined hands in front of his face, elbows up, and right knee bent. A householder smiles, exhibits two inches of tongue, and gives a Napoleonic salute as we pass by, pulling his cap down over his face to his chest. Rosy-backed and breasted sparrows fly in a twittering company before us through the gray-white sallowthorn brake, and a vivid golden wagtail flirts his tail beside a puddle. Redstarts sit on the top of prayer poles, and hoopoes flash black and white wings by the stream. Ruddy sheldrake and bar-headed geese barely move aside from a wet patch of recent plow-land as we approach, and iridescent black-green magpies, half as large again as our English luck-bringers, keep pace beside us with their dipping flight. The sun is hard and vivid, and the flat plain shivers a little in the heat, confusing the lines of leafless willows beside a whitewashed mill. There is promise of foliage, but no more. The houses are streaked perpendicularly with wide welts of Indian red and ash-gray, and long strings of many-colored little flags droop between their housetops and the nearest tree. Tibetan " mastiffs " bark from every roof until the housewife quiets them with a stone. She throws better than her European sister, in spite of a grimy coral and turquoise halo round her head and a baby on her left arm.

The story of the last Sinchen Lama is one which it is worth while to tell. He was the seventh in succession of one of the most important secondary reincarnations of Lamaism. His abode has always been at Dongtse, but his predecessors were buried with great ceremony each under a gilded chorten at Tashi-lhunpo, the metropolis of the province of Tsang. The last Sinchen Lama was the man who in 1882 received Sarat Chandra Das, and extended to him continual patronage and hospitality. In the narrative of his journey the famous spy refers to him repeatedly as "the minister." He was, as a matter of fact, minister of temporal affairs of the province of Tsang at this time, and a most important man. On his way to his first interview with his patron Chandra Das passed in the market place of Tashi-lhunpo a party of prisoners loaded with chains, pinioned by wooden clogs, and in some cases blinded. It was an ugly omen of the end. To the Sinchen Lama's influence Chandra Das owed the facilities which enabled him eventually to make his way to Lhasa, and that he was not ungrateful is clear in every line in which he refers to his patron. The minister seems to have been in his way strangely like that enlightened Grand Lama of Tashi-lhunpo who received Bogle in 1774; he was anxious to improve his knowledge of the world, and especially of English affairs; he even attempted to learn our language, and he seems throughout to have been a broad-minded, intelligent, and sympathetic man. Chandra Das stayed with him for some time at Dongtse, on his way to Lhasa. A year or two after Chandra Das had returned to India the truth leaked out about his individuality. The Lhasan Government threw the entire blame upon the carelessness of the authorities in the province of Tsang. Upon the Sinchen Lama they visited their anger in a fearful manner. His servants were taken—all except one—they were beaten, their hands and feet were cut off, their eyes were gouged out, and they were left to die in the streets of Tashi-lhunpo. The Sinchen Lama was reserved for another fate. He was taken to Gong-kar, a fort on the right bank of the Tsaṅg-po, a few miles below the confluence of the Kyi-chu.

The rest of the story must be told as it is believed by the common people, who had known and loved the Lama in his life. A message was received from Lhasa to the effect that the Sinchen Lama must commit suicide. This he quietly refused to do. He said, "I am indeed in your hands; you will do with me what seems good to you. But I will not kill myself, and if you kill me, you will incur for yourselves a terrible reincarnation." This answer produced another peremptory demand that the Lama should lay violent hands upon himself. To this the Lama made no reply at all. The days went on, and at last the authorities in Lhasa determined to take his life, though they still hoped that they might avoid the awful consequences to themselves of blood-guiltiness. A boat was taken, and innumerable holes of different sizes were bored in her. In this the Lama was placed, and he was sent spinning down the current of the great river. Thus he would be drowned, but to the ingenious minds of the hierarchy it seemed that the responsibility lay perhaps with their victim, whose weight would have sunk the unseaworthy craft. Blood, at any rate, would not have been spilled. But the Lama was in no way dismayed; he raised a prayer, and fishes innumerable came; they intruded their blunt noses into the holes in the boat, and slowly propelled it safely to the shore. The Lama disembarked and walked quietly back to his prison. The news of this miracle produced but momentary consternation in Lhasa; the brute creation might indeed be at the orders of this holy man, but die he must; they must try another way. Therefore, almost immediately, another attempt was made; large rocks of granite were bound upon his back, and he was once more thrown into the river. But again they had reckoned unwisely. If the Sinchen Lama's life were to be taken, the sin of murder must accompany it. This was the eternal law, and as the sainted Lama's body touched the water, the rocks were turned into pumice stone, and his friendly fishes soon nuzzled him again to shore. Thereafter Lhasa grew desperate. They sent a wicked man, a Kashmiri Mohammedan, for whom the prospect of reincarnation as a louse had no terrors, and the Sinchen Lama's head was hacked from his body.[1]

Nor was this all. Having destroyed the body, the hierarchy at Lhasa proceeded to annihilate the soul. No further reincarnation of the Sinchen Lama has been recognized from that day. In the long gallery of reincarnated Bodisats who occupy the chief place of Lamaism there is one frame, as there is in the Venetian ducal palace, blank and empty. This has been a very serious trouble to the good people of Dongtse, and they are apparently not without sympathizers at Lhasa. A few years after the murder of their loved Lama a child was admitted into the Ga-den monastery. He had been born immediately after the crime, and to the awe-struck amazement of the ruling lamas he exhibited the one final proof of Sinchen Lamaship. His left kneecap was absent. That child lives still, and in sullen determination the peo-

[1] This is the native tale, and it is almost a pity to correct it in any particular. Another story is that the Sinchen Lama with his hands tied behind him was thrown into the river and never seen again.

ple of Dongtse are but waiting till their Lama shall be restored to them. Meanwhile Dongtse is in a parlous state. Its religious life has been broken into and a stranger imported from another province to rule over them. Down in the town below affairs are no better. The Pala family which reigned in the great palace underneath the hill is exiled and expropriated. A government chanzi, or bailiff, collects the rents and pays them over to the man who by auction obtained the beneficiary rights of the deposed family. At Dongtse it is said that those rents are paid over to a member of the family, and certainly the local bailiff seems to be in a difficult position, for the offense for which the Pala family was banished was merely that of having abetted the late Regent in retaining temporal power in his hands after the coming of age of the Dalai Lama. At any moment, therefore, the Pala family may be reinstated in their property with unpleasant powers of retaliation.

Our small party—one of us the only servant of the Sinchen Lama who had escaped death—reached Dongtse about noon, and immediately climbed the hill on which the monastery stands; we were received with the greatest friendliness by the abbot, and one or two of the senior monks. The great temple was hardly as richly endowed with silver and jeweled ornaments as we had been told. It was curious to watch the Shebdung Lama as he wandered round the old familiar halls. For many years he had been an exile, and he had never believed that he would see the home of his loved master again, and as he put his forehead on the lip of the lotus throne, upon which the great Buddha of the place was seated, and so remained motionless for ten seconds, there must have passed through his mind something strangely like *Nunc dimittis Domine.* For this man's love for his murdered master after eighteen years is still as fresh to-day as when they lived at peace on this hillside of the Nyang chu Valley, and in all the time since, the Shebdung Lama's only happiness has been bound up with the memories of his life here. He could hardly speak as we entered the shrine, and was again visibly affected when we ascended to the actual rooms occupied by the Sinchen Lama.

These consist of a set of well-painted chambers, opening out one from another. In the main room, still empty and forlorn, save for a table containing a hundred little brass bowls filled with water, there is one of the strangest things in Tibet. The Sinchen Lama, continuing the series of his ancestors painted round the wall, had also a record of his own life and ministry painted in a series of scenes by an artist. His own portraiture is encircled by these little pictures; the figure of the Lama is purely conventional, a mild-eyed, celestial face with a pursed up rosebud mouth. Round him there is a series of stiff little drawings not without some strength, recording from his birth, passage by passage, the events of his momentous life. Now these were painted in the happy days before Chandra Das came.

At the end of this record there is the strange thing. There is in a corner the picture of a fortified house, and, above it, the picture of a man who has been thrown into a stream of water. But there is no such appended written description as may be seen beneath other scenes depicted on the wall. The artist requested him to dictate the legend for these two pictures. The Lama refused; he said, "These two incidents shall remain undescribed; one day you will understand." We were assured there that the house painted on the wall bears a strong resemblance to Gong-kar jong; the meaning of the last scene is obvious enough. There the two pictures are, and in its main lines the story must be a true one, but it is difficult to explain.

Immediately beyond this series of pictures is the most touching thing I have seen in the country. In sheer gratitude to the only companion of his lonely exaltation, far removed from the common friendship of men, the Sinchen Lama had painted upon the wall his little shaggy-haired dog, feeding out of a blue and white china bowl. I do not know that anything in the record of this man could tell the story of his kindly sympathy and humanity so well as this ill-drawn little figure.

We spent an hour or two there, and had tea, both with the abbot of the monastery and with the occupants of the Pala palace in the town below; then we set off for home in the middle of the afternoon, facing south-east to where the high fort-crowned peak of Gyantse rose indistinctly, amid the daily driving dust-storm which wrapped its base and indeed all the valley in a tawny fog.

Né-nyeng—or, as it was invariably known, Nai-ni—was another place which was afterward to become of great interest and importance to us. Seven miles away to the south, just before the valley opened out from the gorges of the Nyang chu, it commanded our road to India, and was the scene three or four times of fighting between the Tibetans and ourselves. Né-nyeng lies in an amphitheater of steep hills; looking at it from across the river the sight was typically Eastern, and might have been a theater " back-cloth," painted with the deliberate intention of including every suggestion of the Orient; but he would have been a clever man who limned such a scene as this. All round this half-circle of converging spurs the plain hot rock glared at one. The line cut by its upper cornices against the sky was harsh and exact. The blue that descended into the ravines and arched the peaks was cloudless and whitened; on one conical hill, almost inaccessible, sat a square yellow block-house commanding the town from a height of a thousand feet. A little lower down, when the eye got used to the glare, another and stronger fort, built of the very rock on which it rested, could just be made out by the straightness of its lines. In the middle of this great recess the river flats stretched white and dusty, draining down by a slackening gradient from the clefts of the amphitheater. Just where it gained its equilibrium, Né-nyeng rose in a garden of greenery. The square white houses blinked in the sun, the high unchecked line of the square building in the center of the town, half monastery, half keep, showed up dustily above the flat roofs of the houses, which cling to it for protection.

Between us and the town the sweeping river cuts its way, leaving perpendicular banks of pebbled banquette purple in the shades and amber in the sun, for all the world like the moldings of a clustered Gothic pillar. We had little to do with the inhabitants, except in an unpleasant manner. Now and again they fired upon our mail runners, and eventually the place had to be cleared when the relieving force was nearing Gyantse. There was in this monastery, if some of the reports are to be believed, a reincarnation in the form of a little girl, of about six years old. We never heard anything more about her; the story seems unlikely, because there was no nunnery in the place. The only monastery over which a woman presides in Tibet is that of Sam-ding, where the Phag-mo Dorje was reigning many centuries before the coming of the "new woman" in the West.

In this connection one thing was frankly admitted by the Tibetans. We were often surprised to find the monasteries stripped of their valuable and most precious ornaments upon our arrival. Without any hesitation the monks would admit that they had all been taken away, and put in the nearest nunnery, because, they said, the English people do not attack women, and do not enter nunneries. It was a simple device and one that implied no small compliment.

CHAPTER VIII

ATTACKED BY THE TIBETANS

COLONEL YOUNGHUSBAND occupied Chang-lo on the 19th of April with a force of about four hundred and fifty men. He had also about fifty mounted infantry, two Maxims, and two ancient seven-pounder field-pieces, now officially discarded, which, in their popular nicknames "Bubble and Squeak," were at once described and appraised. This force was amply sufficient to defend the place against any attack that the Tibetans could deliver. They, however, seemed in no way willing to test the defensibility of Chang-lo; and nothing could have been more peaceful than the reception of the British force, not at Gyantse only, but for a score of miles up and down the valley. It is true, that for our expeditions beyond the immediate neighborhood of the post, two or three mounted infantry were always taken as an escort, but we imagined no danger, and nothing seemed less probable than that which actually occurred. I am quite certain that the events of the 5th of May were not less surprising—and a great deal more dismaying—to the good people of Gyantse than they were to ourselves. In the last chapter I have described one or two visits paid somewhat far afield in the Nyang chu Valley, and it will be clear that nothing could have exceeded the hospitality and, in most cases, the welcome which we received. At Gyantse itself, the friendliness of the inhabitants was almost excessive. We afterward found that from the date of our expedition till the 4th of May, the servants of the Mission (who were unavoidably under less strict military surveillance than other followers) not infrequently spent the entire night within the town enjoying themselves among their Tibetan kin, with results on the following morning which were more natural than edifying. It need not be said that as soon as this was discovered the military authorities made a severe example of the chief offenders. Shopping in Gyantse was an almost daily amusement. The great Palkhor-choide monastery was willingly opened to us by the abbot, and the members of the Mission looked forward to a pleasant two months' stay in one of the most interesting cities of Tibet, and a full enjoyment of the extraordinary opportunities which the undisguised friendliness of our neighbors promised.

More than this, Captain Walton, the surgeon and natural history expert attached to the Mission, had invited the Tibetans to make the fullest use of his own skill and the medical equipment of the Mission; and, as a result, he soon had as many cases as he could deal with. By preference he selected cases requiring surgical treatment, and many unfortunate wretches disabled by cataract or disfigured by a particularly hideous form of hare-lip, which is common in Tibet, were relieved by him.

Everything was peaceful. There was not a cloud on the horizon. The dak ran through from the Chumbi Valley without interruption, day after day. The British intruders had given commissions freely in the town, and the local artists were working overtime to execute orders for "tang-kas." Carpenters from Pala attended daily in the compound and worked from morn to night upon the furniture needed for the post. Their use of tools, by the way, which seemed in most cases to be of European origin, was extremely quick and certain, and the work which the adze was made to do would have surprised the British carpenter. Planes, saws, bradawls, and, in rare cases, chisels, were also used; but nothing showed originality or suggested any device that might possibly be used to advantage at home except a little machine, simple, ingenious, and compact, for marking a straight line upon wood by means of a thread loaded with black pigment.

Gardeners also were called in, and the courtyard in front of the Commissioner's tent was carefully dug up, divided into beds, and manured. There the seeds which the Mission had brought from home were hopefully planted, and beans, peas, cabbages, scarlet-runners, onions, and mustard-and-cress were sown with an almost religious care—in return for which, it must be confessed that only the last-mentioned vegetables produced any return. Still, the experiment was well worth making, and, incidentally, it had the effect of laying the dust in the compound—by no means a slight blessing. To tend this garden a worthy Tibetan lady, with her two husbands, was hired; and if her treatment of her brother-spouses was characteristic of Tibetan domesticity as a whole there is perhaps more to be said for this strange custom than a somewhat bigotedly monogamous nation like England could be expected at first sight to admit. "Mrs. Wiggs," as she at once came to be known, was certainly the moving spirit in her own domestic circle, and the work that she got out of her pair of semi-imbecile husbands was quite extraordinary.

Outside the compound a bazaar was daily held, and over one hundred Tibetan men and women made it a daily practice to come with the small commodities of the place and spend a cheerful and, probably, not unlucrative morning in chaffering with the Sikhs and Gurkhas of the garrison. The afternoon weather, but for clouds of dust that blew eastward from Dongtse, was perfect; and though the trees were long in showing the first sign of spring, the lot of the Mission seemed cast in a fair ground indeed.

While everything round us was pointing toward peace and good-will, the action of Colonel Brander in clearing the Karo la Pass needs some explanation. A week after our arrival the rumor came from a trustworthy source that the Tibetans were fortifying this pass; but as we had never deceived ourselves into believing that our presence in the country was even acquiesced in at Lhasa, the news was neither surprising nor disquieting. The pass, or rather the actual position across which the wall was being built, was over forty-five miles from Gyantse, and at the moment it lay somewhat outside the sphere of our immediate interest. Round us at Gyantse, there was, as I have said, every indication of perfect tranquillity, and even welcome. All up and down the valley agricultural work had been resumed, and there is no doubt that somewhere about this time the men of Shigatse definitely refused to obey the orders of the Dalai Lama to take the field again against us. Another matter which made it even almost impossible that there should be any immediate friction was the fact that the Amban himself had received, and was still considering, an invitation to negotiate at Gyantse.

Matters, however, seemed somewhat affected by news which came in by a special despatch rider on May 1st—that a reconnoitering party of ours, with a mounted escort of fifty men, had been fired upon two days previously from the Tibetan fortification. The affair in itself was not perhaps of the highest importance. Our own intentions were entirely peaceful, and we had found no unfriendliness at any point on the journey to the Karo la. We sustained no casualties, though the sudden heart failure of one of the Sikhs at the unaccustomed altitude was naturally hailed by the jeering Tibetans as proof of the skill of their marksmen. We made no reply except two or three shots to keep down the enemy's fire while we retired; we inflicted no casualties.[1] But, though unimportant in itself, this encounter was not without its significance. In the first place, it put an end finally to any hope of the Amban coming to negotiate at Gyantse, and,

[1] Of this, however, I am uncertain. It was afterward said in Lhasa that two were killed.

though this refusal was not unexpected, the disinclination of Lhasa to take any steps whatever to open up amicable relations with us was hereby exhibited in a somewhat unmistakable manner. Nor was this all. From the Karo la toward Gyantse, ten or twelve miles of an easy route brings one to Ra-lung. At Ra-lung there is a division of the way, the main road running thence westerly to Gyantse and ultimately to Shigatse. It is, in fact, part of the main thoroughfare between the two capitals of Tibet. From Ra-lung another road runs due south-west through Nyero to Kang-ma, and upon this road we had no post. It was at once obvious that the defenders of the wall on the Karo la might, entirely unknown to us, move in two days upon our line of communication to the south and cause us serious inconvenience by the re-occupation of Kang-ma. The position, therefore, was, that while we had no fear of the least unfriendliness in the Nyang chu Valley, Lhasa was obviously prepared to withstand us by force of arms, and might at any time compel us seriously to weaken the little garrison at Gyantse in order to relieve the post at Kang-ma, and re-obtain control of our communications.

There was, however, an understanding with Lhasa that, until negotiations at Gyantse were shown to be impossible, we should not move further along the route to the capital. The detachment of a force sufficient to clear the Karo la would, moreover, cripple the garrison at Chang-lo; nor could we possibly hold the pass, although we might without great loss secure it for the moment. On the one hand it might be argued that our prestige, as well as our line of communications, was in danger, and that the presence of a large and well-armed body of Tibetans holding the best strategical position between Gyantse and Lhasa might speedily undermine the existing friendliness of our neighbors. On the other hand there is no doubt that popular opinion in England would have been seriously affected by the news that we had again assumed the offensive unless, of course, the necessity were overwhelming.

Such was the situation with which Colonel Younghusband had to deal when Colonel Brander, commanding the post, laid before him an urgent request that he would sanction the immediate dispersal of the fifteen hundred Tibetans who had been located at the Karo la. One of the difficulties which every expedition subject to a twin control must experience is the extreme reluctance of the political authorities to interfere in the slightest degree with the operations of their responsible military escort. Colonel Younghusband appreciated to the full the pros and cons of this proposal, and, in giving his unreserved assent to Colonel Brander's suggestion, he was no doubt influenced by the conviction that all chance of negotiation at Gyantse was not only at an end, but had never really existed. At all costs the Tibetans must be made to respect our strength, and against such an enemy as we had before us, the effect of a successful blow might at any time turn the scales and convince them that further active opposition to our advance was a mere act of folly. Colonel Younghusband therefore consented, and accordingly, on the 3d of May, Colonel Brander, with two companies of the 32d Pioneers, one company of Gurkhas, two Maxims, and almost the entire force of mounted infantry, moved out to Gobshi, seventeen miles on the road to the Karo la. As they set forth news arrived that Tibetan troops were moving up the Nyang chu Valley to occupy Dongtse, a post which, it will be remembered, lies twelve miles west of Gyantse. Almost at the same moment a despatch was received from the Amban, saying that the Dalai Lama had definitely refused either to satisfy his demand for transport, or to answer his request that a properly qualified Tibetan should be empowered to deal with the questions in dispute between the British and himself.

Colonel Brander moved rapidly on. At Gobshi he found the headman of the village seriously disquieted, and, though he had no difficulty in obtaining what he wanted, the wretched villagers clearly realized their position between the devil and the deep sea. Gobshi itself is a picturesque village with an untenable jong, perched upon a tooth of rock half a mile from the Chinese post-house, which had attracted to it the little community of the "Four Gates." As a matter of fact, if ever a village deserved the name of "*Three* Gates" it is Gobshi, for there, hopelessly shut in by mountain spurs and heights almost precipitous, three roads, from Gyantse, Nyero, and Ra-lung respectively, meet abruptly. Here the Ra-lung chu joins the Nyero chu, and shortly below "waters meet" the little town sits precariously on the edge of the river cliff, at the end of a wide alluvial terrace, a mile in length, which presents, perhaps, the best instance of successful cultivation that one can see from the road for eighteen miles. From this place until it descends steeply into the valley of the Tsang-po, cereal crops will not ripen, though here and there they can be used for fodder. After a hasty inspection of the Chinese rest-house it was unanimously decided to make no use of its grimy and obviously populous accommodation.

On the next day Colonel Brander moved on up the right bank of the Ra-lung-po. Threading his way over the two bridges just above the confluence of the rivers, he came in two miles through the gorge and out into the easier road which makes its way through the poor fields of the Ra-lung Valley. The first place one passes is the Kamo monastery, a strange community, in which the monks and nuns live a common life together—a thing permitted by the Dalai Lama and one that causes no great scandal even among the strictest disciples of Lamaism, though it is regarded as a concession to the weaker brethren. This part of Tibet has a Red Cap colony, and the ash-gray, white, and Indian-red perpendicular stripes that characterize the buildings of this community form for miles a peculiarity in the landscape and strikingly relieve its monotony.

Of that monotony, the dead sameness of mountain tracks

across the top of the world, it is hard to give any idea. The blue sky, of a clearness and depth of color that no less altitude can give, vaults over the slippery hill-sides between which the thin stream cataracts or spreads itself in runlets across a waste of sand. There is no verdure at that time of the year except that which is artificially grown on the river-flats where the valley is wide enough. Rich umber and light red, seamed and filmed with gray purples of the clefts; bald ocher of spurs that thrust the water from their feet; bare red of whip-like willows growing over a mud wall; coarse grit-colored road, here grayish with slate, here dun with granite, there again rufous with a floor of limestone—these are all the colors except here and there, when one meets a hurrying lama, wrapped in his habit of dull maroon. As the sun sets the richer pigments, beaten all day by his rays into the hot hill-sides, are cooled out of the rocks; and as the sunlight is slowly lost in the valleys below a faint orange gauze spreads and reddens into carmine on the far snowy peaks to the northeast.

One side of the river is like the other; you may cross it anywhere and find the same view, the same road. Perhaps Long-ma, well placed upon a bluff overlooking an alluvial flat where stunted barley grows, is the most interesting town on the route; and the village itself, though quite as dirty as every other in Tibet, has, at any rate in the distance, a certain dignity of its own, to which, in a rather specious way, the buildings set up on the rapidly ascending slope behind the main path of the town contribute. There is a large house here which was unoccupied and shut up on our arrival, and interested us chiefly because it was said to have recently contained a community of Lamaic acolytes. From Long-ma to Ra-lung the road is comparatively uninteresting. Here and there, in the distance, filling the end of the valley, one saw the great white mass of Nichi-kang-sang; here and there steep jutting pinnacles of red rock; here and there across the river the remains of a house crumbling on the alluvial ledge. The river itself runs entirely round the stone buttresses of the fields, and over the waste of uncultivated ground a few patches of vetch—at that time without even a promise of flower—a few stunted thistles, and the inevitable gray brushes of wormwood star the dun naked slopes. Nothing is more striking up here than the way in which the dark blue of the sky overhead shades quickly down toward the horizon on every side into the palest shade of turquoise. The clearness of the air is such that not the faintest screen of blue is interposed between oneself and the hills four miles away; while the clefts in the glaciers of Nichi-kang-sang himself seem as clearly defined at a range of fifteen miles as those which criss-cross upon the gravel of the further bank.

Ra-lung was reached on the afternoon of the second day. This march of thirty-three miles in forty-eight hours at this altitude was, perhaps, the most creditable feat of endurance of the whole campaign. Such distances as these may not seem of any particular military interest, or of credit to the troops concerned, but it must be remembered that the lowest estimate that one can fairly place upon the additional labor of marching at these high altitudes is a hundred per cent. It is true that the actual fatigue to the muscles is hardly increased, and that though men may arrive in camp almost dead-beat, an hour or two's rest (if they are lucky enough to get it) will always set them up again. But the strain on the heart and lungs is terrible, and nothing but use can accustom a man living nearly all his life in the plains of India to that intense heaviness of both himself and his accoutrements which, in these highlands, is the most conspicuous sensation. I have elsewhere referred in more detail to the physical experiences and sufferings of the troops, and these circumstances of all our work in Tibet should be borne in mind as an ever-present environment, from the first climbing of the heights of Changu or Ling-tu to the scaling of the little ridge between Potala and Chagpo-ri.

Ra-lung is divided by a small stream into two parts. The Tibetan village lies to the south, a mere cluster of common adobe huts whitewashed or in ruins. On the northern side of this affluent is the Chinese post-house, set a hundred yards back from the edge of the river cliff on the very spot where there is one of the curiously marked out camping-grounds used by the two Grand Lamas alone. The bridge over the Ra-lung chu is a typical line of roughly heaped stone piers, bridged across with larger slabs of the same schistose limestone. Crossing the river here the main road to Lhasa keeps close beside it on the northeastern bank for one or two miles of a bad track. Small streams intersect its progress, running in the wet weather in a plashy torrent at the bottom of deep-cut ravines; otherwise the steep cliff wall comes down sharply on to the very path until the last corner is turned and the wide valley of Gom-tang is seen spreading out a mile or two wide toward the northwest. Here the track leaves the river-side and runs northward over the gently sloping highlands beneath the snowy backbone of this great spur of the Himalayas.

Some reference should be made to these hills. A high range rises to the elevation of 24,000 feet, through which a deep fissure between Nichi-kang-sang on the north and on the south a peak, which, I believe, is known in the surveys as D 114, allows the road to Lhasa to creep along far down between the gigantic ice-fields. To the north and to the south this uplifted stretch of snow is carried onward, terminated to the north by the abrupt valley of the Rong chu, to the south curving eastward and forming the snowy southern frontiers of the basin of the Yam-dok tso. This description is necessary in order to make clear the importance and the military skill of the Tibetans' choice of a position to defend. No flanking movement is possible, either to the north or to the south, unless an invading force is willing to wait five days for the co-operation of any mounted column sent round by the northern route to come upon the enemy's rear from a point within a mile or two of Nagartse.

After a march of about seven miles from Ra-lung, the road keeps well away to the right to avoid the marshes covered with hummocky grass, reeds, stunted primulas, and, it must be added, quagmires through which the clear brown waters of the Ra-lung chu run ice-cold from their snowy source. Across the river the plain still extends, sweeping upward between the projecting spurs of the western hills in long ascending plains of bare stone. As our force reached this point, it seemed only possible to continue the march in one direction. The long plain stretched out in front, ascending gently until the farthest limits cut upward into the sky itself. But this was no road for a laden force, and, as a matter of fact, it is not used at all except by shepherds and goat-herds in the brief summer months. As I have said, the real road to Lhasa turns suddenly inward under the snowy shoulders of Nichi-kang-sang; and over 8,000 feet below the gigantic mass of unrelieved ice and snow which forms his highest peak, the ribbon-like track dives abruptly into the river-bed beside a little stream which has cut its way through this gigantic curtain of rock.

The gorge that opens here is narrow and the road bad. Closely hugging the southern bluff the trang[1] makes its snowy way over the boulders and almost through the waters of this ice-fed rivulet. On either side the cliffs rise so steeply that one hardly catches a sight of the eternal snows that slope steeply back from the crest of these frowning heights. Now and again a ravine betrays the sparkling glory of the white ice-cornice against

[1] A trang is a track cut out of the cliff beside a stream. There is a steep rock on one side and the water immediately below. It is a useful word for a feature which is not easily described otherwise.

the deep blue of the upper sky. In May there is nothing to be seen here in the way of plants except the dead sticks of a curious thorny scrub, which during its hibernation is of an unusual pink color, cobwebbed about with the gray dead filigree of last year's leaves. This will burn, and, indeed, it forms the only fuel to be found for many miles.

Sharply ascending, the road after a mile and a half crosses the stream, now sparkling in a noisy shallow between the pebbles of its bed; and a climb of another two hundred yards brings one into an oval plain which, probably from the fact that in the summer the whole extent of it is permeated and saturated with water from the melting glaciers, the Tibetans call the Plain of Milk.[1] In May the cold was intense enough, except in the middle of the day, largely to reduce the volume of the stream, and the force made its way without difficulty over the shales and slate of this lonely little flat-bottomed cup buried away nearly 17,000 feet above the sea, and ringed in by the eternal snow-fields of the Himalayas.

At the farther end, immediately under a great glacier—one infinitesimal projection of the huge land of ice of which Nichi-kang-sang is the highest point—the force encamped. The mounted infantry had, of course, been sent on ahead. They reported that the wall was strongly held by the Tibetans; and Colonel Brander, who had accompanied them to a point a mile or two further on, within range of the wall itself, made his dispositions for the next day. To the east the Karo la itself, the highest point between Lhasa and India, was within an easy climb, barely three hundred feet higher than the Plain of Milk. Beyond that the valley takes a turn to the northwest between precipitous cliffs, all immediately crowned by the snow-fields of the Nichi-kang-sang group; and at its narrowest and most precipitous point the Tibetans had built an enormous wall. This

[1] This is also the name of the plain in which Lhasa stands.

was, perhaps, the greatest triumph of Tibetan construction that we found throughout the expedition. I do not suppose that any other nation in the world, with similar means at their disposal, could hold their own for half an hour against the Tibetan in this one art of wall building. With apparent ease the most enormous stones are collected and placed with unerring judgment, and with a rapidity which seems almost miraculous to the eye-witness. This was no ordinary wall. It was composed of angular and well-adjusted pieces of granite about two feet in thickness; the loopholes, at a height of about four feet, were constructed with wide-angled "splays" permitting an extensive field of fire; and above these carefully made little embrasures there was head cover for at least another twelve inches. Between each man's recess the Tibetans had built up a partition wall of heavy slabs of stone, so that the damage caused by direct shell fire was reduced to a minimum, and loss by enfilading shrapnel almost entirely avoided. At this time the wall was about eight hundred yards long; the enemy had thrown forward two sangars, one on either side, which at once prevented any chance of an easy flanking movement, or, indeed, of our bringing forward without danger either the Maxims or the main body of the force; and secure in this position they awaited our coming on the following morning.

It was by no means a promising task for the small forces to attempt, and whatever anxiety Colonel Brander might naturally have entertained as to the rapid success of the enterprise was gravely increased by two despatches which an urgent messenger, riding through the night, had brought from Gyantse. The first was a telegram from General Macdonald, far to the south, expressing his disapproval and insisting that the force should instantly retire, unless it were at the moment of the receipt of the orders irrevocably committed to an engagement with the enemy. In itself this was not calculated to encourage a man immediately confronted with a difficult military problem. That in any case he would have regarded himself as irrevocably committed there can be no doubt; retreat under the circumstances would have been a serious blunder, even though no actual contact between the two forces had yet taken place. But with characteristic loyalty, Colonel Younghusband, who throughout had accepted full responsibility for the expedition, appended to it the opinion that under no circumstances should the proposed operation be abandoned or delayed.

The other news was much more serious. A postscript to the letter, in which Colonel Younghusband confirmed his instructions, gave the intelligence that before dawn on the previous morning the Mission post at Gyantse had been surrounded by 800 armed Tibetans, and that the attack, although beaten off by the reduced garrison of the place, had been renewed at once by bombardment from the abandoned jong, which had been retaken by another column of similar strength. This was grave indeed, and though it was necessary to dismiss it from all consideration till the day's work in front of him was done, this double intelligence greatly increased the anxiety with which Colonel Brander set himself to secure, not a victory only, but a victory that must be complete at any cost and before nightfall.

As we have seen, the Tibetans had built sangars on both sides of the valley in advance of the wall. Two of these sangars—one on each side—were occupied by about thirty men apiece, and Major Row and a company of Gurkhas were sent forward to the left to secure the northern outwork. At the same time two companies of the 32d Pioneers had been sent down the river-bed toward the wall. One, under Captain Bethune, arrived almost at the barrier itself, but so heavy was the fire from the loopholes, and so impossible any effective reply, that cover had to be taken under the river bank itself, some two or three hundred yards away. The second company, under Captain Cullen, fought its way across an open stretch of ground to comparative security within a fold in the ground, about the same distance from the wall. Further advance was impossible, though Captain Bethune very early in the day made a magnificent but doomed attempt to carry the wall by assault. It was here that he was killed, close under the very wall itself; according to one account he was at the moment of his death even clutching the barrel of a protruding matchlock. He was killed on the instant, and the force thereby lost the most popular, and, perhaps, also the most capable of the junior regimental officers. The Sikhs under his command retreated to their former cover and held their places for the remainder of the day.

A small body of Pioneers had been detached to drive the enemy from the sangar which was being held on the southern slope, opposite to that toward which Major Row was now advancing; but it was almost impossible to climb the slippery shale slopes, which had already assumed their utmost angle of repose; there was no cover, and it was necessary to abandon this direct attack. Thereupon Colonel Brander had recourse to an heroic measure. A dozen men under a native officer, Wassawa Singh, were sent up the almost perpendicular face of the 1,500-foot southern scarp, in order that from the ice field above they might enfilade the sangar which was the chief obstacle to a direct attack upon the wall.

Meanwhile, on the left the Gurkhas had pressed on pluckily over the difficult sliding surface of the northern slope, now glissading for a dozen feet, now helping each other up over a difficult spur; here creeping under a projecting shelf on hands and knees, there making a quick dash across an open space, but always under a steady and pretty well directed fire from the sangar they had been told to clear. After a time advance along their present line was seen to be impossible, and the whole action of the morning was suspended while Major Row detailed a few of his small force to climb the rock face overhead commanding the enemy's sangar. For two hours it was the guns only that answered the fire from the wall and from the sangars. There was a deadlock, and if no means could be found to drive the enemy from the advanced defenses which they were holding so gallantly, there seemed indeed little chance of doing anything more until nightfall. It was an anxious moment, and Colonel Brander did not spare himself. Up with the Maxims, within easy range of the Tibetan rifles, he watched the developments of the fight.

But little by little the almost indistinguishable dots moved upward along the face of the cliff to the south. A deep chimney afforded them both protection from the Tibetans manning the wall, and the bare possibility of an ascent. What the hardship must have been of climbing up to an altitude which could not have been less than 18,500 feet it is difficult for the ordinary reader to conceive. Hampered alike by his accoutrements and by the urgent anxiety for rapidity, Wassawa Singh still gave his men but scanty opportunities of rest. It was such a climb as many a member of the Alpine Club would, under the best circumstances, have declined to attempt, and the Order of Merit which was afterward conferred upon Wassawa Singh was certainly one of the most hardly earned distinctions of the campaign.

Still, in spite of everything, the little figures crept upward, and at last reached the line of perpetual snow, where they could be seen clambering and crawling against the dazzling surface of white. There was still a long way for them to go when an outbreak of fire from the southern slope of the valley showed that Major Row's men had established themselves above the enemy's right-hand sangar. A brisk crackle of musketry broke out; the exchanges were heavy, but the issue was never in any doubt. Covered by the fire from the party above, Major Row led the main body forward over the unprotected glacis, at the upper end of which the little fort had been made. The enemy's fire slackened, broke out again, and finally died down as the surviving Tibetans flung away their guns and attempted to escape down the almost perpendicular slope of the hill. Not one of them got away. The wretched men one after another scrambled amid the pitiless bullets that pecked up the dust all round, and then slid in an inert mass till they lay quiet on the road below.

With a cheer that we could hear with odd distinctness in the bottom of the valley, the Gurkhas sprang forward and captured the post. But even then much remained to do. The holders of the southern sangar kept up as steady a fire as before at any one who showed himself, and it was impossible to move on from the recently captured outpost so as to enfilade the main position, which ended on the north against a precipitous cliff. For upward of an hour the fight again languished. Nothing could be seen of Wassawa Singh and his little force; they had taken a course which was hidden behind the edge of the rock and ice above us.

Nothing in Tibet is more curiously deceptive than the little upright boulders which stand, for all the world like men, against the sky line of the hills, and time after time a false alarm was given that the Pioneers had at last reached the mountain brow from which they could enfilade the enemy. At last, however, one of the stones upon which our glasses had been fixed for so long seemed to move and, half-fainting over it, a tiny figure halted and unslung the miniature rifle into its right hand. He was joined in a moment by another, and his comrades in the valley below gave the first warning to the defenders of the sangar by raising a thin distant cheer. The enemy did not wait; not more than four or five of the escalading force had reached their goal before the Tibetans bolted from their advanced post and ran back across the open coverless slopes of the mountain-side to the protection of the great wall. In a moment the fire was concentrated upon the fugitives, not only from three points of the compass, but from angles which must have varied nearly 180°. There may have been about twenty-five men in the sangar:

of these two or three were hit at once, and the remainder, clambering and sprawling over the slippery shale, made their way back in a rain of bullets. Rifle fire is one of the most unaccountable things in the world. Judging by the standards of the shooting range it would seem impossible that even one man should have escaped from this converging battery; as a matter of fact, though the aim was fairly good, that of Lieutenant Hadow's Maxim being especially well managed, I do not think that of the remainder more than five men fell before the shelter of the wall was reached. But the day was won; for the Tibetans behind the wall, who cannot have lost more than two or three men throughout the whole day, and whose position was really hardly weakened as yet, fled as one man back down the valley of the Karo chu. We afterward heard that all day long there had been a steady melting away of this force, and that in consequence reinforcements of 500 men from Nagartse, sixteen miles down the road, had been sent up to stiffen the courage of the waverers.

We found, on passing over the wall, that the tents were still standing, the fires still alight, and the water in the cooking vessels still boiling. Furs, blankets, horse furniture, spears, powder-flasks, quick-match, bags of tsamba, skins of butter, tightly stuffed cushions, everything was there as the Tibetans had left it in their haste; but almost no rifles or matchlocks were recovered.

By the time the force had secured the position Captain Ottley, with his mounted infantry, was hurrying after the flying hordes. At one time it seemed more than likely that his little force of fifty or sixty men would be surrounded by the compact body of reinforcements which was halting for a rest at Ring-la nine miles away, when the dreaded mounted infantry swept round the corner. Never was the inherent incapacity of the Tibetan as a soldier better shown. There is no doubt that the very names of Ottley and the mounted infantry were associated by this time in the minds of the Tibetans with an almost superhuman strength

PRISONERS CAPTURED BY THE MISSION IN THE KAROLA FIGHT

and invulnerability. These reinforcements, which consisted to a great extent of monks, made almost no attempt to defend themselves, but fled in all directions up the ravines and clefts of the sides of the valley—anywhere out of the reach of the "Nightmare" and his men. The blow inflicted upon the enemy was trebled by this successful pursuit, and in Lhasa afterward we heard that the Tibetans themselves admitted 600 casualties. This is certainly an over-statement, made partly in order to justify their expulsion from so strong a position, partly also to persuade the authorities that it was no longer any use attempting to oppose our advance. We took a few prisoners. Our own casualties, besides the loss of Bethune—a host in himself—were but four killed and thirteen wounded. The day's work reflects the utmost credit on the two out-flanking parties, and if it had been possible to retain any sort of control of the position we had gained, this fight in itself might have been the turning point of the expedition. As it was, there was nothing to do but to return with the utmost speed to Gyantse. Colonel Brander had not the time even to pull down the Tibetans' wall. The tents and the ammunition were destroyed, as much damage to the wall as could be done in the short time was carried out, and then the force returned to their camping-place of the previous night four miles back in the Plain of Milk.

The altitude to which the southern flanking party attained was probably the highest point on the earth's surface at which an engagement has ever taken place, and the accounts given by the men of the terrible labor of climbing, and of the utter inability, at this height of over 18,000 feet, to do more than crawl forward listlessly, were not the least interesting part of this extraordinary action.

Immediately beyond the wall is a very curious freak of nature. The ice-field on the south here comes down to a basin three hundred yards across, the lower or northern end of which is banked up; and the melting of the ice has produced there a deep and almost clear lake, the waters of which on one side lap up against the high glacier itself. The Tibetans, recognizing any natural eccentricity as the predestined home of devils, have taken the greatest pains, with little pyramids of quartz and fluttering flags, to propitiate the evil spirits of this pretty little imitation of the Merjelensee.

On the following morning, the 7th of May, the column began the return march, and Captain O'Connor and I set off in good time to cover before nightfall the forty-four miles which lay between us and Gyantse.

CHAPTER IX

THE DALAI LAMA SHOWS HIS HAND

WHAT exactly we should find when we reached Gyantse neither O'Connor nor myself had the least idea. We knew that the first attack had been gallantly and satisfactorily beaten off; but we also knew that only half the Tibetan force had been employed on the 5th—knew too that the attacking party had bungled things in some way or other. We did not know the size of the guns which the Tibetans had mounted on the jong, we did not know how far the post had been surrounded, and to tell the truth we rather trusted to luck and to the shades of night to get back into the post at all. Rumor reached us when we got to Ra-lung that the Tibetans had determined to hold the gorges through which our little party, consisting of Captain Ottley with ten of his mounted infantry and our two selves, had to pass. If this were found to be the case we could hardly hope to force a way through; but we knew that the earlier we pushed on the better hope there was of being able to make our way to the open plain of Gyantse, which it was impossible for the Tibetans to barricade, and in which we might then be able to hold our own against any number the Tibetans were likely to send out from the jong to cut us off. It was an uneventful ride of fifteen miles from Ra-lung to Gobshi, and we covered it in a little over three hours. We halted at the village of the Four Gates to collect intelligence and to rest. The head men of the village were, not unnaturally, in a state of considerable agitation. It is possible that they knew nothing whatever about the intentions or the actions of their countrymen eighteen miles away; but their nervousness inevitably suggested that they were lying when they so assured us. So we determined not to hurry on, but to take care that the evening should have set in before we reached the last and most difficult stretch of our journey.

Leaving Gobshi at half-past four in the afternoon, we moved on slowly down the valley of the Nyero chu, watching the slow transformation of one of the finest sunsets I have ever seen in Tibet. Luckily we found all the bridges along the road intact. This was a never-ending source of amazement to us throughout the expedition. The Tibetans had never taken the trouble or perhaps even had the idea of impeding our progress by so simple and effectual a device as the breaking of the road in any way; perhaps the most glaring example of this was seen in the way in which they eventually left for our use the two great barges at the Chak-sam ferry. The rebuilding of a bridge is no small matter in Tibet. Of wood on the spot there may be nothing, and in many cases where the bridge is made of timber brought from a distance the space across is much too great for the substitution of stone at a moment's notice. Accustomed as we were, it was a relief to find that the stone causeway at Malang, about three miles from Gobshi, was standing intact. After that there was at least no bridge by the destruction of which they could bar our return to Gyantse that night.

There was not a sign of a Tibetan anywhere. The little houses and rare gompas, nestling here and there in the bare valleys to the north and south, showed no sign of life. So we made our way unnoticed till we faced the crimson blaze of the sunset over the open plain of Gyantse, two miles beyond the big chorten which is the most conspicuous object of the track astraddle of the road just where a sharp turn in the river half incloses a wooded peninsula. We moved on in the dying red light for a couple of miles, and then the night of these high uplands crept in upon us from all sides. As we passed the house of the eldest son of the Maharajah of Sikkim we could still distinguish dimly the houses near Né-nyeng. A mile and a half further on we passed the long ruins of a battlemented wall and were just able to distinguish the jong in the darkness as we moved over the low neck of white quartzite, which here thrusts out into the plain a line of little peaks. After that the gloom deepened and soon we could hardly see each other. It was a moonless night, and four miles from home we literally could not see the ground under our horses' hoofs. Now and then a Tibetan wayfarer ran into our arms before he knew what or who we were; such travelers we questioned and turned behind us. The explanation each gave of his night wandering was not wholly uninteresting. One man had been into the city for a charm for his sick wife, and was returning confident in the efficacy of his closely cuddled treasure. Another man was a lama who had been relieved by a friend at a monastery all day, and was hurrying back to keep his word and release his already over-taxed proxy. A third had an ugly story to tell to us—he was the first who gave us any information of the horrible fate which had overtaken our unfortunate servants. They all agreed that the Tibetans were holding all the houses in the plain past which our road necessarily ran; but more than that none of them honestly seemed able to tell us.

By this time our escort had been reduced to six men. Captain Ottley had decided to remain behind at Gobshi to secure a safe escort for a belated baggage mule and her leader. So we moved on through the night, and for the first time I realized the skill of a native of India as a tracker. There was not the slightest indication of a road anywhere. There was not a light visible in the whole plain, and even the stars were obscured by the light night mist that was rising into the cold air from the still warm fields. By daylight one would have made half-a-dozen mistakes in trying to thread one's way across the three miles of flat country, deeply intersected in every direction with wide and often unfordable water-courses; but now in the dark the guidance of our Sikhs was unfailing. One road there was, and one only, after we had struck out toward Chang-lo from the beaten path. This took a fantastic course over the plowed fields, along the bunds containing the marshy squares where the first barley was beginning to show itself, across the irrigation channels by single-stone bridges, swerving now to the right and now to the left, dipping down into a dry water-course, rising on the farther side at some unindicated point, brushing past little clumps of sallow-thorn, skirting an old reservoir, and often verging too close to be comfortable to some occupied house which was invisible at ten yards, but was betrayed by the furious barking of the inevitable watch-dogs. Along this tortuous path the Sikhs of our escort led us in the darkness without the slightest hesitation or mistake. Even at the end, when a single light could be seen from the window of the upper story of our besieged post, they made no mistake in going straight toward it. A sharp turn to the right along an iris-covered embankment saved us a heavy wetting in the deepest water-channel of the plain.

As we approached Chang-lo we suddenly remembered that we were in considerably more danger from the high-strung watchfulness of our own sentries than from all the forces that Tibet could put into the field. After a while we could barely distinguish against the vague duskiness of the sky the mass of our tall poplars. And then two men were sent on to feel our way into the post—no easy matter. The garrison were not expecting us, and the approach to a defended position is a difficult matter, wholly apart from the possibility of the sentry firing before he challenges. Barbed wire entanglements, well-planned stakes and abattis of felled tree-tops and other impedimenta are no light things to penetrate on a dark night; and in the present case we had no means of knowing what additional precautions the garrison had, as a matter of course, taken. But all was well; and at about a quarter to ten we found ourselves in the Mission mess heartily welcomed as earnest of better things to come.

The story of the attack on the Mission in the early hours of May 5th reads like a romance. As I have said, news had come that a body of Tibetans was moving up the valley of the Nyang chu to Dongtse, twelve miles away to the north-west. These men, 1,600 in number, no doubt had their instructions, and it subsequently was shown that those instructions had been given them by Dorjieff himself. They had to retake the jong and annihilate the Mission with its escort. It may be questioned, however, whether they would ever have had the determination to attempt to carry out the latter part of their orders, if at the last moment they had not received what must have seemed to them the miraculous news that two-thirds of the defenders of Chang-lo had suddenly been called away. Marching in two bands through the night of the 4th of May, one-half reoccupied the jong, while the other moved as silently as shadows up to the very walls of the English post.

Speculation as to what would have happened if another course had been adopted is, perhaps, useless; but there was a fair consensus of opinion in the post that if the Tibetans had simply thrown away their useless firearms, and had contented themselves with rushing the sentries with drawn swords, the issue of that evening might have been painfully different. Actually, the men who reached the post were under the walls by about three in the morning; and there in silence they seem to have remained for nearly an hour. Not a sentry perceived them; and if it had not been for an alarm given by the last joined recruit of the whole force, a boy who had not been thought to have sufficient steadiness for the work of a soldier, and was only accepted because of the unexpected loss of another man, they could without difficulty have made their way within striking distance of at least two of the four sentries. This boy, looking through the darkness, thought he saw the movement of what might have been a man about twenty yards from the southern entrance. It will be remembered that our relations with the Tibetans were of the most friendly character, and as a matter of fact the nightly visits paid by the followers of the Mission to Gyantse, for more or less disreputable purposes, must have been well within his knowledge; he must, in fact, have known that at that moment there were at least eight of the servants of the force in the town; and it says a good deal for his coolness and discipline that, whether he were betraying a friend or not, he did not hesitate for a moment to rouse the echoes of the night by a hasty shot following upon a single loud challenge.

The effect of a shot at night upon a defended post is something which should be experienced to be fully understood; the whole place is galvanized as though it had received an electric shock. And every other sentry realized in a second the danger that lay in the swarming black ring of men, which now, for the first time, were seen clearly enough encircling the whole post. The Tibetans also were naturally startled into action; they stood up under our very walls and actually used our own loop-holes, thrusting the muzzles of their matchlocks into the Mission compound. A doctor was the first man to dash into the place from the redoubt and warn Colonel Younghusband of his danger. His description of the compound is curious; he says that a network of flashes and humming bullets struck in every direction over the inclosure. By some merciful accident not a single man was hit, though several of the tents received four or five bullets straight through them. Captain Walton in particular had a very narrow escape; he said that the first thing that he realized, after this rude awakening, was the muzzles of two or three rusty matchlocks poking down through the wall in his direction. One thing probably saved the situation; the Tibetans, being naturally shorter men than the Sikhs, for whom the loop-holes had originally been made, and at no time paying much attention to fire discipline or aim, simply held their guns up over their heads and fired through the loop-holes in any direction that was convenient. For a few seconds, which seemed almost as many minutes, the walls remained unmanned; then round by the water gate the quick reports of the Lee-Metford heralded a blaze of fire from every point of the perimeter.

From the point of view of the Tibetans, the moment chosen for the attack was most unfortunate. They secured, indeed, for themselves the advantage of an approach in the dark, and, of course, had they been successful in effecting their purpose and forcing a hand-to-hand struggle inside the walls of the post, the coming of dawn might have served them in good stead. As it was, however, the growing light caught them, not only still outside our defenses, but a beaten crowd, for whom there was not a stick of cover, huddled up under the walls of the post. When their inevitable flight had to be attempted some fled at once among the trees of the plantation behind Chang-lo; some hid themselves idiotically in the walled-up bays of the bridge, where they were caught like rats in a trap by the first skirmishing party that set out to clear the ground. The luckiest were the most cowardly; large numbers, as soon as our firing broke out, had made their way back in terror through the shrubs and willows immediately overhanging the river bank toward the white house, 600 yards ahead of us, toward the jong, which was afterward captured by us and known as the Gurkhas' post. Here they were in safety. On the way they passed a small shrine which Captain Walton had been using as his consulting room and hospital for Tibetan patients.

It was from this hospital that the first intimation of anything wrong had been received. On the morning of the previous day

Captain Walton's suspicions had been aroused by the sudden exodus of a very large number of his patients. One and all seemed anxious to get away, and though this might really mean little with a shy and probably mistrustful people like the good folk of Gyantse, there was a unanimity about the whole matter which caused him to make some disappointed comment, and then it appeared that one of his patients had been told of the intention of the Tibetans to make a night attack upon the Mission. Such rumors had, of course, been common ever since our occupation of the place, and had been proved time after time to be the merest canards. Captain Walton paid very little attention to it, but he was sufficiently aware of a change in the attitude of his patients —such of them as remained for treatment—to make him report the matter to Colonel Younghusband that evening, without, however, expressing any belief or, indeed, much interest in the matter. By this time his hospital was empty of all its inmates except, I believe, one or two bedridden men who could find no one to come and help them away.

I have said that the luckiest were the most cowardly, but for the main body of the attacking force there was no help. When their attack failed and flight was necessary they were obliged to make the best of their way back across the flat plain to the jong and Gyantse. The defenders' post numbered in all about 170 men, but this number was to a large extent weakened by the fact that Colonel Brander had naturally taken with him the strongest men of the force, and those who remained behind were certainly, to the extent of forty per cent., either weakened by dysentery or actually in hospital blankets. But, well or ill, every man reached for his rifle and came out to his place. The members of the Mission—Colonel Younghusband, Captain Ryder, Lieutenant-Colonel Waddell, and, it should not be forgotten, Mr. Mitter, the confidential clerk of the Mission—immediately manned the upper works, and a certain number of the followers displayed considerable martial energy in positions of more or less personal danger. About a dozen of the mounted infantry had been left by Colonel Brander, and these men saddled their ponies with feverish haste. Bullets were still singing over the post, but there was no doubt that the Tibetans had been successfully beaten off, and the lesson to be taught them was one which mounted men could best convey. The real flight of the Tibetans did not begin till forty minutes after the first alarm, and though it would be inaccurate to say that the issue was really in doubt after the first five or ten, it will be seen that the engagement was for a time hotly contested, and it is doubtful whether the Tibetans lost many men till they broke and ran. After that it was simply a case of shooting down the flying figures in the gray morning twilight. It is one of the peculiarities of Tibet that as soon as a leafless bush can be distinguished twenty yards away in the dawn you can almost as clearly see a willow tree on a slope a mile and a half distant. The tiny body of irregular infantry, made all the more irregular by the volunteers who aided in the pursuit, were busily and systematically clearing the plantation of the enemy, and preparing to carry a counter attack home to the very foot of the rock from which the first jingal balls were now being fired toward Chang-lo.

The Tibetans left behind them but few under the actual walls of the post, but 180 dead were found within a radius of one thousand yards, and, under the circumstances, at least three times that number must have been wounded. On our own side—besides our wretched servants and the unhappy Nepali shepherd who was caught outside the defenses watching his flock through the night, and fell a shocking victim to the Tibetans' savage lust for blood—there were but two casualties all this time. This is but another example of the immunity which, time after time, was enjoyed by our men against all probability and, indeed, experience.

The work of the mounted infantry was finished about six

o'clock in the full light of the quick Asiatic dawn. The Tibetans flying helplessly over the flat irrigated fields had been scattered to the winds. The luckier ones on horseback made good their escape almost to a man. The others either ran for their lives with the characteristic heavy-shouldered tramp of their race, or hid in vain desperation among the irrigation channels of the fields. One or two fled to the river bank and there immersed themselves, leaving their mouths and noses only above the thick, brown flood, under the friendly shelter of an overhanging shrub. One or two by the banks, with animal-like cunning, feigned death, and when detected pretended to be severely wounded.

An hour and a half after this heavy and responsible work two Sikhs threw the post-bags of the dak across their saddles and moved out to take the mails as usual to Sau-gang. Later in the day another man cantered off on the road to the Karo la. The lesson of the morning was emphasized by a spasmodic bombardment all the day, and a Sepoy was killed while standing almost immediately behind a high adobe wall. Captain Ryder instantly assumed the direction of the additional defenses which had to be made, and the next two days produced an extraordinary alteration in the aspect of Chang-lo. Great traverses of timber logs, interspersed with granite boulders, rose up like magic everywhere. The Masbi Sikh is by nature and intention a lazy man; yet it is possible that no Sikh in the history of his race ever worked with such desperation as the hundred laborers who, in very truth, had to work like the famous artisans under the direction of Nehemiah. There was no time to lose, for the only information we could certainly get from the prisoners was that more men and larger guns were even at that moment being hurried up against us from Lhasa.

Such was the state of affairs when O'Connor and I rode in on the evening of the 7th. The column from the Karo la could not arrive until the afternoon of the 9th; an attack, meanwhile, was threatened for that same night. But the Tibetans had had too heavy a lesson, and nothing, therefore, was done before the arrival of the main body of the defenders had put an end to all hope of carrying the post by storm.

As soon as the place was put in a proper condition of defense we had leisure to consider the extraordinary change in the political situation which had been caused by the attack of the Tibetans. Of course, in one way it simplified the position enormously; there could no longer be any pretense on the part of the Tibetans that they were a peace-loving and long-suffering race; the issues were cleared. It was obvious that no negotiations had ever been intended. We were able at last to estimate the authority of the Chinese suzerains and the influence of the Amban himself—neither existed. Unless we were willing to help ourselves, it was in a moment clear that the Chinese were neither willing nor able to help us. I do not suppose that any one in his senses has ever seriously criticized the right of the Tibetans to massacre the Mission if they could, and if they were ready to accept the consequences of success. It is true that the circumstances of this attack during a period of practical armistice, while we were awaiting, if not perhaps expecting, the advent of the Amban, gave some reasonable ground of complaint; but as we were ourselves tarred with the same brush, reproach was a boomerang-like weapon for us to employ. The situation, as I have said, was undoubtedly cleared, but it may well be doubted whether that was any particular gratification to the Cabinet at home. That it was not is perhaps clear from the fact that Lord Lansdowne seems immediately to have gone out of his way to make a gratuitous re-statement of the pledges which the Government had given six months before to Russia. Herein, perhaps, there is some just reason to demur to the policy of Whitehall. It is an open secret that our policy in Egypt just then demanded that we should be on good terms with Russia, but even so, it seemed common sense to lay every conceivable stress upon an active hostility which was at once recognized as due to the presence of a Russian subject in Lhasa. In any case, whatever the responsibility of an unauthorized representative of the great northern neighbor of Tibet, it was perfectly clear that the attack on the Mission had practically justified to the full the presumptions of active hostility which had seemed to us to necessitate the accompaniment of the Mission by a strong escort. The chief point, therefore, which had excited the mistrust of continental critics was clearly demonstrated as a wise and, indeed, a very necessary precaution on our part.

More than this, the behavior of the Tibetans had justified at a stroke our taking action in the matter at all. It was clear from the kindly reception which the Mission received on its coming to Gyantse from every one except the local representatives of the close Lamaic corporation that governs the country, and from the subsequent attack promoted by that corporation, that our forecast was correct, not only in assuming that the Lamaic hierarchy in no way represented the feeling of the bulk of the population, but also that it was from the priestly autocrats of Tibet alone that danger to British interests was to be feared. It was no part of the business of the British Government to play the rôle of Perseus rescuing Andromeda from a monster; but somewhat to our surprise we found that the policy of the Viceroy, begun for very different and somewhat prosaic reasons, was actually compelling us into a position which was not very different. We had begun, without questioning the form of government which obtained in Tibet, by working for the conclusion of some agreement with a properly accredited representative of the country. We had accepted the peculiarities, not to say the brutalities, which mark this extreme form of religious tyranny, not in ignorance, but as being no affair of ours. With the Grand Lama as the head of the country we had certain business to transact; and if he had been willing to meet us at Kamba-jong, our difficulties would have been over. We should never have moved a mile farther into the Forbidden Country, and, perhaps, the hold of the lamas over the country might have been even stronger than before, inasmuch as our diplomatic relations with Lhasa would have formed an additional proof of the ability of the Tibetans to manage their own foreign affairs, and of the uselessness of continuing the farce of Chinese sovereignty. This the Grand Lama failed to see, and the upshot of our interference has been that the reign of superstitious tyranny has received a severe blow, not only by the prestige we have gained by our successful advance to Lhasa, but by the deposition of the Grand Lama, and by the strength which has thereby been temporarily given to the tottering structure of Chinese sovereignty.

These considerations might perhaps have made the home authorities hesitate before wantonly reiterating to the Russians assurances which were perfectly honest but in their origin applicable only to an entirely different and much less complicated state of affairs. The attack on the Mission was the throwing down of the glove. It was a deliberate challenge on the part of an autocrat who saw that in the slowly increasing friendliness between the foreigner and the "miser" of the land there lurked perhaps the seeds of trouble for himself in the future. We know from an excellent source that the action of the English in paying full prices, and even more than full prices, for the food-stuffs they requisitioned in the Chumbi and Nyang chu Valleys was an unexpected shock to the authorities in Lhasa; they complained of it. And knowing, as we now do, whose influence lay at the bottom of this night attack upon the Mission, we can see not only a shrewd and successful scheme whereby Dorjieff himself might escape from the consequences of his own bad advice, but a not unnatural determination at all hazards to put an end to the growing familiarity between the invaders and the invaded.

About this time in Lhasa there was a wave of mistrust of the Chinese. Actual power the Chinese had none, and the very advice of the Amban was believed to be tainted. Dorjieff had assured the government of Tibet that the English had brought into subjection the Middle Kingdom, and were using to the full the authority of the Chinese representatives abroad when and as it suited their purpose. The earnest and repeated advice therefore to them was merely a confirmation of the serious danger they were in. They left no stone unturned to spur their people on to harry those whom they called the English infidels of Hindustan. The men of Kams at first refused to leave their province to oppose our advance; they argued that they could not leave their own district unprotected, and, as the Dalai Lama's temporal authority over Kams is somewhat nebulous, he very wisely adjured them to assist him on the spiritual ground that the ultimate intention of the Mission was to wreck Buddhism.

The state of affairs in Lhasa at this time was desperate. The Emperor of China had ordered the Tibetans to negotiate with the Maharajah of Nepal and the Tongsa Penlop, the temporal ruler of Bhutan; both had urged upon the Dalai Lama an immediate compliance with the British demands. No help was forthcoming from Russia, and, as a final blow, the good people of Nakchu-ka said with some firmness that the English had already killed many professional soldiers of the Tibetans, and how then could peaceable cattle-drivers like themselves fight against them? Rather than come out they would go on pilgrimage. In these depressing circumstances, the Dalai Lama appears to have acted somewhat hurriedly, and, so far as can be gleaned, the Amban seems to have had a bad quarter of an hour with him. At any rate, upon his return through the green parks of Lhasa, which separate the Potala from the Residency, his cogitations took a definite shape, and the Viceroy of Tibet sent an urgent request to the Maharajah of Nepal that a thousand Gurkhas should be sent at once for his protection.

On the side of the Grand Lama also military preparations were pressed on. The construction of a fort at Chu-sul, forty miles from Lhasa, at the junction of the Kyi chu and the Tsang-po, was ordered. A new water-wheel, presumably for the purpose of turning a lathe, was set up in the arsenal, and, in utter need, the magic powers of the Sa-kya monastery, the awful representative of an old régime of divine tyrants, were called in, and the incantations and charms of the contemned Red Cap faith rose up for the first time from under the golden roofs of the Potala. Finally, two days after our arrival in Gyantse, the Tibetans had determined to rush our post by night and reoccupy the jong. This had been attempted with partial success.

It will be seen that there was no real hope of conducting negotiations in Gyantse even before the morning of the 5th of May. After that eventful moment, with the Tibetans all round us and the guns of the jong playing at their will upon the Commissioner's residence, negotiation was naturally farther off than ever. The determination of the Government to adhere to its policy of concession to Russian susceptibilities now crippled Colonel Younghusband's right hand. The very Sikhs of the garrison came to hear of it, and said gloomily that unless this business were carried through as it should be and in Lhasa, they would never be able to hold up their heads again among their own folk at home. So long, however, as this bombardment lasted, so long as the Tibetans retained possession of the jong, negotiation on any basis whatever was in abeyance—except for Colonel Younghusband, whose weary pen again and again restated the position for the benefit of the Cabinet, scarcely one of whose members, with the exception of Lord Lansdowne, had even a bowing acquaintance with the East.

There is no doubt about it; in the East you must do as the East does, if you hope to achieve anything permanently good or permanently great in it. Had the two things been necessarily incompatible, the jettison of Lord Curzon's policy in order that Lord

Cromer's goods should be safely brought to port might well have been accepted by every one, and certainly would have been by every member of the Mission in Tibet. But this was not put forward as inevitable, and it seemed to us unfortunate that the Government should not have realized that the condition of affairs had changed.

Meanwhile, the daily work of defense had to be done, and better provision had to be made for the mules whose old lines lay under the guns of the jong with scarcely a twig to protect them. They were given a more secure position in rear of the buildings. The abattis and horn-works were strengthened, the Gurkhas' gate was re-staked, wire entanglements surrounded the entire post, traverses rose up in every unprotected spot, the trees in the plantation to the rear were cleared away for two hundred yards, and the sentries were doubled. Captain Ryder's defenses of Chang-lo were subsequently slightly extended by Captain Sheppard, but the latter, on his arrival, found the place sufficiently secure to enable him to devote all his energies to the construction of bridges and covered ways between the main position and the outposts at the white house and Pala village, which had then been secured.

From day to day it became increasingly uncertain whether the little mail-bag, which was taken out every morning to be met at Sau-gang by the dak runners from Kang-ma, would ever reach its destination. Why the Tibetans did not effectually prevent this mail remains a mystery to this day. The bag was usually guarded by four mounted men only, and it had a long road to cover, by villages, from any of which the messengers might with impunity have been shot down; through defiles in which any ravine might well conceal a dozen determined men; or across the open plain, where its distant progress could be watched by a sharp-sighted man six miles away. Once or twice a faint-hearted attempt was actually made. On one occasion, May 20th, it was so far successful that the mounted infantry were obliged to make the best of their way into Chang-lo, leaving behind them one mail-bag and one of their number dead.[1]

The coming of the dak was the one incident that broke the monotony of our daily life. The telegraph wire was with us almost from the beginning, and only once was there the slightest attempt to interfere with it on the part of the enemy. In this connection an incident may be noticed which reflects no small credit upon Mr. Truninger. He, so the story was told to me, with his second in command, was engaged in setting up posts and laying the wires along one portion of the road to the undisguised interest and curiosity of one or two innocent-looking lamas. These men persistently asked what was the use of the wire. It will be seen that this was, under the circumstances, an inquiry the true answer to which might prove disastrous to our communications. We had not the men to defend even ten miles of this long line, and without the slightest question the wire would have been cut in twenty places a day if the Tibetans had had the least idea of the enormous value it was to us. But the answer came simply and earnestly. "We English," said Truninger, "are in a strange land, a land of which no foreigner has ever known anything; our maps are no good, and every day we go forward we are like children lost in a great wood. Therefore we lay this wire behind us in order that when we have done our business with your Dalai Lama we may find the road by which we came and, as quickly as possible, get hence to England." Needless to say, nothing could more effectually have secured the wire from damage, as the single ambition of the Tibetans from the first was to be rid of us as quickly as possible.

The result of this forbearance on the part of the enemy was that we often received the news in the first editions of the evening

[1] This dead man was the only one left in the hands of the Tibetans throughout the expedition. His head was afterward found to have been hacked off and sent to Lhasa to substantiate a claim to the grant of land offered by the Dalai Lama in return for every head of a member of the expedition.

papers in London before we sat down to dinner the same evening. In point of actual time we received such news within three hours of its publication, while the news which we sent westward at times reached London long before the nominal hour at which it had been despatched from Gyantse. Ordinarily, however, messages took about three hours apparent time, that is to say, eight or nine hours actual time, in reaching their destination in London.

Diaries of sieges are dull. There was always plenty to do, but it lacked distinction, although under other circumstances much of it would have been exciting enough. One day, or rather one night, there were water channels, supplying the town, to be cut or dammed; there was a patrol to be sent out, with the general intention of rendering night traveling unhealthy for the Tibetans; later on, there was a two-hundred-yard length of covered way to be made in the exposed plain. Another day some of the houses in the plain behind us, which the Tibetans were holding, had to be cleared of their occupants. Another time there was a bridge to be built beyond the end of the plantation, just within the furthest range of the jingals from the rock. These jingals generally gave the first intimation that the dak was arriving. Besides their regular morning bombardment, and one equally inevitable about half-past four, they reserved aim and ammunition for the dak riders, whom from their high eyrie they could easily see as they crossed the bridge and made their way through the trees of the plantation to the southern entrance of the post.[1] All day long there was something to be done; I spent the late afternoons in acquiring a smattering of Tibetan. The wind used to spring up daily about three o'clock, whirling a shower of catkins from the willows beside the wall of the Mission garden, and driving a penetrating storm of grit through the post. Out across the plain, the long trails of smoke from the burning houses were dissipated into the

[1] I do not think that a single man was ever hit in this way, but the amount of lead the Tibetans thus used was extraordinary.

low-lying blue haze of the distant hills, and added another glory to the sunset scene.

On the 19th of May it was decided to clear what was known afterward as the Gurkha post. This was a white house 600 yards away from Chang-lo straight in the direction of the jong. The Tibetans had occupied it with sixty men, and it was imperative that they should at once be dislodged. Before dawn the storming-party, under Lieutenant Gurdon, moved out, followed by the Gurkhas of the garrison. The main doors of the house were blown in, and the place carried by assault in a quarter of an hour; our casualties were insignificant, and before the sun was well up the house was occupied by a single company of the attacking force, which remained in this exposed position during the remainder of our stay at Gyantse. Against this house the chief fury of the Tibetans was thenceforward directed; night after night it was surrounded and had to beat off the Tibetan forces. Day after day it was pounded by the guns on the jong, which here seemed to rise almost perpendicularly above the house. A wall was built up by the Tibetans from the westward corner of the jong toward the river, and from two embrasures in it a continual bombardment was kept up upon the defenders of the post. On the following day occurred the attack upon the mail escort, to which I have already referred. On this occasion Captain Ottley, who went out with the mounted infantry to the rescue of the dak runners, drove the Tibetans headlong from two farms, but found them so strongly ensconced about four miles further on that he was himself obliged to retire, impeded by the necessity of escorting two wounded and five unmounted men.

On the 21st a small force moved out under Colonel Brander to clear the plain to the south; they captured and burned three farms held by the enemy, and returned to camp on receiving a report that the enemy were moving out from Gyantse to attack Chang-lo. Colonel Brander did not allow the grass to grow under his feet, and five days later he swept the Tibetans from Pala village, the most important position that they held, except the jong itself.

The taking of Pala was one of the most creditable bits of work done by the garrison. In utter darkness, before the dawn, Colonel Brander sent out a small column, composed of three hundred rifles, four guns, and a Maxim. Their objective was this hamlet, where the Tibetans had been strengthening a position and mounting guns for the previous two or three days. This danger at all costs had to be prevented. Pala enfiladed nearly the whole of our defenses, and was barely 1,200 yards away to the north-east. The relative positions of Chang-lo, Pala, and the jong were, roughly speaking, those of the points of an equilateral triangle; the road from Gyantse to Lhasa runs through Pala; and the occupation of this post gave us practical command of all direct communications with the capital. For more reasons than one the place had to be taken, and Colonel Brander's scheme was in its conception admirable. The guns were posted on an eminence, a quarter of a mile away to the north-east, which completely dominated the village. After skirting round the village to the south-east his plan was to develop an attack in the first place upon the house which was nearest to the jong. For this purpose Captain Sheppard and Captain O'Connor were deputed, with half-a-dozen men, to open the assault by blowing in the wall of the next house, which wholly commanded it. At the same time Lieutenant Garstin, with Lieutenant Walker, R.E., was sent a few yards further to breach the house itself. Major Peterson, with two companies of the 32d Pioneers, was to follow up the explosions with an instant rush. This was the plan; what actually happened was entirely different.

The column moved slowly through the darkness, until its leading ranks were within fifty yards of the high road to Lhasa. At that moment a small party of three unsuspecting Tibetans tramped slowly along it, and though Colonel Brander believed that not one of his men was actually seen, it is possible that, in some way, these men were able to give the alarm to the defenders of the post. Certainly there seems to be no reason to charge any member of the attacking column with carelessness, or even an accident. But the Tibetans were on the alert, and, as soon as the first figures were visible in the obscurity, a hot fire was poured upon them from the roofs of all the houses in the village. The two storming-parties had by this time reached a low wall, thirty yards from the house to be attacked, and there was nothing else to be done but to make a dash for it. Captain Sheppard, followed by Captain O'Connor, vaulted over the wall, and ran forward into the narrow lane between the two houses. From a doorway in the foremost house, opening into this passage, three Tibetans rushed out with matchlocks and swords. Captain Sheppard drew his revolver and shot two of them, set the cake of gun-cotton under the wall, and lit the fuse. He then ran back, preceded by the third Tibetan, who, however, escaped into the door again. At the same time, beside the smaller house, Garstin and Walker were setting up their explosive, and everything seemed to promise immediate success on the lines that Colonel Brander had mapped out. Garstin's fuse, however, refused to act, and only Sheppard's effected its purpose. An earth-shaking roar was followed by blinding dust, through which it was impossible to see the full extent of the damage done. But all firing ceased for the moment, and in one house at least a breach, big enough for the entrance of the supporting companies, had been made. No one came.

It appeared afterward that Major Peterson's men had found it impossible to advance in the face of the fire from the houses, and instead of moving westward to the place from which they could carry out the work begun by the storming-parties, they took up a sheltered position to the east in a garden, where they remained until the well-directed fire of "Bubble" and "Squeak" enabled them to advance. The little storming-party was indeed also supported by a company of the same regiment on its flank, which had occupied a position in the sunken road a hundred yards from the house, and did not understand the dangers in which the two small bodies of men under Captain Sheppard were in a moment placed. These men were thus entirely cut off, and both houses were full of Tibetans.

O'Connor acted with great presence of mind. He had his own cake of gun-cotton intact, and, by the merest chance, the door through which the surviving Tibetan had escaped back into the house was left unfastened. Attended by one Sikh only, O'Connor dashed through into the unoccupied house. Luckily every man in it was on the roof; for that very reason he considered it necessary to go up on to the first floor, in order more effectively to explode the charge. Followed by his companion, he dashed up the slippery iron-sheathed ladder, and set his cake in the corner where it would do most damage. The men on the roof had seen him, and in a rain of badly aimed bullets he lighted the fuse and, to use his own phrase, "ran like a rabbit." His Sikh companion in his excitement caught his rifle, to which the bayonet was attached, between a wooden pillar and the hand-rail of the stairs, thus completely barring the descent. Fuses used by storming-parties are, naturally, short, and the stage directions for the descent of O'Connor and his man would have: "exeunt confusedly." Picking themselves up at the bottom they made for the door, which, however, they did not reach before the explosion took place. O'Connor never has given a very lucid description of the moment, but the fact that in his inside pocket a thick cut-glass flask was smashed to pieces by the shock shows that his escape was a narrow one indeed. Sheppard outside saw with horror half of one of the walls of the house subside in yellow dust before a sign of O'Connor was visible at the doorway.

Soon after this a second attempt of Garstin's was more successful, but in the absence of any support, the position of the little storming-parties was dangerous indeed. Soon afterward, as we were to hear with the deepest regret, Garstin was killed outright, and O'Connor was seriously wounded by a ball through the shoulder, before safe quarters could be taken up. In fact, these exposed sections suffered all the more serious casualties of the day, and in number no less than eight out of a total of eleven.

As soon as it was light enough, the guns on the little hill opened fire upon the still strongly held houses to the east of the village, and Major Peterson showed great gallantry in bringing up his Pioneers through the gardens and houses, taking each by storm in turn. The fighting was severe, for with the rising of the sun the Tibetans found themselves caught without the chance of escape. The jong lay 1,200 yards away, but to reach it fugitives were obliged to cross an entirely coverless plain. Their fellows in the town could be of little assistance to them. One plucky attempt on the part of a score of mounted men was, indeed, made, but the enterprise was hopeless; riding straight into the zone swept by the Maxims, hardly three of them escaped back. Nor did the bombardment, which the jong opened at the first streak of light, help the defenders of the village. With an impartial hand the gunners showered their balls upon friend and foe alike, and to this cannonade some at least of the Tibetan casualties among the crowded houses of Pala must have been due. A stout defense against overwhelming odds was made for a short time; but as the morning wore on, the Tibetans abandoned their loop-holes and their windows, and fled to their labyrinth of underground cellars, where they crouched in the darkness, and with their matchlocks ready, formed a far more formidable antagonist than in the open air. The place was practically cleared by one o'clock, though for two or three days afterward a considerable number of undiscovered Tibetans crept quietly away under cover of the darkness of the night.

In the center of the village was a large and comfortable house, owned by the Pala family, one of the most aristocratic stocks in Tibet. Besides a well-built three-storied house, there was also the usual little summer-house beneath the trees of the garden. The excellent workmanship of the few things, such as tea-pots and brass images, which were found in the house gave proof of the luxury of its late occupants. A more significant find, however, was the discovery of two heavy jingals in the cellars. It is a little difficult to account for their presence. They had certainly not been brought there recently, and it is curious that the Tibetans in bringing guns even from Lhasa itself, for the purpose of bombarding our post, should have overlooked within a mile of Gyantse two pieces throwing a ball as heavy as those which they had laboriously transported from a distance. The larger of the two guns weighed over four hundred pounds, the diameter of its bore was three inches, and the outside was curiously fluted. It was made of gun-metal, and altogether seemed serviceable enough for the limited ballistic requirements of Tibetans.

The village was occupied by a detachment of the Pioneers, whose exploits were recognized in their Colonel's orders on the following day. It is perhaps a pity that the work of the storming-parties did not receive acknowledgment, though the survivors of them, wounded or not, were the last people to notice the omission. It was a good piece of work, and Colonel Brander is to be congratulated. The delay of even twenty-four hours in capturing this village might have made a serious difference to the defense of Chang-lo, and when the Tibetans had once been driven out the fullest use was made by us of this second *point d'appui*.

The situation created by the capture of Pala was briefly this: the English force was placed in a strong position with regard to the jong; we were enabled to cut the communications of the Tibetans eastward, and, by holding the bridge at Chang-lo itself, communication with the south was only possible after the river had risen by going five miles down stream to the bridge at Tse-chen. We had for some time been able to keep the Tibetans under cover all the day; a few sharp-shooters and Lieutenant Hadow, with an itching thumb upon the trigger-lever of his Maxim, had long made it impossible for any Tibetan to show himself by daylight on any part of the jong, or in so much of the town as was visible from the roof of the Commissioner's house. But we had hitherto of course been unable to stop steady communication with Lhasa by night. Now, however, we were astride the road, and an occasional patrol was all that was necessary to prevent the Tibetans holding any communication with their capital, except by the circuitous and difficult track, which could only be followed by retreating thirty miles down the valley of the Nyang chu.

On our side we were still surrounded, and it was a daily uncertainty every morning whether our thin line of communications would have continued to exist through the night. We were therefore in a curious situation, both sides besieging the other; and the word investment (which was generally used to describe our position) is not perhaps strictly accurate. The honors were pretty evenly divided; neither the Tibetans nor we were able to storm the others' defenses; a mutual fusillade compelled each side to protect its occupants by an elaborate system of traverses; and straying beyond the narrow limits of the fortifications was, on either side, severely discouraged by the other. The Tibetans had, however, two considerable advantages. They were fighting in their own country, and in numbers they probably exceeded us by ten to one. For them, every village or house that dotted the wide plain round us was a refuge, and might also become a post from which to operate against us. The loss of a few men now and then mattered little to them; they had the whole of Tibet from which to make good their casualties, and from almost the same wide recruiting ground reinforcements crept in nightly in small companies. Sometimes in the past they had ventured in during the daylight, bent double, running from cover to cover like hares, now waiting for a quarter of an hour behind a friendly overhanging bank, now making quick time to the shelter of a white-washed chorten, or a ruined wall. But our success at Pala made a great difference to the relative positions of ourselves and the Tibetans.

CHAPTER X

LIFE IN THE BESIEGED POST

AT Gyantse, from dawn till sunset, there was generally a breeze. Except for an hour or two in the white heat of mid-day the lightly strung leaves of the branching Lombardy poplars in the compound were every moment shifting edge-ways to the faint indraft from the plain, and, overhead, the long strings of prayer-flags, orange and faded gray and gauzy chrome, rocked gently in the stirring air. Silent the post never was by day, not even in the motionless glare of noontide when the wind was stifled and the heat sweated out from the wide empty plains, a teeming mirage veil. These were the hours which the shrill whistle of the kite or the monotone of the hoopoe filled—hours when the petty restlessness of a camp, even in the hour of siesta, assumed ear-compelling importance. Never during the day could one hear the faint rush and race of the Nyang chu over its pebbles a hundred yards away. At night there was no other sound.

Gyantse under the stars will remain an impressive memory for every one in the little post at Chang-lo. Perhaps the picture of the nights there is worth giving so far as one can. Close behind the fortified parapet of the Commissioner's house the trees stood up with their sable branches sharply etched against the powdered spaces of the night sky. One had to look upward at them to be sure that it was not, indeed, their rustling, but the voice of the river that hushed the silence and was itself muted by the distant bark of a dog or the lifted heel-chain of a restless mule in the lines below. Far behind, straightly ascending like a column of phosphorescent smoke, the Milky Way ribbed the sky to the south-southwest. Beneath it, the heavy sloping buttress of the redoubt stood out boldly, the outer angle cutting sharply across the line of the river as it flowed westward in its shadowy channel, only a little brighter than the sky, till a curve carried it behind the thin fringe of sallows, where all day the rosefinches chattered in a crowd.

Looking downward over the sand-bags, the thick tangle of the nearest abattis is barely seen, and beyond it the plain is only certainly broken by an acre patch of iris, or by the darkness under a clump of trees. These, uncertain in the gloom below, are blackly silhouetted above, over the outline of the distant hills which are clear against the sky of the horizon round; for in these pure altitudes the stars invisibly assert themselves, and interstellar space has a half-latent illumination of its own, against which the peaks and saddles of these Himalayan spurs are better defined than on a moonlight night. At the end of the parapet is a sheeted Maxim, and beside its muzzle the motionless sentry looks out into the night toward the jong. All day long the high rock and its forts, clean cut in the bright air, have towered up against the ash and ocher of the distant mountains, scored and scarred with sharp water channels, cut fan-wise by a thousand of the brief rains of these high uplands. Six hours ago every stone of it could be counted; now it had vanished and the blank levels run to the foot of the distant ranges. Other familiar things but a few yards away—a worn foot-path, a clay drinking-trough, or a half up-rooted tree-stump—have vanished with the jong. Pala village is faintly betrayed in the distance by its whitened walls, but even of that there is no certainty. Six hundred yards to the front the position of the Gurkha Post is only distinguished by the trees which cut the sky line over it.

As one peers out into the warm night, a long monotone is

faintly droned from the darkness ahead. It is one of the huge conch shells in the jong and it may only mean a call to prayer —the "hours" of Lamaism are unending—but as the moaning note persists softly and steadily, a vivid speck of flame stabs the darkness across the river. A second later the report of the gun accompanies a prolonged "the-e-es" overhead. There is another and another, and the balls chase each other through the trees. The Tibetans are out for the night. A heavy fire breaks out for two or three hundred yards along the further bank, the neater crack of the European rifles in their possession blending with the heavy explosion of matchlocks an inch in bore, and the malicious swish of the conical bullets with the drone of leaden lumps.

The sentry moves inward shadow-like and rouses an officer sleeping in a corner of the parapet. It is only a word or two, "Water-gate, sir." As the fire increases, the garrison, a ghostly company of half-seen men, move silently and mechanically to their posts from their beds behind the traverses. After a little, the officer of the watch comes round and one hears a few whispered words in the compound below. But this has happened so often, night after night, that there is not much to do; the defenses are manned without question needed or answer given. A minute or two later there is hardly a change to be noted in the quietness of the post, except for the wail of the bullets overhead, and the occasional inevitable cough of the awakened Sepoys. But the post is ready from end to end, and the officer at his Maxim traverses her snub muzzle once or twice to see that she runs easily.

The conch drones again from the hidden jong. Nothing is easier now than to people the darkness with creeping figures. One seems to have seen them—one always seems too late actually to see them—here and there in the obscurity, but the small force betraying its front by the flashes across the river is the only certain thing. These men keep up a persistent but useless fire, though not a shot is returned. The spots of flame jerk out of the night along a widening front, but there is no sign of an advance, and, failing to draw any response from us, the aimless fusillade slackens after a time. From the enemy's position, Chang-lo must seem a sleeping, almost a deserted, post. But the Tibetans have been taught a severe lesson time after time, and they will not easily come on. Two or three, indeed, of their hardiest come right up to the other side of the bridge and, at a range of sixty yards, fire straight into the mud walls of the water-gate. There is a rifle muzzle out of every loophole that commands the bridge, of which the seven sagging bays may just be seen against the dim stream from a corner of the redoubt. But not a sound of life is betrayed. The Tibetan "braves" fire half-a-dozen shots along the roadway and then go back to urge on their reluctant followers. There is a momentary increase in the firing, but the sparks of flame have not moved up a yard, and the faint sound dies down again into silence. It is difficult to convince oneself that anything has happened, so completely has the night swallowed up everything except the chuckle of the river over its stones.

After a lull of twenty minutes it is clear that no attack is to be brought, at least against the central post. There was perhaps no real intention on the part of the Tibetans to follow up their volleys; we are much too strong and they know it; their real object is disclosed as we watch. Round the detached Gurkha posts the darkness is suddenly pierced by a hundred tongues of flame, and upon the rattle of the muskets, a babel of excited shouting follows. The enemy have surrounded the house. Again and again the Tibetan war-cry is caught up. It is like nothing in the world so much as the quick and staccato yell of a jackal pack, and it carries for two miles on a still night. One from another the Tibetans take up the weird cadences in an uprising falsetto, reviving and again reviving the hubbub whenever there seems any chance of its dying down. But the Gurkha house is mute, though its walls re-echo with the din. Then the Tibetans adopt another course. Shouting together in groups, they pour forth challenges and contempt upon the little garrison of forty or fifty Gurkhas. One or two swaggerers come up within fifty yards of the very loopholes and scream out a flood of foul abuse. There is never a word or a shot in reply, and the braves retire. The fire re-opens and the enemy advance a little. Even the most timid Tibetan takes heart and looses off his piece a little less wildly.

Inside the post, the Gurkhas stand aside in the darkness beside their loopholes, through which a bullet whizzes every now and then, burying itself in the mud wall opposite. Two men keep watch for the rest, and Mewa, the jemadar, bides his time till he has word from them. The war-cry breaks out again, rising and falling like the bellowing falsetto of the mules' lines at feeding time, and the Tibetans grow confident and move forward, until a dim ring of them can just be seen from inside the post. The fire re-doubles, and a Gurkha is hit in the neck, but still there is not a sign of life about the house. The excitement of watching this attack from the roof of the post is as fresh to-night as if it were the first time we were seeing one.

There must be about a thousand of the enemy. From Chang-lo we can hear them chattering and shrieking together, keeping their courage up with noise. One thinks of the fate that awaits every soul in that little garrison should they be caught unawares some night, and one blesses the foolishness of the noisy Tibetans.

But the time is almost ripe. Mewa takes the place of one of his watchmen and looks down keenly through the dark. After a while, he is reluctantly convinced that the enemy cannot be induced to come forward again for some time, and he knows that the strain on his men has become severe. There is suddenly a movement among twenty or thirty Tibetans; they move round almost out of sight for a rush at the stake-protected door. From the parapet, we can hear a quick double whistle. It is the awaited signal, for the Gurkha post will risk no storming-party.

In a moment there is pandemonium. From every window and loophole, and from between the sand-bags and through the crevices on the roof, a burst of Maxim-like fire is poured into the misty ring of men, which envelops the building, and the air aches with the incessant snap of the rifle and the very short scream of the bullet. In another moment all is over. The Tibetans have broken and are flying into the night, leaving five or six dead behind them. Their road back to the jong lies flat and free before them, and they never look back. The Maxim fire has stopped as suddenly as it had begun. Silence falls upon everything as before. Only the first rays of the rising moon strike full upon the upper terraces and towers of the jong, and the mass of it emerges from the distant darkness edged with silver and strangely near. It is still some two hours before sunrise, but as the moon frees herself from behind the hills to the east, the first faint ripple stirs the leaves overhead, and the silence of the night is lost.

After the sun had risen the day became monotonous, and the monotony was repeated daily, from week's end to week's end. Even the poor interest of watching the first appearance of the vegetables in the garden palled. There was a day when nine little green points promised nine bean plants to come. Day after day added two or three to this number, but after the appearance of thirty-eight, there was not only a cessation of further evidence of fertility, but a lamentable check in the development of the plants already above ground. At one time the peas, two little square plots planted with a generosity of seed which would have scandalized Messrs. Sutton, arose in ranks almost in a single night, and a few days afterward were about three inches in height. Captain Walton, to whose hands the Mission had intrusted this responsible duty, assured us that all was going well. Both the beans and peas were, he assured us, of a dwarf variety. Indeed, he seemed to suggest, with apparent self-conviction, that had these two plots exhibited any further intention of growth he would have despaired of the dishes we were looking forward to. The carrots made no attempt to justify their credit, except in a prodigious growth of green feathery leaves. To them, and to the radishes, one fault was common. Where one expected to find the best part, a thin leather-bootlace-like root descended weedily into our carefully prepared loam. Nor, so far as I was ever able to ascertain, was a single dish of any vegetable, except mustard-and-cress, produced from our carefully tended and certainly Eve-less garden.

There was very little to do from morn to night. Captain Ryder planned the defenses of the post. Construction and demolition were alike in his hands; and the ultimate result of his care and technical skill was quaintly embodied one day by Colonel Brander in a sentence in the orders,—*Si monumentum quaeris, circumspice.* The original phrase referred, indeed, to a structure which served as a tomb, nor perhaps was the quotation strictly accurate, but Colonel Brander's intention was delightfully clear, and every soul in the garrison of each one of the many races there represented most cordially echoed the phrase.

The direction from which most danger was to be expected was that of the jong. Every morning and every afternoon the usual bombardment broke out. It is possible that the Tibetans had secured some knowledge of the hours during which, from one reason or another, there was generally more movement inside the post than at other times. The free intercourse which the Tibetan visitors to Kamba-jong enjoyed must, at least, have taught them something of our habits, and, without doubt, they made whatever use they could of this information. We early received news that the Téling Kusho was directing operations. He had been allowed to see a good deal of us at Kamba.

There was one thing in connection with this bombardment which may throw some light upon the ability of beleaguered garrisons in old days to hold their own until starvation compelled them to surrender. The fact that the report of a gun of an ancient pattern invariably precedes the ball was, we found, of the most invaluable assistance. There was always time to go four yards at least under cover of the nearest traverse before the ball crashed into the compound. There was one jingal, however, which was christened "Chota Billy," which only allowed three yards and in extreme cases of over-charge of powder only two. The naming of the bigger guns mounted on the jong was curious. From a large jingal, throwing a ball four inches in circumference, and immediately receiving the name of Billy, two Chota Billies, one big Billy, and finally two Williams successively took their names. In all, there may have been at most nineteen guns mounted on the jong, of a bore ranging from one inch to three and three-quarter inches. All of them ranged easily some two or three hundred yards beyond Chang-lo. William, the heaviest of all, would sometimes kick up the dust 600 yards in our rear, and 2,400 yards from the jong; that is to say, from 800 to 1,000 yards beyond the post was the utmost range of any gun, except one of the two Chota Billies, which at a pinch could reach the bridge at the end of the wood 2,800 yards from the gun positions of the rock.

But most of their missiles fell short. The ground immediately in front of Chang-lo was scarred and seamed with hundreds and even thousands of futile jingal balls which had dropped uselessly into the "football field" or the field outside. Only eight or ten of their best weapons threw projectiles with accuracy and certainty. The others heaved their muzzles up into the sky and trusted that elevation would counteract economy of powder and the amazing escape of gas all round the ill-fitting bullet. Bigger guns made an astonishing report, and a second and a half later a lump of lead from William, as big as a Tangerine orange, would moan through the air, sometimes with unpleasant accuracy whipping down into the compound, or sometimes tearing its way through the high trees over our heads. Altogether about four men were killed by these misshapen projectiles, which looked like sections of a solid lead bar with the edges roughly filed down. At first lead alone was used, but the appearance among us of balls composed of a heavy stone wrapped with lead suggested that the supply was running short. Later on, this surmise was justified, for a curious substitute for lead was found in the use of pure copper. During the last two weeks of the siege lumps of this glittering red-gold metal were used almost as constantly as those of more humble material.

At one time the Tibetans adopted the principle of firing volleys. At a given signal fourteen or fifteen guns were fired in a ragged *feu de joie*. There was little additional danger to us even from the first of these concerted pieces. But it is clear that to follow such a volley by another, five minutes afterward, was sheer waste of ammunition. Still, almost everything in the post which could be struck was struck. Tents, sand-bags, traverses, house-walls, and trees were pounded alike. The trees suffered most; the Tibetans never seemed to be perfectly certain of the direction of any ball unless it betrayed its billet a hundred yards in front of our defenses. Naturally, therefore, in order at least to insure that no such obvious failure of aim should be noted against them by the Commandant, they preferred to elevate their guns at an angle which often only resulted in a shower of twigs and leaves from the lofty poplars over our heads.

In those trees the kites whistled and the ravens croaked all day. Both species were twice the size of ravens and kites elsewhere.

Captain Walton would not admit that this enormous difference in size justified him in setting them down as a new species, but the practical results of having these double-powered scavengers probably contributed in no small degree to our comfort. Outside our defenses the unclaimed pi-dogs roamed all day and howled nearly all the night. By day they were probably engaged in unearthing the long-buried limbs of some wretched Tibetan killed during the attack upon the post on May 5th. By night they seemed to be disputing among themselves the possession of the disgusting spoils they had secured during the day. At one time Colonel Brander arranged for the destruction of some scores of these parasites. But this was found to be a somewhat dangerous proceeding when carried out within half a mile of the camp. Two charges of attempted assassination were brought by a person of no small importance in the post, and, though these cases were smilingly dismissed, there was undoubtedly a certain element of danger in permitting this indiscriminate dog-slaughter with rifles which were capable of inflicting serious harm at a range of 4,000 yards. So the dogs were permitted to grout in the ground as they liked, and as a set-off against the intolerable nuisance of their howls by night, it was remembered that they might perhaps thereby give us useful warning of any second attempt on the part of the Tibetans to creep up in the darkness of a moonless night.

Of the dogs within the defenses "Tim" was perhaps the best known, and certainly in his own eyes the most important. He was an Irish terrier belonging, so far as any dog very certainly belonged to any one there, to Captain Cullen, but the members of the Mission, making a contemptible use of the few occasional titbits which were found in their mess-boxes, successfully seduced him away from his true allegiance for some time. Of other dogs mention must be made of "Mr. Jackson," a little beauty of an Irish terrier, who we were assured enjoyed every minute of his life in spite of a permanently dislocated shoulder. He undoubtedly limped, and he even more certainly enjoyed life; but we could not help hoping that some mistake had been made in the diagnosis of his complaint. "Major Wimberley," a fearsome hound, had undoubtedly bull-dog and fox-terrier as his chief ingredients, but it was difficult finally to exclude his claims to any other breed of dog, except perhaps a greyhound or Pekinese pug. I do not remember what the real name of this entirely attractive dog was, but he used to go, on the below-stairs principle, by his master's name, and I am sorry that no photograph I possess seems to include his sober countenance. "The Lama" was a snarling, bad-tempered little beast, who produced a litter of pups of such appalling vulgarity and ugliness that, in spite of the real need which we then had of the companionship of even an animal, they were drowned by her native owner without a protest from any one.

To many it may seem unnecessary, and perhaps silly, to make even this passing reference to the dogs that shared our captivity. But without going more deeply into the matter, I would only say that a critic should experience even the slight investment which it was our lot to undergo before he speaks slightingly of the right of a dog to grateful recollection.

For the rest, one day succeeded another without change, and except for the uncertainty of the arrival of the daily post, without variety. There was little actual danger, but we were of course restricted to the narrow limits of the defended posts for the greater part of the time of the investment. Toward the end, when we had secured and were holding Pala village and the Gurkha post, and after Sheppard had constructed his covered ways between us and them, more exercise was possible. But for the greater part of the time we could not stray beyond our own perimeter, and that in itself became somewhat of a burden. Perhaps the want of exercise contributed in no small degree to the irritation caused by this sense of captivity, but whatever the cause, an observant man might at times have noticed a slight tendency toward what we believe was called, in Ladysmith, "siege temper." In fact, with the exception—and in justice I must say the absolute exception—of Colonel Younghusband himself and Captain Sheppard, there was hardly any one in the little force who was entirely free from a touch of this pardonable frailty.

It is a pity that there were not more men with the force who were able to sketch. The most rudimentary skill in color would have found scope indeed at Gyantse. As it was, there was hardly a paint-box in the force, if we except the little old-fashioned cakes of color which officially provide for the sappers the reds and grays and ochers needed for their plans. However, even had there been more skill and better equipment, there would have been little time for the mere work of the artist. It is perhaps worth while to try to catch in words a little of what the finest photograph must fail utterly to record.

The color of Tibet has no parallel in the world. Nowhere, neither in Egypt, nor in South Africa, nor even in places of such local reputation as Sydney, or Calcutta, or Athens, is there such a constancy of beauty, night and morning alike, as there is in this fertile plain inset in the mountain backbone of the world. Here there is a range and a quality in both light and color which cannot be rendered by the best of colored plates, but which must always be remembered if the dry bones of figure and fact are to be properly conceived.

During the mid-hours of a summer day, Tibet is perhaps not unlike the rest of the dry tropical zone. Here, as elsewhere, the fierce Oriental sun scares away the softer tints, and the shrinking and stretching shadows of the white hours are too scanty to relieve the mirage and the monotony. All about Chang-lo the contemptuous shoulders of the shadeless mountains stand blank and unwelcoming. All along the plain as far as the eye can see the stretches of iris or barley and the plantations of willow-thorn are dulled into eucalyptus gray by the dust; the trees lift themselves dispirited, and the faint droop of every blade and every leaf tires the eye with unconscious sympathy. Far off along the Shigatse road a pack-mule shuffles along, making in sheer weariness as much dust as the careless hoofs of a bullock, that dustiest of beasts. One does not look at the houses. The sun beats off their coarse and strong grained whitewash, and one can hardly believe that they are the same dainty buildings of pearl-gray or rose-pink that one watched as they faded out of sight with the sunset yesterday evening. Everything shivers behind the crawling skeins of mirage. There is no strength, there are no outlines to anything in the plain, and even the hard thorn trees in the plantation are flaccid. As one passes underneath them a kite or two dives downward from the branches. He will disturb little dust as he moves, for your kite mistrusts a new perch, and the bough he sits on must be leafless both for the traverse of his outlook, and for the clear oarage of his wide wings. Also, you may be sure he has been to and fro fifty times to-day. See him settle a hundred yards away near that ugly significant heap of dirty maroon cloth, and mark the dust thrown forward by the thrashing brake-stroke of his great wings. It hangs in a petty cloud still when we have come up to him and driven him away in indignation for a little space.

Under foot the dwarf clematis shuts in from the midday heat its black snake-head flowers, and the young shoots of the jasmine turn the backs of their tender leaflets to the sun, drooping a little as they do so. Veronica is there in stunted little bushes; vetches, rest-harrows, and dwarf indigo-like plants swarm along the sides of the long dry water channels; and here and there, where the ditch runs steep, you may find, along toward the southern face, what looks for all the world like a thickly strewn bank of violets.

Violets of course they are not, but the illusion is perfect, in color, growth, and size alike. Near them tall fresh-looking docks have found a wet stratum deep below the dusty irrigation cut, and away in a sopping water meadow by the river stunted Himalayan primulas make a cloudy carpet of pink.

Late in the afternoon the change begins. Details of flowers and fields and trees vanish—and surely one is content to lose them in the scene that follows. First, the light pall of pure blue which has all day gauzed over the end of the valley toward Dongtse deepens into ultramarine ash. Then, in a few minutes as it seems, the fleeces of white and silver in the west have gathered weight, and a mottled company of argent and silver-gray and cyanine heaps itself across the track of the setting sun. The sky deepens from blue to amber without a transient tint of green, and the red camp-fires whiten as the daylight fades. But the true sunset is not yet. After many minutes comes the sight which is perhaps Tibet's most exquisite and peculiar gift: the double glory of the east and west alike, and the rainbow confusion among the wide waste of white mountain ranges.

For ten minutes the sun will fight a path clear of his clouds and a luminous ray sweeps down the valley, lighting up the unsuspected ridges and blackening the lurking hollows of the hills. This is no common light. The Tibetans themselves have given it a name of its own, and indeed the gorse-yellow blaze which paints its shadows myrtle-green underneath the deepened indigo of the sky defies description and deserves a commemorative phrase for itself alone. But the strange thing is still to come. A quick five-fingered aurora of rosy light arches over the sky, leaping from east to west as one gazes overhead. The fingers converge again in the east, where a growing splendor shapes itself to welcome them on the horizon's edge.[1]

[1] Travelers have more than once referred to this curious phenomenon, and the Tibetans have a word, "Ting-pa," for this rosy and cloudless beam also.

Then comes the climax of the transformation scene. While the carmine is still over-arching the sky, on either side the horizon deepens to a still darker shade, and the distant hills stand out against it with uncanny sharpness, iridescent for all the world like a jagged and translucent scale of mother-of-pearl lighted from behind. Above them the ravines and the ridges are alike lost, and in their place mantles a pearly underplay of rose-petal pink and eau-de-nil green, almost moving as one watches. Then the slowly developed tints tire and grow dull; the quick evening gloom comes out from the plain, and a sharp little wind from the southeast is the herald of the stars.

These sunsets are as unlike the "cinnamon, amber, and dun" of South Africa as the high crimson, gold-flecked curtains of Egypt, or the long contrasting belts of the western sky in mid-ocean. So peculiar are they to this country that they have as much right to rank as one of its characteristic features as Lamaic superstition, or the "bos grunniens" itself; and to leave them unmentioned, however imperfect and crude the suggestion may be, would be to cover up the finest page of the book which is only now after many centuries opened to the world. That alone is my excuse for attempting what every man in this expedition knows in his heart to be impossible.

CHAPTER XI

RELIGION: MANNERS AND CUSTOMS: ART

IN Tibet the line of division between the layman and the priest is sharply drawn indeed. The domestic life of the country, its government, its cultivation and even, in some degree, its commerce, all are colored to a greater or less extent by the strange religion centered in the divine person of the Grand Lama of Lhasa; and the line of honorable demarcation, so far as persons are concerned, permits of no mistake. If a man is a layman he belongs to an inferior caste; however high his rank he does but the more point the contrasts which exist between the rulers and the ruled. The Lamaic hierarchy have succeeded in creating a religious caste unparalleled in the world.

What that religion is, demands therefore more than a passing notice. There is, or rather there has hitherto been, a belief that the Buddhism of Tibet is a lawful descendant of the Buddhism which the Master preached beneath the pipuls of Bengal. Extravagant it was known to be; it was obvious that it had become incrusted in ritual, and both adorned and humbled by traditions; it was clear also that for the common folk the letter had almost killed the spirit, and the use by the priests of their sacred position to secure entire tyranny over the laymen had not escaped notice. But after all, the same things, each and all of them in some form or another, are to-day true of Christianity also. And yet the flame of Christianity, however strange or tawdry the shrine, burns perhaps as steadily to-day as ever it did. This ever-ready parallel—one which the student carries with him almost unconsciously to the consideration of Buddhism—has obscured the truth.

But the Buddhism of Tibet has no longer the faintest resemblance to the plain austere creed which Gautama preached. It is doubtful if the great Founder of Buddhism would recognize in its forms or formulæ any trace of the purity and sobriety of his own high creed. It is hard to say whether he would be more offended by the golden cooking-pots of the Potala palace or by the awful self-mortification of the immured monks of Nyen-dé-kyi-buk and other extreme hermitages. Except in so far as that Buddha's face of quietism personified still gazes down from wall and altar upon the rites of Lamaism, that religion can claim little connection with the faith upon which their reputation and power are wholly based. Under a thin mask of names and personifications suggested by the records of the Master, or by the reforms effected by Asanga, a system of devil-worship pure and simple reigns in Tibet; the monkish communities spare no effort to establish their predominance more firmly every year by fostering the slavish terror which is the whole attitude toward religion of the ignorant classes of the land. The wretched tiller of the soil is always the ultimate supporter of a religious tyranny, because in a manufacturing community the faculties, and a sense of independence, are necessarily developed too strongly for its toleration; but of all such superstitious servitudes the unhappy "miser" of Tibet supplies us to-day with the classical example. Not even the darkest days of the Papal States, nor the most bigoted years of Puritan rule in New England, not the intolerance of Genevan Calvinism, not Islam itself can afford an example of such utter domination by an abuse of the influence upon men of their religious terrors. The line between religion and superstition may be a fine one and hard to place. But wherever it may be drawn the Buddhist of Tibet has long crossed it.

From a political point of view, the importance of the religion of any country lies less in its moral or ethical excellence than in the extent to which it exerts a real influence upon the lives of its professing members and in the use or misuse of that influence in the government of the country. Apart, therefore, from the actual doctrine or ritual of this so-called Buddhism, the degree to which it enters into the public and private life of the Tibetans is worth studying. It may be said at once that, so far at least as the lower classes are concerned, it is paramount: no other influence is of the slightest importance. But whether that influence deserves to be called religious is another matter. The distinction between northern and southern Buddhism is one which is far more than geographical. The common people of Burma and Siam still apply the standards of Gaya to their daily life, but northern Buddhism has long abandoned, except in name, the Indian faith. In their vain repetitions and mechanical aids to self-salvation, in their gaudy and frequently obscene ritual, in their hells full of demon spirits and fearsome semi-gods, Buddha's simple creed has long been dead. The doctrine of reincarnation, rather implied than taught by him, is still politically useful, and therefore remains as almost the sole link which still connects the two Churches. Brushing aside the films of ritual and the untruthful suggestions of tradition, one finds in Lamaism little but sheer animistic devil-worship.

To the Tibetans, every place is peopled with the active agents of a supernatural malice. Always in this country—at the summit of a pass, at the entrance of a village, at a cleft in the rockside, at the crossing of a stream by bridge or ford—one is accustomed to find the flicker of a rain-washed string of flags, a fluttering prayer-pole, or a gaily decked brush of ten-foot willow sprigs; evil spirits must be exorcised at every turn in the road. Wells, lakes and running streams also are full of demons who visit with floods and hailstorms the slightest infraction of the lamas' rules. Tibet is peopled with as many bogies as the most terrified child in England can conjure up in the darkness of its bed-room. A natural cave, a chink beneath a boulder, a farm-stead, the row of willows beside an irrigation channel, or the low mill house at the end of them, a doorway or a chorten—every habitation of man teems with these unseen terrors. The spilling of the milk upon the hearth-stone needs its special expiation, and the birth and death of men are naturally perhaps made the opportunity of securing oblations from the people of the land. For there is but one way of exorcising these powers of ill. Prayers are not of themselves the defenses of the poor in Tibet; they can only be lively and effectual when sanctioned by the priest; and the fluttering prayer-flag, the turning-wheel, or the muttered ejaculation is valid only after due consultation at the local gompa. And not a pole is set up, not a string of flags pulled taut, not a water-wheel or a wind-wheel set in motion without the payment of the customary fee. The priestly tax is not paid in money alone. The labors of the people's hands are at the disposal of the ruling caste. The corvée is known in Tibet as it was known in ancient Egypt, and no feudal seigniory of the Dark Ages in Europe ever exacted its full rights as mercilessly as this narrow sect of self-indulgent priests.

Invariably there will be found outside a house four things. The first is the prayer-pole or the horizontal sag of a line of moving squares of gauze; the second is a broken teapot of earthenware from which rises the cheap incense of burnt juniper twigs—a smell which demons cannot abide; the third, a nest of worsted rigging, shaped like a cobweb and set about with colored linen tags, catkins, leaves, sprigs and little blobs of willow often crowning the skull of a dog or sheep. The eyes are replaced by hideous projecting balls of glass and a painted crown-vallary rings it round. Hither the spirits of disease within the house are helplessly attracted, and smallpox, the scourge of Tibet, may never enter there. Last of all is the white and blue *swastika* or fylfot, surmounted by a rudely drawn symbol of the sun and moon. This sign marks every main doorway in the country.[1]

Other more public charms against evil are the chortens or cairns which piety or terror has set up at small intervals along the road to be a continual nuisance to the impious traveler. Like the "islands" in Piccadilly or the Strand, they may only be passed to the left, and their position on the edge of a cliff often renders this in one direction a hazardous proceeding. There are, of course, no carts or wheeled vehicles of any kind in Tibet, or this superstition would long ago have become extinguished through sheer necessity. As it is, the chorten remains till the cliff itself falls, but to the last there is generally foothold on which to climb round the outside of a cairn. It may be noted as a psychological curiosity that, after living in the country for a few months, the least thoughtful man in the force usually adopted this superstition as he walked along, though, of course, when riding it is not unnatural for Englishmen.

Here and there one finds long walls, composed for the most part of inscribed stones; these *mendangs* or *manis* represent the accretions of many years, and some in Tibet are reported to be half a mile in length. They do not, however, assume the importance in the province of U that they possess farther to the west. To other pious memorials also the passer-by adds his contribution of a stone. A few white pebbles of quartzite carefully selected

[1] A good deal of inaccurate statement has been made about the swastika. To nothing did I pay more attention than in noting the color and shape of religious emblems as we penetrated deeper and deeper into the country. It is said that the swastika which revolves to the right is consecrated to the use of orthodox Buddhists of whatever school, and that the swastika which kicks in the other direction, that is to say which revolves to the left, is used only by the Beun-pa, the aboriginal devil-worshipers, whose faith was ousted by the adoption of Buddhism. This is not borne out by the relative frequency of position of the two swastikas in Tibet. The left-handed swastika (*i.e.*, that which turns to the dexter) is, if anything, the commoner of the two, and the commonest use of this symbol is in the opposition of the two kinds: thus the two halves of a doorway, or the pattern of a rug, will generally offer an example of the two kinds confronted.

from the neighboring stone-strewn field will acquire for him no small merit if heaped together in a little pyramid, or piled with careful balance one on the top of another. Prayer-wheels offer their fluted axles to the hand of the traveler in long rows, hung up conveniently beside the wall of a house. The poorest may thus accumulate merit. I have before referred to the use of prayer-wheels, but it may be added here that besides the hand-turned wheels and those moved by water, the principle of the anemometer has long been known for the purposes of Lamaic devotion, and the essential principle of the turbine is found in little gauze-sided stoves which drive a tiny rotating tun by hot air forced through a spiral.

The walls of the merest hovels are plastered with yellow paper charms; and round their necks the people carry amulet boxes, without which no Tibetan ventures far. These are packed with a cheap little image of clay, a few grains of sanctified wheat, two or three written charms and a torn scrap of a sacred katag, originally thrown over the shoulders or head of some famous image. Pills, too, may be found in the box, red pills certified to contain some speck of the ashes of the Guru Rinpoche. For the special purposes of this year, one often found a small, sharply triangular piece of flint. This was guaranteed to be a perfect protection against the bullets of the foreigner. For all these things the lamas have to be paid, and we soon realized that their control over the souls of their flock was used solely to secure an unlimited tyranny over their worldly possessions. The riches of Tibet are, almost without exception, enjoyed by the priestly class.

It may be not without interest to draw attention to a curious and special use of the one doctrine which connects Lamaism still with Gautama by a fundamental dogma. It is a cynical misuse of the theory of reincarnation, the employment of it as a political lever. Augurs do not look at augurs when they meet, but when they quarrel they sometimes afford the onlooker some amusement.

The present Dalai Lama (at the time of writing it does not seem at all clear that we have succeeded in weakening his hold upon place and power) made for political reasons a sudden and convenient discovery, that Tsong-kapa, the great reformer of Lamaism, was reincarnated in the person of the Tzar of Russia. This announcement was, of course, intended to smooth the way to that closer union between the two states which Dorjieff had so successfully managed to begin. As a statement in itself by the reincarnation of Avalokiteswara, it was difficult to deny or even to discuss the truth of the proposition. But the indignant Tsong-du were equal to the occasion. They countered gracefully. In effect they said, "How interesting and how lucky for the Tzar!" But the guardian of this country, the Chinese Emperor, is also a reincarnation. He, as they reminded the forgetful Tubdan, is, poor man, the existing representation of the god of learning, Jampalang, and therefore is not lightly to be ousted from his predominance in Tibet.

Here matters remain, though the Grand Lama had no reason to regret the extension of this graceful courtesy to the Tzar. It is a fact beyond dispute, deny it as the Russian individual may, that the "Little Father," in virtue of his position as head of the Christian Church in Russia, sent with all ceremony a complete set of the vestments of a Bishop of the Greek Church to the Dalai Lama. This is perhaps the most extraordinary thing of all the strange incidents in connection with this odd expedition. A Russian would probably prefer to deny than to explain the fact. It does not seem probable that it was caused by any similar lapse from common sense as that which the early Christians displayed when they raised Buddha to a place among the saints of the Church. (This is a fairly well-known fact, and, if evidence were needed, the life of St. Joasaph, as told in the "Golden Legend," would convince the most skeptical.) Still, it is a long step from including the personality of a very holy pagan by inadvertence among the pillars of the Early Church to the symbolic acceptance as a Christian, and subsequent appointment as an apostolically descended bishop, of the most typical character in the heathen world to-day.

Among these freaks of politico-religious strategy, one of the most amazing was the reincarnate representative which, by universal consent, was found for the soul and spirit of one of the terrible guardian deities of the land and of the faith. Palden-lhamo is a dark-blue lady with three eyes who sits upon a chestnut mule drinking blood from a skull and trampling under foot the torn and mutilated bodies of men and women. Her crown is composed of skulls, her eye teeth are four inches long, and the bridle, girths, and crupper are living snakes kept in position by the dripping skin of a recently flayed man. Of this atrocity the Tibetans found a reincarnation in Queen Victoria. This they did without the slightest wish or intention in the world to do anything but convey the highest possible personal compliment. The "horrible" aspect of these guardian deities does but increase their virtue and their efficacy. They represent the old heathen tyrants of the land who were brought into subjection by Buddha, and left with all their horrible attributes to scare away every evil, especially the intruder and the enemy. This last reincarnation was so well known, that a lama will think an Englishman ignorant if he does not know it; and he will explain that, after all, if proof were needed of the truth of what they believe, it is to be found in the fact that Tibet, during Queen Victoria's long reign, was saved from invasion, saved even from that intercourse which they hate nearly as much, and that after her death and her return to be reincarnated again in a little child in Tibet, the English troops immediately bore down upon their sacred capital.

As I have said, no priestly caste in the history of religion has ever fostered and preyed upon the terror and ignorance of its flock with the systematic brigandage of the lamas. It may be that, hidden away in some quiet lamasery, far from the main routes, Kim's lama may still be found. Once or twice in the quiet unworldly abbots of such monasteries as those of Dongtse or Ta-ka-re, one saw an attractive and almost impressive type of man; but the heads of the hierarchy are very different men, and by them the country is ruled with a rod of iron. The vast aggregation of symbols and ceremonies which have strangled the life out of the simple and beautiful faith of Buddha is but a barrier which the more effectually separates the priestly caste from its lay serfs. To educate the latter in any way would be to strike at the root of Lamaic supremacy, and, therefore, the whole land is sunk in an ignorance to which it would be difficult to find a parallel. To these unlettered hinds the awful figures which scowl from the gompa wall, blood bespattered, with dripping tusks and bloated and beastlike bodies, are as veritable as were ever the pictures of a medieval hell to the frightened catechumen. To them the muttering or the fluttering of the strange charm, *om mani padme hum,* is the easiest, and for them the only, pathway to a vague well-being after death, provided spiritual pastors shall have sanctioned and hedged about with charms their earthly life.

These simple people are a pleasant race. You will always meet in the poorest hut with unfailing courtesy; not only is it an unquestioned duty, but you would believe it also to be a pleasure, for them instantly to bring forth an offering of their best. It may be small enough—a little bowl of barley, three or four eggs in the hand—but there it will always be. Eggs may cost but twopence a dozen in the nearest village, but it is only fair to remember that pennies are scarce among these poor people. They live a toilsome and hard life uncomplainingly, without the wits to realize that any other could be their lot. The ordinary villager sleeps and eats on the floor of the hut. Furniture he has, of course, none; two or three brass or copper bowls, a big unglazed red porcelain teapot, a few lengths of thick red or gray cloth are (besides the implements of his trade) all you will ever find in a Tibetan house.

Perhaps the best known thing about Tibet is the habit prevalent throughout the country for a woman to marry all her husband's brothers as well as himself. This is a curious custom and I do not think that any sufficient reason has ever been given for it; naturally it fills the nunneries, and the population of the country, whether due to this fact alone or not, is steadily decreasing. The plan, however, seems to work well enough so far as the family is concerned. Perhaps they expect very little, but the fact remains that these many-husbanded ladies seem able to keep a comfortable enough home for their changing housemates. That, I think, may be the reason why friction rarely or never occurs. If there are three sons in a family the third will become a lama, the eldest will remain chiefly at home, the second son will tend the flocks on the grazing grounds or carry the wool to the nearest market; the two brothers, therefore, do not very often meet, and the good lady apparently chooses which of the two she would rather look after for the moment. The result is apparent in one way; the women have developed a distinctly stronger character than the men. No layman or laywoman, of course, has any opportunity of public influence—that is entirely reserved for the lamas; but in the realm of commerce the women are usually supreme. Both at Gyantse and at Lhasa my experience was the same. It was the woman who managed the family trading, and if the man were there at all it was only to help in carrying the goods backward and forward between the bazaar and the town. I have at times known a woman refer to her husband before she would sell me any unusually good turquoise-studded charm box or other jewel, but as a rule they seemed to dispose of the family possessions without consulting any one. Any one who knows India will appreciate from this fact alone the vast difference that the barrier of the Himalayas causes. Some of these women are not bad-looking. I say this with some doubt, because beneath the dirt of many years it is impossible to do more than guess at their complexions. Their children are charming little things.

Into the home life of the Tibetans our almost complete ignorance of the language, coupled with the state of armed neutrality, if not actual war, which so often characterized their attitude toward us, made it difficult for us to enter. So far as I could—far more than any one else except O'Connor, with whom I generally paid such visits, and whose fluency in Tibetan was as invaluable to both of us as it was exasperating and coveted by me—I made a point of seeing the Tibetans, both lay and clerical, in their homes.

On one occasion we went out for luncheon to a somewhat interesting family. The man was the eldest son of the Maharajah of Sikkim. At a period of stress in the relations between the Indian Government and the royal family of Sikkim, this young man had been given the choice between returning to the territory of Sikkim, or of forfeiting his succession. He elected to remain in Tibet, and from that day he has never seen his relatives. The present Crown Prince of Sikkim—one of the best known to Europeans of all the young princes of India—assumed the position, and, thanks entirely to the prudence and sympathy of Mr. Claude White, promises to become a useful and loyal Rajah. To his brother's house O'Connor and I went. Taring, his residence, is situated seven or eight miles from Gyantse along the road to Lhasa. It is a house of no great pretensions, prettily hidden among trees. The young couple entertained us hospitably; Prince Namgyel was simply but richly dressed, his wife was wearing a fine *kincob* and an exquisite head-dress in which the high aureole commonly in use was barely recognizable under the strings of pearls which webbed the whole thing. Servants there were in half dozens, and the meal we had was full of interest. It began with tea.

Tea in Tibet is a thing entirely after its own kind. It bears not the vaguest resemblance to the pale, scented beverage of China and Japan, nor to the milkless and lemon-flavored glassfuls of Russia; still less to the sugared slops which one finds in London. Tea in Tibet is imported in the shape of bricks, which vary very much in quality; they are made in the province of Sze-chuan and the tea-leaves are glued, with something that looks suspiciously like sawdust, into hard blocks of which it would puzzle Mincing Lane to distinguish the various grades. But for the veriest Tibetan child *du-nyi* is unmistakable for *du-tang*. Next to *du-nyi* comes *chuba,* and the last and worst kind is known as *gye-ba.*[1]

A corner is knocked off a five-pound brick and it is infused with boiling water in a teapot. The tea is then poured into a cylindrical bamboo churn and a large lump of salt is churned up into it; the amount of energy which is spent upon this churning is extraordinary. I suppose the reason is that the heat should not be lost before the tea is drinkable. The moment this is well churned up, a pound of butter is also slid down into the bamboo and another minute's furious work produces the liquid as it is drunk in Tibet. If you are expecting the sweetened milky brew of England, when you put your lips to it you will be disgusted. It is a thickish chocolate colored mess, sometimes strengthened with a little flour, to give it greater consistency. But if you will regard it as soup you will find that it has certain very sound qualities as a meal in itself. I have been actually glad to drink it after a long day.

After tea our exiled hostess gave us the real luncheon. It began with a heaped bowlful of boiled eggs. The worst of these meals in a new country is that you never know either how, or

[1] It is characteristically Eastern that these four grades of quality, first, second, third, and fourth, should in Tibetan be called first, second, tenth, and eighth. I make a small note like this in order to deter the matter-of-fact European from contradicting the statements of Central Asian travelers merely because they are logically impossible.

how much to eat. The first question solves itself in Tibet because, except as curiosities, there are no spoons or forks. But we did not know how many courses were to follow, and it must be confessed that the first draught of Tibetan tea is extraordinarily effective in damping one's appetite. We tried two eggs apiece out of the white heap and waited. The servants did not so much change the dishes as accumulate them, and little by little other things came straggling in from the kitchen. The next course was composed of sweet chupatty-like things which had absolutely no taste whatever and were rather mealy in the mouth. Then came little balls of forcemeat skewered by fours upon a straw. These we eat conscientiously, but a following dish of twenty different kinds of sweets did not prepare us for the *mo-mo* which, as the Tibetan *pièce de résistance,* we should have anticipated. These are dumplings of thick pudding wrapped round strange meat. I would not for the world suggest that any mistake had been made by the cook, but after the sweets, this mixture of suet and carrion was almost more than we could stomach. However, the dish had to be eaten, and eaten it was. Prince Namgyel was hospitality itself and the drink he offered us was extraordinarily good. It was a home-made whisky with all the peat reek of Irish potheen. Only too conscious of the diminishing stores of the Mission, both of us made a mental note of this excellent stuff and determined that we would take off our host's hands as much as he was willing to sell when our own supplies ran short.[1] I remember noticing behind me, nailed up against a pillar, two colored photographs. One was of the new palace at Gangtok, the other, somewhat to my surprise, was of our host's stepmother, the present Maharani. This lady, still one of the most attractive looking of Tibetan women, was a daughter of the great aristocratic Lhasan family of

[1] Unfortunately, before another week had elapsed the Tibetans were bombarding the Mission, a state of war was declared, and poor Namgyel and his wife had fled to his father's other property on the shores of Lake Tsomo.

Lheding. The circumstances immediately preceding her marriage with the Maharajah, about seventeen years ago, drew a good deal of attention at the time to a personality, the strength of which is apparent after an acquaintance of five minutes. In other circumstances she might have exercised the same power as the Empress Dowager of China or as the mother of Queen Su-pi-ya-lat; as it is, the political officer of Sikkim will, if you ask him, assure you that she has long been a factor in our relations with Tibet which by no means could be disregarded. Her two eldest children were born to her husband's younger brother before she reached Sikkim. This lapse cannot be explained away as an instance of Tibetan polyandry, as no "wife" of a younger brother is shared by the elder brothers. However, the matter was overlooked.

The walls of Taring were painted with minute delicacy, and the design of the invariably present animal acrobats—the bird on the rabbit, on the monkey, on the elephant—was the best I ever saw. We took leave of our kindly host and hostess, and the former a day or two later rode into camp for a luncheon, which this time was less of a change from the usual diet of the guest.

The servants of Tibetans, even of the highest, are abominably dirty. It was a curious thing to see outside the tent, in which the gleam of gold and brocade and light-blue silk mingled, the waiting attendants with grimy faces and torn and dirty clothes. At Chema I obtained permission from the lady herself to photograph the belle of the Chumbi Valley. I wanted her to come out to the doorway of her house, but she was much too aristocratic a young woman to be so taken. I was asked to come into the women's apartments, where, in an almost dark room, the lady, most beautifully dressed and certainly looking extremely handsome, was seated on a raised platform, with her dirty maid standing behind her. I did not want the maid in the picture, and said so. But Lady Dordém was firm; she had three husbands in the room at the time, but she would not be taken without a chaperon. She very properly argued that no one who saw the picture could know that her natural protectors were at the photographer's elbow. The photograph was not a success, for an enormously long exposure was necessary and no contrast of any kind could be obtained.

Tibetan women of the highest class travel very little, but when they do, they wrap themselves in a huge shapeless rug, which almost conceals the fact that they are riding astride. The saddles of the Tibetans are curious high structures, under which a beautiful cloth is placed, and the whole is then concealed by rug after rug. The rider is thus raised eight or nine inches from the horse's back, which gives his mount a camel-like appearance. No Tibetan rides very fast, but the ponies are trained to amble at a pace which gets over the ground as fast as any one would care to trot. Shoes are not used, and the bits are merciful; but there is the inevitable Oriental insensibility to the sufferings of a galled and sore-backed brute. At these altitudes sores will not heal. When the skin is broken the want of oxygen in the air delays the healing of the wound, but "out of sight, out of mind" is as true in Tibet as elsewhere, and the beast is still ridden day after day. On the crupper and bridle there are often fine filigree plates of brass and sometimes good Chinese enamel. The stirrups are unnecessarily heavy; a handsome dragon design is often embodied in them.

I have said that the Tibetans are a courteous race. Unlike Hindustani races, they not only have, but continually use, the words for please (*ro nang,* literally "good help") and thank you (*tu che*). The greeting to a visitor, corresponding roughly with "how do you do," is literally "sit and adhere to the carpet," while the farewell of a visitor may be translated "sit down slowly." His host speeds his departing guest with an adjuration to "walk slowly." The language is entirely distinct both from

Hindustani and Chinese. It is an agglutinative, monosyllabic tongue, and neither the structure nor the fairly large vocabulary is difficult to acquire. But the trouble is that almost from the outset the practical colloquial language is found by the learner to be an inextricable tangle of idioms. Experience of the East should long have taught one never to say "why?" but the eccentricities of the Tibetan wrench it from one at every turn. A thing which is at once apparent is the indistinctness with which it is muttered. If you were to say to a man "call me to-morrow morning at six o'clock," "*nga-la sang-nyin shoge chutseu druk-la kétang,*" deliberately and slowly, he would smile politely, but make not the slightest attempt to understand; but if, on the other hand, you threw at him something like "*nyalsannin-shoshutsu-dullaketn*" you would be understood in a moment.

Some words used in Tibetan are very expressive; the word for a duck is "mud fowl"; to awaken is to "murder sleep"; a flower is a "button (or canopy) of fire"; a general is a "Lord of the Arrow"; bribery could hardly be more neatly defined than by the Tibetan "secret push." One peculiarity of the language is the use of two opposites in conjunction to express the quality in which they differ—thus: distance is literally "far-near"; weight is "light-heavy"; height, *to-men,* is "high-low," and *dang-to,* "cold-warm," means temperature. The honorific vocabulary is an additional stumbling-block. For ordinary traveling purposes it is hardly necessary; the stranger will always be pardoned if he prefaces his remarks with an apology for not being able to speak the language of courtesy; but as every remark will instinctively be made to him in that language in spite of his protest, he will find himself very little advantaged. The vocabulary of the Tibetan language is enormous, and it is very widely known; such comparatively delicate shades of meaning as are required to express slightly varying color shade in horses are ready in abundance, and in Tibetan a chestnut horse with a black mane can be described in a word. It is not, perhaps, necessary to say more than that there is ready for use in Tibetan a single word which signifies "the interdependence of causes." [1]

The literature of the country is almost entirely religious. It consists of the Kan-gyur, or sacred scriptures, in over one hundred volumes; the Ten-gyur, or commentaries thereon, in three hundred volumes, and countless tomes filled with the tales, parables, biographies, and legends of the great teachers of the Lamaic Church. These books are wonderful things. It is not the least of the oddities of Tibet that in this unlettered country more beautiful books are produced than anywhere else in the world. Before the volume is opened, the covers alone present an example of beauty and loving care which Grolier could never have secured from the best of his binders. The outer cover is about thirty inches by eleven inches; it is of hard, close-grained wood, divided into three panels; each panel is carved with minute and exquisite workmanship. In the center of each is one, or perhaps two Buddhas seated on the lotus throne, cut in a quarter-inch relief. Round him, with strong and free grace, the conventional foliage of the Bo-tree fills the entire field, except immediately overhead, where the *garuda* bird, all beak and eyes, sits keeping watch. Above and below are rows of smaller images carved in exquisite detail. The three panels are said to refer to the three conceptions of the Buddha. If that be so it is the only instance of Maitreya, or the coming Buddha, being represented squatting tailorwise in the Oriental fashion.[2] The whole cover is heavily gilt, and one turns the leaf to find a silk veil, probably of olive-green, carnation, and rose-madder, protecting the first page of the manuscript itself.

[1] This is hardly the occasion for a full account of either the written or the spoken language. I may, however, in reference to the former, point out the difficulty of the spelling. Thus the province of "U" is spelled "DBUS" and "DÉ" (rice) is spelled "ABRAS." This is the spelling of the first syllable of De-bung monastery.

[2] This statement, like most statements which have long been accepted about things Tibetan, is probably open to correction.

This page is made of fine stout paper, bearing in the middle what looks exactly like the depressed plate mark of an etching; the whole is of deep, rich-glazed Prussian blue, and in the inset panel in the middle the opening words of the book are written in large raised gold characters. The next page contains to the left a miniature, and then the book begins. From one end to the other it is painted in large regular letters of gold, some of the choicer books having alternate lines of gold and silver. Although they are no longer used, the holes through which the binding strap originally ran through the leaves themselves in two places are still left clear and indicated by a thin gold circle. Cumbersome, of course, these books are, but the care which is bestowed upon them would have delighted the heart of William Morris.

Art in Tibet is still in a conventional state. It is true that the technique of miniature painting upon an enormous scale has been thoroughly mastered by them; and, as I have said elsewhere, the only parallel to the microscopic work used on the walls of such buildings as the Palkhor choide, or the Nachung Chos-kyong temple outside Lhasa, is that of the seventh and eighth century illuminators of the Irish school.

A figure of Buddha in color was copied by myself from the wall of the dining-room at Chang-lo. The original is of life size and was evidently painted by one of the most capable artists in Tibet. I do not remember ever having seen another similar figure as strongly designed, minutely finished, or delicately colored. The use, indeed, of gold, which it is impossible adequately to reproduce, was both restrained and effective, and the transparent brown mastic which covers it mellows the semi-burnished surface. The rest of the wall was taken up with figures almost as carefully painted by the same hand. The disciples of the Master stand or sit round him in varying attitudes bearing the symbol of their identity, while the great teachers of Buddhism smile blandly from the side walls dividing the

Master from the "terrible" guardian monsters which confront the outer world in every Buddhist shrine.

The general effect of a painted wall in Tibet is not dissimilar from that of Italian tapestries of the best period, and I am inclined to think that the object of the designer in both cases is the same. In spite of the enormous amount of work brought into the smallest details of dress and the delicacy with which the flower work is done, I doubt whether the intention of the artist in either case is to produce figures to be examined by themselves. The general arrangement and composition of a Tibetan fresco is masterful. The ground is well covered, but never crowded; the subordination of the less important to the more important is never mistaken, and in the greatest as well as the smallest matters the symbolism is unerring and full of significance. But the veriest stranger might go into such painted courts as those of the first floor of the Palkhor choide and remain perfectly contented with it merely as an almost moving carpet of color and light.

Convention reigns supreme, but it does not take long for the most prejudiced European to realize that these golden and blue and red faced figures are essential to the artistic balance of the picture, as well as the meaning of the legend before his eyes. Of the color there is less to say. It is intensely strong, and though one rapidly realizes that it is justified in the mass, it is not only as open to criticism in the detail as a holiday crowd of natives in India, but the secret of the extraordinary harmonies so successfully produced remains as completely beyond the power of European reproduction.

In the general arrangement for the internal decoration of an important room in a good house, Gautama will always be found in one form or another, seated either as a statue or in paint. The upper wall is sometimes furnished on either side with the close rows of pigeon-holes which serve the Tibetan for library shelves. At times a more realistic form of ornamentation is attempted, and here the limitations of the artist are plain indeed. The religious subjects have, in the course of centuries, had their treatment crystallized into a purely national style of representation, and the moment the artist strays beyond this preserve he leans heavily upon the Chinese for support. Chinese perspective is used by them; Chinese landscape, Chinese dresses and faces are helplessly copied by Tibetan artists, careless of the fact that neither in feature, robes, nor surroundings are the two races alike. Once or twice I have seen a Tibetan attempt to represent some well-known natural feature in the country. In these cases it is necessary to read the description which generally accompanies the object to be perfectly certain what it is intended to represent.

The Sinchen Lama, as has been said, caused an able artist to record upon the walls of his room the incidents in the lives of preceding reincarnations, and the story has been told of the strange way in which he thereby foretold his own death and of a pleasant proof thereby of his affection for his little dog. The picture is difficult to photograph, and the only picture I was able to take is marred, not only by the reflected light from the windows behind, but by the fact that it is partially concealed by the open door to the right, through which alone sufficient illumination could be obtained. All but the head of the dog is hidden. But that dog is in a way the test of art in Tibet; there is apparently no conventional method of representing a dog, and if there had been one, it is clear that the Lama would not have been satisfied with it, so this man was forced face to face with nature as he had perhaps never been compelled before. The portrait of the master of the dog is a piece of pure convention, but the painting of the dog, intensely bad as it is from every point of view but one, remains the touchstone of Tibetan art. There is such a minute and laborious representation of every curl of hair that one would hardly be surprised to find that the artist had attempted to paint both sides of the dog at once. Bad as it is, that picture at any rate achieves its purpose, for that dog is as living, as recognizable, and as pat-able an object as ever Briton Riviere created, and the affection of the lonely reincarnation, cut off from the living world from birth to death, for his one fearless and disinterested companion is apparent in every stroke of the brush. But I must confess that of all the acres of painted surface which I saw in Tibet this dog remains the only attempt to represent a subject naturally.

At Gyantse the chief local artist received several commissions from us which, as I have said, were never fulfilled, but I suspect that a good deal of his earlier work afterward fell into the hands of our men at the taking of Little Gobshi. Hundreds of *tangkas*[1] were then found, but as they were of no interest or value in the eyes of the native troops, the vast majority of them were thrown on one side, and the heavy rain of the following night disfigured the majority almost beyond recognition. These *tangkas* are the most characteristic and portable expression of modern Tibetan art. It says something for their good taste that those which they account most highly are the plain-line drawings in Indian red upon a gold background, or of gold upon Indian red. Here the artist owes nothing to color or shade, and some of the work is as strong and quaint as that of the "Guthlac" designs in the British Museum.

The majority of these *tangkas* display a large central figure surrounded by smaller flame- or smoke-framed pictures of the deities of Lamaism. These pictures often leave much to be desired on the score of propriety. It is one of the things which must be taken into consideration with regard to Lamaism that decency forms no part of it whatever. Immoral the Tibetan

[1] A *tangka* is a roll painting on canvas or silk, framed in rich Chinese brocade, and generally resembling the kakemonos of Japan.

EXAMPLES OF TIBETAN-CHINESE WORKMANSHIP

religion certainly is not, but to Western eyes its manifestations often assume the strangest shape.[1]

Unfortunately a change has recently come over Tibetan draftsmanship. There is a falling away from the austere standard of other days, and there is a distinct tendency toward merely pretty and pink and white designs of a Chinese type. This is apparent not only in the coloring but in the choice of subject. The colors used are curious; they are undoubtedly water-colors ground up with a large amount of body color, and stiffened with glue or some such material. They last indefinitely and, so far as can be guessed, the tints do not fade. I do not think that the names of any artists are preserved.

The jewelry of Tibet is exquisitely finished, and in a slight degree suggestive of Byzantine work. I have in my possession several objects that will serve as examples of the finest work in the country. The crown came originally from the head of a Buddha in Né-nyeng Monastery. Nothing can exceed the delicacy with which the figure of Buddha in carved turquoise is inset into the central leaf. The foliation throughout is strong, clean cut, and decided, and the general balance of the diadem will, I think, be universally admitted. It is a good specimen of the best Tibetan work, and the sparing use of turquoise in its composition is the more satisfactory because it is clear that neither time nor money was spared in its manufacture. I bought two earrings in Lhasa. They are of gold and of the usual design set with large pieces of turquoise. A square charm box was also procured in Lhasa. It is of typical design, but the stones and general workmanship are undoubtedly above the average. I also obtained two beautiful charm boxes of gold and

[1] It is interesting to notice that of the two more valued kinds of *tangka* those on a gold background are always austerely chaste, while those on a red field leave much to be desired on the score of decency. I think that those also on a dark blue background should be classed with the latter kind.

turquoise. Both workmanship and stones are of the finest class. The single earring touching the crown is that worn by men, and it is worthy of notice that the lower drop is never real turquoise. Even in the case of the highest dignitaries this pendant is invariably blue porcelain-like glass. The encircling necklace is of raw turquoise lumps set in silver and separated one from another by large coral beads.

The brass work of the Tibetans exhibits their art in its highest form. The little gods which sit in rows along the altar shelves of Tibet are models of good and restrained convention. The finish is delicate, and the sheer technical skill with which the artist manipulates his material is undeniable. The same delicate workmanship is carried also into other objects of their daily life or religion. Tibetans are capable of producing pottery of a fair quality, but it is quite beyond their powers to watermark a design into the material.

The woven stuffs of Tibet are extremely interesting, and the patterns are indigenous. I have elsewhere suggested that in rugs alone a thriving and successful trade might be carried on with the neighborhood of Gyantse. Most of their silks are imported from China. It may fairly be said that nothing manufactured in Tibet is positively ugly, and though the hierocratic tendencies which have checked the political independence of the people of the country have also tended to confine its artists within narrow channels, the very stiffness of the style has not been without its definite use in educating the natural taste of the people. The blaze of color inside a Tibetan gompa might be thought garish by a student of the half tones of Europe, but it must be remembered that in this land of thin pure air and blinding light, harmonies and discords are to be judged by other standards than those of Europe.

Of the music of Tibet it is impossible to say much. The temple services are intoned on three or four notes, which, I should say, approximate fairly well to those of our own scale. But

SPECIMENS OF CHINESE-TIBETAN WORK IN SILVER

the Tibetans have not reached the stage at which noise ceases to be the first aim of the musician. By this I do not necessarily mean that the noise is always an ugly one. The sound, heard a mile away across the plain, of a temple gong beaten, or the long seductive purr of a well-blown conch, comes into the pictures of one's memory as not their least attractive feature. But heard close at hand the music of Tibet is merely barbarous. The temple orchestra usually consists of seven men; two of them are occupied with one of the big trumpets, one to hold it up, the other to blow it. These trumpets furnish a grating noise approximating in depth to the length of the instrument. As this is anything up to twelve, or, in the case of one trumpet in Potala, eighteen feet, the note produced is low. Two other men blow as seemeth good to them upon shorter trumpets, one about four feet in length, the other a small sixteen-inch instrument, generally made out of a human thigh-bone with copper end pieces. Two men also will devote themselves to *gyalings;* these are short reed-blown clarinets. The last and most important member of all is he who beats the drum. The drum is a kind of warming-pan-like structure, and the parchment of its three-foot head is struck with a sickle-shaped stick. By a convention, which is like that of Europe, the drummer manages the cymbals also. Powerful instruments these are, taking unquestioned command of the babel whenever used.

Besides all these the officiating Lama will from time to time ring a sweet silvery-toned bell at, no doubt, the accurate intervals, but it must be confessed that the general effect of a Tibetan service is not unlike that of a farm yard, or a nursery, and it may still be many years indeed before order is given to these sounds confused. One or two tunes they have which can be recognized. One of them is *par excellence* the melody of the Orient. I do not know if it has a name, but Mrs. Flora Annie Steel has sufficiently indicated its scope and cadence by wedding to it the words, "Twinkle, twinkle, little star."

The marriage customs of Tibet are like those of the vast majority of mankind—the lady is bought. But one feature in the preliminaries differentiates them strongly from the methods of modern England. The girl's mother will firmly and repeatedly insist upon the ugliness and uselessness of her *débutante* whenever a suggestion is made by the professional matchmaker of the village. This modesty, however, can be overcome by a little negotiation. Groomsmen and bridesmaids are, I believe, as necessary to a smart wedding in Tibet as in America, and, if Chandra Das is to be believed, the difficulty of knowing whether a wedding present is expected or not is overcome in Lhasa by a simple device. The maiden presents a cheap little katag or scarf to every one from whom she would like a wedding gift. There is a slight religious service at the actual marriage. The officiating lama, after prayer, declares the woman to be from henceforth the bride of her husband alone—and his brothers. The usual Oriental overeating accompanies the rite. Divorce in Tibet is expensive, but easily obtained, though the necessity for any such annulment of the marriage tie is greatly reduced by the frequency of "Meredithian" marriages.

In private life the Tibetan is a cheerful body with, of course, the defects of that amiable quality. Not infrequently he gets drunk and he has at no time many morals. But he is a hard worker, capable of enduring for weeks extremes of physical discomfort which would incapacitate a native of India in a day, and, above all, it must be set down to his credit that he is merciful to his beast. The tail-twisting of bullocks stops at our frontier. He has, of course, no nerves, or it is possible that the dogs which swarm over the country and form one of its most prominent features would fare badly even at the hands of a Buddhist.

They are an unmitigated nuisance, savage by day and noisy by night. Every breed of dog known to the fancier seems to

TIBETAN CHILDREN CHARACTERISTICALLY EMPLOYED IN A GYANTSE STREET

have been mixed in this sandy-coated pack. It is curious, however, that in spite of the out-of-door life which is led by them, the type to which they have reverted is not that of the wolf or collie, but rather that of the Esquimaux sledge dog. Some of them are easily domesticated, and the puppies are friendly little things only too anxious to be adopted. The typical Tibetan terrier, a long-coated little fellow with a sharp nose, prick ears, and, as a rule, black from muzzle to tail, we found but seldom in a pure state.[1]

[1] The finest specimens of this breed are owned by Mrs. Claude White—"Tippoo," "Jugri," and scantily coated "Nari" came up with us to Lhasa with their master. But "Sebu," a sable freak in the same family, and beyond question the most beautiful of them all, remained at Gangtok.

CHAPTER XII

INTERNAL HISTORY OF LHASA 1902–4

BEFORE taking up again the story of the Expedition I propose to sketch the internal affairs of Lhasa for the last few years with somewhat greater detail than before. The key to the situation in Tibet, which was now becoming desperate, is to be found in the deliberate and steady determination of the Tibetans to do away with the Chinese suzerainty. This is a policy of long standing. Thirty-five years ago the spirit of independence was already abroad in Tibet, and there was a recognized progressive party, headed by no less a dignitary than the treasurer of Gaden monastery. Under the old régime, as is well known, a consistent policy of regency, made possible only by the equally systematic assassination of each successive young Grand Lama before he reached the age of eighteen, resulted in a continual regency, and therefore also a continual opportunity for the assertion and reassertion of the Chinese suzerainty, for no regent could be appointed without the sanction of the Chinese Emperor. The very election of the Dalai Lama himself was theoretically subject to the approval of Peking, but this prerogative was seldom, or never, exercised. In other parts of his dominions the Chinese Emperor made undoubted use of his rights. At Urga, a new Taranath Grand Lama, the third in importance in the Buddhist world, was, on one occasion, peremptorily disqualified by his majesty on the grounds that his immediate predecessor had been a turbulent and seditious fellow, and that there was no good ground for supposing that he had been reincarnated in any human being. Against this the good people of Mongolia entered a violent protest. They said that such a contention cut at the root of their religion, and so much trouble did they give that eventually the Emperor compromised; he said that as the monks of Urga had chosen a Mongolian to be their chief he would allow the election to stand, but that on no account thenceforward was a reincarnation to take place in the body of a Tibetan. The descent of the spirit is thus regulated to-day. Again it is necessary to remind the European reader with a sense of humor that these apparent absurdities are the source of very real and often very bitter political feeling in the Far East, and that the application of European habits of thought to these circumstances can only result in a total misapprehension of the whole situation. The Tibetans see no absurdity in situations thus created at a time when in other ways their national aspirations were shaping a shrewd and Occidental policy.

The leader of the party died indeed before achieving success, but it is worth notice that in the election of the present Dalai Lama, in 1874, a change directly attributable to the dead reformer's personality was made in the devolution of the spirit of Avalokiteswara. In the old days the names of all babies born at the time of the assassination of the previous Dalai Lama were written on slips and put into a golden urn, which, it is reported, levitated itself and thrice cast forth the slip of paper bearing the name of the chosen child. This miracle is supposed to have been somewhat assisted by the writing of the same name upon every slip, and it was to guard against any such political manipulation of this all-important choice that a new plan of selection was then adopted. Acting upon the counsels of the chief magician of Nachung choskyong, the discovery of the new Dalai Lama was intrusted to the pious clairvoyance of the Shar-tse Abbot of Gaden. This man, acting upon instructions, went to the Chos-kor Plain, to the east of Lhasa, and there on the surface of the Muli-ding-ki lake the new reincarnation was seen in his mother's lap upon a lotus flower. After a brief search for mother and child, Tubdan Gyatso, the present pontiff, was found at Paru-chude in the district of Tag-po. This method of choosing a successor to the divine authority checkmated the ordinary intrigues by which family influence as well as official guardianship secured to the Chinese suzerain no small voice in the acts of the doomed child's government. The last regent, as has been said, was chosen from Gaden, though he also had some connection with the Kun-de-ling in Lhasa.[1]

Eighteen years afterward, when, under other circumstances, his life would have been brought to a sudden conclusion, Tubdan Gyatso was spared. This has been attributed by some to the unrest prevailing during our troubles with India at that time; the treaty was then actually in process of construction in Calcutta, and it is very likely that the recent war with ourselves had suggested to the shrewder Tibetans that the time had come finally to take their affairs into their own hands. China had been of no use to them in their dispute with India, and to have "reincarnated" the Dalai Lama at that moment meant a repetition of the usual opportunity for the exertion of Chinese influence which would have been peculiarly inopportune and even disastrous. He was therefore allowed to survive maturity, but only as a religious pontiff, the temporal power remaining in the hands of the regent. But as soon as the treaty was signed the last vestige of Chinese influence in Tibet was thrown off by a *coup d'état,* in 1895, strangely resembling that of King Alexander of Servia under similar circumstances: Tubdan Gyatso declared himself temporal sovereign as well as religious autocrat, cast the regent into prison, and poisoned him almost immediately.

[1] It is impossible to obtain very accurate information upon a point like this. A Tibetan has his "La-lis" out of his mouth before a name is even mentioned.

Such was the position in 1901. There were at this time three important men in Lhasa: the Dalai Lama, Dorjieff, and the "Premier"—the Shata Shapé.[1] The last of the triumvirate was a man who had been brought into prominence some years ago by an unfortunate incident in Darjeeling. The story is well known: a Tibetan was ducked in the fountain for insolence displayed by him or by one of his countrymen toward an Englishwoman in a rickshaw. The man's rudeness did not, perhaps, justify so drastic a punishment, but it was not altogether unnatural, and it was our misfortune rather than our fault that we thus incurred the perpetual and bitter hatred of the man, who, in the course of a few years, was destined to become prime minister of Tibet; for the victim was no other than the Shata Shapé, then exiled and under a temporary cloud. He never forgot or forgave, and it is not surprising that when the opportunity presented itself he flung himself heart and soul into the change of policy advocated by Dorjieff. Sufficient reference has already been made to the career of Dorjieff; of the Dalai Lama, we only know from Chinese sources that he is a headstrong and somewhat conceited man, not without strength of character, but intolerant of restraint in any form. Physically he is a tall and powerfully built man with unusually oblique eyes.

Opposed to them stood the various representatives and delegates of the ruling priestly caste, greatly swayed by the traditional respect and homage which the Grand Lama's position inspires in the least dutiful of his subjects, but stubbornly refusing to depart from their ancient principles and the policy of seclusion which had stood Tibet and themselves in good stead for so long. In all else the Dalai Lama was able to have his way, but neither the introduction of a Russian protectorate, nor the presence of Russian representatives in Lhasa, would the Tsong-du tolerate in any form whatever, or for an instant. To neither side

[1] He is also known as Shaffi Phen-tso Dorje.

were the claims or the opinions of the Chinese of the slightest moment. The return of Dorjieff in December with the unofficial understanding between Russia and Tibet was, therefore, the inauguration of a difficult period for the Dalai Lama.

The existence of this understanding was a fact that he could neither openly avow nor, on the other hand, entirely conceal. The solemn anti-foreigner covenant, signed by the Tsong-du, was obstinately pleaded by the opposition and nothing could be done. The Dalai Lama changed his methods. Not for a moment did he abandon the policy which promised to secure for himself and for his country the apparently gratuitous protection of Russia and freedom from the ever-present dread of the English; and he did not attempt to conceal his not unnatural dislike for the short-sighted policy of the Tsong-du, by which he now found himself as much thwarted as by any possible interference of China. But in their existing mood it was impossible to coerce the members of the National Council, so for the future he determined to use the wide powers he was able to wield without reference to it, and he believed that their scope was extensive enough to carry through his matured Russophile policy, not so much by the deliberate choice of the Tsong-du, as of necessity, and he set himself determinedly to bring about that necessity. This was no easy task. There was no trouble then with India, and the self-confident Tibetans attached small value to any inducements that Russia could hold out. Tibet had succeeded easily in regaining her independence of China, and could conceive no reason for putting herself again under obligation to any man. But with shrewder foresight the Dalai Lama saw that some such protection from the north or from the south was ultimately inevitable. He chose to make a truce with Russia. Apart from the practical inducements offered by Dorjieff, it must be remembered in his choice of an ally that he was acting upon a principle well known in the East. Long before his days the worn out shoes and moldy bread of the men of Gibeon had persuaded Joshua that it was safe to make a treaty of peace with so distant a tribe. The moral effect of an alliance with either was, as he knew well, a guarantee for the non-interference of the other. Now India is but a fortnight away, while Russia, by the quickest route, is full four months' journey distant.

So soon, therefore, as he could make the Tsong-du recognize the necessity for outside support, he knew that the assistance of Russia, as being the more distant friend, would, as a matter of course, be preferred by it to the traditional and imminent menace of Indian influence. He set himself to bring this recognition about, and it was clear that if friction could in some way be established in his relations with India, he would have gone far toward obtaining his end. In achieving his purpose, he had neither scruples nor difficulty. Reference has been made before to the policy of aggression he adopted, but the acts may be briefly recapitulated here. The frontier regulations of Sikkim were violated in a flagrant manner; the grazing rights near Giao-gong were encroached upon in a way which he was well aware we could not much longer suffer. A customs house and a barrier were actually erected and occupied, and British subjects kept out by force from a small portion of the British Empire. Eventually the arrival of a letter from Lord Curzon, in the middle of 1902, offered him an opportunity he was not slow to use. The letter was returned unopened, without apology or comment of any kind. Such, it will be remembered, was the situation immediately before the arrival of the Mission at Kamba-jong.

Under this new régime the Tsong-du were little consulted. It was Tubdan's intention to use them afterward, but rather for the mere purpose of ratifying an inevitable policy than of asking them their opinion upon its wisdom. No definite information of their attitude seems to have been sent to Russia. Rifles were from time to time received and stored at Norbu-ling under the Dalai Lama's personal supervision, and Dorjieff continued to distribute small but valuable European-made gifts among the leading men of Lhasa. The action of the Indian government in sending Mr. Claude White to enforce the rights of the Sikkimese over their grazing grounds was interpreted by the Grand Lama as an act of overt hostility, and was used to hasten the catastrophe—all the more readily, perhaps, because of the repeated warnings of the old Amban Yu-kang that the Tibetan policy with regard to the English was both foolish and *ultra vires:* his protests were, however, consistently and insolently ignored. At last, however, it seems that the Shata Shapé recoiled before the lengths to which the Dalai Lama, now utterly in the toils of Dorjieff, was prepared to go. The exact circumstances of their quarrel are not known, but it is clear that in 1903 the Shata Shapé was deposed from office and thrown into prison; where, I believe, the unfortunate man remains. The story of this incident is not without interest.

We get glimpses of the internal affairs of Lhasa about this time, which reveal sufficiently clearly the chaos which was then reigning. To any demur on the part of his colleagues in the government, the Dalai Lama opposed ill temper instead of argument, and soon made the unfortunate discovery that the slightest threat of resignation from temporal affairs—which one might have supposed to be no unwelcome idea to his harassed colleagues—speedily reduced the most insubordinate member of the Tsong-du to submissiveness.

But the dissatisfaction of Tibet with the Russophile tendencies of the Grand Lama could not thus be checked, and the cooperation of England and China in the advance of the Mission to Kamba-jong was a rebuff for the Grand Lama that could not be misinterpreted. The great astrologer of Tibet, the Lama of Re-ting, was asked about this time to interpose the influence of the stars against the encroachment of the British. It is remark-

A TIBETAN POLITICAL AGENT

able that in his answer he makes the definite charge that the troubles from which Tibet was suffering were due to the fact that bribes of European money had been unlawfully accepted by Tibetan officials.

On the 3d or 4th of October, it was asserted that 150 Russian rifles[1] were brought to the Potala by Dorjieff. At this time the latter's influence reached its highest point, and it was regretfully admitted in Lhasa that even the Shapés themselves were obliged to curry favor with him to get anything done or even listened to by the Dalai Lama. About this time, owing to the direct intervention of Dorjieff, the Dalai Lama took the arbitrary and high-handed step to which we have referred. On the 13th of October he sent for and imprisoned at Norbu-ling the four ministers of state and the representatives of the Three Monasteries. He accused the Shata Shapé of having taken bribes; the other members were charged with having concealed from the Dalai Lama important facts connected with the boundary dispute, with having taken money from Ugyen Kazi[2] on the occasion of the presentation of an elephant, with being behindhand in their biennial reports, and, in general, with disobedience to his Holiness, and with attempting to carry on the business of the country contrary to his intentions and orders. In order to carry through this *coup-de-main,* he once again threatened to resign and adopt the meditative life unless his action were indorsed. He was completely successful.

[1] It was believed in Lhasa that weapons were continually arriving in camel loads, but it is more probable that they were barrels only. The Tip arsenal across the river was working at high pressure, and even during our brief experience of Tibetan munitions of war it was possible to observe a very distinct improvement in the manufactured cartridges; the rifles here made consisted, as a rule, of a local Martini lock adjusted somewhat carelessly to an old European-made barrel of some discarded pattern.

[2] Ugyen Kazi, horsedealer and diplomatist, is the most conspicuous figure on the Tibetan frontier. He was used by the Indian Government in 1902 as the bearer of the letters to the Dalai Lama which were returned unopened to Lord Curzon. A commanding presence and a quick humor also has this man, who might use Elizabeth's scratching on the Hatfield window for his motto.

Almost the last act of these unhappy men was a refusal to attend the annual review on the plain between Sera and Lhasa on the day when the Emperor of China is customarily saluted by obeisance made toward the east. It is probable that they refused to attend this yearly ceremony in order to avoid offending either the Emperor or the Dalai Lama, either by abandoning or persisting in the old custom which the latter seems now to have forbidden for the future, and it is not without significance that, in order to save themselves from internal treachery, the four deposed Shapés had bound themselves by an oath to stand or fall together.

The points were put upon the i's of the situation by a remark of the Amban's about this time that even if ambassadors were sent to meet the British at any point, and even if they succeeded in coming to an agreement, the Tsong-du would refuse to ratify the treaty. Of the four Shapés or Kalons, the monk official Te-kang, the Shata Shapé, and Sho-kang were the more responsible and respectable officers; the last, by name Hor-kang, a man of somewhat weak character, who had been in office but four months, committed suicide almost immediately in terror. Their places were taken by the Ta Lama as ecclesiastical member, the head of the house of Yutok, the Tsarong Dépen, and the Tse-chung Shapé; none of them, with the exception of the Yutok Shapé, of any social position or strength of mind.

The Ta Lama, whom we repeatedly met at one time or another, was a gentlemanlike old priest, verging on his second childhood and incapable of keeping his attention fixed on any subject for more than a minute or so at a time. The Yutok Shapé was a phlegmatic fatalist who seemed fully aware of the impossibility of doing anything for his country with the scanty authority he possessed. The other two were negligible quantities and were clearly appointed for the sole purpose of allowing a freer hand to the Dalai Lama's personal eccentricities.

THE TA LAMA AT TASKI-TSE

The chief executive member of the hierarchy under the Dalai Lama

With this ramshackle government the affairs of Tibet were carried on; every now and then the Amban, who had already received notice of his dismissal, tried, in a weak manner, to settle the matter by a personal appeal to the Grand Lama or the Tsongdu, but the treatment of the Mission at Kamba-jong is witness enough to the small importance that was attached to Chinese representations at this period. In December, 1903, the Shapés, by instruction of the Dalai Lama, definitely refused transport to the Amban. This, by preventing his approaching Colonel Younghusband, was tantamount to an active refusal to allow China to interfere in any way. It was the last straw; he angrily demanded that their refusal to obey the orders of the Chinese Emperor should be set down in writing. It was probably somewhat to his surprise that the Dalai Lama instantly acquiesced and assumed full responsibility for the action. Tibet had decided to act as an independent kingdom, and as soon as the gauntlet had been thrown down, troops were moved out from Lhasa along the southern road to Phari. Yu-kang then rather weakly offered to pay his own transport expenses, but this was as steadily refused as before. For some time now the Amban had been unable to obtain an answer from the Dalai Lama even to questions wholly unconnected with the dispute with ourselves; from this moment he was an insignificant and ultimately a disgraced man.

The arrival of the new Amban, Yu-tai, was about this time announced from Chyando, and Yu-kang made his preparations to return. His degradation was no loss to us. He had been acting upon the confidential orders of Yung-lu for many years and undoubtedly supported the Tibetans in their refusal to negotiate with the English, relying upon assurances received from Yung-lu that Lhasa would be occupied by Russian troops in the spring of 1903. This corroborates Dorjieff's boast, and our minister in Peking obtained from Prince Ching an admission that he had heard the report. Nor when pressed did the Russian minister in

Peking deny that there was a certain *rapprochement* "on religious grounds"; but Yung-lu's death shortly afterward and the first rumblings of the Japanese war cloud effectually held the hand of Russia. The Dalai Lama therefore found himself in the position of having paved the way for advances on Russia's part from which nothing was to be expected, while from our side he could only await that demand for satisfaction and a clearer understanding which he had himself deliberately provoked.

By this time even the pious citizens of Lhasa were grumbling against their divine ruler. They whispered that the Potala Lama, as he is not infrequently called in Lhasa, after having murdered the regent of Tibet and imprisoned the Shapés, was about to consummate his folly by losing the country itself as well. The wildest confusion prevailed in official circles; no man trusted his nearest friend; the Amban, trying perhaps to retrieve his credit at the last moment, appears now and then in a whirl of fussy and impotent ill temper, making demands that his master must be obeyed, that transport must be provided for him, that the La-chung men must be released at once.[1] No one paid him the slightest attention, and at last he seems to have subsided upon receipt of an unpleasant communication from Peking, intimating that his punishment would be decided upon after he had returned; and this is the end of Yu-kang.

Meanwhile the new Amban was slowly making his progress toward Lhasa. He had started in November, 1902, and fifteen months seems an inordinate time for even a Chinese official to take in covering the distance which separates Lhasa from Peking. He

[1] Two men from Sikkim had been caught by the Tibetans and detained by them during our stay at Kamba-jong. It was almost universally reported that they had been tortured and put to death in Shigatse, but on our arrival in Lhasa they were found to be still in prison there, and on the 17th of August Colonel Younghusband had them released. This incident at one time seemed likely to give rise to serious complications, but thus it ended happily, and the men themselves made no charge of brutality against their Tibetan jailers.

had asked for an escort of 2,000 men to accompany him, but as a matter of fact he found it difficult to provide for the needs of the bare hundred whom he was allowed to take. He had been selected for the post because he was the brother of Sheng-tai who had concluded the unfortunate treaty of 1890, and it was regarded as only fitting and just by the Oriental mind that the harm done by one member of a family should be rectified by another. On his way he met Mr. Nicholls, an American, at Ta-chien-lu, the frontier city, where he seems to have spent some time in extracting money from the Chinese prefect and the Tibetan "gyalpo" alike. He seems to have asserted his intention of restoring Chinese authority, and he admitted no sympathy with the Tibetan desire for seclusion, arguing that if Sze-chuan was open to foreigners there could be no reason why the pretensions of the Tibetans should be permitted for a moment. He moved on to Batang for the same dubious purposes that had detained him at Ta-chien-lu.[1]

On the 12th of February, the belated official reached Lhasa and assumed the reins of government. Later in the same month Dorjieff's influence began to wane. The intrigues with Russia had been overdone and were the common talk of the town. It was known and widely resented that the Dalai Lama had sent back to St. Petersburg a Buriat who had come to Dorjieff, bringing with him a large sum of money. Moreover, the new Amban, whatever his moral deficiencies, had at least some energy at first. He tried to carry things with a high hand, and one of his first actions was severely to censure the inaction of a Chinese representative, who had been ordered south to confer with Younghusband; he seems also to have given our Kamba-jong acquaintance, Ho, a bad

[1] Mr. Nicholls notes that at this place the hair and scraps of the finger-nails of the Dalai Lama were sold at enormous prices in the market, and Mr. Wilton tells me that there is a constant demand in Peking for scraps, however dirty, of his Holiness' clothing, and even more repulsive relics of the great Reincarnation

quarter of an hour on the ground that he had misappropriated Government money. A week after his arrival he made an official visit to the Dalai Lama, and for three hours attempted to bring him to reason; it was not, however, of much use, and on his return to the Residency the Amban set himself to the re-organization and reform of the military arrangements in Tibet so far as the Chinese soldiery was concerned. On one point at least he failed as completely as his predecessor; he, too, first requested and finally demanded that he should be allowed transport to go to Tuna to meet Younghusband, or Yun-hai-phun, as they transliterated the name. This the Dalai Lama courteously but firmly refused. At a subsequent visit the Amban seems to have moderated his tone, but to no effect; the Dalai Lama again cheerfully accepted the responsibility for every obstacle that was placed in the way of the Amban's intended journey, and refused to permit the strengthening of the Chinese garrisons at the frontier and in Lhasa. The mood of the Tibetans at this period was anything but conciliatory. The Tongsa Penlop, who had written offering his services as mediator once again, was told that only after a retreat to Yatung and payment of damages for our trespass at Phari would the question of negotiation be opened.

But the display of temper was not confined to officials. About this time levies from the province of Kams were called up, but they refused to come, alleging that no proper rations had been served out to them; a promise of proper supplies (which, by the way, was never performed) induced them to send about a thousand men for the defense of Lhasa, but in other parts of the country the demands of the Dalai Lama were met with a blank refusal. Upon the top of this came the news of the disaster at Guru and of our occupation of Gyantse jong. The discontent redoubled. Dorjieff felt that, now or never, the time was come for action if he wished to save his life. He seems to have argued to himself that if a successful attack could be made upon the small British garrison at Chang-lo, time would be gained and his policy justified, for the moment at least. On the other hand, if such an attack were unsuccessful his own liberty and even his own life would be in danger; he therefore planned and ordered the attack on the Mission post on May 5th, and straightway fled the country, posting north along the Sining highway, and ultimately branching off along the Urga road.[1]

About this time the Tsarong Dépen asked that troops should be sent to Nagartse to oppose the advance of the British troops. He especially objected, it is said, to the English habit of taking photographs. The Paro Penlop in Bhutan was stealthily approached by the Dalai Lama at the same time with the object of inducing the Bhutanese, in the absence of the Tongsa Penlop, to destroy the British lines of communication,[2] and a second messenger was sent in haste to Russia as the former envoy had not returned.

High officials now began to talk among themselves almost without concealment of the foolishness of the Dalai Lama, but no one dared to say much to him. The news that Russia was getting the worst of it in Korea had reached Tibet. A report of the fight on the Karo la was received with consternation in Lhasa, but the Grand Lama merely observed that it was time to send forward the Golden Army[3] and, if necessary, all the male inhabitants of Lhasa also. The rumor that Gyantse jong had been retaken and the British garrison there exterminated to a man helped to restore public confidence a little, and about the same time a letter of sympathy came from Bhutan causing disproportionate satisfaction. It is significant that the Chinese Amban re-

[1] Rumors of a subsequent meeting between himself and the Dalai Lama have as yet no confirmation, but it is not improbable that at Urga or some similar place the two men have since met.

[2] The Paro Penlop ranks second, and consistently opposed the Anglophile tendencies of the Tongsa Penlop. He is, however, now discredited.

[3] This is the monkish reserve which supplies a personal escort to the Dalai Lama. It is often loosely used to describe the fighting lamas as a whole.

fused to believe in the killing of even a couple of Chinese at Dzara during the Karo la fight, pointing out that the English had not killed one of his countrymen throughout the expedition, and bluntly declaring his belief that these two had been assassinated there by Tibetans.

Such, then, was the position until the middle of July, when the Dalai Lama heard that Gyantse jong had been again recaptured and that the English were on the point of starting for Lhasa. He lost no time. Disguised in the plain dirty crimson of a common monk the mortal body of Tubdan Gyatso fled away from his ancient residence and hallowed cathedral in Lhasa, carrying within him the incarnate soul of Avalokiteswara. He set his golden feet along the Nakchu-ka road and never looked back till he was eight days' journey from the capital. With him went the Chief Magician, he who many years ago had helped to place Tubdan upon the throne, and in later years had foretold only too truly that the "year of the wood dragon" (*i.e.*, 1904) would spell disaster for Tibet. These two men at the present moment are at Urga, where a religious jehad is being organized, and it is quite clear that no finality in our relations with Tibet can be secured until they are persuaded of the foolishness of opposing the rights of India, or until, as is far more likely, they have been quietly put out of the way by the hierarchs whose ancient régime they have so rudely offended.

As to the negotiations which we had so far vainly endeavored to begin, it should be remembered that the terms which Colonel Younghusband was instructed to demand from the Tibetans were in themselves neither burdensome nor indeed as heavy as we had a right to demand. Briefly stated, they included a demand that the frontier should be rectified, that an indemnity should be paid of an amount and in a manner to be subsequently decided, that foreign political influence should be totally excluded from Tibet, and that no concessions for mines, railways, or telegraphs should be granted without the knowledge and the assent of the Indian Government. Trade markets were to be established at Gyantse and Gartok, a place far on the road from Shigatse to Leh, and another clause permitted trade from India to pass freely along any existing highway of commerce. A Resident in Gyantse was to be appointed, but no representative of British interests, political or commercial, was to be posted at Lhasa. As a guarantee for the payment of the indemnity the Chumbi Valley was to be occupied by the British. The suzerainty of the Chinese was frankly recognized throughout the document, and it need hardly be said that Russia was not referred to. Colonel Younghusband had frankly expressed his opinion that it would be cheaper and more effectual in the long run to have a Resident in Lhasa, and if the Government had not committed themselves to an opposite policy by their promises to Russia it is possible that this suggestion, which to some extent commended itself to Lord Curzon also, might have been adopted. We shall see later the actual course of negotiations and the form which this treaty eventually assumed. For the moment it is only necessary to remember that Lord Curzon's absence from India on leave from the end of April to the beginning of December placed him somewhat at a disadvantage. He has, however, in the fullest manner, acknowledged his indebtedness to Lord Ampthill, Governor of Madras and acting Viceroy of India during Lord Curzon's furlough, for the steady way in which the policy, which had been begun and shaped by himself, was consistently pressed forward by his successor. The latter, who was thus in office during the actual advance to Lhasa and the signing of the treaty, is a man of capacity far beyond his years. Difficult as his position was—and the difficulty was added to by the ultimate uncertainty prevailing as to the length of his tenure of office[1]—it was uni-

[1] Lord Curzon's return to India was indefinitely delayed owing to Lady Curzon's sudden illness. She had been ailing for some time. On the 21st of

versally recognized that he had dealt with a new and increasingly difficult situation with firmness and restraint, and the Home Government regarded themselves as under a deep obligation to him.

One advantage of the sending of the expedition has been, as Lord Curzon is probably very well aware, that public attention has now been definitely drawn to a matter which had been allowed to be shelved almost too long. However much some of the less responsible members of the Opposition in England may regret it, it cannot again seriously be contended by them that our position on the northern frontier of India was this time safe. I have referred to the warnings that reached Lord Curzon of the gradual insinuation of Russian influence at Lhasa, and the expedition proved conclusively that those rumors considerably underestimated the importance of the occasion. There is no reason in the world why Russia should not obtain a predominating influence in Lhasa except the plain one that it is incompatible with our own clearly recognized interests. If such a consideration is held not to have justified the sending of the Mission, there is little more to be said, but to those who recognize the importance of safeguarding our Indian frontiers without possibility of mistake, a few more considerations as to the policy to be observed in the future with regard to Tibet may here be offered.

To begin with, we have discovered for the first time the true nature of southern Tibet. It is far from resembling the dreary waterless deserts of the north, so well described by Sven Hedin and others, and it must also be admitted that it in no way substantiates the impression left upon the mind by the reports sent in by the secret surveyors. Apart from the fact that the native

September she developed peritonitis of an aggravated and complicated kind. For three weeks she lay in Walmer Castle between life and death, and few indeed of those who watched the struggle day by day had any hopes that she could ultimately throw off the disease. However, to the sincere relief of every one who had at heart the best interests of India, Lord Curzon, on the 24th of November, was able to leave her to continue her convalescence at Highcliffe, and returned to take up the threads of his work at Calcutta.

of India has no eye for the beauties of nature, and would as soon make a day's journey across a desert as a park, it must be remembered that the very manner in which these invaluable men were obliged to carry out their work precluded the possibility of much observation. To go on walking from day to day, intent only upon counting every footfall and faithfully registering the hundreds and the thousands upon a Tibetan rosary, naturally debars a traveler from such observations as would have suggested to the Indian authorities both the stored-up and the potential wealth of the great alluvial river-flats of southern Tibet.

I do not know that there are many feats in the world of adventure, endurance, and pluck that will compare favorably with that of the Indian native intrusted with the work of secret exploration in Tibet. In the first place it must be remembered that to secure the brains necessary for the work a class of native has to be employed which, by tradition at least, is not the pluckiest in the peninsula. The wonder therefore is doubled when one remembers the splendid work of such men as Krishna (better known as A.K.) or Kintup (K.P.), for the moral courage needed to persist in an enterprise like this can hardly be overestimated. The men employed are of necessity entirely without companions and without resources; they are engaged upon one of the most hazardous occupations that remain in the world, that of a spy in a barbarous country, and should they fail for one minute in all those months and years of exile, they know that no mercy will be extended to them; and I think it but fair to add that not one of them would in any emergency betray the Government whose servant he is. There is a known case of a man who actually consented to be betrayed by his colleague as a spy in order that one at least of the two might be able to escape and bring back to India the priceless notes and calculations collected during a year of travel. For three years Kintup was sold into slavery and endured it without complaining.

But this is not all; a life of exploration, apart from the dangers and hardships of it, is one of unremitting toil; the mere physical endurance needed to travel in this brain-benumbing way, counting each step, hardly daring to raise the eyes from the track at one's feet lest a number should be missed, or lest suspicion should be aroused, is incredible. One man measured the length of the Ling-kor, the road round Lhasa, by counting the prostrations necessary, afterward solemnly repeating the whole process over a measured mile. Another man is known to have traveled 2,500 miles, counting every footstep over mountain ranges. Atma Ram did the same thing in one of Captain Bower's expeditions for a distance of 2,080 miles. Nain Singh counted his steps from Leh to Assam—look at it on the map. When the story of Asian exploration is finally and worthily written, the work of these lonely spies, twirling incessantly within their wheels rolls of blank paper instead of prayers, which are laboriously and minutely filled up night after night with the day's observation, must receive a place of honor second to none. Hurree Chunder Mookerjee in "Kim" is a character drawn, I believe, immediately from the record of Krishna's work.

To return to the question of protecting the northern frontier of India. It seems a fair estimate that, so far as supplies are concerned, a force of a hundred thousand men could without difficulty rely upon the produce of the luxuriant valleys of the Tsang-po and the Nyang chu. It was no friend of England's who remarked that the natural frontiers of India were less the Himalayas than the impenetrable deserts which lie a hundred miles north of Lhasa, and it is a serious consideration for us that if Russia's influence should ever predominate in Lhasa, the actual ground to be fought for, diplomatically or otherwise, is that which lies across the barrier formed by the Himalayas. The advanced base, whether of the defending or of the encroaching force, must lie in these valleys. If the fertile fields of southern Tibet cannot enter into the calculations of an invading nation, that nation will have to rely upon the trans-Siberian railway as its base, and I need hardly say that this is tantamount to ridiculing the whole danger of invasion through Tibet. Such, baldly stated, is the situation.

To secure immediate access to this glacis of granaries is the obvious policy for the British Government to pursue, and it cannot be said too insistently that the recognition of this necessity in no way whatever involves interference with the internal affairs of Tibet. As to a protectorate, the very idea of undertaking responsibility for an additional eighteen hundred miles of frontier is ridiculous. This, however, is a different matter. To secure this advantage there is little constructive work needed. An alternative route to the prohibitive hardships of the Natu la is now being surveyed along the valleys of the Di chu and the Ammo chu. It is proposed to push rail-head from some point on the line in the neighborhood of Dam dim as far up the lower slopes of the Himalayas as is feasible without a rack; and then to construct a cart-road, with an easy gradient, along the valley to the head waters of the Di chu, crossing into Bhutanese territory near Jong-sa, and at a height of 9,000 feet, overpassing at its lowest point the great mountain wall which here hems in the right bank of the Ammo chu. From this height there is almost a level run into Rinchen-gong. Once in the Chumbi Valley the difficulties of a second expedition will have been largely overcome, for even as this work is published the road from Rinchen-gong to Kamparab is receiving the last touches from the engineers who have worked on it so long. From Kamparab there is a level natural road which has been steadily used throughout the present expedition for wheeled traffic as far as Kang-ma. The road is practicable for carts for a few miles further still, and the construction of the road I have mentioned over the Jong-sa la would enable stores, unloaded at rail-head, to be carried, without bulk broken, on wheeled carts to within thirty miles of Gyantse itself. It is hardly necessary to comment upon this. We have, I repeat, no wish in the world to interfere with Tibet so long as Tibet does not imperil our tranquillity in Bengal. While we ourselves seek no exclusive rights in the country, we have at the same time no intention of allowing any other power to secure them. So long as the Tibetans cordially co-operate with ourselves in excluding foreign political influence, so long will we assist them to the best of our power by doubling the existing barriers along the common frontier. But it must be patent to the shallowest that the simple laying of this road will in future put us in a position to insist, should our friendliness be insufficient to win the loyalty and good faith of the hierarchy of Lhasa. It is but bare justice to credit Captain O'Connor with the original suggestion of its construction in any practicable form.

Inseparable from this cart-road is the question of trade. Elsewhere I have referred to the staple products of the country. On our side it seems clear that tea is beyond all competition the chief export from India which the Tibetans would buy profusely and with gratitude should the opportunity be fairly presented to them. But a curious and unfortunately not an extraordinary thing is the unwillingness of the Darjeeling tea-planters to recognize the real necessities of the case. They are ready to supply their ordinary tea in its ordinary form to any extent, but they seem quite unwilling to manufacture the tea in that shape in which alone the Tibetans recognize the article. I believe that after some pressure the institute of planters in the Darjeeling district have sent two men to the Chinese tea fields to learn the method of making bricks of tea, such as the Tibetans require, but it seems strange that it should have required an expedition to teach them such an obvious act of commercial prudence.

This, then, is in brief the truth about our future relations with Tibet, and in whatever terms the treaty now signed may eventually be ratified, the fact remains unalterable, that by the simple construction of a road the northern frontier of India can now be safeguarded at an expense which is ridiculously small in comparison with the millions lavished on the north-west, and one which by sheer encouragement of trade will be recouped within ten years. Roads are the great pioneers of peace, and those who know their north-west frontier best will be the first to admit the almost instant result of their construction even in the most hostile districts. But the matter may safely be left in the hands of Lord Curzon.

CHAPTER XIII

LAMAISM

NO account of an expedition to Lhasa would be complete without some reference to the technical side of the religion of the country. I have before referred to its application to the people and the effect it produces upon their life, but a certain amount of information as to the ecclesiastical aspect of Lamaism is necessary to a full understanding of the real position which Buddhism occupies in Central Asia. I have no intention of wearying the reader with minute formulæ, but the spirit which underlies this Buddhism is worthy of some study.

The origin of Buddhism in Tibet is explained by the Tibetans themselves in a somewhat amusing way. It is said that in old days Tibet was a country of ravines and mountain tops and torrents, varied by huge lakes. Buddha in person then visited the land, and found that the inhabitants were monkeys. He questioned the monkeys and asked them why they were not men and good Buddhists. They answered, not without reason, that with the country in its existing state there was no opportunity for the development of their own bodies, let alone their religious impulses. To this Buddha replied: "If you will promise to become men and good Buddhists I will give you a good and fertile land to live in." The agreement having been struck, Buddha there and then drained off the waters from the land which is now known as the plain of Gyantse by an underground channel through the Himalayas into the Ganges near Gaya. The Tibetans on their side kept their promise, and though of course they knew not Darwin, became both men and, as they assert, good Buddhists.

As a matter of fact, the moment at which Buddhism became the established religion of Tibet can be ascertained with some approach to certainty. The Tibetan King Srong-tsan-gambo, to whom reference has been made in the first chapter, must have been a man of considerable foresight. It is not in the least likely that it was the influence of his two wives, one of whom was a Chinese, and the other a Nepalese princess, which decided him to adopt Buddhism as the religion of his country, though both of them may have helped to strengthen him in his intention. The truth is that he recognized the enormous value which would attach to the identification of Buddhism with his new capital. In India, as he saw clearly enough, Buddhism was being driven headlong before the re-encroaching tides of Hinduism. Had Buddhism remained a living force in India, no other place in Asia could have attempted to compete in local religious importance with, say, Gaya. But when Buddhism became an exile from the land of its birth, Srong-tsan-gambo made use of his opportunity. He recognized both the importance of having its central authority located in Lhasa, and the peculiar suitability of that place to his aims. In the seventh century, therefore, the official metropolis of Buddhism was transferred from the plains of Northern India to the mountain fastnesses of Tibet, and here in a couple of centuries the new religion established itself in the mystic and fascinating seclusion which veils it to this day.

This King of Tibet sent to India for learned Buddhist fathers, and, with the unquestioned autocracy of an Oriental tyrant, he imposed the new faith upon his people. There are few relics, except, perhaps, in the cathedral of Lhasa itself, of this primeval state of Lamaism, but that it underlies and was the foundation of all that we now see is beyond doubt. The Buddhism which was first introduced into Tibet was of the ampler form taught by the school of Asanga. It was in its original state the "greater vehicle," without any other accretions than those which Asanga's opportunism compelled him to adopt from the Hindu ritual and mythology. But, as I have said before, the present condition of Lamaism is such that Buddha himself would hardly recognize a phase or a phrase of it. The interesting part of this development is that it has been going on without any outside interference whatever. Secured by their geographical position, securer still by their overweening pride in the sacro-sanctity of their capital and the learning of their doctors, the Tibetans developed Lamaism along lines which betray no foreign influence. But this does not imply that the new religion was not severely tested and tried. There were molding forces enough in the religious party strife to distribute countless lines of cleavage through the fibers of the parent Buddhist stock. From the first the difficulty of communications in this country and the laxity which necessarily followed when the strong hand of an autocratic monarchy slackened, produced a large number of special and local developments of the Buddhist faith. It would be tedious to do more than note again that the first universal supremacy of any church in Tibet was that created by Kublai Khan in the middle of the thirteenth century, when he recognized the spiritual autocracy of the Grand Lama of the Sakya Monastery.

Sakya lies well to the south of Tashi-lhunpo, far from the influences of Lhasa, and here the Red Cap faction flourished exceedingly. There is a legend in connection with Kublai Khan's action which is credible enough. In wide sympathy with all forms of religious endeavor, Kublai Khan determined to put the claims of the various creeds to a practical test; none was excluded. A certain miracle—it was the levitation of a wine cup from the table to the Emperor's lips—was to be performed if possible by the representatives of the different creeds. Those championing the Christian faith were perhaps unwise in accepting this challenge

MONKS WALKING ON A TERRACE BENEATH LINES OF PRAYER-FLAGS

to make a public advertisement of supernatural powers. The lamas, on their side, no doubt, took private and material means to secure the success of their own incantations, and the failure of the Christians to achieve the marvel put the coping-stone to the strength of Buddhism in Central Asia.

It is not unlikely that the supernatural powers claimed to this day among certain sections of the lamas had their origin in this curious legend. Madame Blavatsky has drawn attention to these claims, and it may be doubted whether much popular enthusiasm would ever have been displayed for the shadowy tenets of Theosophy if it had not been for these attractive suggestions. Personally, I only once came in contact with a lama who made, or had made for him, a definite claim to supernatural power. Nyen-dé-kyi-buk is from time to time called upon to produce lamas of unusual sanctity. They are always forthcoming. These men have their spiritual capacity proved by their ability to pass certain tests, of which several were described to me. The first thing to be proved is their capacity to transmit their personality in a visible form to Lhasa, Gyantse, and Tashi-lhunpo within the space of a few seconds. Another and probably a more difficult feat upon which to satisfy their examiners consists in their ability to crawl through the keyhole of their locked cell. The Abbot of Nyen-dé-kyi-buk had successfully passed these tests, but one felt that the rules of courtesy forbade one from making any direct request that he should repeat on the spot even the simplest of his miracles. But supernatural powers are, of course, claimed in a very definite manner by all the wizards and magicians of the country, and also by the Dalai Lama and other high officials.

It is perhaps unfair to class the pretense of the magician to keep off hail from the crops by his prayers as an illustration of witchcraft, for a not dissimilar claim is implied even in Christian services; but it would be difficult to find a hard and fast point at which to draw a dividing line between such a pretension as this and that which underlies the claims of the austerer members of the Red-cap faction to the supernatural powers to which I have just referred. The earlier teachers of Lamaism are undoubtedly credited with curious non-human capacities, and the manner in which these mighty men of old encountered and defeated the obstacles devised by their enemies, or put in their path by the conditions of nature, is probably the basis of the Theosophist contention.

I have been at some pains to ascertain the origin of this belief, which Madame Blavatsky has been perhaps chiefly responsible for spreading. The following most learned teachers may be quoted here as having been the source of much of her doctrine:

1. *Nub-chen-nam-kar-ning-po.*—A Red-cap Lama, who transported himself at will through the air.

2. *Nub-chen-sang-gyi-ye-she.*—This man had even dared to see Shin-je himself, the god of Hell. He was also able to split rocks with a stroke of his purbu.

3. *Nal-jor-gyal-wa-chok-yung.*—A mighty teacher of the Red-cap school.

4. *Khan-dro-ye-she-tso-gyal.*—A woman disciple of the Guru Rinpoche. She exercised supernatural powers.

5. *Dog-mi-pal-gi-ye-she.*—He meditated on a snow-field with such success that the welfare and the misery of the world alike were visible to him, and he was obeyed by the goddesses themselves.

6. *Nyak-chen-ye-she-scheun-nu.*—A Lama of the Red-cap sect, who obtained water from a rock in the desert by touching it with his finger.

7. *Tub-chen-pal-gyi-sing-ge.*—A Bhutanese, whom the gods and goddesses were compelled to obey.

8. *Nga-dag-cho-gyal.*—This Lama lived at Samye. He lived without eating and made himself invisible at will.

9. *Nal-jor-wang-chuk-chempo.*—A pupil of the Guru Rinpoche, of great but unspecified supernatural powers.

10. *Na-nam-dor-je-dud-jom.*—A pupil of the Guru Rinpoche, who could project himself through the air.

11. *Ba-mi-ye-she.*—A pupil of the Guru Rinpoche. This man, like Enoch, passed into Nirvana without going through the pains of death.

12. *Sok-po-lha-pal.*—This man, the fourth of the Guru's great disciples, had the power of killing a tiger by touching its neck with his hands.

13. *Na-nang-ye-she.*—This Lama was learned enough to be able to fly through the air like a bird.

14. *Khar-chen-pal-gyi-wong-chuk.*—This great interpreter of Khar-chen wrought wonders with his purbu.

15. *Shu-po-pal-ki-sing-gé.*—A Tibetan "doctor," who controlled the sea.

16. *Ko-wa-pal-tse.*—A Hindu. His supernatural gifts are not specified.

17. *Na-jal-den-ma-tse-mang.*—A Hindu magician of the Red-cap school.

18. *Gyal-wo-lo-deu.*—A Hindu pundit (who brought brass images to life!).

19. *Kyu-chung.*—A youthful Hindu interpreter, who spoke the language of birds.

20. *Kun-chok-jang-né.*—A Hindu pundit who controlled the elements.

21. *Nul-joy-pal-gyi dor-je.*—This man was able to walk as easily over precipices as over the ground.

22. *Lo-che-ma-thog-rin-chen.*—With his magical powers he was able to tear off great boulders from the mountain side and crush them to powder in his hands.

23. *Wo-den-pal-gyi-wang-chuk.*—This teacher could swim through water as quickly and as easily as a fish.

24. *Nal-jor-den-pa-nam-khe.*—This great Lama was so skilled in magic lore that he could catch by the ear even the "flesh-licking" bison. (This is the repeated statement of a Tibetan lama, but if the yak is intended, it neither "licks flesh" nor much minds being held by the ear.)

25. *Dub-chen-gyal-wo-chang-chub.*—While meditating he was levitated into the air and so remained.

I have given these uncouth names in order to place upon a proper footing the supernatural claims of theosophists for Tibetan Lamaism. I have myself no doubt that in these traditions lies the origin of many of their beliefs, and I am glad to provide such material for acquiescence or argument as these supply.[1]

The word Mahatma is not known in Tibet, and, though he must know little of the East who will definitely say that any apparent variation therein of the ordinary course of nature, whether due to hypnotism or not, is incredible, I do not think, on the whole, that any particular occult knowledge will come to us from Tibet. Formulæ and details of ritual we did indeed find in overwhelming numbers, and the credulity and superstition of the common people may once have suggested that there really is something in these claims to theurgy, but the success with which a monotoned imprecation impresses a crowd of worshippers in a Tibetan gompa is, we found, due merely to the policy of extinguishing knowledge which the lamas have adopted.

To return to the history of the Church, Buddhism, in its earliest shape, was an agnostic rather than an atheistic form of religion. Buddha's scheme of retribution implies a belief in a First Cause, but when on a certain occasion he was asked to express an opinion upon the validity or otherwise of the traditional

[1] This list is, I believe, a complete one of all the "red letter" doctors of the Lamaic Church who wrought miracles. It is included in the full "ong kur-wa" or "power-sending" equipment of a Lamaic wizard.

deities known to Asia, he declined to admit the necessity of a categorical answer. He may have thought that it was convenient for common people of low intelligence, whose minds could only grasp a truth objectively, to have some external and tangible crystallization of truths, however far they might be from that which he saw. More than that cannot, I think, be found in the earliest form of Buddhism. There were, however, few even among the earliest Buddhists who were strong enough to drink this pure milk of the Word, and we find that even before Asanga had fused the two creeds, Buddhism was peopled with many semi-deities.

After the "Buddhas" and the Bodisats—a large class, consisting of those who have, so to speak, qualified themselves to be Buddhas, but whose self-denial has not yet and may never be called upon—there is a class of divinity which is very strikingly prominent in Tibet. These are the tutelary or guardian deities, chiefly of the "Towo" or "terrible" aspect. These were the original gods of the country, and after Buddha, who is always conceived as having made a personal mission tour through the land, had converted these hideous human monsters to his own austerer faith, he permitted them to retain their aspect and even their powers of doing harm, in order, as he said, that they might defend the faith and the chosen people from outside attack. This retention has had a natural result. There is no doubt that the inclusion of these "terrible" guardians in the Lamaic Pantheon has been the chief cause of the people remaining at heart devil-worshipers. We can imagine that at first the apostles of Buddhism found their work considerably smoothed for them by accepting the devil-gods of the aboriginal inhabitants. In this they after all only carried out Asanga's own policy in India, but the result, which they might have foreseen, has been that, except for the external veneer of Buddhism, devil-worship has absorbed its conqueror.

These terrible deities are the gods of the common people of Tibet. The mild-eyed Buddha is to them only a vague means of escape from the tyranny of these loathsome and misshapen monsters, aureoled with the fire of hell, who with dripping fangs and beastly deformities are far more present and practical than the master. They are placed, naturally enough, at the gates and in the forecourts of temples, either in actual carved shape, or, as is far more common, painted upon the walls. Upon these the eye of the passer-by rests, and it is probable that he rarely asks for any higher sanction for his religious duties than that which they afford. They terrify him into obedience to his lama, and that is all that the lama requires. For an adequate conception of the real effect of Lamaism upon the Tibetans, it is hardly necessary to go higher up in the scale than these tutelary deities.

Vaguely known to the common Tibetans by their colored figures upon wayside rocks are such semi-deities as Dolma, in her three hues of green, red, and white, and in the same class may perhaps be placed the eight ladies in whom Colonel Waddell recognizes aboriginal deities adopted *en bloc* by the incoming Buddhists. They are of comely complexion, and certainly do not look as if butter would melt in their mouths. This, however, is not the case if the fearsome tales which were told to me by one of our interpreter lamas have any foundation in fact. They are probably merely the spouses of the male tutelary deities, and derive any importance they may possess from the reflection of their consorts' terrors. A very common figure in wall paintings is the god of wealth. He is represented with a red face, and down his left forearm runs the mongoose by which jewels[1] are fetched from the center of the earth. Conventionally there is a rank and degree for every member of this supernatural company; but even the educated Tibetan is quite willing to allow

[1] Jewels are conventionally represented in Tibetan art like turnips of different colors.

these complications of mythology to be understanded of the priests alone, and it is practically sufficient for the traveler to recognize at sight the four terrible guardian deities of the four quarters of Heaven, Tamdin, so called because of the horse's head and neck which are always to be found in the flames with which his head is crowned, Shin-je, the god of Hell, and Palden-lhamo.

Besides these are the mischievous gods which the lamas use to subjugate the common folk—gods of lesser and local influence. They are malignant sprites with strictly limited powers. They have a thousand different shapes. Some are gnomes or hobgoblins, creeping and peeping among the rocks. Some are gigantic brutes a mile in height, with tiny mouths which prevent them swallowing even the smallest crumb; naturally they suffer from hunger, and in their agonized writhings they are the immediate cause of earthquakes. Others again confine themselves to peaks and passes—the noi-jins [1] are of this class. They do not, however, do much harm to mankind except that of course avalanches are their work, and they seem also to be responsible for breathing out what the Tibetans call *la-druk*—"the poison of the pass." This, of course, is merely the attenuated air which even in the hardiest Tibetan will bring on mountain sickness and nausea. Then there are imps who hide themselves during the day and come out and hold high revels all the night. They ride over the hills and plains on foxback, and if you hear one of these animals yelping in the distance, you may be sure that it is being over-driven and beaten sorely by one of these "lan-de." However, as the only whip which they are allowed to use is the hemlock stalk, the wounds cannot be very severe.

Every village and every district has its own particular god, and it is part of the duties and the emoluments of the lamas to

[1] The first word in Nichi-kang-sang is really Noi-jin, but it is never so pronounced.

instruct travelers (for a moderate fee) as to the deity proper to be invoked at the entrance of each commune. Fevers and diseases of all kinds are caused by minute but malignant sprites. Thus, when you see a rainbow, you may know that these infinitely small folk are sliding down it Iris-like to the water at its foot, and then beware of that place, for ague lies thereby. If one wished to put into a fanciful form the last theories at home about malaria, this would be as pretty a way of telling them as any. They amuse themselves (here, perhaps, we have the missing anopheles) by playing on guitars. Some of these spirits live solely on odors. They inhabit the air, and flit like fairies to and fro. They feed upon any kind of scent or stench, good or bad, and butchers burn offal round their shops in order that by a more overpowering smell than that of their own wares, these spirits may be attracted away. Finally, there are the *shri*, the commonest and perhaps the most dreaded spirits of them all. It is to be noticed that they are chiefly dangerous because they attack children.[1]

These spirits really represent to the common Tibetan peasant all the religious influences that he knows, and for him the elaborate structure of Lamaism is only a shield and defense against a very real terror which waits for him a hundred times a day beside his path and about his bed. For the lamas, on the other hand, there is much in the ritual of their church, and if they do not actually disbelieve in the existence of these malignant spirits, they feel perfectly secure behind the protection af-

[1] Children are very well treated in Tibet. Of course they are left unwashed, and if they have any kind of disease they are left to grow out of it if it is so ordained. The result of these two customs is that skin disease among the children is unpleasantly common. But they are well-fed, never ill-treated, and have, on the whole, a very good time. From the very beginning they were never afraid of our troops, and the first word of Hindustani that was learned by the Tibetans as a whole was the "salaam" which the three-year-old mites ran beside us and squeaked continually. Afterward "salaam" was a well-recognized form for exchanging salutations among their seniors.

forded by their rites and ceremonies. But for them an entirely different set of emotions and motives comes into play. The attitude of the lamas is in its way not less credulous and untaught than is that of the poorer people, but the spur which drives them to religious observances is not the fear of earthly mischief, by whomsoever caused; it is a very different and a very interesting goad of their own making—a blind horror of the consequences of that reincarnation upon which the whole fabric of Lamaism is built. This is a most interesting question.

It is difficult for a Christian to realize how terrible a weapon this article of faith can become. For him this world, good or bad, is at least the last world in which things earthly will affect him. Of the next he knows only by the eye of faith, and the terror inspired by the most material conception of hell is unquestionably mitigated by the fact that the most earnest Christian believer cannot really know what it is that awaits the wicked after death.[1] Indeed, if it were not so, if there were no such modifying circumstance attached to the formulæ of Christianity, life for a devout man could hardly fail to be—if on his own behalf perhaps, certainly on that of his friends—an agony of pain. This, I fancy, it rarely is—at least, on this account. There is another distinction to be remembered. The human mind is notoriously incapable of conceiving the notion of eternity. But the Oriental can throw his conceptions forward in a vastly greater degree than the European. Whether we deny it or not, our conception of time is dominated by our habitual method of measurement. For us a year is not merely a convenient form of expression, it is a hampering unit from which we cannot shake ourselves free. For a Tibetan the life is the unit of repetition, and it must be remembered that a lifetime is an

[1] I am aware of the Roman article "Ignis Inferni est corporeus et ejusdem speciei cum hoc nostro elementari." But this statement is so much qualified by the many supernatural properties claimed for the flame that even a Roman Catholic cannot clearly fix his conception of the means of punishment.

infinitely longer time for a man than are his seventy years. A lama's conception of eternity is, therefore, of a terrible depth compared with ours, and, what is far more, he believes from his earliest days that failure on his part to acquire merit in this world will result not in an instantaneous and irrevocable judgment, after which at least no action of his own can do him good, but in a never-ending repetition in some form of life *in this world* of the very same struggle that he is now enduring. And the ingenuity with which the lamas have conceived the lowest, filthiest and most obscene envelopes in which the sentient and intelligent human mind and soul may, after death, be re-imprisoned, would do credit to a monkish theologian anticipating cases for the canon law. Herein lies the rub of it all.

The means of punishment is ever under his eye. Here is an example. The ordinary man in the country will slip his outer garment down over his shoulders and spend a lazy hour, in the heat of the sun, in detecting and exterminating the almost invisible vermin which inhabit his robe. But to the lama this is forbidden, for there can never be an hour in his skin-tormented life in which he does not remember that his loathsome parasites may have deserved their present fate by carelessness in some point of ritual during their life on earth—nay, that he may even himself be then awaiting the imminent moment in which he shall join their creeping company.

If the reader can seriously understand that this is not a mere theoretical truth, but an actual daily terror to the educated classes in Tibet, he may go some way toward understanding one at least of the myriad terrors which a belief in the theory of reincarnation necessitates. If, then, it is clear that the mental terrors of the Tibetans, whether they are called by the name of superstition or of religion, have provided for the professing Buddhists, high and low alike, an ample sanction for the due observance of the rules of life, it remains to be seen what general effect these rules have upon the life and morals of the inhabitants.

One thing at least is clear in the case of nearly every religion of importance. The influence of religion has in almost every case been used to inculcate not only such virtues as tended to secure the material prosperity of the nation, but such also as make for the permanence of society and the sanitary benefit of the members of the faith. As an example, it is sufficient to point to Islam. Mahomet, whatever his spiritual deficiencies, had a keen and certain eye for the necessities of a nation living in the tropics, surrounded by hostile tribes in every direction. The trend of his regulations is obvious enough. Every line of the Koran breathes of sanitation on earth, and, after death on the field of battle, of the hope of an eternity of pleasure. It is easy to understand why the devotees of so straight a creed have never ebbed from their widest flow. But in Tibet, after a sanction had been obtained, which for strength has been surpassed by nothing elsewhere held out for the admiration or terror of men, we find that the religion thereby enforced is not merely neglectful of the development or even of the continued existence of its professing members, but is even detrimental to it.

Buddhists are, of course, confronted with the same difficulty by which Christians also are faced. Nothing is more characteristic of the two faiths than the repeated injunction to suffer injuries meekly and take no life. I do not propose to discuss so difficult a theological compromise as that at which the Christian nations of the world have arrived in this matter, but it may be pointed out that Buddhists must again and again have found it difficult to adopt even an approximation to this rule of life, surrounded as they are by races to whom such laws were patent foolishness. Christianity in Europe, strong within itself and its friendly co-religionists, is in a different case. In Tibet the sacrosanct character of the country has saved the inhabitants again and again from hostile attack; and this, combined with the necessity of keeping a serf people in an unarmed condition, has made of the Tibetans a quiet race unused to war. I do not for a moment wish to say that the Tibetan was found by us wanting in individual pluck, but it is a long step from the innate courage of an untutored and misled barbarian to the effective self-confidence of the same man properly officered and buoyed up with all the confidence that religion and discipline can instil. Herein lies a characteristic of Buddhism which, from a political point of view, cannot be classed otherwise than as a serious fault. So long as the earth remains divided into races whose first duty is self-preservation, so long, deplorable as it may be from an ideal point of view, a religion which does not also help to protect the nation as well as defend the family, stands little chance of propagating its own good influences. Now, Lamaism has no such tendencies. It does not make of the man a good fighter, and it certainly does not make of him either an intelligent citizen or a good father of a family. I suppose that under these three heads almost every human virtue can be classed. That it does not help him in his civic life is obvious enough, for absolute servitude, mental and physical, is the political result of Lamaism upon its flock. So far as concerns his domestic relations, it seems clear that the polyandry practised in Tibet is not likely to lead to a high standard of morals. The results of the large proportion of women who, in consequence, have no chance of becoming wives, and the complication in family relationships that results from these strange marital customs, might be less harmful if, as happens in Sumatra and on the coasts of Malabar, the women undertook also the government of the country. But they do not; far from it; they have no voice whatever in the government of the country; they still remain merely the toys or the beasts of burden of their male acquaintances. It need not be said that, in the conventional sense of the word, morals are unknown in Tibet.

But it must not be supposed that Tibetans are therefore devoid of characteristics which, after all, may rank as high as the virtues of sterner moralists. They are courteous and hospitable, and so long as they do not feel that their wits are being challenged, their word may be relied upon and their kindliness taken for granted. They are industrious and, as we have seen, capable of extraordinary physical activity. It is true that this activity finds its vent rather in the muscles of the legs than in those of the fingers, but this is only to be expected. They remain dirty, but dirtiness is a merely relative expression. If you must have your daily tub you will not travel far, except on the high roads of this world—I had almost said of England. But far more than this fact, which must be known to a traveler within even a limited radius, there remains the fact that dirt—so far, I mean, as affects the human being—is far less offensive in high and cold altitudes than it would be in London, and it is hardly too much to say that there was no one in the expedition who did not, after a comparatively short time, come to look upon the dirtiness of those who surrounded him with a mere mental shrug of the shoulders.[1] It has been before suggested that the cold of Phari was one of the reasons of its supreme filth, and this is borne out by every experience of Tibet.[2] I do not think that many of even those stalwarts who bathe in the Serpentine on Christmas morning would cut a valiant figure on the Tang la, where the thermometer is sometimes fifty-nine degrees lower than the freezing-point they defy in Hyde Park.

But in other ways than those of ablution, the religion of

[1] It is not uninteresting to remember that for days at a time on the plain of Phari in January and February it was foolhardiness to attempt to wash one's hands before midday. I remember once reaching out, in the early hours of the morning, for an aluminium cup which had had some water in it over-night and thoughtlessly trying to drink from it. My lips stuck to the aluminium, and the skin came away with it. The water was, of course, a block of ice, and the temperature was $-15°$.

[2] Andrada politely remarks "e se bene nelle proprie persone non hanno molto riguardo alla delicatura."

Tibet makes no attempt to enforce healthiness. It is beyond question that the ophthalmia of Tibet is due directly and the prevalence of hare-lip [1] indirectly to the physical inadequacy of the Tibetan race. Pyramidal cataract is another very common disease; this is mainly caused by neglect of ophthalmia, of which the origin is again neglect of cleanliness. These physical deficiencies or deformities might easily be supplemented by a reference to the prevalence of smallpox and similar dirt diseases; but at the moment I wish simply to emphasize the fact that a religion which neither directly nor indirectly encourages cleanliness, is one which requires artificial fostering if it is to remain a power among mankind. That artificial fostering Lamaism has always received. Partly from its inaccessibility, partly from the superstitious veneration with which the country and its god-king have always been regarded, and partly because of the stubborn exclusion of foreign influences, Lamaism has been allowed, if I may use a common phrase, to stew in its own juice until the goodness has entirely departed from it and from the people who are its official ministers. It is difficult at this moment to point to a single recognized and observed ordinance peculiar to Lamaism which is of the slightest use or virtue.

It is odd to remember that an early explorer in this country found, as he thought, every sign of Christianity except the essence of it. In the first half of the seventeenth century Father Andrada, in the following words, reported what he believed to be the truth in this connection:

"L'immagini sono d'oro, & una, che vedemmo in Chaparangue, stana à sedere con le mani alzate e rappresentana una donna, la quale dicono che e Madre di Dio: riconoscono il misterio dell' incarnatione dicendo, che il figlio di Dio si e fatto huomo: tengono di piu il Misterio della Santissima Trinita molto distincto,

[1] Hare-lip is a symptom of a physically under-developed human being.

e dicono, che Dio e trino & uno. Usano di confessarsi, ma solamente in certi casi col suo Lamba Maggiore. Hanno vasi d'acqua benedetta molto politi, da quali pigliano i particolari per tenerla in casa."

There is without doubt a curious resemblance between the ritual of the two great autocratic churches. The arrangements inside the gompa might well be regarded as owing their origin to Christian usages. The sanctuary, especially at night, bears a curious resemblance to that of a Roman Catholic shrine. And the antiphonal chant of the singing men and boys, ranged just as with ourselves in lines, decani and cantoris, the monotoned voice and the rare tinkle of the Sanctus, combined with the genuflexions before the altar, carry on inside the church a merely ritualistic resemblance which adds color to the fanciful imaginings in deeper matters of Father Andrada of the Society of Jesus. Nor does the similarity stop here. The orders within the Church, the relative positions of pope and cardinal, abbot and parish priest, all have their equivalent in Lamaism, and the use of the cross gammadion as the badge of the faith cannot but strike as curious the most careless observer. Indulgences also are freely used, though it must be admitted that in Lamaism these approximate more nearly to the erroneous view of their intention taken by Protestant communities than to their real function in the Roman Church. The Dalai Lama on one occasion somewhat overstepped prudence in this matter. To induce the men of Kams to come down and fight us, he offered them plenary indulgences which should not only absolve them from sins past, but safeguard them against the penalties for sins to come for the next six months. The men of Kams, furnished with this spiritual armor, did not fail to make use of it, and on their return from the Karo la ran riot among the Grand Lama's own temples, looting and sacking everywhere they went.

The practice of blessing small articles distributed among pious pilgrims is, of course, common to all religions in the world. The spiritual brigandage of the lamas finds its counterpart in many other creeds, for the purse of superstition lies at the mercy of the first comer; but it would be unjust not to record in the strongest terms the great radical difference that exists between Lamaism at its best and Christianity at its worst. There has never been absent from the lowest profession of our faith a full recognition of the half-divine character of self-sacrifice for another. Of this Tibetans know nothing. The exact performance of their duties, the daily practice of conventional offices and continual obedience to their Lamaic superiors is for them a means of escape from personal damnation in a form which is more terrible perhaps than any monk-conjured Inferno. For others they do not profess to have even a passing thought.

Now this is a distinction which goes to the very root of the matter. The fact is rarely stated in so many words, but it is the truth that Christianity is daily judged by one standard and by one standard only—its altruism, and this complete absence of carefulness for others, this insistent and fierce desire to save one's own soul, regardless of a brother's, is in itself something that makes foreign to one the best that Lamaism has to offer. Kim's lama may exist to-day; that is, there may be, and indeed I have no hesitation in saying that there are, in Tibet at the present moment members of this priestly caste of whose sanctity and austere detachedness from mundane pleasures there is no doubt, men of kindly heart, unsullied by the world, struggling so far as in them lies to reach back to the great Example beneath the quivering leaves of the pipul tree of Gaya. But apart from the fact that these men are rare indeed, and were they commoner could exert little or no influence upon others, it is to be remembered that there is only one way in which the pious Buddhist can hope to help his fellow-man, and that the very structure of Lamaism decides for him whether or not he is destined to be one of the helpers before a conscious thought moves through his baby brain.

The doctrine of the reincarnation of Bodisats is perhaps a theory which in conception is not unworthy to rank close behind even that great sacrifice upon which Christianity is based. For the Bodisat has earned the right to eternal rest; for him, and he knows it well, there need be no more "whips and scorns of time"; everlasting quietude, so peaceful that the soul does not know even that it is at peace, the Paradise to which all Buddhism stretches out and, as it may, creeps from point to point, all this he has most fully and most fairly won. But having reached the goal of all desire, the Bodisat turns again, with deliberate purpose, to descend into the arena of the world and the flesh, there to help onward along the thorny road some few at least of his fellow-men. And this is not a single choice. He elects so to continue in an eternal cycle, bound down by the cares and pleasures of the flesh, generation after generation, in order that some of his fellow men may have their feet set straighter on the road that leads to the blissful abyss.

But, as I have said, this is no goal for the ordinary man. If he is not born one of the reincarnate saints of Buddhism, he has no further interest in his fellow kind, and even the best of them have no other incentive to action or piety than that of saving themselves, bodily as well as spiritually, from that life which to a Buddhist is the truest eternal punishment. This is the underlying flaw that vitiates the spiritual value of Buddhism, just as it vitiates that of every other religion of the world, except Christianity.[1]

[1] If there is one result of this doctrine of reincarnation more unfortunate than another it is the theory that a man who is physically deficient has deserved his punishment by his behavior in another world. Browning's remark in "Childe Roland,"

"He must be wicked to deserve such pain,"

might have been written—and perhaps should only have been written—by a Buddhist of Tibet.

It cuts at the root of human sympathy. It isolates the individual in his life and in his death, and it says a great deal for the innate beauty of the character we found among the simple Tibetan peasants that they remain kindly, hospitable, and courteous in spite of the debasing influences of the only religion they can know.

CHAPTER XIV

THE RELIEF OF THE MISSION

THE relief of the Mission at Gyantse was the beginning of the last movement in our operations in Tibet. For seven weeks, day after day, the bombardment of the post had continued. It was an ignominious position for the King's Commissioner to be placed in, and there is no doubt that our prestige suffered considerably during this period; still, our own absolute confidence in the successful termination of our operations was perhaps somewhat reflected in Lhasa, for as soon as news came of the advance of the troops from the Chumbi Valley, representatives were actually deputed by the Tsong-du to negotiate in Gyantse. Colonel Younghusband had been ordered to send in to the Tibetan Government a polite ultimatum, the terms of which were simply that unless negotiations were opened with an accredited representative of high standing at Gyantse before the 25th of June, he would be compelled to proceed to Lhasa and there conduct the necessary *pourparlers*. It was generally felt in the post that the India Office had failed to understand that, from an Oriental point of view, it was a display of weakness even to mention the word "negotiation" before the jong, from which we were daily fired upon, had been completely evacuated and full apologies and reparation offered for the insults we had suffered so long. But the orders that Colonel Younghusband received were explicit. Even while the lumps of lead were viciously tearing through the trees of his compound, the British Commissioner despatched the invitation to negotiate which he had been instructed to forward. It was carried into Gyantse, most unwillingly, by a prisoner on the 1st of

June.[1] The Tibetans merely waited till daylight on the following morning and returned it unopened. This action on the part of the Tibetans cleared the issue considerably. It is true that the Colonel took care that the Amban should be informed of the contents of his letter and of the action of the Tibetans in the matter, but the responsibility for renewed hostilities on our own side was at an end. It is possible that the abrupt discourtesy of the Tibetans saved us from a serious dilemma; for had they been more polite the situation, as it then presented itself, still would have demanded a different and a stronger handling than that which might have been suitable in the early days of our dispute with Tibet. Younghusband, however, as was made abundantly clear by the reiterated assurances of Lord Lansdowne, would not have been allowed to depart one iota from the policy as laid down in November. That policy, in fact, the Government adhered to till the end, and we have not yet fully reaped the consequences.

The real answer to the demands of the Commissioner was given in a redoubled bombardment that afternoon. There was nothing more to be done until the arrival of Brigadier-General Macdonald. Covered ways extending out across the plain to Pala, or zigzagging up toward the Gurkha Post or to the bridge across the river at the end of the plantation, made communication between all parts of our lines easy and secure. During these last few days the Tibetans began firing into our position jingal bullets made of pure red-gold copper. The use of this metal seemed an extravagance and probably indicated that the supply of lead was running low. They were pretty little things about as big as a large Tangerine orange, and possibly present an unique use of this metal for such a purpose.

[1] Nothing terrified the prisoners in Chang-lo more effectually or got better work out of them than a threat of release. This man asked that, if he carried out this commission, he might be given a safe conduct to return to captivity in Pala.

On the 6th of June, Colonel Younghusband started from Chang-lo with a strong escort of mounted infantry on a return journey to Chumbi, in order to be within easier communication with the Indian Government; he arrived at Kang-ma in the afternoon of the day, and on the following morning, before light, found the post half surrounded by a party of about 1,000 Tibetans, who had come down overnight from Nyeru by the short cut to Ra-lung. They made a bold attack in the mist of the early dawn, and succeeded in killing one Gurkha who refused to take refuge on their approach. They stampeded the yaks and even managed to come to a hand-to-hand struggle with some of their drivers. But after a moment's delay in rousing the garrison, they were easily beaten off and lost over 100 men; their retreat was turned into a rout by the pursuit of the mounted infantry. Most of them made their escape by the mountain nullahs in all directions, but though they remained in the neighborhood, no further attempt was made to oppose the Commissioner's return journey.

At this time the Tibetans, so far as could be ascertained, had a force of about 10,000 men in or round Gyantse; of these, 6,000 were holding the points of vantage in the immediate neighborhood of Chang-lo. There were 1,500 on the jong itself, a similar number at Tse-chen monastery, 500 at Dongtse, and the remainder were either in the Palkhor choide or in the town and villages hard by. A rumor reached us of a large camp just hidden from us by the curving spur which forms the amphitheater within the sides of which the monastery is built; these men, however, must have abandoned their encampment soon afterward, certainly before the arrival of our troops. Perhaps another 3,000 men may have been distributed along the road between Gyantse plain and the Tsang-po. There was also a report of an additional 2,000 men from Kamba-jong who had been awaiting our advance near the Kala tso. However, in spite of frequent alarms, these last remained a spectral body to the end. The Tibetans were commanded by a Dépen of the name of Chag-pa; associated with him in supreme political authority was an old friend of Kamba-jong days, the Téling Kusho.

The relieving force arrived on the 26th of June, having had an uneventful march from Chumbi. There was, indeed, a rumor that the Tibetans had concentrated not far from Nyeru and a halt was made at Kang-ma, while a small party went out to test the truth of the story. Evidently, however, the Tibetans had got wind of this reconnaissance, for they abandoned their position overnight; all that the reconnoitering party found was the still warm embers of many fires and a few cooking-pots beside them. The march was continued through Red Idol Gorge without incident, but shortly after leaving Sau-gang on the morning of the 26th, Captain O'Connor brought them the news that Né-nyeng, between them and Gyantse, was strongly held. He and I had come out of Gyantse and passed Né-nyeng by a circuitous course; it had been re-fortified and partially rebuilt where necessary. Colonel Brander had demolished its defenses about a month before, as a punishment for an attack upon the mail runners. But he could not, of course, occupy a place so large and so remote from our small garrison, and with a nation skilled in building like the Tibetans, the amount of harm which we could do by the chary use of our small stock of gun-cotton had easily been made good by them.[1] The walls of the monastery here are thirty feet sheer, and the Tibetans had strengthened them by the erection of sangars; Né-nyeng would have been a strong little post had it not been commanded by the hills which half encircled the little plain in which it lies. Colonel Brander on this morning co-operated with Macdonald by leading a small force from Chang-lo up the hills in rear of the town; he had with him two guns and a Maxim. He

[1] It was discovered that for our engineering and military requirements the whole stock of explosives in Calcutta had by this time been exhausted. From Karachi and elsewhere a little could still be obtained.

reached his destination without being detected, and then awaited the action of the General in the plain below, outside the walls. The latter, after reconnoitering the position, sent up a detachment of the 40th Pathans under Colonel Burne; in the face of a heavy but badly aimed fire, these men, supported by a contingent from the 23d Pioneers, succeeded in effecting an entrance by scaling an almost perpendicular buttress of adobe and mud. Forcing their way on, they found the monastery inside to be, as usual, a human rabbit warren. The recesses and underground chambers were innumerable, and it was impossible finally to clear the post of its inhabitants. Many, however, were killed, and a lesson was taught the survivors which the people of Né-nyeng respected till the end of the campaign. After the monastery had been taken a few shots were fired from a stubbornly held house just outside the walls; there were in it about six men, and they, with indomitable pluck, kept up a steady reply to the volleys of rifle bullets which must have penetrated clean through and through the thin adobe walls. Brigadier-General Macdonald then ordered up the ten-pounders and the improved seven-pounders, and 60 or 70 shells were fired into this house; the men, however, escaped, and were seen making their way through the bushes and inclosures to the north of the village. The column then started again, and about ten o'clock that evening the last stragglers arrived in camp near Chang-lo. There was a day's halt and then the clearing of the Gyantse neighborhood began.

On the 28th Macdonald sent a strong force down the valley. The 32d Pioneers were on the right bank of the Nyang chu, the 7th Royal Fusiliers and the 23d Pioneers were on the left bank, and they moved down the wide open space, clearing it from end to end as they advanced. There was no great resistance, and at last the valley of Gobshi, where the carpet factory is, was taken and occupied. Here there was a long pause, and the battalions forming the left wing of the attacking force found themselves unable to proceed to the capture of the most important position of the day. This was the fort-like monastery of Tse-chen, crowning the sharp knife-edged spur which here runs out from the west, separated from the hills only by the narrow strait in which Gobshi lies. The importance of this operation was obvious, for by securing Tse-chen we cut off the main and, indeed, the only remaining road to Gyantse which the Tibetans had in their possession.

It fell to the lot of the Gurkhas and Pathans to capture, by one of the most picturesque actions that is possible to imagine, this western barrier which had for so long screened from our sight the movements of the enemy along the Shigatse road. The *mise en scène* of the fight it would be hard to parallel; the key to the position was a squat, strongly built stone keep, astride the crest between two fortified peaks. Immediately below it, the ascending tiers of white monastery buildings, all well occupied, prevented direct approach. On the other side of the crest, toward Dongtse, the rock descended headlong. By the time the movement began, the sun was low and heavy indigo clouds were coming up from Shigatse. The jagged outline of the spur was clearly silhouetted against the lemon-yellow of the sky, and, after a long wait, one could see very clearly the little figures of the Gurkhas moving along the sky-line from the west.

It was a difficult task; they could only advance in single file along the very teeth of this rocky jaw; again and again they halted; once they signaled down to ask for the guns' help to clear a strongly held sangar across the road; it was instantly given, beautifully timed, and thoroughly effective. Then the little dots crawled forward once more over the evacuated wall. At last, just as the leaders reached the left-hand peak overlooking the jong, a stubborn and somewhat unexpected resistance was encountered. The defenses of the peak were still held, and the curious vision of men hurling down enormous rocks over the steep sides of the peak was etched sharply against the glow of the western sky. It could not, however, last long, and the Gurkhas forced their way through to the main position only to find it empty. Meanwhile, the Pathans had been sent zigzagging up the slope to the north, passing through the houses of the monastery almost unscathed. To the great regret of all his colleagues, Captain Cr'aster was here killed by a matchlock ball fired at point-blank range. The Pathans reached the top almost at the same moment that the Gurkhas descended upon the jong, and the mingled figures of the lanky Pathans and the small Gurkhas were clearly distinguishable one from the other against the red glow of the dying sunset. It was a beautifully executed manœuver, and from first to last it was thrown into prominence in a way which rarely indeed occurs in military operations in these khaki days when gallantry and capacity in the field are rarely to be detected at the distance of a mile.

On the 29th a white flag approached Chang-lo. An armistice was demanded for the purpose of negotiations. Colonel Younghusband consented to a cessation of hostilities until sunset upon the following day, in order to allow time for the arrival of the Tibetan representatives in Gyantse. It was agreed that everything should stand *in statu quo* during this armistice, but Colonel Younghusband made it abundantly clear that no negotiations would be entered upon by the British until the Tibetans had evacuated the jong and had retired from the neighborhood of Gyantse.

It was obvious that General Macdonald's action in clearing the valley was the immediate cause of these overtures. Subsequent events seem to suggest that the whole scheme was a device to gain time; certainly the evacuation of the jong was never contemplated, and the only practical use which the Tibetans made of the armistice was to increase the strength of their fortifications in direct contravention of the terms under which it had been granted. Just before the expiration of this armistice a messenger arrived asking for an extension of time, because the Ta Lama, the chief monk official and one of the four members of the Tibetan Cabinet, could not press on beyond Dongtse till the following day. The armistice, therefore, was extended by Colonel Younghusband till noon on the following day, the 1st of July.

On that day ceremonial visits were paid to Colonel Younghusband, both by the Ta Lama and by the Tongsa Penlop,[1] who had now joined us with a large retinue from Bhutan.

The Tongsa Penlop is the actual ruler of his country, and is a man of considerable capacity. At the present moment the position of Deb Raja or King of Bhutan remains unfilled. It would be the easiest thing in the world for the Tongsa Penlop to have himself elected to the vacant post, but he is of that masterful race of men which prefers to have the power rather than seem to have it. He sees no particular advantage in being nominal as well as actual sovereign of his country, especially as there is a certain penalty of exclusion imposed upon the position of Deb Raja. He is obliged to live the life of a recluse, he is separated from his wife and family, and he rarely has the chance of seeing either them or any other of his acquaintances. The Tongsa Penlop is distinctly of a jovial type, and demurs to these penalties, though at the same time he is not entirely willing to sanction the election of any other Bhutanese chief to the kingship. He is a small man with a powerful but plebeian cast of countenance, and his habit of perpetually wearing a gray uncloven Homburg hat pressed down all round his head to his eyebrows, instead of his official crown, does not increase his dignity. That crown is a very handsome ornament. It is composed of a circle of gold, bearing in four places the representation of a skull, and, Cleopatra-wise, it is arched over the top by a peacock's head in gold and enamel. In theory, he came to act as mediator between ourselves and the Tibetans, but his unblushing and openly admitted preference for the Eng-

[1] The "p" is barely sounded in this name.

lish was not entirely satisfactory even to us. It suggested a biased mind that was likely to interfere with the discharge of his delicate and impartial duties, and it almost became too much when we found that his men, with his full sanction, took advantage of the presence of our troops to harry the land far and wide, and do what looting they could on their own account. On the whole, he was a cheerful, but not a particularly dignified adjunct to the Mission.[1]

He appeared soon after two o'clock, and in the course of a long conversation explained to Colonel Younghusband that the Dalai Lama agreed that further war and bloodshed must be stopped, and had, in a letter written to himself, nominated the delegates for the purpose of negotiating with the invaders. These delegates were the Ta Lama and the Yutok Shapé, both "Kalons" or members of the Cabinet, the Tungyig Chempo, one of the Dalai Lama's personal secretaries, and, with them, representatives of the three great monasteries outside Lhasa. Of these, however, we saw the full number only after a long interval, during which the advance to Lhasa was in progress. In the middle of the discussion the news arrived that the Ta Lama was actually approaching under a flag of truce. He was given a formal reception, and the following day was appointed for the first audience for the purpose of negotiating.

The proceedings of the 2d of July were picturesque enough, but on our side Colonel Younghusband, Mr. White, and Mr. Wilton, in their official dark-blue and gold and silver, made a barely respectable show beside the dazzling brocades of the Tibetan visitors. The room in which the Durbar was held is decorated from end to end, and the rich oil paintings which cover the walls

[1] Looting by his attendants in the Nagartse district caused such widespread distress that the inhabitants came in to us for food. We had been careful to leave enough food in the houses to supply their needs through the winter, and to pay for all we took. The Bhutanese came after and deprived the wretched peasants of grain and money alike.

formed a splendid background for the vivid silks of the delegates, chrome, copper, and scarlet. The Ta Lama himself was arrayed entirely in figured gold silk, except that he wore a golden Chinese silk hat turned up with black velvet. The Tungyig Chempo was similarly dressed; the Tongsa Penlop's attire was a closely woven Bhutanese stripe, gay enough in itself, but sober beside his splendid companions'. He had bare legs and the Homburg hat. He was deferred to by the Tibetans with the utmost respect, and, though the Tungyig Chempo, probably the bitterest hater of England that lives in the world, did most of the talking, the Tongsa Penlop was always consulted before the Ta Lama assented to his young companion's eloquence, or answered a direct question of the Colonel's. Very little was done in the way of business; official compliments were exchanged, a formal re-statement of the Tibetan case was once again elaborately made, and then Colonel Younghusband announced the conditions under which alone negotiations could proceed. The only feature of any importance was that the Tibetans appeared anxious to settle the affair with the English themselves, and no reference of any kind whatever was made to the Chinese.

The visitors went away, and the question immediately became acute, whether or not the first and primary condition laid down by Colonel Younghusband would be conceded. Was the jong going to be evacuated or not? On the 3d of July, the Durbar arranged for twelve o'clock fell through, because of the non-appearance of the Ta Lama. He appeared later on in the day and with old-fashioned courtesy apologized for his lateness, urging as his excuse the infirmities of his advanced age. The Tungyig Chempo made no comments or apologies. This Durbar also ended without any definite assurances on the part of the Tibetans as to the evacuation. They made every attempt to gain time and to postpone the moment when they would have to decide this all-important question. Colonel Younghusband finally gave them till the 5th of July, at twelve o'clock, to come to a decision; if they had not surrendered the fort by that hour, he assured them that the bombardment would instantly be begun, and a state of war would again be declared.

Thus deprived of any chance of further delay, the delegates adopted the fatally easy course of abstention altogether. The time, of course, lapsed, and on the 5th of July, at twelve o'clock, no sign whatever had been made. General Macdonald was slow to begin the work of assault, and, in spite of Colonel Younghusband's warning to the Tibetans, it was not till two o'clock that the first gun was actually fired. Little was done that day, and the Tibetans were allowed ample opportunity to get the women and non-combatants away from the jong. A small party of Pioneers reconnoitered to the west of Gyantse town and came in contact with the enemy who were defending the encircling wall of the monastery, but only a few shots were exchanged. The day passed almost quietly, but there was the bustle of preparation overnight.

There had been rain for some days before, but the night of the 5th was clear and cloudless. The moon did not rise till between two and three in the morning, and as the three columns advanced eastward across the plain to Pala, they had her light low in their eyes, over the jagged outline of the distant hills. They started from the encampment, about two miles west of Chang-lo, at about one o'clock, and making a wide detour, concentrated at the village about three o'clock in the morning. By this time the moon was in strength, and as the men turned again westward to their objective, the masonry of the high, steep rock showed up clearly in its light. The dark masses of gardens and trees at the foot of the jong were to be occupied first by our men.

No time was lost, and twenty minutes' silent march brought the first attacking parties to their positions a few minutes before four. The alarm was given, and a few shots were fired, but it was a wild and badly aimed salvo, and no casualties resulted. Two gardens are thrust forward on either side of the eastern or Lhasan road as it curves round the rock and strikes out into the plain. In the darkness there was some confusion, and an unfortunate incident occurred which resulted in the re-organization of the storming-column into two parties instead of three, as had been originally intended. That under Colonel Campbell and Captain Sheppard occupied the garden to the right, where they were for some time held in check by a spirited fusillade from the housetops before them. At the earliest streak of dawn use was made of "Bubble," who had been brought along with the column and was now used with terrific effect at point-blank range. On the left, Lieutenants Gurdon and Burney, of Major Murray's party, gallantly and successfully carried out their storming work, and four or five explosions cleared the way for a general assault, which rapidly gave us possession of all the houses along the southern foot of the rock. While carrying out this all-important duty, Lieutenant Gurdon, to the deep sorrow of all, met his death. The loss of a man of his caliber was, in itself, a severe blow to the force, and the regret was doubled by the friendly intimacy which acquaintance during two months of investment had necessarily strengthened. He was struck on the head by a piece of stone dislodged by his own charge of gun-cotton, and death was instantaneous.

By this time the entire jong was alarmed, and the defenders joined, as well as they could, in the fray that was raging at the base of the hill, but the steep sides of the rock, and the sangars with which they were crowned, made it difficult for them to bring their full armament to bear. From a distance our guns and Maxims kept a keen look-out for any parties of Tibetans who exposed themselves along the upper slopes or defenses of the rock, and their fire, though persistent, was almost unaimed.

When the sun was fully up, the earlier part of the day's work was done. Resistance had been crushed out along the eastern and southern bases of the rock, and the Gurkhas had succeeded in establishing themselves at a point some fifty feet above the houses just where the direct approach to the main gateway, now barricaded heavily, turns the last corner. They there came in full sight of the Tibetans swarming upon it, and found the *cul de sac* in front of them to be an almost impassable barrier even if undefended.

At this point the day's operations languished; indeed, as much had already been done as the General had intended for the first day. He had effected a lodgment in the houses which commanded the south and east of the rock, and on the west the 32d Pioneers had pushed forward and were holding two or three of the houses to the west of the main street of Gyantse. The jong itself remained untouched, and that it was strongly held a continued fusillade from the upper works still proved clearly enough. These shots were fired chiefly at the two ten-pounders and the new seven-pounder guns, under Easton and Marindin, fifty yards in front of the Gurkha post. Except for these, all sounds of fighting ceased, and the sun blazed down with oppressive heat. The men had been now at work since one in the morning, and were tired out. After a while, the enemy themselves realized that they were only wasting their ammunition, and silence reigned over the entire position. The Tibetans, just before this lull began, concentrated the fire of two small jingals upon our right, where the ten-pounders were placed, on the north of Pala—between that village and the spur of the hills girdling the plain.

About two o'clock Colonel Campbell, to whom had been committed the command of the attacking force, sent across to Pala village, where the General was watching operations with his staff, urgently recommending that an attack should be made at once upon the extreme east of the upper works of the jong. The rock of Gyantse is so steep that it seemed accessible nowhere except along the main approach, which, as has been said, was well defended. Any direct attack here would have been made not only in the teeth of the gun-fire of the Tibetans holding the gate, but also at great danger from the stones rolled down by the enemy from the high bastion which flanked the road. The postern gate descending to the town on the northern side we were not in a position to attack, and we had not, at the moment, sufficient men to press round on that side and hold the houses which commanded this avenue.

But at the point which Colonel Campbell chose there was just a bare possibility of scaling the rock. It was a fearful climb, and the top of it was crowned by a well-made wall flanked by two projecting bastions. At first the General was unwilling to press forward any farther that day, and was in some doubt whether to accede to this request. He determined, however, to be guided by the advice of Colonel Campbell on the spot. At a little past three, a concentrated fire from all points was ordered to be directed upon the wall at the head of this steep climb. The common shell used by the ten-pounders was now employed with terrific effect, and one could see, second by second, a larger ragged hole being torn open in the wall at this point. Clouds of dust rose and slowly drifted away to the west in the slight breeze, and whenever a lull in the cannonade allowed a clear sight, the breach was wider by a yard or two. A constant cataract of dislodged masses of stone and brick fell down the face of the rock below, which here was almost sheer for forty feet. It was not shell only that did this work. Magazine fire was concentrated at the same point, and under this whistling canopy of ball and shell, the Gurkhas were soon seen moving upward and onward from the houses at the base of the rock. It was a moment tense with excitement. Lieutenant Grant was in charge of the storming-party, and soon the first figures appeared over the belt of houses and trees which hem in the rock on this side. Instantly the fire redoubled, and from three points a converging fire hammered and bit upon the wall above their heads.

Absolutely confident in the skill of the gunners, the Gurkhas climbed on. Not a Tibetan was seen on the wall above, but through the loopholes of the bastions a few shots were fired which, at what was becoming almost point-blank range, caused one or two casualties among the little figures clambering upward on their hands and knees. To those who watched from a distance, it seemed as if more loss was being inflicted when again and again one of the escalading force was knocked backward by the masses of stone and brick dislodged by our shells. The steepness was so great that a man who slipped almost necessarily carried away the man below him also. But little by little the advance was made, and conspicuous in front of the small company was Grant, with one Sepoy, who was clearly determined to rival his officer in one of the pluckiest pieces of work ever known on the Indian frontier. The men had now reached a point fifteen or twenty feet below the level of the breach, and it was no longer safe to allow the cannonade to continue. The guns had been tested with a success which almost surpasses belief. The chief danger lay in striking too low and exploding the shells on the outside, but not a single missile had struck the rock at the base of the wall. The marksmanship displayed was astonishing; inferiority in the gun itself was the only real danger to be feared, but these new screw ten-pounders seem to have reached mechanical perfection for all practical purposes.

Just at this moment, when the General himself was issuing orders that the fire should cease, the thin, high pipe of the Gurkha bugler cried again and again from the distant rocks in the four shrill consecutive notes which call for silence, and silence reigned. Then, uncovered by our guns, the last desperate climb was made, and up the higher ridges of an ascent so sheer that it was almost impossible for our men to protect themselves, one or two of these little figures scrambled. They reached at last the crumbling wreckage of the Tibetan wall. Lieutenant Grant and his faithful follower were the first two men over, and the great semi-circle of the watching British force held their breath for a second to see if they would be at once shot down. For the moment it was two men against all the enemy that were in the jong—for the third man slipped and carried away in his fall his immediate successor—and it was patent enough to all of us that if the Tibetans had but reserved their fire and waited in the bastions, they might well have picked off, one by one, each man as his head appeared above the breach.

But hardly a shot was fired. The Tibetans had apparently seen in the cessation of the cannonade only a lucky opportunity for their own escape, and forty or fifty of them were seen crawling and clambering back up and across the rock face to the sangars near the barrack and the postern gate. Here, for a moment, they did indeed turn and use their matchlocks, but these were their last shots. Dividing in a panic into two streams, part made for the postern gate, part for the extreme western cliff of the rock, where a way had been beaten through the wall of the citadel, and two long ropes were hanging down over the precipice below, their ends resting on the shelf a hundred feet beneath. From this coign the Tibetans could, with danger and difficulty, scramble down to the shelter of the houses at the foot of the rock.

Meanwhile, Gurkhas, to the number of some twenty or thirty, had collected at the breach on the east, and slowly moved forward, carefully testing the absence of the enemy from each building and sangar as they went. Some of the Tibetans fled into hiding among the cellars of the rock. The jong, like most

THE CHINESE WALL ACROSS THE AMMO CHU AT CHORTEN KARPO

other Tibetan buildings, is, underground, a labyrinth of dark rooms, tortuous passages, and low storehouses. Into them the remnant of the enemy fled, hidden in the impenetrable obscurity or concealed beneath stacks of dry grass or heaps of rubbish. It was dangerous work getting them out, as most of them still retained their arms. One small party pushed on straight ahead into the citadel, and at last, after meeting with a few spasmodic attempts at resistance, climbed from story to story up the rickety, slippery ladders, to the topmost roof of all, where, attached to a prayer-pole which the Tibetans had but recently put up, the Union Jack was again seen rippling in the strengthening breeze.

It was a gallant and successful finale. The climax was a dramatic scene which those who saw it will never forget. And though it may be invidious to mention them, the names of Lieutenant Grant, Colonel Campbell, and Captain Sheppard should not be forgotten in connection with the exploit. The recapture of the jong in this absolute and final manner had a practical importance which was even greater in a political than in a military sense. The confidence of the Tibetans in the impregnability of their newly strengthened position was perhaps the prime cause of their obstinate refusal to negotiate on equal terms with us. And there is no doubt that if they had been allowed to retain their fort during the negotiations at Chang-lo, it would afterward have been interpreted as evidence of our inferiority. To have defended it successfully for some days, or even to have inflicted heavy loss upon the expedition during its capture, would have encouraged the Tibetans to defend to the utmost every other post of vantage along the route to Lhasa, but, as it was, a lesson of the first importance was taught the Tibetans, and the absence of all opposition henceforward is unquestionably due to the exploits of the gunners and the Gurkhas on this day.

This recapture closed the Gyantse episode of the expedition. It was now imperative that an advance should be made to

Lhasa. Mr. Brodrick cabled from home to that effect, and after twelve days' preparation the General was able to continue the advance. During that time reconnoitering parties were sent out in all directions, Dongtse was occupied, and a small force pushed on down the valley till Pénam jong was reached. This is an imposing structure, but, from a modern point of view, is open to every objection to which the apparent impregnability of Gyantse had been proved to be liable. Enormous stores of grain and tsampa were found in Dongtse. Pénam, too, was found to contain about twelve thousand pounds of butter[1]—a fact which cast some doubt upon the *bona fides* of the monks of the Palkhor Choide in having asked that the fine of twenty-five maunds might be remitted.

Contradictory reports about the Karo la, about the willingness of the monks to fight, about the attitude of the Dalai Lama, and, indeed, about everything connected with the Tibetans and their policy, were now rife. In the course of these days I made a careful inspection of the jong. The scene of the breach itself is a striking illustration of the effect of rapid sustained fire. Hardly a square yard was left untorn by bullet or fragment of shell. The jong itself had not been greatly altered, except by the low sangars and the other improvements introduced by the Tibetans during the days of armistice. Very few of the bigger jingals were found in place, and an explosion which took place during our assault had set fire to, and destroyed, some part of the timbering of the casemates in which they were placed. Two or three of the larger ones were afterward found where the Tibetans had buried them. One of the most extraordinary features of the fight was the amount of casualties suffered by the enemy on the postern descent of the jong. This was regarded

[1] This Tibetan butter is kept in tight cornered leather sacks firmly stitched down. It is strengthened with fat and lard and seems to keep indefinitely, though from the first the smell of it is somewhat rancid.

by us as almost completely protected by the walls which had been built during the investment of Chang-lo, but I counted nearly forty dead men down this descent, fifteen of them lying together in such a way as suggested that one exploding shrapnel shell had accounted for all of them. Our casualties during this week were low indeed. Cr'aster and Gurdon had been killed and, in all, six officers had been wounded slightly, one more seriously. Of the men, we had lost but three killed and twenty-six wounded, of whom, however, two died of their wounds within twenty-four hours.

A rapid interchange of communications ensued between Younghusband and the authorities at Simla and in London, and at last, on the morning of the 14th, the advance to Lhasa was definitely begun.

CHAPTER XV

THE ADVANCE TO LHASA

THE force moved out from Gyantse for the march to Lhasa on the morning of the 14th of July; rain had fallen for two or three days, and the road, especially where it crossed the fertile valley of the Nyang chu, was bad; later on the sharp cut trang by the side of the Nyeru chu afforded a good enough passage. In spite of the drizzling rain, which delayed the march for one hour, and lasted well on into the later hours of the morning, the outlook of the great Gyantse plain was changed for the better indeed since we had seen it last. For more than two months we had been shut up at Chang-lo, and during that time the vegetation and the cultivation of the valley had advanced by leaps and bounds.

Nothing is more vivid in Tibet than the glaring patches of chrome yellow mustard flower at this period. Square cut, and always level, they light up the dark gorges and the river flats, in a way of which it is difficult to give any idea. For the rest, clematis and larkspur are the most noticeable varieties of plants. The rain, which had kept off during the middle of the day, fell again during the evening, and tents were pitched at Ma-lang, in a dull and depressing downpour. The exact position of the camp could be ascertained by a traveler who noticed a curious series of horizontal flaws of vivid pink-stained limestone, crossing through the cliffs on the northern side of the valley, just where the valley flats open out in a sandy, stone-strewn stretch. There are a few ragged and neglected adobe walls here, evidences of a long-abandoned village, and across the stream there is a small group of houses, perhaps four in number. Nothing of any importance occurred, except that the rain, which held off during the night, descended again at six o'clock on the following morning.

To some readers, rain may seem a small matter in these altitudes, and so long at any rate as the march is conducted over hard rock floors, there does not seem much danger of its causing either ill-health or delay. But where speed is of the utmost possible importance, and where the transport has therefore been cut down to its utmost necessary compass, rain is one of the most dangerous accidents which can befall a flying column. Sleeping in wet clothes, night after night, is not after all as dangerous an occupation as dwellers in cities are apt to think. But the real crux is, that where tents must of necessity be used by troops on the march, the difference in sheer weight caused by the saturation of canvas is almost incredible, and where every beast of burden is already loaded with the last additional pound which common sense permits, a steady rain-storm daily will of itself ruin an expedition's mobility, and almost its chances of success. Still there was a sufficient margin, for Bretherton and Macdonald had allowed in their calculations for the extra strain of a long forced march, and therefore had seen to it that comparatively light loads were originally distributed among the beasts. They had also carefully weeded out the weaker animals from the various corps, and had, in consequence, a thoroughly well-equipped transport service for this 150-mile dash. Thus it was that the rain proved no worse than an inconvenience, though only those who have experienced it can know the intolerable dreariness of sitting down on wet earth in pouring rain, waiting hour after hour for the arrival and the pitching of the already soaked tents. My own servants were, perhaps, for this particular work, the best in the Mission camp, and though in all human probability neither of them will ever read this book, I should like to render them a moment's tribute for the constant cheerfulness and alacrity with which they generally managed to set up my tent among the first.[1] After tents had been pitched, and beds screwed together, or valises unrolled, the native servants set to work to prepare the evening meal. This is a business in which the Indian servant stands unrivaled; at a time when there was absolutely no dry thing within a quarter of a mile, except the interior of one's boxes and one's bed—and not always those—these servants will somehow manage to obtain a fire from wood that is demonstrably wet, and when an Indian cook has been given a fire and a couple of stew-pans, there is very little that he cannot perform, within the conventional limits of camp cookery.

There is not very much to report about this second passage by the side of the river to Ra-lung. On the next day, we passed Gobshi, and encamped a quarter of a mile west of Long-ma in a pitiless downpour. On the third day from Gyantse, we reached Ra-lung, and encamped a little way farther along the same plateau upon which Colonel Brander had pitched his tents in the first week in May. The short vegetation was rank, and surprisingly bright, but no trees, of course, were to be seen after we had left behind the willows of Kamo and Long-ma. The mounted infantry, of course, preceded us day after day, and by their reports the length of the next day's journey was decided. On the evening of the 16th, news was brought in

[1] Really good servants are rare indeed on the Eastern Himalayan frontier. One of mine, the syce Tsering, has been taken into the service at the Residency of Sikkim. The other, my bearer, is, I believe, still attached to the Rockville Hotel at Darjeeling. His name is Singh Bir, and if this slight mention of his services to me during this expedition may recommend him to others who wish to obtain a thoroughly capable personal and camp servant, I shall be glad. At a time when other servants were deserting daily in sheer terror, Singh Bir remained steady, though when pressed he admitted his conviction that we were as good as dead men already if we tried to reach Lhasa.

that the wall on the Karo la had been lengthened and reinforced by a parallel wall 200 yards behind it. Great activity on the enemy's part was reported, and the small column prepared for a sharp engagement on the 18th. The composition of the little force may as well be set down here; it consisted of six guns of the 7th Mountain Battery (ten pounders), and two guns of the 30th Mountain Battery (seven pounders), with the Maxim of the Norfolk Regiment. There were also half a company of the 3d Sappers, and the first and second companies of mounted infantry—200 men in all. Of infantry, there were the headquarters and four companies of the Royal Fusiliers; one company of the 23d Pioneers; headquarters and four companies of the 32d Pioneers, headquarters and six companies of the 40th Pathans, and headquarters and six companies of the 8th Gurkhas. There was one section of a British Field Hospital and two and a half sections of a Native Field Hospital, while about 3,000 mules drawn from the 7th, 9th, 10th, and 12th Mule Corps acted as transport. Besides these beasts, there were also about 250 yaks, and two Coolie Corps.

This was a well-equipped and self-contained little force, and there was no doubt whatever, that what Colonel Brander had been able to do with less than 350 men in May, this column could easily achieve in the middle of July. But the peculiar difficulty of forcing the Karo la lies, it will be remembered, in the fact that the wall built by the Tibetans crossed the gorge just where two ice-fields 2,000 feet above the floor of the valley render a turning movement impossible on either side. The wall itself was, as we know, of magnificent proportions, and as we were, from the reason mentioned, almost committed to a direct attack, if full use had been made by the Tibetans of their unique position, we naturally expected that some severe loss on our side was inevitable. We moved on from Ra-lung, on the 17th, to the Plain of Milk.

Over the Gom-tang plain foxes and gazelles moved away as we approached. Fine grass covered the quagmires with which the plain is carpeted, and in between the tussocks, where the clear brown water straggled, tiny pink primulas lay out in the sun; through the gorge below the glaciers of Nichi-kang-sang, we passed young tender nettles and purple flowers, which looked like drooping cowslips; saxifrage was there, with white blossoms, and vetches, both purple and blue. Almost on the same spot as that on which Colonel Brander's force encamped a halt was made for the night. Macdonald himself went out, and from a distance reconnoitered the position. He found that the reports were true, and that a second wall had been built almost across the valley; but this was not all, for the Tibetans had learned the use, for the purpose of defense, of advanced sangars, and these had been built on both sides of the gorge, right up to the crowning cornice from which the Pioneers two months before had, after a terrible climb, dislodged the defenders of the single sangar down below.

But the Tibetans' courage was oozing away. They have since admitted that the fame of our guns was widely spread in all parts of the country, and the fact that the cornice above referred to was held may, perhaps, have been the reason why our opponents did not stay to defend the position they had chosen with such care. For from that cornice they could see over the Karo la itself on to the Plain of Milk, and there they could see with unpleasant plainness the slow accumulations of men, munitions, beasts, and tents which accompanied our march. It is difficult to say when the bulk of the enemy deserted their defenses, but on the following morning, when the first line, composed of four companies of the Fusiliers, flanked on either side by Gurkhas, moved out of camp to the attack, the only position that was still found held by the enemy in any way was the high cliff to which we have repeatedly drawn attention. They indeed fired but one or two shots, but they could no longer be allowed to remain in their position to threaten our advance or our communications, and the Gurkhas were sent up to clear them out. On this occasion, actual fighting took place at a height of nearly 19,000 feet above sea-level. One of the officers engaged on this day told me that the physical strain thereby involved was almost intolerable. On one occasion he had succeeded in hauling himself up to a small plateau, defended at its farther end by a Tibetan sangar; he had with him five men: there was no cover available, so he at once gave the word to charge. The space was not more than thirty yards long, but before they had gone fifteen, the little force of six men, careless of the Tibetan fire, had flung themselves on the ground almost fainting, and in some cases positively sick. But in spite of these obstacles the work was done, and very well done, and slowly the remaining Tibetans, who were for the most part men from Kams, were driven out from their rocky eyries, from which they had kept up an ineffectual fire upon our men, to seek refuge across the bitter white slopes, or in the aquamarine crevasses of the snow-fields behind them. After a long delay the General moved on down the valley, beyond the wall, which was totally undefended, only to find that some of the enemy were still escaping by the steep shale slope, immediately to the east of it. The Pathans were sent up this height, which overlooks the ice-bound tarn to which I have before referred; here, also, many of the Tibetans escaped by plunging boldly across the ice-fields of the glaciers to the south, where none of our men were able to follow them. But the position they had held was cleared, and the column moved on in safety, two miles down the valley beyond Dzara, to the night's halting ground.

Below the Karo la, the aspect of the valley undergoes a marked change; of trees there are still none, and only the appearance of the vivid sky-blue Tibetan poppy distinguishes the flora of this pass. This is beyond question the most striking flower that we saw throughout the entire journey. It was found expanding its crinkling *crêpe-de-chine* silk petals in the sand among the rocks at the Karo la, and it remained with us until we descended to the valley of the Tsang-po. The height varies from five inches to fifteen, the leaves and stalks are covered with sharp, stiff spines, and the color is the most vivid blue I have seen in a plant, far exceeding in strength and purity the forget-me-not, or the germander speedwell.[1] Aconite or, as we know it in England, monkshood, is unfortunately common, and the utmost care was needed to prevent the beasts of the transport from cropping the tall pyramids of gray-purple and gray-green flowers which spring beside the roads and dot the damper levels of the plain. Blue five-inch gentians grow in profusion here, and stout patches of the little sunflower gardeners know as Gerbera Jamesonii.

But the Alpine flora was not yet fully out; the rocks which hem in the valley of the Karo chu dominated the scene. They deserve special mention, for the high bastions and curtains of these thousand-feet precipices run for miles. The little cones of rufous débris which reach upward from the ground to every chimney and channel of the cliff do not detract from the extraordinary abruptness with which these red barriers leap upward to the sky, towering aloft sheer from the stream on either side. The river, too, is worth a note. All morning, after the bitter frost has bound up the leaks of the encircling but invisible glaciers overhead, the stream runs clearly enough, but toward evening the main flow from the eastern side of the ice-fields of Nichi-kang-sang hurls itself into the river like a flood of antimony, so black and leaden are the waters.

In these scenes we pitched our camp for the night, and considered the advance we had made.

[1] I sent roots home to Madresfield and Burwash, but I am afraid nothing has survived.

The official estimate of the importance of this operation seems misleading; it is probable that not more than 200 Tibetans were holding the southern cornice west of the wall, and about the same number tried to escape by the slope of shale to the east.[1] On the next day, the 19th of July, I went down the stream on the right bank with Mr. Claude White, who was taking a series of photographs. The long line of the column crept along under the high scarp to the north. As we rode beside it all day long we saw partridges, foxes, hares, and marmots of a larger kind than those which honeycomb the Phari plain. The flora of the valley itself remains inconspicuous here, for the high cliffs which bind it in prevent the growth of plants; only jagged slate edges and grasses moving in the wind decorated the trang along which the column moved. On the other side of the river we found much dwarf edelweiss and some stumpy reeds. But the rocky formation of the ground was still the most important feature of the scene. At last the Yam-dok tso appeared in the far distance, a blue, quivering line, which one could swear was but a mirage. Soon after that, on turning the corner, Nagartse jong was seen, three miles away across the plain. We moved slowly upon it, and thereupon heard that the Tibetan delegates, who had fled from Gyantse, were ready to meet us, and requested an audience. We went on, and camped a quarter of a mile from the jong on a rising patch of dried ground. The Yam-dok tso and its little sister, the Dumu tso, were glittering in the sun below the unfolding hills.

Twenty years have passed since Ugyen Gyatso, one of the best of our native explorers, corrected, inadequately enough, but to the best of his ability, the traditional delusion as to the shape of the Sacred Lake of Tibet. Traveling in disguise and almost by stealth, his opportunities were limited, but his map of the

[1] This latter number alone was, however, reckoned as 800 by the headquarters staff. I have throughout this book given numbers and facts that seem to me to accord with observations taken during the day, and generally accepted by impartial eye-witnesses.

Yam-dok tso was the first improvement upon D'Anville's 1735 design, and it is probable that to this day the common conception of this strange sheet of water is that originated by the Jesuit-taught Lamas of 1717, and repeated without any great variation by every atlas down to 1884. But the Yam-dok tso is by no means a symmetrical ring of water surrounding a similar ring of land.[1] Lieutenant-Colonel Waddell uses the happy expression "scorpionoid" to describe its real shape.

It is not, perhaps, surprising that our ignorance of what is undoubtedly the most interesting inland sea of Asia should have been so profound. Its claim to sacred isolation has been respected far more than that of Lhasa itself. For every one who has ever set eyes on the Yam-dok tso, four or five foreigners have seen Lhasa. Indeed, we do not certainly know that before this expedition any Europeans except Manning and della Penna's company had ever passed along the margin of the long, narrow waters which mean so much to the superstitious Tibetan peasant, and from Manning, the incurious, we learn little indeed, except that the water is bad—a wholly misleading statement, for though the taste is somewhat alkaline, neither salt nor entirely fresh, it is wholesome and clean.

The Tibetans themselves, besides the name Yam-dok tso, or "High Grazing Lake," use another, "Yu-tso," or the "Turquoise Lake," and it is impossible to describe more exactly the exquisite shade of blue-green which colors the waters under even the most brilliant azure skies. Near inshore the innumerable ripples are, indeed, blown in over the white-sanded floor as colorlessly as wavelets on a South Pacific strand of white coral, but twenty yards out the bottom drops suddenly, and the lake glows deeply with the color from which it takes its name.

On shore, dotted severally over the wide, clean shelf of sand and grit and pebble, a white drift into which one sinks to the

[1] Some maps recognized that this "island" incloses an inner lake.

ankles, great nettles grow rudely, only yielding place to the waving hoof-track—there are no wheels in Tibet—which follows the curve of the beach. Above it, feathery green plants of wormwood, transfixed by the dead brown bents of last year, crowd downward from the steep banks, on which sturdy bushes of barberry and wholesome English dog-rose flourish as well as the crowding weight of "traveler's joy" allows. Over that again, in the clefts of the flawed rocks or between the tussocks of the grassy hill slopes, where the yaks and goats graze, spring prickly poppies, sky-blue and purple, spikes of lemon-yellow foxgloves, and primulas and oxlips of half a dozen shades. Here and there is cultivation, and wherever the stunted barley crop is sown comes, too, a sweeping carpet of forget-me-not, eighteen inches in height, and blue with a virility and strength unknown to the pale myosotis of English ditches. In the grass flats of fine closely cropped turf, which here and there join the foreshore to the hills, is a jetsam of green, low-growing lilies, as yet only starring the ground with their flat leaves, but bearing aloft on their stalks a promise of sturdy flowers to come. Opposite, across the mile-wide strip of water, the steep, green-velveted hills of the "island" rise out of their own reflections, checkered here and there by the vivider green of cultivation or the dull moving contrast of cloud shadows.

There is, perhaps, much excuse for the old belief that the Yam-dok tso is indeed a ring of water, for in the two wide places where the great circle is broken the shaking stretch of black mud is even now more kin to water than to land. It is fair enough to see, with its wastes of green reeds and hummocks of primula-strewn grass, but it is merely a quagmire, across which it is dangerous to walk, and impossible to lead a horse. A hundred years ago it must have been shallows—a thousand years ago, perhaps, the old level betrayed on the hillsides to this day was awash. Forty feet added to the present height of the water would change the shape of the lake curiously indeed.

As it is, perhaps to Tibetan eyes the quagmires that represent the retreating lake have their special value too, for three miles of bog separated the orderly tents of our camp at Nagartse from the thrice-holy buildings of Samding convent, where the reincarnated Dorje Phagmo, or pig-goddess, bears rule over one of the most venerated foundations in the land. While we were in the neighborhood the buildings were deserted, but the occupants will return to find them untouched. Not a turquoise has been taken from their shrines, not a dainty little brass image will be found missing from their inventories; hardly a foot has been allowed to cross the threshold, because unconsciously the lady abbess once nursed in sickness a subject of Queen Victoria. They will never know the reason, and beyond doubt a special miracle will soon be credited to account for the stern prohibition which saved the monastery from violation of any kind.

It may be a vain piece of advice, for there is no doubt that even now as I write Tibet has again been trebly barred against the foreigner; but if by force or fraud another traveler shall find himself at Nagartse, let him go ten miles to the southeast and climb the saddle of the Ta la.

There are few sights in the world like that which is seen from the peak in which the saddle ends to the east. Below lie both the outer and the inner lakes, this following with counter-indentations the in-and-out windings of the other's shore-line. The mass and color of the purple distance is Scotland at her best —Scotland, too, in the slow drift of a slant-woofed raincloud in among the hills. At one's feet the water is like that of the Lake of Geneva. But the tattered outline of the beach, with its projecting lines of needle-rocks, its wide, white, curving sand-pits, its jagged islets, its precipitous spurs, and, above all, the mysterious tarns strung one beyond another into the heart of the hills, all these are the Yam-dok's own, and not another's. If you are lucky, you may see the snowy slopes of To-nang gartered by the waters, and always on the horizon are the everlasting ice-fields of the Himalayas, bitterly ringing with argent the sun and color of the still blue lake. You will not ask for the added glories of a Tibetan sunset; the gray spin and scatter of a rain-threaded after-glow, or the tangled sweep of a thunder-cloud's edge against the blue, will give you all you wish, and you will have seen the finest view in all this strange land.

Here and there along the shore to north and south rise half-ruined castles as harmonious, as inevitable, as everything else in this high enchanted valley. There they stand, foursquare, reddish-brown bulks of native quarrying, crumbling everywhere and sometimes fallen, now laying bare the long abandoned economy of an upper story through a shattered corner, now, lower down, betraying the emptiness of a bastioned courtyard at the base of the tower. The rock-cresses and the saxifrages have long established themselves between the crevices of the stones, and on their old, worn surfaces the somber mosses and vivid orange and black lichens spread themselves in the pure air and sunlight. Overhead, among the beflagged sheaves at the corners of the keep, the ravens hop heavily and cry, and along the shore the seagulls dip and squeal.

Hidden behind Pe-di or Nagartse jong, against the slope of a hill, are a few white, straitened hovels in tiers, banded mysteriously with red and crowned with brown cornices and broken parapets. On the door of each is a kicking swastika in white, and over it a rude daub of ball and crescent.

At the street corners the women stand, one behind another, peeping and curious. Men, too, are there, who stare with eyes that cannot understand. Nowhere in Tibet has our incursion meant less to the people than here, up at the Yam-dok tso, and one feels that in years to come the passing and repassing beside the holy waters of the unending line of our quick-stepping, even-loaded mules and tramping, dust-laden men with light-catching rifle barrels, will only take its proper place among the myriad other and equally mysterious legends that wrap with sanctity the waters of this loveliest of all lakes.

Nagartse is the best-known town between Gyantse and Lhasa; it is placed upon a neck of land, which joins the jong to the hills behind. The rock on which the jong stands must at one time have been lapped by the waters of the lake, but at the present time the Yam-dok tso has retreated so far, that a quashy stretch of vivid green quagmire spreads between the road and the shore. The jong itself is of no great interest. It is the usual ramshackle congeries of unsteady walls and uneven floors, and, except the rooms which were at this time occupied by the Ta Lama, and afterward tenanted by Lieutenant Moody, who was left in command of the post, two small chapels are the only rooms which are still rain-tight. As I have said, Samding lies five miles across the plain—five miles of quaking bog, intersected by the deep-cut channel, whereby part of the waters of the Karo chu are led into the lake. As an illustration of the mistake made by other surveyors in asserting that the lake in the center of the so-called "island" is 500 feet higher than that of the Yam-dok tso itself, it may be mentioned that the Karo chu divides itself just where it debouches into the plain, and one section glides placidly into the waters of each lake. There is, as a matter of fact, not a difference of six feet in the level of the two waters.

One has to go some way to convince oneself that the Dumu tso and the Yam-dok tso are indeed distinct pieces of water. Only a narrow neck of land, a hundred yards in width, divides them, and this obstacle cannot be seen until you approach very near. On the top of a promontory hard by, Mr. Claude White and I took a series of photographs, including a panoramic view of the lakes. These photographic excursions had a special interest of their own.

At the wise discretion of the Indian authorities, the transport of the column was burdened to the extent of three mules' loads, with the large 13 by 10 camera and innumerable plates. Mr. White's servants have become experts in the art of carrying and setting up this cumbersome instrument, and Mr. White himself is a first-rate photographer. Sending the plates back to India was a tedious and uncertain process, but I am glad to hear that from this cause very few plates were broken or lost.

As I have said, the Ta Lama again met us at Nagartse jong, and with him were the Tungyig Chempo and the Chi-kyap Kenpo. Their position had now become desperate; their instructions had been from the beginning to stop our advance to Lhasa. They were given no powers to carry on final negotiations. The views of the Dalai Lama were repeated to them in one unvarying order: "Get these English out of my country again at once." How this was to be done they neither knew nor cared in Lhasa; the unhappy delegates were given no authority to make a concession of any kind, and they knew better than to act in this matter on their own initiative. One would have thought that a man like the Dalai Lama would at last have realized that he was dealing with an opponent who was not in the least impressed by his religious pretensions. He should have realized that at last we were in earnest, and whether he was willing or not to come to any definite arrangement with us at the time, he should at least have sent men armed with sufficient authority for them to open up a discussion, which would soon have shown whether it was wiser or not for the Lamaic hierarchy to make a total surrender of their claims. As it was, these unhappy men, the Ta Lama, the Chi-kyap Kenpo—and here the Yu-tok Shapé also—were reduced to the useless expedient of repeating a parrot-cry without arguments or authority of any kind. It is significant that at one moment during these negotiations of the 19th of July the Ta Lama, poor old man, burst out with an unveiled threat. He said, "If you will make an agreement elsewhere we will observe it; if you will go to Lhasa, and make an agreement there, you may get it signed, but we will not observe it."

During one of these meetings a skirmish took place between Captain Souter and his mounted infantry and the armed retinue of the delegates, who, in defiance of an agreement, were attempting to escape and give information of our numbers and composition. The Tibetan officials were much mortified at the detection of this scheme.

It was increasingly apparent that Nature had come to the assistance of the Tibetans' determination to keep their country isolated in more ways than by mere physical obstacles. How could one carry on negotiations with such men as these; and, in the circumstances in which we found ourselves, how could we insure that relations, even of the friendliest sort, would continue for even a year after our departure? General Macdonald made no secret of his personal opinion that the political ends of the expedition could be better arrived at by instant negotiation, than by carrying out the letter of the orders which had been received by Colonel Younghusband. To this the Colonel could only reply, again and again, that even were he of Macdonald's opinion, which he most emphatically was not, he was still compelled to carry out the definite orders of the Government; he was to go to Lhasa, and make a treaty there. Simla was somewhat amused at this spectacle. As a rule, it is with the utmost difficulty that a political Commissioner can restrain the military aspirations of his escort, and generally has to fall back upon the distinct orders of the Government, to compel his acquiescence in a non-military solution of the difficulties. Here the rôles were reversed with a vengeance.

At Nagartse jong we stayed one day, and on the 21st we moved on by the side of the lake, past the little fishing villages of

Gya, Tu, and Badi,[1] to the Bridge of Good Luck, or Kal-sang Sampa. This bridge has been referred to by Chandra Das, but his description of it as an embankment more than 100 yards long is wholly inaccurate. There is here a small pond of a level somewhat higher than the lake, and divided from it by a neck of land, with one sluice gate cut through it, over which a roughly piled stone causeway, twenty yards long, is carried. It is often believed that the Rong chu runs through from the lake into the Tsang-po. This is not true, for there is a rising fold of ground, about three miles above this pond, which makes a watershed between the two. Yarsig lies a mile west-north-west of the Kal-sang Sampa, but it was not visited except by a few mounted infantry. It is a squalid collection of huts and houses. At the Bridge of Good Luck we encamped after a march of twelve miles from Nagartse. On the next day, the 22d, a short march of five miles brought us to Pe-di jong, which stands prominently on the very edge of the lake, just where the mountainous "island"[2] approaches most nearly to the northern shore. Pe-di jong is not one of the official fortresses belonging to the Tibetan Government, but we did not discover the name of its private owner. Like so many other Tibetan buildings, this one is fast falling to pieces, and one or two small demolitions, necessitated by our subsequent use of the place as a fortified post, will probably hurry on the inevitable ruin of the whole. One threads one's way past slippery stones, through which the nettles rise rankly, skirting a pool of liquid filth by getting close under the wall, then up some slimy, broken steps into the darkness of a passage, wherein you stumble along till a grayish square of light at the farther end shows you where the stairs

[1] The names of these villages as they appear on maps are entirely inaccurate. On my return journey at Nagartse I took pains to find out the real names from Lieutenant Moody (in whose district they all lie), as he had made it his business to find them out from their headmen.

[2] The native name for this peninsula is "Do-rang," or "stony house."

are placed. Tibetan staircases are no ordinary things. The angle at which the stairs are placed is somewhat steeper than that at which an English ladder is ordinarily used; the treads are long and very narrow pieces of poplar wood, either worn into a slant, at which no foothold is possible, or tipped with iron, upon which the nails in one's boots slide mercilessly. The only handrail is a highly polished wooden willow-pole, which slants from the lowest step at an angle more perpendicular than that of the steps. They are more difficult to come down than to go up, and this is saying a good deal. On the third story of Pe-di jong are the living rooms, the only really habitable ones in the place; the rest of the building keeps the rain out, and that is about all. Here, however, Lieutenant Dalmahoy, with a company of Pathans, was left in charge, while on the 23d the force moved to their camping-ground, a mile short of the little village of Trama-lung. From this point the road over the Kamba la rises abruptly to the north; the road beside the lake presents no very interesting features, and two things alone arrested our attention. The first was a curious example of the cup marks which indented an artificially smoothed surface at shoulder height above the road, just where it doubled a rocky spur. These cup marks are referred to later as a characteristic of Lhasa also. A mile and a half further on we found that the Tibetans had built a wall across the road, choosing its position with some skill. The sharp-cut fresh turfs with which they had crowned the wall and a little house, just where it terminated over the lake, proved that it had not been built for long. We arrived at our camping-ground before twelve o'clock, and I went up to the summit of the hills which divide the Yam-dok tso from the basin of the Tsang-po in order that I might, if possible, catch the first glimpse of the Potala.

Kawa-guchi, the Japanese traveler, reported that from the Kamba la he had seen the palace, and the villagers of Trama-lung proudly claim for this spot the first sight of the Forbidden City.

There can be no question of the direction in which, if at all, this first glimpse of Lhasa is to be obtained. Looking carefully through glasses, I saw a minute, symmetrically shaped dot of gray, just visible over one of the intervening spurs. I do not know to this day whether that were really Lhasa or not. It was certainly in the exact position, but it was entirely impossible from that distance for a stranger to be sure, even had the day remained clear. Afterward, nothing was certainly distinguishable. There were so many subsequent misstatements made as to the identity of Potala, that I would not do more than suggest to another traveler, following upon our track upon a clearer day, that it may be worth while to substantiate or refute the claims of the villagers of Trama-lung.

The remainder of the day was spent by a good many officers in fishing. At Yarsig, on the evening of the 21st, the waters of the lake were found to be full of fish, which had rashly crowded into the shallows by the shore, and were easily captured by the hand. Major Iggulden and Mr. Vernon Magniac were the most industrious fishermen of the force, and it may be news to some of the disciples of Izaak Walton that in Lhasa these two men habitually caught from 60 to 70 fish in an afternoon. These fish were generally called trout, but this was merely a convenient misnomer. The essential feature of a member of the family of Salmonidæ is the presence of dorsal fins, which were wanting in these trout-like fish. The presence of minute barbels also disproved their claim to belong to the salmon tribe. In color they varied. Some were of glittering silver, heavily mottled with splashes of rich blue-black; others were of a quieter pattern of greenish and yellowish gray. Their bones are bifurcated and innumerable, and the flesh was consequently hardly worth the trouble of eating.

On the 24th, we crossed the Kamba la, and descended 3,000 feet into the valley of the Tsang-po. There are two passes over this cup edge of the Yam-dok tso. The other, the Nabso la, was used by the troops on their return journey. There is not much to choose between them, but the ascent of the Kamba la from the Tsang-po is terribly severe, the entire rise of 3,000 feet being accomplished in about five miles. From a halting place about 200 feet before the pass is reached from the Yam-dok tso, a wide view can be had of the lake from east to west, and I suppose that few travelers, even the most unobservant, have ever reached this last point without halting to look at the magnificent scene at their feet. Trama-lung lies below one in a deep, short valley of which the head rests against the barrier of the Kamba la itself. It is a plainly built little cluster of flat roofs, bearing every sign of poverty and insignificance. To right and left of it sweeps the blue of the lake, which had deepened in intensity with every step upward that we took. Once on the other side of the pass, the cultivated fields of the Tsang-po valley stretch out beneath the traveler on either side of the sandy river-bed, intersected with its innumerable channels. The ferry by which we had to cross at Chak-sam was not now visible, but we could see a hide boat being slowly manœuvered across the yellow waters of the great river. The road to Shigatse branches off at the very level of the pass, and curves by a very slight gradient to the west; its course is invisible in a quarter of a mile behind a projecting spur.

The track to the Tsang-po descends abruptly to the little village of Kamba-partsi, where, compared with those we had left behind, the greater prosperity and comfort of the buildings on the shores of the Tsang-po and its tributaries were at once apparent. Poplars, willows, and large thorn trees dotted the lower slopes of the valley, and there were several cultivated fields, lying immediately round the hamlet.

As we came down the slope of the valley we could see more closely the body of the great river which barred our passage. It was a fast-running yellow stream, swirling even then with deep-toned irritation round the jutting rocky promontories of the shore, and tearing away at the crumbling cliffs of sand within which it was confined. The volume of water, even at this date, was considerable, for though narrow the main channel is very deep. But it was not so much the existing state of the river that gave us some prospect of anxiety, as its obvious liability to an enormous expansion; the sand islets and eyots that parceled out the waters of the Tsang-po were bare of vegetation, and it was easy to see that in a few weeks' time they would be swept a foot deep by the swollen waters, which even then were gathering strength, far to the west, beside Lake Mansarowar.

Kamba-partsi is a prettily placed little village under trees of considerable age; the sentinel is a double-willow of great antiquity, writhen into the shape of an 8, keeping guard at the entrance of the hamlet. Lower down, divided from the water's edge by a level strip of sand, was a rectangular plantation of willow-trees with a low wall running round it. Here the camps of the Mission and of the headquarters of the escort were pitched; outside there is a more than usually elaborate camping-ground for their Holinesses when traveling. The altar and reredos are of adobe, set up facing the ravine down which the Kamba la descent drops, with its sanctuary in front, carpeted with a neat cobble of white quartzite, edged with raw splinters of basalt. Inside the inclosure the most striking things were the cockchafers; I have never seen so many cockchafers in my life; they lay in thousands, either dying on the ground beneath the trees, or clinging, like diseased growths of pink and gray, to the branches of the pollarded willows above. When they flew there was a flash of pink underwing, and the sudden extinction of the color when they alighted on the self-tinted ground made their disappearance almost uncanny. They buzz round and round the trees during the sunset, with the note of a thrashing machine, and make a clumsy little holocaust of themselves in the cooking fires and, alas! in the cooking pots as well. Here General Macdonald, who had been sick for a long time, was taken seriously ill during the afternoon, but he pulled himself together for an advance on the following day.

Sunset over the Tsang-po from Kamba-partsi was a magnificent sight. The valley was closed in to the west by two snow-capped mountains, the last northern promontories of the Nichi-kang-sang range. Below them, as the orange of the sky deepened, the conformation of the rock was lost in a veil of purple gloom, and the river ran from beneath their feet, a perfect mirror of the deepening colors of the west. Muddy water will always give you a truer reflected color than a clear running stream, for the same reason, no doubt, which enables a black-backed piece of glass to be used as a mirror. Anyhow, it is so, and the brilliancy of the Tsang-po might almost have been taken for a gash clean through the earth, meeting the sunset again beneath the distant barriers of rock, for this vivid light on the face of the water ceased with a sharp line at a sudden rapid half a mile away, and became just a swirling river. Here the water became indistinguishable from the land until it was almost at our feet, and then it had lost almost all the charm of water, except its sound and motion. The snow on the hills turned complementary colors in contrast to the deepening carmine behind them. Clouds, touched with orange-fire, ranked themselves a mile above the earth, forming a glowing canopy all the way to where the sun was setting. In England the effect of a sunset is generally of two dimensions only; at its best it does but rear itself up against the sky, a blazing curtain of dissolving color. But in these intensely clear altitudes, the fact can be well perceived that the sunset effect is really created by serried ranks of the lower edges of illuminated clouds, each hanging motionless by an immutable barometric law, at the same appointed height. They are, in fact, like the flies and floats of a theater sky. J. W.

M. Turner, probably as a result of his travels, was the first painter to recognize this atmospheric truth. At last, as one watched, the crimson footlights of the west were turned down, and one found that half a hundred stars were already blinking whitely in the gray-blue depths.

On the next day we went on to Chak-sam ferry, a distance of about six miles. The valley of the Tsang-po is different indeed from what one had been given to expect. Instead of a full and racing sweep of water, cutting its way, like the southern Himalayan streams, through a densely forested gorge, the yellow volume, almost without a ripple, swerves and divides itself across and between a mile-wide stretch of sand, bordered on either side by a broad strip of well-cultivated fields of barley, wheat, and peas. Here and there are openings between the hills dotted with the white and blue of the surrounding houses, and encroached upon by the wastes of billowy sand, which the tide at first, and the wind afterward, have banked and shelved against the base of the hills.[1] Beside the cool lush greenery of the road, the whitening barley fields were edged with rank growths of thistles and burdock, and "black-veined whites" and "orange-tips" fluttered over the opened dog-roses. Where the vegetation ceased, the arid waste of triturated granite running up to the mountain buttresses is dotted with a kind of mimosa which seems rarely to obtain a height of more than two or three feet, but is useful in binding together the shifting sands of the river bank.

Chak-sam is so called because of the iron bridge which was made many years ago to span the deepest and narrowest channel of the river; the chains are all that now remain, but these are magnificent enough to deserve a moment's notice. Prince

[1] Mr. Hayden, the geologist of the Mission, is of opinion that these enormous blankets of sand are due to the local disintegration of the hillsides, and that they remain *in situ* till they fall or are blown away.

Tang-tong [1] put up this bridge in the fifteenth century. It consists of four heavy chains of links, which at a guess, I should say, were each eight inches in length; the span of the bridge is, approximately, 200 feet, and in mid-stream it descends upon an island rock, covered with thick willows, which in the dry season stands on the edge of the permanent river-bed; from this rock to the northern shore a stone causeway runs slant-wise, which for more than half the year is free of water, but now the river made a weir of it, pouring over it in a dirty, clouded stream, and you might hear the roar of it at the ferry half a mile up the river. At the shore end the abutments and anchorages rise at the foot of a tidy-looking monastery, set among the steep rocks of the basalt hill, here cut and painted with raw images in white and blue, daubed with raddle, crested with chortens, and flagged sheaves of carving innumerable with the inevitable *om mani padme hum.* The bridge itself is gone, only the chains remain; slings and footway alike have disappeared, but there is scarcely a sign of rust or clogging to be seen on the iron.

The Tibetans themselves have long been accustomed to rely upon the ferry. In their retreat from their southern and western positions, they had neglected to destroy the two ferry-boats, to our great advantage. It is difficult to imagine what we should have done without them. Each of these great arks is an oblong lighter, forty feet by twelve, with a four-foot freeboard, and a quaintly carved horse's head at the bows. The transport of the troops across the river was enormously hastened by the device used by Captain Sheppard. He turned these two boats into swinging bridges, by the aid of stout ropes running on a

[1] This learned pillar of the Church was long averse to encountering the pitfalls and delusions of the flesh. He therefore remained for sixty years *in gremio matris* cogitating upon the vanity of worldly things. Eventually it occurred to him that his inaction was causing serious inconvenience to another, and he consented to be born. The whole story is a bitter but unconscious satire upon the selfishness of Lamaism.

carrier backward and forward along a steel wire hawser, which he here threw across the 120 yards of whirling and swollen brown water. In this way the interminable waste of time, caused by the necessary drift down stream of the big boats in their passages across, was prevented, and what had previously taken an hour—with occasional intervals of three hours, during which the boat had lumbered two miles down stream, and had to be painfully retrieved and towed back—now took but twenty minutes for the return journey. The mules were swum across under Captain Moore's charge, half a mile higher up stream.

On the second day the force suffered the greatest loss which overtook them throughout the entire expedition. General Macdonald, remembering his Central African experiences, had provided rafts, supported at either end by Berthon boats; these carried ten men and their kits at a time, but owing to the velocity of the current, which caused a series of whirlpools, gyrating in a curve from the corner of the bluff under cover of which the ferry-boats came to rest, more freeboard was here needed than in still water, and after the sixth or seventh passage had been hazardously but safely performed, the nose of one of the boats was caught in the stream, and before one could have believed it possible, the whole raft, water-logged, with its occupants clinging to it, was floating helplessly down stream. All except two men caught hold of the raft and were ultimately saved; but one of these two was no less important an officer than Major Bretherton; he was a good swimmer, and made one or two desperate efforts to keep from going under: he was seen to go down twice, and from that moment he was never seen again. It is a difficult thing adequately to assess the loss caused by his death. The department of which he was the brilliant chief was that upon which the success of this expedition almost wholly depended, for supply and transport were as necessary to the force as the very air they breathed. Cool, capable, and untiring, a thorough believer in the necessity for personal superintendence of the smallest detail, Major Bretherton's thorough grasp of every department of supply, and his unfailing willingness to help the individual, had long before earned for him the admiration of every one and the personal gratitude of most men. Only a few minutes before I had met him walking up to the landing-stage. I asked him where he was going, and he told me that he was going to make a search for food-stuffs in the little house which could be seen a mile away on the other side of the river. It seemed to me, under the circumstances, a needless exertion for the chief of so large and so well-managed a department. He only answered, with that curious half-stammer with which he often began a sentence, "They always miss a few maunds if one is not there oneself; I had better go over." This was the last I saw of him, and I should like to record here my deep personal regret at the death of one whom I had come to admire and like most unfeignedly. In him was lost the most brilliant of the younger service-corps chiefs in the Indian army.

CHAPTER XVI

THE LAST STAGE

ON the third day after our arrival at Chak-sam Colonel Younghusband and the Mission crossed the river, and took up their abode in the garden of a little house of which the local name is Pome-tse. The work of transporting the entire force across the river occupied a week, and during that time I made one or two expeditions to interesting points beside the river. On the 28th of July, O'Connor and I rode out to Ta-ka-re, about two and a half miles along the north bank of the river to the west; the road ran through barley fields dotted with forget-me-nots and plantations of willows and poplars until we came in sight of the large pyramidal chorten which stands just outside the village of Tse-gang-tse. This is a curious structure built up of receding tiers and crowned with a large drum. No one was able to tell us anything about its origin, but it is interesting because of a slight resemblance to the Pyramid of Saqqara.[1] It is called a Pum-ba locally, and I noticed that in the innumerable reiterations of *om mani padme hum* round the structure the conventional order of colors was varied in one particular, the second syllable being a dull apricot instead of green. Otherwise it was normal.

We rode on under the white wall of the village, passing a splendid walnut-tree standing just where a ravine flawed with

[1] One of the interesting things in Tibet is the frequency with which one may see in almost, if not entirely, contemporary history the existence and development of processes and ideas which in other parts of the world are almost prehistoric.

slowly trickling water afforded shelter to a rich profusion of flowers and ferns. A mile on we mounted a short-cut over a little spar of quartzite, which here deflects the road, and came down within sight of two extensive monasteries built up against the rock. At their feet was a walled-in inclosure, half-swampy, half-firm grass, in which were growing some of the most enormous willow trunks I have ever seen. These trees must be of immense age. Without seeing them, it is difficult to form an idea of the unusual size which these writhing and gnarled monsters attain. We visited the Ta-ka-re gompa, the entrance of which immediately faces the willow grove, and were well received by the little company of monks. It is the smaller of the two monasteries, and does not perhaps differ very much in construction or in ornamentation from the usual Tibetan lamasery. The Umzi, or manager, took us over the buildings. They are not of very great interest, the place being somewhat overshadowed by the reincarnate divinity of Jang-kor-yang-tse next door, but there was one particularly interesting room, in which were collected some of the older or disused objects of ritual in the monastery. These they were perfectly willing to sell, and we both secured two or three objects. In front of the seat of the Kenpo or Abbot was a very handsome skull bowl set in turquoise-ornamented silver, the finest, I think, that I ever saw in Tibet; near by was a European looking-glass which the Tibetans regarded with especial pride; and there was also one of the cinerary chortens in which the mortal remains of only reincarnate lamas are allowed to be preserved. This was of silver.

It is never entirely satisfactory, as no doubt the reader will have discovered by this time, to ask a Tibetan too closely as to the meaning of some of the stranger sights in a gompa; our own lama confessed himself beaten when he was asked what was the meaning of some objects arranged in the innermost sanctuary here behind a pane of glass of considerable size. In this, the most sacred position in the temple, it was certainly surprising to find, after pulling aside the dirty and greasy katags which hung over the front of the shrine, three irregularly shaped pieces of common rock and a wasps' nest. All four were crowned with gold and turquoise, and from the interior of each crown rose a torma, a marvel of dexterity and patience. We had tea with the Umzi, the Abbot being absent in Lhasa, and came back in the company of two cheerful lamas, who were carrying our purchases. We arrived back at Pome-tse, or North Camp as it is called on the military maps, in time to join the Mission mess at dinner out in the open air under the trees. I doubt whether very many people have ever before deliberately chosen to dine out of doors at an altitude of 12,600 feet.

On the 30th of July, as the passage of the river was still delaying us, O'Connor and I went out again on the same road to pay a visit to the larger monastery next door, Jang-kor-yang-tse. This is a far more pretentious establishment than its neighbor; as I have said, it boasts the proud distinction of having an incarnation of its own, and we were lucky enough to find his Saintship at home. We went up to an open courtyard in front of the main entrance of the gompa. Immediately facing this was the usual frescoed arcade and overhead a great siris tree, a species of acacia, which the Tibetans call *yom-bor*.[1] Inlaid in the courtyard in front of the temple was a boldly designed swastika. The bosses and ring-plates of the doors of the gompa were of the finest filigree work, and the design and finish of the great key of iron and inlaid silver was remarkably good; it was

[1] The last syllable of this name contains an unusual sound in Tibetan speech; it is a deep and prolonged note, and is found again in such words as Jo, the great golden idol of Lhasa, and in towo, meaning "terrible." I have, perhaps, been inconsistent in rendering the sound in the former word by a single letter and doubling it in the latter, but "towo" is so constantly used by writers upon Tibetan ecclesiology that I have preferred not to alter it.

about 18 inches in length. Inside the temple one noticed particularly the profusion of hanging katags and gyan-tsen. The place resembled an alley in a Chinese market, so obscured was it with hanging cloths. Among them I noticed a singularly fine tang-ka, the finest in workmanship that I had seen.[1] In a wide and high dark court behind it, divided in two by a half-floor, was sitting a gigantic Buddha. He was probably made of clay, but the surface was finely finished and gilded as successfully as if it had been made of copper. Over the huge shoulders costly silks were thrown, and it was singularly effective to encounter the impassive gaze of those inscrutable eyes gleaming out in sharp relief against the surrounding darkness; the entire image was, perhaps, thirty feet in height; in some respects it resembled the inclosed Buddhas of Japan, and, perhaps, by sheer contrast, reminded one of that most effective image in the world, the great bronze Buddha in the sun among the pine-trees of Kama-kura. After making a thorough inspection of all the buildings, we leaned over the parapet of the flat roof beneath a gilded cupola and let our eyes run up and down the river, which here is seen more splendidly than from any other place.

We had tea with the Lama. He told us the story of his life, and it is not without interest. He said that it was a long time before his sanctity was recognized. He spoke in a low, sweet voice, and I am not certain that there was not a tinkle of humor to be detected now and then. His earliest remembrances were unfortunate; he was then as a child attached to Pénam monastery, twenty miles west of Gyantse, and his life was made so miserable there by the brutality of the lamas that, while still a

[1] The size of these tang-kas varies greatly, but few are more than eight feet in length; they are generally protected by one, two, or even three curtains of thin tussore silk, the outer one being of curious but characteristic coloring. In rainbow tints, merging imperceptibly one into another, some of the "eight sacred emblems" are mistily indicated.

THE MOUNTAINS THAT SURROUND LHASA
Viewed from the Jong-kor-yangtse

CHAK-SAM MONASTERY
Showing the cable for the ferryboat to the opposite bank of the river

boy, he ran away and went to Lhasa. He must have been a boy of character and audacity, for such insubordination as that is almost inconceivable in a lamaic acolyte. Arrived in Lhasa, he attached himself to a doctor, and after some years of apprenticeship he came to practise in this village of Jang-kor-yang-tse. Three years ago, tired of the small scope which this little village afforded him in his profession, he had intended to return to Lhasa. The lamas, with whom he was on the friendliest terms, were in despair at the thought of losing his services. In Tibet there are ways and means unknown to western nations, and as the succession of incarnations in this gompa happened then to be in abeyance, a hurried despatch was sent to Lhasa, with the result that our friend was, to his own intense amazement, hailed, in his twenty-fourth year, as the long-lost successor of the Bodisats of Jang-kor-yang-tse. Sitting cross-legged on his little dais in front of the square latticed windows which kept the bright heads of hollyhocks from falling into the room, he told us his story, and I confess I wondered at the time whether he were not, even then, yearning for his old life of less sanctity and greater freedom. He explained that he had intended to pay a visit of courtesy to Colonel Younghusband, but had been restrained through fear of the Lhasan Government. Turning to O'Connor, he asked, with unaffected simplicity, "Tell me, under which government am I? Are the English or the Tibetans lords of this valley?"

During the interview a dozen of the senior lamas crowded the end of the room, and two of the younger ones busied themselves hospitably by filling our tea-cups after every draught. O'Connor assured them they had nothing to fear from our troops so long as they attended to their religious duties; he explained to them exactly what we needed and were ready to pay for in the matter of provisions, and to each succeeding sentence the listening crowd of monks bent forward with hands upon their knees, and chorused the one cry of obedience and respect in Tibet, "La-lis, la-lis."

We returned to Pome-tse, watching the blue smoke drifting across the river from the now dwindling encampment by Chak-sam. There was but one more day of waiting, and that I spent in reading lazily under the shadow of the trees in a plantation two hundred yards up the river-flat from the house. The place was like an English wood, except that big water-worn boulders emerged here and there through the grass. Forget-me-not and hemlock bloomed carelessly under the tall poplars, and homely "meadow-browns" spread their wings upon the dark-blue dead nettles; all round, outside the walls containing this little wood, the wheat fields rustled silkily in the breeze, and the hum of bees murmured drowsily in the pauses of the ringdoves' urgent suggestions that two cows might as well be taken as one. It was strangely English, and from that time till I once more regained the high grazing-grounds of the Lake, I became more and more used to finding the least expected sights and sounds of England among these lonely uplands. Wild carrots grew in rank profusion, looking up to the white undersides of the leaves of the poplars, and round a raw country altar—Pan's very own, all sods and turf—Michaelmas daisies starred the grass. The roofs of a white farm-house a quarter of a mile away rose *en échelon* through the foliage. The house was made of the usual sun-dried brick, for it is not possible to use the round alluvial pebbles of the spot for more responsible work than a field boundary; their shape denies them stability and cement is unknown. Patches of golden light checkered the turf under the willows, and here and there a tiny five-starred blue passion-flower climbed the stouter plants, and a common "blue" chased his dowdy spouse, zigzagging a foot above the grass.

This quiet little elysium was owned by the Jong-pen of Nagartse, a man of great importance and brutality. Upon our arrival all his servants and serfs implored us as one man to take this opportunity of cutting off his head.

We set off again on the 31st, and welcome indeed were the cheery war-cries of the Sikhs and Gurkhas as they set their feet upon the road again.[1] We moved on to the east along the northern bank of the Tsang-po, threading through fields of grain and sometimes through villages nestling among trees. Far across the river in the long distances there were heaped up sand-drifts, nine hundred feet high, against the mountain precipices, and now and then a slow dust rose from them toward a white silver slant of threaded rain, caught like a skein of spun silk in front of the heavy indigo clouds. Ten minutes later the storm would come to us also, but passed as suddenly as it came.

Here the signs which befit the last stages of a pilgrim's road were beginning to increase in number and in beauty. It was not merely that, as always in Tibet, one found beside a village, at a cleft in the rock-side, at the crossing of a stream, on every place which looks a likely home of devils, a rain-washed string of flags, or a gaily decked brush of ten-foot willow sprigs, but from here until its end, besides the great Buddhas cut deep into the point of each spur, round or over which it drives its stony course, innumerable mantras are cut in light relief upon every offering-stone along the road. "*Om mani padme hum*"; the monotonous ejaculation seemed to cry out from rock to rock—"This is the way of salvation; by this alone shall you escape from earth.[2]

[1] The Sikhs' war-cry, raised in chorus by the entire company as the first foot is advanced, is as follows:—Wa guru ji ka khalsa! Seri wa guru ji ki futti! Sut seri akhal! (*Hail, God of the liberated! Victory to the holy ones! My body is to thee, O God!*)

The Gurkhas' adjuration is:—Seri Ghurkh' Nath baba ki jai. (*In the name of our holy father Ghurkh' Nath, victory!*)

[2] An occasional sequence of colors for the six syllables of this mantra at Chusul, and later on also at Ne-tang, is white, blue, yellow, green, red, and black; but from continuous notes I am able to say that white, green, yellow,

Before we reached the point which hides Chusul, Gonkar jong, where the Sinchen Lama was done to death, was conspicuous on a little bluff five or six miles down stream, and the sight of it brought tears to the eyes of the Shebdung Lama. However, we came no nearer to it. Our course turned off to the left here, and we soon passed through the little green-clad village of Chusul. Here the Ta Lama awaited the arrival of Colonel Younghusband, who, with ever-ready patience, granted him another, but, of course, a fruitless interview.

Chusul is dominated by two peaks on which the ruins of two strong forts may be still seen. In a cavern of the mountain-side beyond the inner peak it is said that the Tibetans condemned to death were walled in until such time as the scorpions which infest the spot had done their deadly work. This is probably wholly untrue, though we did, indeed, notice scorpions more than once in this part of our route. Thence we moved on up the valley of the Kyi chu, leaving behind us the Tsang-po sliding heavily to the south toward the defile where its waters vanished from our sight. The point of land which runs out between the two rivers was explored by Mr. Magniac, and found to be an impassable morass. The road keeps on at the foot of the hills, but before these are reached a wide plain is crossed through which a deeply cut canal carries off the snow waters from the mountains on the left. A monastery stands near the mouth of a dry and unfertile valley. At Tashi-tse, a mile or two short of Tse-pe-nang, we halted for the night, just underneath a detached fort-crowned pinnacle of rock thrust out from the mountain-side. The ground swarmed with little black beetles, spotted with white and red like a Tibetan domino. On the 1st of August, the eight-mile-long line set out betimes for the last stretch of the journey which was to be still uncheered by the sight of Potala's golden roofs; the distance to be

blue, red, and indigo (rarely black or purplish blue) is beyond comparison the commonest sequence of color throughout the country.

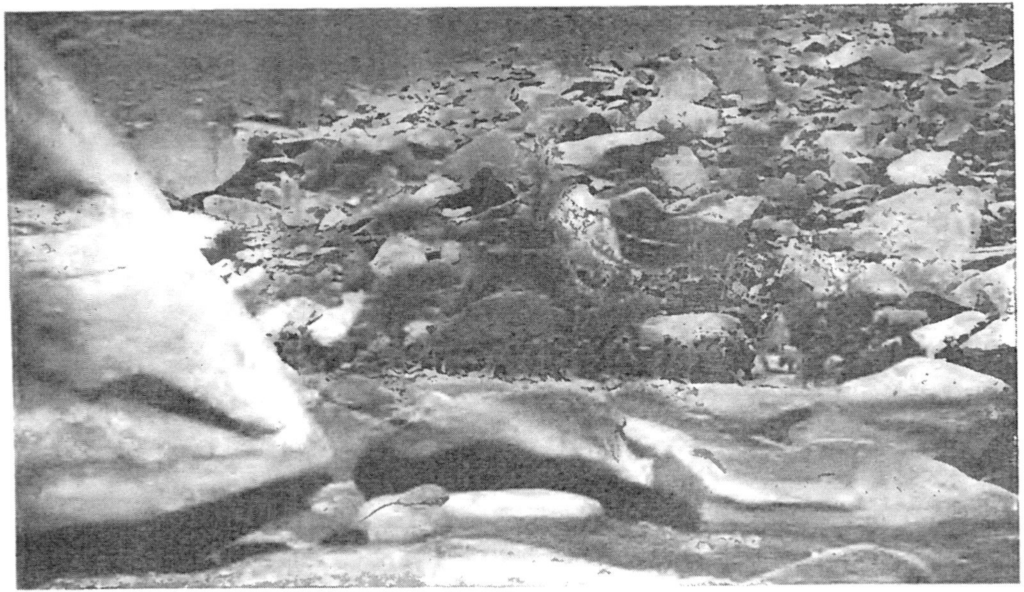

THE MARCH TO LHASA

The omnipresent prayer-flags and cairns beside the road to exorcise evil spirits

marched was about eleven miles. The road lies at first over flat and marshy ground, but in view of the subsequent narrow and difficult trang, it was impossible to make use of this advantage by advancing otherwise than in Indian file all day.

The expeditionary force upon the march must have been an impressive thing for the natives who peeped toward it from the distant rocks. One is so apt to think of an army from one's remembrance of a parade ground or a review, that it is difficult to convey an impression of the enormous length to which even so small a force as that with which we were now advancing stretches out upon the road. The first result of this is that the greatest danger to be guarded against, apart, of course, from hostile demonstrations from the enemy, is that of irregularity on the march; for a second's delay, caused, say, by a deep water-cut, multiplied, as it must be, by the number of files in an eight-mile column, becomes, at the end of the line, a delay of twenty minutes. It was a striking sight, this long filament of men and beasts stretching and shrinking themselves forward—for all the world like a worm upon a path—as the gaps were lengthened and made up, between the high cliff and the tumbling water below. You would, in the morning, find the Pioneers striding with long legs until the Gurkhas' officers had to protest against the pace; but later on, in the same day, you would find a Pioneer or two sitting exhausted beside the road, but rarely would you find a Gurkha in distress. The dust crawls out slowly from under the changing feet, hanging in the air for a mile behind the last files of the rearguard. In front will go the mounted infantry, inquisitive and at wary intervals, and then a detachment of Sikhs, long drawn out—interminably, one thinks, as one waits beside the path to let the men go by. Then with a brisk clank of new trappings, up steps nearly a mile of mountain battery, composed of great upstanding mules specially chosen for their work. Some, those carrying the heavier pieces, are necessarily "top-loaded." This is the most trying of all ways of porterage, because there is no natural balance of the loads and the breastplate and breechings press heavily indeed against the animal's steadiness unless the road be flat. Still, to those good beasts, this was but a little matter. One mule carries one half of the gun and the breechpiece follows behind, racketing backward and forward with the jerky mule step, but secured inexorably; then comes the trail, and then the whéels, two and two, all separated by a man or two on foot. After these, the endless ammunition train, each train of leather shell-boxes close up beside its own gun, and you would think that there were twenty guns instead of six in the battery by the time you had waited for a quarter of an hour only to find the *disjecta membra* of these all-important weapons still slowly trailing by. Behind them, the Commissioner might be found. Of him one could never say positively his position or his pace, for he would sometimes remain in camp working with a dak orderly in attendance until the rearguard were on the point of starting, and then he would manage somehow to climb up the slow-moving force of which the vanguard was as he started within sight of their evening's camping-ground. Not far away from the battery you would always find the General, jogging along with bent shoulders—a mile away you could tell that he was a sick man.[1] Bignell you would find near him, mounted on a horse that looked fitter for a circus than a campaign, but was useful enough at a rough-and-tumble scurry up and down rocks, down the face of any nullah of any angle, through brakes of sallow thorn or across the stony bottom of a tumbling river. "Hippo" and his rider did yeoman service, and though, by his own confession, Bignell is not a Ritz, before the campaign ended the Headquarters' mess had been brought to a state of almost unnatural excellence—so at least Bignell claimed, and he should

[1] For three or four days Macdonald, during his advance from Chumbi to the relief of Gyantse, was so ill with gastritis that he had to be carried in a dandy, and repeatedly afterward he was compelled to take to his bed by attack after attack of this weakening and lowering sickness.

know. Major Iggulden might be there too, but more probably he would be found well in front, watching the road. Lieutenant-Colonel Waddell, with his strangely laden attendants, would be hard by, and not far away O'Connor on his strawberry and cream mount. After the latter's exploits at Pala, Colonel Younghusband set a grim foot down on the aspirations to any further military glory of the most irreplaceable man in all that force. Here you are to imagine a well, but somewhat slightly, built man of more than the average height, with an offhand courtesy which masks an attractively unselfish nature and a quick and observant eye. I think, like every one else who is worth knowing, he needs to be known, for it is truer of few people in the world than of O'Connor, that he attends strictly and exclusively to his own business; a touch of the recluse—shown in a disinclination to attend meals—he is still a man with whom no other man, except by his own fault, could fail to be on the best of terms. A steady judge of most things is this young gunner, and I know that the Commissioner rated his opinion very highly. I must have written badly indeed in these pages if they do not already confess the great and continued debt which they owe to O'Connor for any interest they may possess.

Still the column stretches on; after the fighting men come the interminable trains of laden mules, linked together four by four, tail to nose, and swerving aside for no man and no thing. I have had my pony swept off a bridge into a river because I foolishly attempted to make one of these mule-trains see that there was ample room for both of us; their instinct, which, no doubt, has been developed by generations of pack-carrying along dangerous trangs, is not to give way when they meet an obstacle; they seem then to put their heads down and make a determined rush inward in order to put an extra foot or two between themselves and the edge of the path. There is no greater fallacy than that of supposing that a mule prefers to walk on the edge of a precipice. He is no fool, and if he gets his load entangled with a passing rider he will simply shove straight through the obstacle. The only occasion on which he becomes reasonable and docile is when his pack slips, when he will stand perfectly still and refuse to be hauled forward, however much his companions in front pull at him; it need not be said that this they immediately do with all their strength.

One conceives a very genuine liking for these uncomplaining half-breeds; the work they do is something which no other beast could attempt, and they remain well and fit for work long after every other animal known to man as a baggage-carrier has given way. We tried on this expedition most of the world's beasts of burden; the ponies were, perhaps, hardly given a fair chance because the larger part of their drivers bolted the night before we crossed into the Chumbi Valley. Of the rest, the story of the yaks is one of the dreariest histories of a waste of animal life in military records; but it is difficult to apportion the blame for this.[1]

[1] The original corps of yaks were three in number, under Wigram, Tillard, and Twiss respectively; they came from the Nepalese frontier, where they were taken over to Chumbi by the highest possible route that could be found across Sikkim. About 3,500 started in November, but as their numbers melted away under stress of every disease known to the veterinary surgeon, the scanty remnants of these herds were united into one under Wigram. I do not think that any record of the expedition would be complete without at least some reference to the work done by this officer. Exiled from speech with his own kin for many months on end, with only the half-savage yak-drivers of Nepal to talk to, he tended his miserable beasts with a care that deserves recognition. He was not allowed by the exigencies of the case to draw upon the commissariat for any fodder, and when it was eventually necessary to find some other sustenance for his charges than that which bare snow and rock provided, he paid for it out of his own pocket. In spite of all he could do himself, his beasts dwindled away, dying in tens and twenties at a time, and I well remember seeing the last remnants, 150 in number, of these 3,500 yaks slowly wending their way into Chumbi, with the drivers themselves actually carrying the little loads which the yaks were no longer able to support. Subsequently another corps was made up of 600 beasts from Phari, 150 from Tuna, and 500 from other places. At the end of June, of this new corps of 1,250, 209 alone were alive in Gyantse; about 170 were picked up afterward, and with greater success than had ever been achieved before, they were divided into two corps, one of about 240 at the ferry, the remainder being

We had in the column two curious beasts—zebrules. They were not a success; pleasant and docile animals, a cross between a zebra and a Clydesdale mare, they were physically unable to stand the pack work because they were longer in the back than any horse, or any zebra, or any mule has ever been before, so, as a rule, they were allowed to accompany the battery more as curiosities than as workers. Camels were even at one time proposed, and, I believe, actually used, but their immediate failure was predestined. Donkey corps were used successfully; but in these cases the contracts were given out locally to Tibetans in the habit of transporting goods on these little animals. The Supply and Transport Department, indefatigable in their researches, offered 100 rupees for any kyang which could be brought in. This can hardly have been seriously meant, though it certainly was seriously taken by the native troops. A kyang is a tortoiseshell-colored wild ass confined to this part of the world's surface; it has never been tamed, and the Tibetans, who should know, say that it is untamable; herds of them are found on the Tuna plateau; and again, outside Lhasa, there are some which are regarded as the peculiar and semi-sacred property of the Dalai Lama.

Excepting of course coolies, the only other means of transport employed during the expedition was the ekka, a brilliant inspiration of Major Bretherton's. These light two-wheeled carts, a mere platform upon wheels, were laboriously hoisted up over the Natu la in detached pieces and toward the end of the time were running regularly and without undue mishaps on the level plain between Kamparab and Kang-ma, a distance of 90 miles. There was some difficulty at first in harnessing the ponies of Tibet to a thing they had never seen before; the yaks, on the other hand, took to it at once, and four or five of these beasts could be seen

stabled at Pe-di jong. This, in bald outline, is the fate of the yak corps, and the S. and T. Department have learned never again to place their reliance upon these burly and delicate beasts.

any day solemnly trudging along with the weary persecuted look on their face which entirely belies the innate contentment that a yak feels when he has succeeded in inducing his master to believe that he cannot go more than a mile and a half an hour.[1]

So the far-stretching column creeps along, leaving behind it a trampled highway and a low hanging canopy of dust.

Three times in the march to Nam the road creeps painfully between the rock and the river, three times it stretches across a wide and cultivated plain; one passes Jang-ma, where a stagnant and picturesque reed-swamp separates the village from the mantra-adorned rock. The village is pretty enough in its fields of deep barley. At last we turned the steepest spur of all, to double which the road runs 100 feet up the high projecting shoulder of granite. Here there was to be seen a gleam of gold in the far distance, and we thought that Lhasa was at last in sight; but it was in reality only the gilded roof of the Chief Magician's temple, two miles distant from the Ling-kor. Descending to a plain, we made our encampment for the night just where the curving river, here a mile wide, was eating into the alluvial flats so fast that, as we watched, another and yet another piece of fresh green turf fell helplessly into the muddy stream. The view from Nam to the north-east—and no one would look in any other direction—is shut in by two

[1] The language of the yaks is a thing in itself: it must be heard to be believed. These yak-drivers, almost as well qualified for stuffing as curiosities of natural history as their charges, carry on a conversation with their beasts which astounds an outsider. I here append two or three of these sounds. The command to quicken their pace is indicated to the yaks by the same sound as that produced by a small boy in London whistling through his teeth with the fullest power of his lungs; the signal to stop is a triple "ugh" thrust from the lowest recesses of the chest. More interesting are two other commands. If you are approaching a yak from behind, and you do not wish him either to get alarmed or quicken his pace, all you have to do (and he will recognize it at once) is three or four times to make that sound with the tongue and teeth with which a nicely brought up lady will express the tiresomeness of a trifle. I do not know much more about the language, but I doubt if in their vocabulary they have a more surprising word than "yea-milly." At this order the yaks will actually return again to the path if they have strayed too far from it up the mountain-side.

converging spurs from north and south, in the middle of which an islet of rock rises, nearly joining the two. Between this and the southern spur the river ran; our road was to take us on the northern side of the islet. These barriers shut off all sight of the plain of Lhasa, and in spite of the repeated claims of those who went forward with the mounted infantry, the fact remains that Captain Peterson or Captain Souter must have been actually the first man to see the Potala, long after the force had been persuaded that the credit belonged to Captain Ottley, who had a race up a height with Major Iggulden, and beat him by a head in obtaining the first glimpse of—Sera Monastery! They returned to camp vowing they had seen Lhasa, in spite of the steady assurances of a Tibetan interpreter.[1]

On the next day, the 2d of August, we still followed the difficult track along the indentations of the hills and emerged at last into a wide, well-cultivated plain. There, moving along a sunken road between wide fields of peas and wheat, we soon reached the well-wooded village of Nethang, which boasts the distinction of having been the residence of the great reformer, Atisha. The road runs straight through the town, making two sharp turns at right angles as it does so; a few lamas gathered at the door or on the roof-tops to watch us, a few children stood in the doorways with their fingers in their mouths and their eyes wide open. There was no other sign of life.

We made a short halt beyond the village to enable the proper intervals to be made up, but it was with impatience that we waited the order to continue our march. Before us the two spurs of intervening rock still closed the view of the Plain of Milk completely, and there was a mile to be traversed before we could make our way between these forbidding barriers. Once set moving again, the column crawled forward under the rocky

[1] If it is of any interest to record these details, the town of Lhasa itself was first seen by Captain Ottley from the spur joining Potala and Chagpo-ri.

sides of the northern spur and at last threaded through the defile.

Another disappointment was in store for us. Once inside the gate of the plain, even from that point of view not a stone nor a pinnacle of Lhasa is to be seen. We had to possess our souls in patience still. But that we were near our journey's end was clear enough. Here at our left elbows, hacked out on the inner surface of the rock, was the famous Buddha of which we had so often heard; this great monster, thirty feet in height, and cut in thirty-six-inch relief in the natural flattened surface of the raw rock, gazed over our heads toward the Holy City. It has had built over it a roof supported on two jutting walls of granite, and it is undoubtedly of a very early, even possibly of a prehistoric, type; it marks the entrance to the plain in which Lhasa lies, though, as I have said, a projecting spur from the south still conceals the Potala from one's eyes. It is for this reason of great religious interest and veneration, and in front of it stands a twenty-foot heap of pebbles raised by pious pilgrims in thanksgiving for the nearness of their long-expected goal. It is bedaubed coarsely with yellow and blue and red, and, it must be confessed, is one of the ugliest things we saw in the country.

Close as we thought ourselves to be, it was nearly two miles yet, two long miles impatiently covered—past strange strata of gneiss jutting out perpendicularly from the hillsides like huge armor-plates—past an interesting example of the strange "cup marks" which are found all the world over in the Eastern and Western hemispheres alike, which no living man can even attempt to explain, and at which no one just then even wished to look—past treacherous swamps of vivid green grass growing on soil more water than earth—two miles that seem like ten, before that interminable southern spur is outridden, before the place of our desire was reached.

You may see from afar the spot at which the first glance of the Potala may be obtained. Beside a barley field is a low mud-colored chorten, and beside the chorten is a heap of stones larger even than that before the great Buddha behind us. There is not much else to mark the place, but assuredly nothing more was needed on that day.

It was about three o'clock in the afternoon, and a light-blue haze was settling down in between the ravines of the far-distant mountains that to the east ringed in the plain, and nearer to hand on either side threw their spurs forward like giant buttresses from north to south. There was a smell of fresh spring earth and the little rustle of a faint wind in the heads of barley; the sun was merciless in a whitened sky wherein from horizon to horizon there was never a flush of blue. It was all common, and yet the hour teemed with a fierce interest of a kind that no man will perhaps ever feel again. I took off my smoked-glass spectacles to see the clearer, and it was bright indeed.

Then, as we rode on, it came. In the far, far distance, across and beyond those flat fields of barley, marked here and there by the darker line of low-wooded plantations, a gray pyramid painfully disengaged itself from behind the outer point of the gray concealing spur—Lhasa.

. . . . . .

Here at last it was, the never-reached goal of so many weary wanderers, the home of all the occult mysticism that still remains on earth. The light waves of mirage dissolving impalpably just shook the far outlines of the golden roofs and dimly seen white terraces. I do not think any one of us said much.

The mounted infantry were, of course, ahead of us, but we had outridden the main column by some distance, and we stood a moment on the road just where a sudden flight of dragon-flies pierced the air with lines of quick blue; then we rode on. Even supposing we had found Lhasa to be a handful of hovels scattered on a dusty plain with just such distinction of palace and temple as one had time after time seen in Tibet before, one side of our natural curiosity would, no doubt, have been slaked sufficiently, but we were to find a different thing indeed. Here, in these uttermost parts of the earth, uplifted high above humanity, guarded by impenetrable passes of rock and ice, by cliffs of sheer granite, by the hostility of man and by the want of food and fuel, here was no poor Oriental town arrogating to itself the dignity which mystery in itself confers. Judged by the standards of the East and West alike, Lhasa is a city which can hold its own with most; we were to find it unique, dowered with a mingled magnificence and green luxuriance for which no step of our journey had given us warning.

There at last it was, and for the next half mile O'Connor and I allowed our beasts to find their own way over the pebble-strewn road while little by little we devoured with our eyes the outlines of the twin rocks which stand as sentinels to hide from the traveler the sight of the Cathedral which lies low on the plain to the east. For the city of Lhasa is not visible until you shall have climbed up the neck of land which almost joins Chagpo-ri to Potala. But there the great palace of the god-king was, and a shaft or two of light from the golden canopies burned whitely upon us for a few yards as we went.

The remainder of that day's march was simple enough; we made our way past whitened houses lurking here and there under the shade of Lombardy poplars and begirt with the green and rustling ranks of barley, until at last Tö-lung was reached.

Tö-lung is but a house or two by the western approach to the bridge over the Tö-lung-chu. This bridge is one of the most creditable pieces of Tibetan labor, for not only is the bridge itself well constructed of granite with its piers protected by long sterlings up stream, but for more than a mile on either side the very course of that stream is guided beneath it from the hills where its springs are. Two well built containing walls ten feet in height curb the snow waters coming from the long valley to the north.

It is, perhaps, as well to describe at once the unusual conformation and consistency of the plain in the middle of which Lhasa lies. The Tibetans themselves will assure you that there is an underground lake, and that unless these waters are annually propitiated, not only by services and obeisances rendered to the serpent who lives in the island sanctuary of Lu-kang, but also by ceremonies calculated to mollify the vague personality who dwells beneath the very shrine of the Jo itself, Lhasa would be inundated by its unseen waters. There is this much to be said in justification of this theory, that, from end to end, the plain round the capital is almost without exception a water-sodden morass on which it is almost impossible to travel for a hundred yards without encountering a quagmire. The road by which one approaches the capital is a causeway built four or five feet up from the surface of the marsh and pierced a dozen times by culverts through which brown peaty water flows apace. Only in two places are these waters confined within their proper channels. The Tö-lung revetments make it possible on the west to build a bridge across the collected waters that would otherwise undermine the firm earth for half a mile on either side, and farther on, under the western gate of Lhasa itself, another great work of sand binds in the spasmodic floods which oppress the Kaling chu. These two works drain the Plain of Milk, so far at least as Tö-lung and Lhasa are concerned; for the rest, the waving rushes of the plain conceal a treacherous depth of slime.

In length the Plain of Milk is about 15 miles, in width it varies from two to five, and in upon it from all sides strike the spurs of vast mountains which even then, in July, were snow-capped in the morning hours. In the recesses between these spurs lurk the villages and the monasteries of which we had heard so much. Lhasa itself lies out in mid-plain under the eastern lee of the two hills I have described. Through the plain, immediately to the south of the capital, the Kyi chu meanders vaguely through its wide and sandy course, and, thanks to this luxuriance of water and to the shelter which is provided by the mountains round from every wind that blows, the unpollarded vegetation of the plain grows rank and free. A little road creeps along the northern mountain-side, following the ins and outs of the mountain contours from Tö-lung to Sera, but this is only a side track—the main road strikes fairly and straightly across the center of the marsh from Shing-donkar to the Pargo Kaling, or western gate of the Sacred City.

At Tö-lung we halted for the night, but long before the camp was settled a great deputation arrived from out of the capital. An audience was granted, and for two hours and a half the Mission camp was thronged with the bright silken habits and hats of the more important dignitaries. There were the usual arguments, the usual prayers; in their recommendations that the force should advance no further toward the city of which the guardian hills were now clearly visible to the east, the Tibetan envoys enjoyed what must have been to them unexpected support from the General. But it was the same old game on the part of the Tibetans, and I do not think that anything throughout the campaign reflected so much credit upon the Secretary of State for India as that when he at last realized at all the necessity of this advance he recognized also its imperative nature. Accepting the representations of Colonel Younghusband, he did not hesitate a moment; the treaty, he ordered, was to be signed in Lhasa itself, and signed not even one mile short of it. As the afternoon wore on, the fruitless durbar slowly dissolved, but not until the leading men had thoroughly satisfied the curiosity which almost every article of dress or mechanism excited.

Personally, I amused myself by showing to them several illustrated weekly papers; it was curious to notice that they thoroughly understood the course which the Russo-Japanese war was taking, and they looked with great eagerness at the plates in which the incidents of the struggle were depicted. But other things in the papers puzzled them extremely. They did not seem at all impressed by the large portraits of well-known beautiful and partially unclad ladies which constituted no small part of the attractions of most of the periodicals we had with us, but a representation of Dan Leno, seated, if I remember rightly, on a pillar with a guitar in his hands, a crown of flowers round his head and a skirt round his legs, was something they would not allow me to pass by. I confess I found it difficult to explain to them exactly all that Dan Leno but two months ago represented to the Londoner. Another picture about which they wished to know the whole truth was that of His Majesty the King walking down a quay-side in Germany. I explained to them that the figure to the right was that of the "Pi-ling Gyal-po Chempo," and in a moment the attention of twenty of them was called from all sides to it; they crowded round with their chins on one another's shoulders. After they had sated their curiosity about the Emperor of India—that unknown majesty in whose omnipotence they were slowly coming to believe—I was abruptly asked who his companion might be. It was the Kaiser. I tried to explain the family and the political relationship between the two Emperors, but found that I was not entirely understood, so I summoned an interpreter and told him to explain to the Tibetans that the German Emperor was a very great sovereign in Europe and that he was the King's nephew.[1]

[1] My intentions were, however, somewhat misunderstood, for some time afterward, when I asked the interpreter what he had actually said, his answer was to this effect:—"Sir, I told them that this was a nephew of the Emperor, and a great and mighty monarch possessing wide territories. And I

So, in a drizzling rain ended the last day of our weary march from India, for there remained but seven miles to cross and every yard of them was lightened by the distant view of the palace and roofs of our long-sought goal.

said that because of the especial love with which our Emperor regarded him, he had of his goodness granted unto his nephew all the wide territories which he possessed." This was not exactly what I had meant, but it was too late to correct the impression.

CHAPTER XVII

LHASA, I

THERE was a light rain in the early hours of the morning of the 3d of August. All round the amphitheater of hills a light-gray Scotch mist was draining itself imperceptibly into the plain, and it was not until just before the start that the rain stopped, and the lower edge of these clouds became a clean-cut white line slowly receding up the mountain-side as the morning passed. Our course was almost due east. We crossed the bridge and made our way by the well-defined though somewhat weed-grown road between high fields of peas and barley to the spur which ran out from the north and hid from our sight the monastery of De-bung. It was to be in all a march of about seven miles, and after the first three had been passed without incident a halt was called just on the western side of the town and ruined fort of Shing-donkar. This is a picturesque little place nestling at the foot of a high precipitous spur, of which the almost horizontal and razor-like summit is supported on a roughly columnar edge of granite. Even from Lhasa itself it stands out boldly against the sunset, and its jagged edge is a small feature in the scenery of which I am somewhat sorry to have taken no photograph. The road passes between Shing-donkar and the first of the many "lings," or thickly planted inclosures, which are characteristic of the plain in which Lhasa lies. Immediately afterward the road ascends the stony spur, and dropping quickly on the other side follows the contour of a recess in the hills before the last point is reached and De-bung Monastery is clearly seen.

De-bung, the home of all the misplaced political intrigue of Tibet, lies in tightly packed tiers of houses far up into the stony amphitheater made by a recess in the hills. From a distance it is a somewhat imposing object; the very compactness with which it has gathered into itself, without a straggler far or near, the dormitories and chapels needed for nearly 8,000 monks is, in itself, a striking thing. In the middle the golden Chinese roofs of the great gompa shine above the friezes of maroon and brown yak hair curtains, whereby the golden badges hang. For the rest, De-bung presents but few features of interest. It is like every other monastery in Tibet. Once inside it there is nothing to see which differentiates it from the Palkhor choide, from the Potala, from Tse-chen, from Dongtse, from a dozen more. But all the same, in this monastery of De-bung there has been for some years, and there still is, hatched all the trouble which the present Dalai Lama has brought upon his country and his faith.

Not far from it on the eastern side of the amphitheater, and so hidden from the sight of Lhasa, in a small tree-clad ravine through which a fresh stream tumbles among its boulders, lie the house and temple of the chief wizard of Tibet—the Na-chung Chos-kyong. This building is finished with more beauty and luxury than any other in Tibet, and a full description of it is reserved for a later chapter.

At Cheri the column halted upon the road a mile across the débris-littered plain from De-bung. Here Mahommedan butchers carry on their work, and the first signs of habitations made of the horns of slaughtered beasts are to be seen. Soon, however, we stretched on again across the causeway between the marshes from which teal and wild duck flew up now and then. Slowly the two western hills of Lhasa raised and extended themselves along the horizon, and when at last, after some deliberation and reconnoitering, a dry patch of ground was found about a mile from the still invisible gate of Lhasa and a camp was pitched there, the sharp outline of the great palace towered over us against the gauzy whiteness of the noonday sky.[1]

Looking eastward from the camp, Lhasa was still completely hidden by the twin hills and the neck between them. On the left Potala raised its great bulk, though the full size of this gigantic building is nowhere less to be seen than from the spot on which our camp was pitched. One had a view of it on end which failed to give any suggestion of its real length and importance, but what we did see even so was huge enough. A white round-tower crowned the serrated wall of bald white masonry which divides off the palace from the almost perpendicular scarp of the rock on which it stands. Behind that rose another great white bulk of square grim masonry pierced with a row of stiff small windows; above that rose yet a higher rim of white roof; over that again the square red outline of the central palace of the Dalai Lama himself; and, above all, the great golden roofs glittering in the sun. Immediately below it the slanting way up the rock passed between the dark green foliage of trees and the sienna and ocher of the Red Hill,[2] relieved by spaces of wild grass. Toward us to the south and south-west the hillside sheers down steeply before it again rises with almost the same abruptness to form the lion-

[1] For sheer inaccuracy the following description by Chandra Das of the approach to Lhasa can hardly be paralleled in serious literature. "At this point the road nears the river, and the whole city stood displayed before us at the end of an avenue of gnarled trees, the rays of the setting sun falling on its gilded domes. It was a superb sight, the like of which I have never seen. On our left was Potala, with its lofty buildings and gilt roofs; before us, surrounded by a green meadow, lay the Town with its tower-like white-washed houses and Chinese buildings with roofs of blue glazed tiles." One would think that the middle sentence was literally true.

[2] The original name of this hill was simply Marpo-ri, and the palace built on the site in 1032 was evidently constructed of blocks quarried on the hill itself, for it was known as the Phodang Marpo.

shaped mass of Chagpo-ri.[1] Chagpo-ri is crowned with a small square yellow jong, and immediately hidden from view by the topmost pinnacle on which the jong is placed is a medical college resting, as it were, on the lion's withers. Immediately on the south again runs the stream of the Kyi chu. So much could be seen or guessed from the halting-ground, whence the high road leads straight into the western gate between the two high rocky citadels. The first thing that the traveler notices is the embankment of sand constructed by a Dépen of the name of Karpi in 1721. This man, by order of the Chinese conquerors, had immediately before pulled down the walls which defended Lhasa more from the assaults of nature than of man, and he found it necessary to undertake the construction of these enormous retaining walls—to which I have referred in the last chapter—to save Lhasa from the encroachment of the water-sodden plain around. The Kaling chu is an artificially constructed waterway which diverts from the town itself all the water coming down toward it from the two valleys lying immediately north of Lhasa, in one of which Sera Monastery, two miles away, is clearly to be seen, a small nest of white houses buttressing the foot of the rock and ensigned with a gilded roof or two. This double embankment is a striking feature; the road runs parallel along the northern side of it for 500 yards, and one can see the tops of the trees which fill the square "ling" or plantation abutting on to it to the south. At last the embankment turns northward, and we cross it by a primitive bridge under the wide branches of a poplar tree. After crossing it the plantation on our right is seen to be a tangled jungle of thorn and willow and poplar, over all of which the thick-petaled orange clematis grows in rank profusion. A hundred yards on a road sweeps into our route from the right. As we approached, two monks, one of them of extreme age, came slowly along it twirling their prayer-wheels

[1] It will be remembered that at the first view of Lhasa, Potala and Chagpo-ri stood out like two pyramids across the plain.

THE WESTERN GATE OF LHASA

and muttering incessantly the one phrase of Lamaism as they went. This is nothing less than the famous Ling-kor, the ribbon of road which separates as with a knife the sacred from the profane. In all the world there is, perhaps, but the Via Dolorosa its equal in tradition. For miraculous renown the Ling-kor stands alone, for even an infidel who dies while making the sacred circuit is saved from the penalties of his sins.

To the left, after crossing the highway, it runs beside the sandy embankment of the Kaling chu to the north, and then, sharply turning, it is hidden behind the trees outside the garden wall of the Lu-kang seven or eight hundred yards away. On its surface, immediately to our left, are a few beggars' huts, mere patched rags of dirty cloth supported on sticks. We crossed the road and were in the sacred territory at last. Immediately on the farther side we passed the gate of the Kun-de-ling Monastery with its woods and gardens and a long rocky eminence crowned with a Chinese temple; at its foot a hundred cocks were scratching up the sacred dust awaiting a purchaser. The mass of Potala now hung above our heads, and between us and the western gate there was only a straight stretch of road bordered on the one side by a little patch of barley and a small orchard of willows, and on the right by the still waters of a stagnant willow-edged pool. Over the willows rose the mass of Chagpo-ri. Another two hundred yards, and after a half-turn to the right round the end of the water, we find facing us the western gate of Lhasa, or Pargo Kaling. We left the gate on our left and at once began the ascent of the neck of rock which joins the two hills. There is a steep climb of about two hundred feet, and then, with breath-taking suddenness, the panorama of Lhasa burst upon the gaze.

As I have said, Lhasa would remain Lhasa were it but a cluster of hovels on the sand. But the sheer magnificence of the unexpected sight which met our unprepared eyes was to us almost a thing incredible. There is nothing missing from this splendid spectacle—architecture, forest trees, wide green places, rivers, streams, and mountains all lie before one as one looks down from the height upon Lhasa stretching out at our feet. The dark forbidding spurs and ravines of the valley of the Kyi chu, up which we had come, interlock one with another and had promised nothing of all this; the beauty of Lhasa is doubled by its utter unexpectedness. It is true that we had only yesterday and that very day passed through green fields and marshes cloaked shoulder high with rushes; it is true that here and there a densely matted plantation had swung slowly beside our road to meet us as we moved along; but there was nothing—less perhaps in such maps and descriptions of Lhasa as we had than anywhere else—to promise us this city of gigantic palace and golden roof, these wild stretches of woodland, these acres of close-cropped grazing land and marshy grass, ringed and delimited by high trees or lazy streamlets of brown transparent water over which the branches almost met.

Between the palace on our left and the town a mile away in front of us there is this arcadian luxuriance interposing a mile-wide belt of green. Round the outlying fringes of the town itself and creeping up between the houses of the village at the foot of the Potala there are trees—trees sufficiently numerous in themselves to give Lhasa a reputation as a garden city. But in this stretch of green, unspoiled by house or temple, and roadless save for one diverging highway, Lhasa has a feature which no other town on earth can rival.

It is all a part of that splendid religious pride which has been the making, and may yet prove the undoing, of Tibet. It was right that there should be a belt of nature undefiled encircling the palace of the incarnate god and king, and there the belt is, investing the Potala even inside the loop of the Ling-kor with something of the isolation which guards from the outer world the whole of this strange and lovely town. Between and over the

LHASA, DOMINATED BY THE TOWERING BULK OF THE POTALA

The western gate is in the foreground below

glades and woodlands the city of Lhasa itself peeps, an adobe stretch of narrow streets and flat-topped houses crowned here and there with a blaze of golden roofs or gilded cupolas; but there is no time to look at this; a man can have no eye for anything but the huge upstanding mass of the Potala palace to his left; it drags the eye of the mind like a loadstone, for indeed sheer bulk and magnificent audacity could do no more in architecture than they have done in this huge palace-temple of the Grand Lama. Simplicity has wrought a marvel in stone, nine hundred feet in length and towering seventy feet higher than the golden cross of St. Paul's Cathedral. The Potala would dominate London,—Lhasa it simply eclipses. By European standards it is impossible to judge this building; there is nothing there to which comparison can be made. Perhaps in the austerity of its huge curtains of blank, unveiled, unornamented wall, and in the flat, unabashed slants of its tremendous south-eastern face there is a suggestion of the massive grandeur of Egyptian work; but the contrast of color and surroundings, to which no small part of the magnificence of the sight is due, Egypt cannot boast.

The vivid white stretches of the buttressing curtains of stone, each a wilderness of close-ranked windows and the home of the hundreds of crimson-clad dwarfs who sun themselves at the distant stairheads, strike a clean and harmonious note in the sea of green which washes up to their base. Once a year the walls of the Potala are washed with white, and no one can gainsay the effect; but there is yet the full chord of color to be sounded. The central building of the palace, the Phodang Marpo, the private home of the incarnate divinity himself, stands out four-square upon and between the wide supporting bulks of masonry a rich red-crimson, and, most perfect touch of all, over it against the sky the glittering golden roofs—a note of glory added with the infinite taste and the sparing hand of the old illuminator—recompose the color scheme from end to end, a sequence of green in three shades, of white, of maroon, of gold, and of pale blue. The brown yak-hair curtain, eighty feet in height and twenty-five across, hangs like a tress of hair down the very center of the central sanctuary hiding the central recess. Such is the Potala. In a way it recalls the dominion of the Shwé Dagon over Rangoon, though in every aspect of construction, ornamentation, and surrounding it would be hard to imagine two buildings more entirely different in every detail than these two greatest erections of modern Buddhism.

The utter disproportion between the palace and the town remains a wonder, but a wonder devoid of a trace of falsity or ostentation, rather a wonder full of a deeper meaning. The petty town which lies a mile away beyond the trees helps, by its very insignificance, to emphasize the tremendous gulf that in Tibet yawns between the people and their priests. In that town there was indeed the true sanctuary of the faith; in that town there was the idol which the largest faith of all the world holds sacred beyond all earthly things, and underneath those far distant golden roofs of the Jo-kang the wealth and tradition of the whole creed lay enshrined. Moreover, there is nothing inside the Potala particularly sacred, particularly rich, or particularly beautiful. But unconsciously it thus symbolizes all the more the vast erection of power and pride which separates the priestly caste of Tibet from the real truths of the religion they have prostituted. The fearful sanctity which hedges about the person of their divine ruler is here in Lhasa demonstrated in a manner that must impress the dullest pilgrim. That double-edged weapon seclusion, which the Pope, in magnificent retirement in the Vatican, is now using with doubtful success at Rome, has long been in the armory of the Grand Lama of Tibet. The Tibetan policy of isolation receives here its only possible justification by a success that is startling in its sufficiency, and one can well understand that a visit to Lhasa "satisfies the soul" of the most recalcitrant subject of His Holiness. I have said much in these volumes to the discredit of La-

THE AMBAN, THE CHINESE REPRESENTATIVE IN LHASA, COMING TO CONFER WITH COLONEL YOUNGHUSBAND

Of all the inhabitants of Tibet, only the Dalai Lama and the Amban are allowed to use a chair

maism, and I have said it with deliberation and conviction; but this panorama of Lhasa batters down helplessly the prejudices of a quieter hour. Lamaism may be an engine of oppression, but its victims do not protest; and there before one's eyes at last is Lhasa. It may be a barrier to all human improvement; it may be a living type of all that we in the West have fought against and at last overcome, of bigotry, cruelty, and slavery; but under the fierce sun of that day and the white gauze of the almost unclouded sky of Lhasa, it was not easy to find fault with the creed, however narrow and merciless, which built the Potala palace and laid out the green spaces at its foot. In this paradise of cool water and green leaves, hidden away among the encircling snows of the highest mountain ranges of the world, Lamaism has upraised the stones and gold of Lhasa, and nothing but Lamaism could have done this thing. To Lamaism alone we owe it that when at last the sight of the farthest goal of all travel burst upon our eyes, it was worthy, full worthy, of all the rumor and glamour and romance with which in the imaginings of man it has been invested for so many years.

If you will tear your gaze away from the Potala you may see the Ling-kor lying below you like a thread, betrayed here and there by a gap in the leafage of the gardens. Before you in the distance the turquoise Kyi chu, "river of delight," moves lazily between its wide white dunes, here elbowed out of its course by a spur of the hills, there shorn and parceled by a heavy outcrop of water-worn stones and the miniature cliffs of a dazzling sand-bank. Across the mile-wide bed of the river cultivation begins again, and you may see plantations, fields, and houses all the way up to where the wind-blown buttresses of sand blanket the hollow scarp of the southern hills. Far away in the distance beyond the town the plain still stretches, always the same marshy expanse jagged and indented by the spurs of the encircling hills; six miles away it closes in to the east at the point to which the curving thread of the high road to China makes its uncertain way, banked high across the morass.

Just where the dun town encroaches upon the greenery you may see clearly the famous Yutok Sampa or Turquoise-roofed Bridge. To the right is the Amban's house, almost completely hidden in its trees, and on the other side of the Jo-kang's gilded canopies, far away to the left, rise the steep, unbeautiful walls of the Meru gompa, the last house in Lhasa to the north-east; to the west of it, amid the greenery of its plantations, flash the golden ridge-poles of Ramo-che, after the Jo-kang itself the most sacred of all temples in Tibet. But, believe me, when you have marked these historic points the eye will helplessly revert again to the Potala; it is a new glory added to the known architecture of the world.

Nothing in Lhasa, excepting always the interior of the Jokang, comes up to this magnificent prelude. If a traveler knows that the cathedral doors are hopelessly shut to him, his wisest course would be to sit a day or two upon this spur of Chagpo-ri and then depart, making no further trial of the town; for he will never catch again that spell of almost awed thanksgiving that there should be so beautiful a sight hidden among these icy and inaccessible mountain crests, and that it should have been given to him to be one of the few to see it.

The camp was by this time pitched, and the Amban paid Colonel Younghusband a formal visit. He and the Dalai Lama are the only two in Tibet who are allowed to use the sedan-chair, and the sight of the Amban making a formal visit is not uninteresting. He is preceded by ten unarmed servants clad in lavender-blue, edged and patterned with black velvet. Immediately behind them come forty men-at-arms similarly dressed in cardinal and black, bearing lances, scythe-headed poles, tridents, and banners; after them come the secretaries and their servants,

THE CHINESE REPRESENTATIVES IN LHASA MEETING COLONEL YOUNGHUSBAND FOR THE FIRST TIME

and then, borne by ten men, his Excellency in his chair.[1] There was no great importance in this first visit of ceremony. But it was returned by Colonel Younghusband on the following day, and, if you please, we will ride behind the Colonel as he passes through the streets of Lhasa on his way to and from the Residency. Now instead of passing to the south of the Pargo Kaling, we go underneath the gilt-ribbed and celestially crowned chorten which tops the western gate between the two guardian hills.[2] There is a protective railing of timber along both sides of the interior of the gate and a blue deity in his most "terrible" aspect is painted on the left-hand wall.

Immediately inside the gate the road turns to the left, and a good view is to be had of the Potala palace rising above the walled square of houses and stables and prisons at the foot of the rock. Between the gate and this inclosure is a small village tucked up under the rock, not more than thirty houses in all, dirty, squalid, and stinking, although it is under the very threshold of the Grand Lama's magnificent residence. Five hundred yards on an obelisk rises in the middle of the road; this, which is almost opposite the center of the palace, was set up to record the pacification of Tibet and the domination of the Chinese in 1720. The inscription was carved three years later, and it is noticeable that in it the name of the Tashi Lama precedes that of his brother of Lhasa. The road continues for a little space and then divides abruptly into two tracks, that to the left keeping straight on toward the palace of the Yabshi family and the northern part of the city, that on the right continuing between

[1] It is interesting to note that the Chinese have such a contempt for Tibet that the viceroy never takes full official dress with him to Lhasa; negotiations were, therefore, carried on with the Amban with less formal ceremony than would have been considered necessary under other circumstances, though the Commissioner and his staff, to their great discomfort, always wore correct diplomatic uniform in their intercourse with both Chinese and Tibetans.

[2] This is in shape a typical "stupa," with the exception that the road passes through it, making a clear tunnel in the center.

fields and green swamps, acres of barley, and willow plantations to the Yutok Sampa.

This bridge is reckoned by the Tibetans and the Chinese to be one of the five beauties of Lhasa.[1] It is a plain structure, and its general character is excellently shown by Countess Helena Gleichen's picture. The tiles must have been brought from China, and in the course of many centuries the blue glaze, which has given the bridge its name, has been worn off from projecting edges and points, and the rich Indian red of the clay mingles most beautifully with the prevailing color. Inside it is painted with the same dull greenish blue as that with which the Pargo Kaling is decorated. There are small sacred images under the projecting roof at either end of the bridge, and inside there is a decorative design on the lintel of the gates. It stretches across a swampy marsh through which at that season the water was cutting small channels, gay with vivid grass and primulas. Through the Yutok Sampa the road turned sharply to the left and the gate of Lhasa proper was before us; it is a plain hole in the wall without decoration, and without even a door.

Immediately in front as one penetrates through the wall is a wide open space with a stream of water running down between weeds and bushes from the left; following up this direction with the eye, the street is seen to turn into a small square, and at one end of it a gigantic willow-tree towers high above the flat, low-lying roofs. This is the famous tree that grows opposite the western front of the Jo-kang, of which one can from the gate see but the tops of its golden roofs towering above the dull, flat buildings with which the cathedral is surrounded. In front, and indeed in all other directions, are the squat, uninteresting mud houses of Lhasa. The Chinese quarter, immediately to our right,

[1] These five sights are believed by the Chinese to be, with the exception of the Jo-kang, or, as they call it, the Ta-chao, itself, the most ancient remains in the capital.

THE AMBAN COMING OUT FROM LHASA ON HIS WAY TO MEET THE MISSION

which in general is far better kept than other parts of a Tibetan community, is as bad as the others. We turned off in this direction through the quarter and emerged immediately into another wide space of which the unevennesses were indicated by great pools of black-scummed water. Under some squalid willows dividing this open space from the gate, the main drain of the town runs fetidly between black banks, passing beneath the very walls of the Residency. On these stinking eminences herds of black pigs were grouting about among rubbish heaps more than usually repulsive in their composition. Across the square rose the timber gate of the Amban's reserve, and we cavalcaded across to it, splashing through the water-pools and jostling from their filthy meal the privileged scavengers of the town.

The Residency deserves no long description: you enter and turn to the right between the two usual Chinese "lions," and after passing through a couple of courts overhung with poplars you arrive in the durbar hall, with its red and green hangings and green and gold-flecked doors. It is a poor little room and the ceiling is adorned with irregularly shaped pieces of paper with a red all-overish pattern. Here we had a durbar, and some excellent little cigars were handed round alternately with tea—made, we were glad to find, after the Chinese habit—and Huntley and Palmer's biscuits. Colonel Younghusband intimated to the Amban that it would be as well for all concerned if immediate attention were paid to the reasonable and proper demands of the English. The Amban, as usual, deprecated the foolishness of his Tibetan flock, but seemed more preoccupied with the precariousness of his own position than anything else. His memory dwelt somewhat persistently upon the assassinations which had overtaken two of his predecessors in office; and there could be no doubt about it that he was honestly relieved when our force encamped outside Lhasa.

The concealed band was playing when we arrived, and this

again struck up the Oriental melody as we left the place, but the bombs which had been exploded in the Commissioner's honor on our arrival were not repeated, greatly, I think, to every one's relief, for as the first went off we all feared that Macdonald in the camp outside would take it as a sign of treachery, and we knew that he had his guns laid on the Potala as we sat in durbar in the city.

We returned by another route, again crossing the black swamp which, it will be remembered, constitutes one of the "five beauties" of Lhasa. We passed into the other open space, which we crossed diagonally toward the sacred willow. We turned up the street I have referred to and passed to the left of the tree in its walled inclosure. This diverted the course of the small column—300 rifles had come in with the Commissioner, and we had as well forty of the comic-opera guard of the Chinese Residency—from passing the actual front of the Jo-kang. I was, however, able to inspect the Do-ring, and get the first glimpse of the Cathedral from inside the small paved inclosure bounded to the east by the timbered and painted portico and hanging draperies of the Jo-kang. A crowd of villainous-looking monks were gathered sullenly before the great barred doors. A description of the Do-ring will be found later on in the chapter dealing with the Jo-kang. I rejoined the column which was making its way up toward the Yabshi house, and thence struck off sharply to the left along the wide road, or rather the continual puddle, which, running between the adobe walls of monasteries or well-wooded gardens, brings you back to the foot of the Potala and thence to the Pargo Kaling gate. It must be confessed that to judge from this itinerary the town itself of Lhasa would compare but badly with the capital of even a third rate petty chief in India. The buildings lack distinction, though on a closer examination it must be confessed that the walls of the better houses were often soundly built and of strong material. Granite is

A STREET SCENE IN LHASA: NEAR THE CHINESE QUARTER

used in large splintered blocks for nearly every one of the bigger houses of the town; but if the original description of the place by Father Andrada had any real foundation, the capital of Tibet has changed sadly for the worse, for not even the kindliest advocate could find in the slosh and filth of every street, or in the ramshackle structures which cumber every available inch of ground beside the heavier houses, the well-paved thoroughfares and dignified architecture which he describes.

About three hundred yards north of the Jo-kang, before reaching the Yabshi turning where the chorten stands, the street edges along a wide open space, chiefly swamp and ruin, across which the Meru gompa can easily be seen. The only interest attaching to this gompa is that, so far as can be ascertained, it has been built over the site of the old Christian chapel. If the actual site of the chapel is not covered by the monastery buildings, it can safely be asserted that the chapel and the surrounding buildings of the mission have been totally destroyed, for a space, clear of all but a few trees, exists on every side of the present Lamasery. The bell of the mission is still in existence in Lhasa.

The story of this mission has been well told in a recent volume by the Rev. Graham Sandberg. Briefly stated, its somewhat inglorious history is this. In 1708 the Propaganda sent four Capuchin friars from India through Katmandu and Gyantse to Lhasa to found a mission. Three years later the adult conversions claimed by the whole chain of outposts of the "Tibetan mission" were two in number, and as the report from which this is taken included the results of proselytization in Bengal and in Nepal as well as Tibet, it is perhaps possible that no Tibetan had seen reason to change his faith. In 1713, after a gap of two years, missionary effort was again attempted, and in 1715 we find the mission once more established in Lhasa. But these were troublous times, and the active hostility between the Dalai Lama and the Chinese Emperor prevented that tranquillity in which alone lay any hopes of successful work for the worthy friars. They were in continual danger, and even the valiant claim of Father della Penna to have half converted the Dalai Lama himself does not convince the student that any serious ground had been gained. Mr. Sandberg gives in full the terms of a document granting permission to build a Christian chapel to the Capuchins. Unfortunately a flood in Lhasa in the following year, 1725, was attributed by the people to the desecration of the sacred soil of the city by the erection of a heretical place of worship. Things became so serious that the regent of Tibet himself issued a proclamation affirming that the cause of the late floods had been declared by the head of the Sam-ye monastery to be not the erection of this chapel, but the sins and wickedness of the Tibetans themselves. The little church was finished and eleven Christians were present at its consecration; of this number four or five were, of course, accounted for by the monks themselves, and by the admission of della Penna himself, the majority of the eleven were Newaris—that is, half-caste Nepalese, whose previous religion was almost certainly Mahommedanism. It is even said that the Grand Lama himself visited the chapel.

Some years before, the Jesuits in Rome, with their proverbial jealousy, had prevailed upon the Propaganda to send two of their number, for no other purpose than that of spying upon the work of the mission in Lhasa. It can be imagined what effect was caused by the presence together in Lhasa of rival representatives of two Christian communities, who could not carry on the sacred work with which they were intrusted without betraying to the inhabitants the unfortunate dissensions of their Christian visitors. Ippolito Desideri, with a Eurasian companion, Manuel Freyre, arrived in Lhasa for this purpose on March 18th, 1716, and although a kind of armed neutrality subsisted between the two factions, it was probably a relief to all concerned when Pope

THE ENTRANCE TO THE CHINESE AMBAN'S RESIDENCE AT LHASA

Clement sent a peremptory order in 1721 that Desideri and his companion should leave the country. After a long stay in India he returned to Rome and set forth the case for the prosecution. The Propaganda, however, after four years' deliberation, decided in favor of the Capuchins, but this was only twelve months before the flame of Christianity again flickered out in Lhasa in the year 1733.

In 1740, as the result of a direct appeal to Rome by Father della Penna, this worthy man again set out with one Cassiano Beligatti, of Macerata, and reached Lhasa on the 5th of January, 1741. The old buildings were re-occupied, but the opposition of the lamas was destined to achieve its end, and on April 20th, 1745, after four years of dispiriting ill-success, that fine old warrior, della Penna, with tears in his eyes, turned his back for the last time upon Lhasa and the darling project of his life. It was the death of the poor old man, who three months later was laid to rest in the little cemetery of Pathan.

By any one who has seen the place there can hardly be conceived a more despairing and disheartening field for missionary effort than that provided by Lhasa.

Lhasa, it has been said, must be conceived as a town of low uninteresting houses herded together in an aimless confusion, but beyond question the most ragged and disreputable quarter of all is that occupied by the famous tribe of Ragyabas, or beggar-scavengers. These men are also the breakers up of the dead. It is difficult to imagine a more repulsive occupation, a more brutalized type of humanity, and, above all, a more abominable and foul sort of hovel than those which are characteristic of these men. Filthy in appearance, half-naked, half-clothed in obscene rags, these nasty folk live in houses which a respectable pig would refuse to occupy. The characteristic type of hut is about four feet in height, compounded of filth and the horns of cattle.[1] These men exact high fees for disposing ceremonially of dead bodies. The limbs and trunk of the deceased person are hacked apart and exposed on low flat stones until they are consumed by the dogs, pigs, and vultures with which Lhasa swarms. The flesh of the pigs is highly esteemed in Lhasa; and indeed to the taste it is as good as most pork; but after you have seen the Ragyaba quarter and heard the story of the manner in which the Tibetans dispose of their dead, you will be little inclined to eat it again.

Chandra Das reports that these Ragyabas are recognized by the authorities as a tribe of refuge for all the rascals in the country, whose place of origin cannot be ascertained; he also mentions a curious legend that if a day passes without a burial, if the word may be used, ill-fortune is certain to overtake Lhasa.[2] Recruited from such sources, accustomed to live among surroundings more disgusting by far than those of the Australian aborigines, this guild presents a study which cannot fail to be

[1] This horn masonry is one of the best-known characteristics of Lhasa. So far as I know it is found nowhere else in the world, and therefore deserves a passing mention. It is of two kinds. One sort shows the exquisite regularity and care with which these horns are at times inserted into the mortared surface of a wall, which internally is also strengthened by a rubble also composed of the same material. In other cases no outside covering is attempted, and the horns are simply thrust into a mass of mud wall which probably does not survive the year. Of this latter class are the Ragyaba huts.

[2] Three other incidents are said to portend disaster to the country:—(1) It has long been a proverb that when the snow ceased to fall the English would arrive in Lhasa. This, of course, was tantamount to never, but it was so far justified on the present occasion that never within the memory of the oldest Tibetan had so little snow fallen upon the passes to the south. (2) Disaster shall overtake Tibet when rice grows at Phari. If it were true that disaster could only come in this way the Tibetans might indeed feel themselves secure, though I believe Mr. Walsh made an amusing but entirely unsuccessful attempt to make use of the short Tibetan summer at Phari for the purpose of planting a miniature and carefully tended paddy-field. (3) The lowness of the waters in the great lakes is a further sign of impending trouble. By common consent the waters of the Bam tso and of the Kala tso had never been lower.

ORNAMENTS OF A TIBETAN ALTAR

A HORN HUT

In vile hovels like this live the Ragyabas, or breakers-up of the dead, in Lhasa

of interest to the ethnologist: the more ordinary traveler will soon have seen sufficient of this loathsome tribe.[1]

These men compose the only community peculiar to Lhasa. For the rest, lay and cleric alike, the inhabitants are similar to those of the rest of Tibet. There is indeed but one difference even in the dress. In the province of Tsang, as will be remembered, the women use a turquoise studded halo as a head-dress; in Lhasa a fillet ornamented in the same way is bound close down over their Madonna-parted hair. The two braids are then fluffed out on either side and fall down over the shoulders. It is one of the most becoming ways of doing the hair that I have ever seen, and for a certain type the entire dress of a woman of Lhasa would be a not unbecoming costume for a fancy-dress ball at home.

The dress of both men and women is very similar; there is a single undergarment and one heavy native cloth robe, dun or crimson in color and usually patched, which both sexes pull in round the waist with a girdle—the men pouching it at the waist to form the only pocket that they use. Into this fold of the over-garment the Tibetan slips everything which he will need throughout the day, the little wooden bowls in which he eats his meals, a brass pot with which to do his cooking, a pair of shoes perhaps, and certainly one or two gau-os or charm boxes. These last are at Lhasa larger than elsewhere, and are often finished with extreme delicacy; the silver front of the better class of gau-o is often beautifully chased in a design which strongly resembles good Italian work of the seventeenth century. A good specimen will sometimes measure five inches by four by two, and it will contain a heterogeneous mass of paper prayers

[1] They are, as a rule, considered outcast from every profession or circle except their own, but on one occasion the Dalai Lama enlisted the Ragyabas into the Lhasa regiment to replace the losses which that corps had sustained at Guru.

and charms and objects specially blessed, such as grain, or pills containing the remains of the body of deceased lamas, just as in other parts of Tibet. The high officials of state add gold and brocade to their dress in an increasing amount until the position of shä-pé is reached, when the entire robe is of vivid orange yellow brocaded silk, lined with blue; the hat of the sha-pé is a Chinese cap of yellow silk turned up with black velvet, and the coral or second-class Chinese button is almost invariably worn upon it.[1]

The variety of hats at Lhasa is extraordinary. Almost every conceivable form of headgear is to be found there, from a yellow woolen Britannia's helmet to a varnished and gilded wooden pot with a wide circular brim. One shape suggests an inverted flower-pot bearing upon the top a much larger flower-pot the right way up; others are high Welsh hats of yellow silk with a "cap of maintenance" turn-up of black or yellow, while one most remarkable of all is nothing else than a circular pleated crimson lamp-shade with a four-inch valance or flounce of the same material. The most artistic headgear in Lhasa is that of the servants of the Nepalese Resident. These men wear tightly fitting black leather caps with a plain band running round them, bearing a flame-shaped ornament of gold or silver, held in its place in front by a plain twisted claw of the same material running back on both sides to just above the ears.

[1] In China itself the use of these buttons is carefully regulated, though every man is permitted by custom to wear the button of one higher class than his own; this, however, does not apply to the use of the first-class button, a transparent red color, which is used by the royal family alone. The second-class is of opaque pink, the third of transparent blue, the fourth opaque blue, the fifth of transparent crystal, the sixth opaque white. Below this comes the gold button, which may be worn by any one, and is, therefore, hardly worn at all. The use of these buttons in Tibet by officials of different classes is very clearly laid down, but no attention whatever is paid to the rules. The coral button, which is the highest permitted to any one in the land, is apparently used by any and every one who cares to buy it. These remarks do not, of course, apply to the Chinese Viceroy and his staff, who naturally keep to the stricter rules of their own country.

THE LUKANG GARDEN

A spot in Lhasa which reminded the Mission of home

The Tongsa Penlop himself still went abroad with bare feet and his uncloven Homburg hat.

The Nepalese Resident met us when we reached Lhasa. One is reminded of him at this moment because his overcoat was one of the most gorgeous pieces of Oriental embroidery I had ever seen; quietly dressed in all other respects and personally an unassuming man, his outer garment made him recognizable at a distance of a mile. It was of delicate pink satin sewn all over with silver and gold lace and imitation pearls, latticing down some really very fine flower embroidery in myrtle green and rose. He is a shrewd man, and we owe him a debt of gratitude for the common-sense advice he always gave the Tibetans.

To return to the features of Lhasa. The Ling-kor, or sacred way, incloses the city and Potala palace, as has been described, with a loop of road, sometimes twenty feet wide, sometimes hardly three. It is now a wide sandy expanse from which the noonday sun is fiercely beaten back; now a cool firm path under the shade of the poplars of the Lu-kang; now an up-and-down bridle-track worn smooth and slippery by millions of naked footfalls along the limestone cliffs overhanging the Kyi chu itself; now a part of the filthy swine-infested street which skirts the dirty Ragyaba quarter, three inches deep in black iridescent mud.

From dawn to dusk along this road moves a procession, men and women, monks and laymen. They shuffle along slowly, not unwilling now and then to exchange a word with a companion overtaken—they all go round the same way and therefore they meet no one—but, as a rule, with a vacant look of abstraction from all earthly things they swing their prayer-wheels and mutter ceaselessly beneath their breath the sacred formula which shuts for them the doors of their six hells. Let us go round with them.

Coming in from the west, one turns off into the road just

by the patch of cocks, passing the grimy and squalid yak-hair tents of the beggars, where dogs crawl in and out, and in the intervals give themselves up to the same necessary and Oriental occupation as do their masters and mistresses. A field of barley and peas is on the right hand, and on the left the sand revetments of the Kaling chu. Four hundred yards on, the Ling-kor takes a sharp turn to the right after passing a green swamp in which the pollard willows stand ankle-deep in clear brown pools; on the left the sand-bank which we here leave still hides from the pilgrim all sight of the valley to the west. Hard by there is a group of tall poplars standing sentinel at the corner of a plantation of lower trees, and the glaucous willow-thorn at their foot is weighed down with yellow clematis, partly in flower, partly in silver-threaded fluff. Over all towers up the wide back of the Potala. The turn of the Ling-kor here incloses the Lu-kang, which lies at the foot of the Marpo-ri. This is beyond question the most beautiful thing in Lhasa, and the Chinese, as we have seen, have recognized it by putting it first among the five beauties of the place. It is a still lake of clear brown water, fringed with reeds and overhung with willows and other trees of great age, and it lies low in green-wooded glades, where overhead the branches meet. Under foot the turf is fine and springy, and in every direction the wealth of undergrowth hides from one the fact that it is after all a comparatively small garden. In the center of the lake is an island entirely covered with trees and margined all round with huge rushes. An old flight of stone steps betrays in the foliage a scarcely visible pavilion with a blue-tiled and gilded roof; here a teal rises from the reeds as one approaches, and over them the "thin blue needle of the dragon-fly" is poised in myriads. Scarlet, green, dun, light-blue and dark-blue, barred, ribbed, transparent, or mailed, the dragon-flies vibrate motionless over every piece of water in this water-logged city, but the Lu-kang and Lha-lu are their

THE SACRED ELEPHANT IN THE LUKANG GARDENS IN LHASA
The one elephant in Tibet

favorite haunts. The Lu-kang, or serpent-house, is so named because of the common belief that in the central island lives a serpent devil who needs an annual propitiation to keep flood waters from the town; the tradition re-appears also in a part of the Jo-kang itself, where the underground waters can be reached through a narrow and dark channel, and at the Lha-lu house a quarter of a mile away from the Lu-kang across the swamps. In each of these places there is approximately the same tradition connected with the supposed underground lake, which is ever ready to engulf the sacred city.[1] Immediately to the left as one enters the Lu-kang is the courtyard, in which the solitary elephant of Tibet is kept. He had a companion on the journey up from India destined for the Grand Lama of Tashi-lhunpo, but that one died—it would naturally have been that one.

The Ling-kor runs on through barley-fields to the east until it reaches the green trees overhanging the wall of the Royal Pastures at Re-ting, where the late regent, put to death in prison by the present Grand Lama ten years ago, had his residence. The temporary regent, whom we found in occupation in Lhasa, did not take up his residence here, as he had been appointed for a special emergency only. Soon after this Ramo-che is passed on the right hand. This somewhat uninteresting temple is reckoned in Tibetan eyes as inferior to the Jo-kang alone, and claims a clearly impossible antiquity; it is a medieval building of an undistinguished type, and the gilded roof is the prettiest thing about it. It contains, according to Chandra Das, only a collection of military relics, shields, spears, drums, and swords,

[1] It is not unlikely that this bogy has been created, or, at any rate, perpetuated, at the Lu-kang to scare away trespassers from the favorite picnicking ground of the Dalai Lama. His windows look out from the back directly down upon the Lu-kang. No well in Lhasa need be more than six feet deep, a fact which undoubtedly lies at the root of the subterranean lake theory.

and the image of King Srong-tsan-gambo's Nepalese wife. Nothing is more remarkable in Lhasa than the interior destitution of every temple except the Jo-kang itself. Nothing has been allowed to compete in even the most timid way with this august repository of the faith. The only other temple which is of peculiar interest besides the Jo-kang is the temple of the Chief Magician outside the walls, of which a full description will be given elsewhere.

Still going onward, the Ling-kor, now a pebbly length of banked-up causeway, curves round to inclose the Meru gompa on the extreme north-east of the town; here it touches the deep irrigation channels which drain off the water from the swamps in this direction, flat, treacherous, and wickedly green. This water-course is bridged by the Min-duk Sampa, or bridge of the Pleiades, over which the Chinese trade route runs into the city. The Ling-kor here becomes acquainted with strange surroundings, and it becomes but a dirty and befouled track running between houses of increasing squalor and disrepute. Thrust out on the eastern side are the shambles of Lhasa, for life may not be taken within the sacred precincts of the city, as was noted by Friar Oderic more than five hundred years ago. But this respect does not prevent the *via sacra* of the faith from being used as a refuse heap for the raw scraps of bone and skin and ugly red flesh from the butchers' shops which are thrown here to be mouthed and quarreled over by mangy dogs and the outlying scouts of the pig battalion.

The Ling-kor, now curving round the eastern side of the city, skirts the quarter where, as everywhere else in the world, the poor are congregated, and there are on all sides broken-down hovels with unrepaired holes, and empty window-holes grimy with the continual fog of smoke inside. On our left hand as we go round beside the swampy flats of Pala, which stretch out westward toward the distant river, the treacherous quagmire comes right up to the causeway on which the Ling-kor is now raised, though here and there a square plot of ground has been reclaimed from the morass and nourishes good barley, or a small plantation is set about a tiny poor house. But bad as this quarter is, it is respectability itself compared with the Ragyaba quarter, which we shall reach the moment we turn the corner to the right and begin to retrace our steps westward to Chagpo-ri and the Pargo Kaling. But before we reach the corner we notice the great heap of stones, another relic of the piety of pilgrims, who here lose or catch their first sight of the Potala palace.[1] As we retraverse the Ragyaba quarter the remembrance of a previous day is outrun by the reality of the moment; the foulness of these homes is equal to but, I think, more repulsive than that of Phari. It is true it is confined to a small quarter in Lhasa, but there is not here the saving grace of bitter cold to excuse, and possibly mitigate, the dirt and stench, and as one rode through them one could hardly imagine that one's own brothers and sisters of the human race were actually content to live in these low piggeries scattered here and there over the reeking black mud, which had long been churned into a greasy soup by the picking feet of the black swine that swarm throughout the quarter. Yet,

[1] I have said that pilgrims on the sacred way move always the way of the sun. But if the explanation of the heap of stones, which was given me by a lama, is true, it is clear that a certain number must go in the opposite direction, for the heap of stones to which I refer is placed exactly where the sight of the Potala is lost, not gained, by one going round the sacred way in the usual manner. On this whole question of the rotation of Lamaism I have throughout given the conventionally held view rather than a personal one. It is perfectly true that chortens and such things are passed on the road, as a rule, by the wayfarer keeping to his left. It is true that prayer-wheels are generally swung in the same direction, but on two occasions I have noticed on the sacred way itself an intelligent-looking monk briskly wheeling his prayer instrument in the opposite direction, and the ready explanation of some that this was a monk of the Beun-pa will not hold good, for the men were certainly following the usual circuit. The question of the swastika I have already alluded to, and I am inclined to think that although what I have said is, without doubt, the general rule of the faith, yet less importance is attached to it than is generally supposed.

strangely enough, here are the flowers of Lhasa. In these foul surroundings they bloom better than elsewhere—clean, upstanding hollyhocks, radiant of gentility; old-world stocks, with dainty crimson flowers and fine gray-green leaves; nasturtiums trailing their torn trumpets of fire, opal and gold, over the carrion filth of these decaying walls. It reminded one of the jeweled butterflies wheeling over the dirt of the Riang road.

On the left is a row of willows hedging about a water meadow, across which are two of the "lings," or gardens, which surround Lhasa.[1] Soon after this the wide black pools which mark the clearing in front of the Amban's house appear to the right, but the Ling-kor runs on below the willow-trees on the left, to the green plantations which have now taken the place of the houses; for now Lhasa proper has been left behind and we are moving along the southern side of the woodland waste between it and the Potala palace. The town has given place to the woodland, and the woodland will soon give place to the rock. Seven hundred yards on through this green avenue with a stream beside us moistening the roots of the willows brings the pilgrim to a sharp upstanding spur of stone.

It is not one of the least extraordinary things connected with Lhasa that no visitor, traveler, or spy seems to have made the complete circuit of the Ling-kor. Not only are the maps we possess consistently wrong in a matter about which no mistake can possibly be made by any one who has seen the place, but no account or description has hitherto been given of one of the most remarkable features of Lhasa. The steep limestone cliffs fall sharply down beside the running stream which here is merged into the wide flood of the Kyi chu. One of the channels of this river actually washes the base of this limestone

[1] It was in one of these that the Commissioner was invited to take up his residence on his arrival in the city, but the place was inconvenient for many reasons and the Lha-lu house was chosen instead.

outcrop, and the path has been cut out of the rock three feet wide in the manner of the ordinary mountain trang. It slowly rises to a height of nearly a hundred feet, almost every yard of the way being marked by images, chortens, or deep-cut mantras on the rock. Flat stones in innumerable quantities, bearing the unvarying formula, are carefully set up on end; tens of thousands of little clay medals, bearing some religious impress, are strewn on every ledge. On the top of this ascent one looks away over the wide waste of the Kyi chu river, and there are few sights in the world more beautiful than that which here meets the eye. Far and wide the sunlit river stretches its shallows; one could almost believe that Lhasa was an island in a lake, and the picturesque foliage of the trees and flowers that rise at the foot of the long slaty cliffs, just where the southern sunshine washes them all day and the rock gives out its warmth to them all night, are more luxuriant than anywhere else beside the sacred way. The Ling-kor descends here somewhat abruptly, finding a foothold at the base of the rocks by which you may climb from here to Chagpo-ri—it is as it were the sprawled near hind-leg of the couching lion of stone.

Now the most impressive sight of all the Ling-kor is in front of us. It is a gigantic rock, flat and facing the stream squarely; the whole surface is a close-set gallery of Buddhas of all sizes and colors, jostling each other's knees in their profusion; at a distance in the sunlight it looks as if a vast carpet of vivid color has been thrown over the face of the rock. There can hardly be less than twenty thousand of these figures, the majority being small images but two inches high, cut in symmetrical rows by hundreds upon a convenient surface of the rock itself, or propped up on detached slabs against the cliff side. Others, from nine inches to two feet in height, cover the entire surface of the great rock disposed round the big Buddha in the center. He is twenty feet in height, and below him in enormous gaudy letters of the deepest relief is the parent mantra of all the "*om mani padme hums*" of Tibet. Each letter is cut six feet in height out of the living rock, and the total length of the text must be thirty feet at least; the colors of the letters follow each other in this order—white, green, yellow, slate, blue, red, and dark indigo.[1]

Twenty yards on there are two small flat houses in a garden of their own, where the road turns inward a little, and the path passes away into a wide and well-kept road, fringed on either side by green plantations overhanging adobe walls. A hundred yards later a common is reached, which the Ling-kor incloses by making a sharp right-angled turn at the opposite side of it. Strictly speaking, the pilgrim should throughout his circumambulation keep to the actual track, but the slant across the common which cuts the corner is suspiciously well worn. Another point at which a deviation is apparently made is in the omission of that part of the Ling-kor which goes outside the Lu-kang. Here my syce met an old friend whom he had known in Gangtok in former days, and though she was obviously off the main route, she still assured Tsering that she was performing the ceremonial circuit. After all, your Tibetan is a very human person.

A quarter of a mile further on the road, still running north, meets our starting-point underneath the rock on which the Chi-

[1] This is the sacred sequence, and I was glad to find in this classical example in Lhasa corroboration of the frequent notes that I had made on the way up. It is to be noted that the coloring of the last symbol but one carefully distinguishes between the D and the M of which it is composed, the upper symbol D belonging strictly to the previous syllable *pa;* the coloring of the vowel sound above it indicates the relationship of the vowel to the underwritten M. The Lamaic tradition attaches considerable importance to the proper distinction of the vowels of this great formula.

This difference in color between the D and the vowel mark above it is in this case almost the only remaining proof that there ever was an M at all, for the whole of the rock at this most holy point has been worn into the most gigantic "cup-mark" in the world. There is a smooth, worn hole three or four feet in depth and height and five feet in length, from or into which the pious either throw, or take, a pebble, for the dust of it is accounted miraculous in its efficacy for diseases of both soul and body.

nese temple stands. At this point, it will be remembered that the buildings and gardens of the Kun-de-ling press upon the road itself. These "lings"—the word literally means a garden—are four in number; they represent four lamaic colleges from among whose members the regent of the Dalai Lama was in old days invariably chosen. From this rule an apparent exception was made in the middle of last century, and if the sudden demise of the Dalai Lama should make it necessary for the hierarchy to elect a new regent, it is more than probable that they would select some one from De-bung or another of the great monasteries outside the walls in whose hands the political power is now wholly vested. The tradition, however, has in the past been a useful check upon intrigue. Of the other lings, Tengye-ling is a large but uninteresting building which one passes on the right, if, instead of branching down to the Yutok road from the Potala palace, one keeps straight along by the road which, as I have noticed on the occasion of our first entrance into Lhasa, is as a rule one continuous puddle. Here the Tongsa Penlop took up his abode, with unerring judgment, for Tengye-ling is quite the most comfortable of the four. If, however, his followers adopted the same methods in Lhasa as had marked their progress to the city, it is more than likely that the sacred treasures of Tengye-ling have been seriously reduced in number by this time. Chomo-ling is an insignificant structure, almost concealed in trees, not far from Ramo che, and the fourth and last is Tsecho-ling, which is outside the city altogether, across the river to the south.

With this brief survey of the course taken by the Ling-kor this chapter must end, though we shall have to return across its sacred ribbon when the gem of all that lies within it is to be described, and the reader will be asked to penetrate with me into that holiest of all holies, the Jo-kang, or the very "place of God" itself.

CHAPTER XVIII

THE ENVIRONS OF LHASA

IMMEDIATELY after his arrival in Lhasa, Colonel Younghusband had asked that a proper residence should be provided for him. To this request there was, of course, the usual Tibetan demur, more the result of habit than intention, whereupon the Colonel announced his willingness, and, if some action were not at once taken by the Lhasan officials, his intention to occupy Norbu-ling, the summer residence of the Grand Lama just outside the Ling-kor and within a few hundred yards of the point on which our camp had been pitched. This veiled threat brought the Tibetans to some sense of the respect that must be paid to the English representative, and they even went so far as to say that any one of the houses of the Sha-pés was at his disposal if only he would leave Norbu-ling alone. In the end Lha-lu house, the finest private residence in Tibet, was placed at the Commissioner's disposal, and the Mission moved into it on August 12th. The reason of this perturbation on the part of the Tibetans was simply that Norbu-ling is the summer residence of the Dalai Lama. It has a perfectly square garden or plantation, surrounded by a well-built wall, each side being a quarter of a mile in length, and to secure greater seclusion—though it is difficult to imagine what trespassing can be possible over this stout barrier—a second wall has been built inside the outer barrier for nearly its whole extent. Inside this again is a house and a temple of no pretensions whatever, save that, from the distance, a small gilded roof and half-a-dozen golden "gyan-tsens" distinguish it somewhat. The only

TIBETAN WOODS AND MEADOWS NEAR LHASA

acquaintance we ever had with the interior of Norbu-ling was that obtained by looking down upon the whole plain of Lhasa from the high crest of the hill across the river. No member of the force penetrated into the inclosed garden, and therefore the vague stories we were told about it by the natives are all that there is to report. They really seemed to know as little of the interior as ourselves. It was built in its present form only eight years ago, and as a residence for the Dalai Lama does not claim a greater antiquity than 1870. The trees bear out this statement, for they are nearly all of small dimensions. The Dalai Lama lives here for two months in the summer, observing the same state as before, and hedged about with an even greater seclusion than that which marks him at his palace on the rock a mile away. There was a rumor during our stay in Lhasa that the Dalai Lama was actually in hiding in Norbu-ling, and it is beyond question that a large number of European rifles were stored in this pleasure house. The Dalai Lama, however, when once he had turned his back upon the people committed to his charge, never looked back, and if the latest reports, at the time of writing, be true, the soon-to-be-deposed pontiff must have made his way hot-foot to Urga, in Mongolia, where he remains the unwelcome guest of his spiritual brother, the Taranath Lama.

The outer walls of Norbu-ling are, as I have said, of splendid workmanship, and they offer a good example of the peculiar stone-laying of Lhasa. Divided by lines, three "stretchers" deep, of stone almost as thin as a tile, the greater blocks are ranged in courses separated from each other by splinters of granite set horizontally and symmetrically between the bigger lumps. This is the universal method of laying the masonry of Lhasa; it will be found throughout the province of U and in rare cases in Tsang also, but we found it is specially characteristic of Lhasa, though I do not know how far the custom has extended to the East. The upper part of this wall is friezed above a string course with maroon red and at the south-east corner there is a curious and unexpected symbol of a religion with which Lamaism should have nothing in common. Half-way along the southern side, where there is but fifteen yards between the water of the Kyi chu and the wall, is a latticed projection containing about 430 small, well-designed images of the Master, and one strangely inconsequent white china figure of a lady on a beast, which might have come from Germany. Here there was good fishing, and beside this little shrine the "Nightmare"[1] put off his panoply of war and deftly drew the mud-barbel from the waters of the Kyi chu.

As we have said, this haunt was left inviolate, and the Mission established itself at the Lha-lu house. This is a large and substantial building, seven or eight hundred yards away from the Lu-kang ford of the Kaling chu, twelve hundred yards north-west from Potala. There is a road across the marsh to it so that one may arrive there dry-shod, but, like most other places on the Plain of Milk, the luxuriance of its gardens and plantations is greatly due to the fact that the soil is saturated with water. This, it will be remembered, is one of the five beautiful things, and well it deserves the name. Always excepting the Lu-kang, there is nothing in Lhasa, not even the vegetation near the Sacred Rock, that equals the luxuriance of this spot.

The house itself is built round a large, open quadrangle with galleries on three sides of it in the usual way; the northern side of this quadrangle is the southern wall of the main house, and here Colonel Younghusband took up his quarters. Some description of a typical Tibetan house should be given in these pages, and a better example than Lha-lu cannot, as I have said, be found.

[1] This we found to our amusement was Captain Ottley's recognized name among the Tibetans. There is a good deal to be said for the applicability and picturesqueness of the title, and its universal adoption by the Tibetans betrays the terror with which the ubiquitous mounted infantry inspired the people along the road. The work done by Captain Peterson and Lieutenant Bailey in the same corps was invaluable.

THE ELABORATE DETAIL OF TIBETAN ARCHITECTURE

Over a small stream in front of the house one passes by a bridge obliquely into the courtyard. The outer walls of the house are of no importance, and the quadrangle itself, though paved, is muddy and generally heaped with odds and ends; all round the base under the first balcony the horses and mules of the owners are as a rule ranged, but on our arrival in the place our beasts were banished to more convenient quarters outside. Hence, immediately in front of one rose the considerable mass of the main residence; on the left, a door led into an inclosed garden and toward the summer-house and temple, beautifully set about with foliage. On the right a similar doorway led to the menials' buildings and lesser stablings. Crossing the courtyard, one enters the house by a small and insignificant door in the center of its southern side. The mud, through and over which one has gingerly to pick one's way, stepping from stone to stone, enters the house as freely as ourselves, and in the sudden dark one can only just distinguish the corner down which a precipitous ladder slants. It is impossible here to choose one's steps, so one plunges through the mud and stones to reach the base of the ladder, which, it must be remembered, is the only way in which a visitor or resident, high or low, can reach the house itself. Up the slippery iron-sheathed treads one goes, clinging desperately to the polished willow hand-rail, and at the top one is confronted across the passage by the durbar room of the house.

This is also the chapel, and three seated figures of gilt bronze, properly draped with katags, are ranged in recesses along the opposite wall. On either side of them the wall is pigeon-holed for books. No photograph can even suggest the decoration of this room. Color covers every single square inch of wall space or pillar from end to end. Scarlet and emerald green, gold and Reckitt's blue predominate to the exclusion of half-tones, harmonizing, however, more than would be thought possible. Above this room, which is lighted by a vertical opening in the roof, is the floor on which the family lives, and it is curious to emerge from the mud and untidiness of the ground level to the dainty finish of this beautiful series of rooms. There were seventeen living rooms, and of these ten were decorated in the same lavish manner as below. Ornament was not confined to the walls; latticed screens of paper, silk, and even glass separated one part of a room from the other, and all and everything were figured with richly tinted specimens of local or Chinese draftsmanship. Colonel Younghusband took up his abode in the central room overlooking the courtyard. From immediately above his window ran many ropes on which huge sun-blinds should have rested. But these, with all the other furniture of the house, had been taken away by the young representative of the Lha-lu family before we came to occupy the family mansion. This clearance was done at our request, as we had, or could obtain, sufficient furniture for our own needs, and we did not wish to run the risk of damaging our host's property.

Almost the only thing left in the house was a cheap pendulum clock made by the Ansonia clock company. These very rare recurrences of Western civilization never influenced the intensely Oriental seclusion of Lhasa. One noticed them from time to time with a shock—a shock of regret, it must be said—for if Lhasa be not free from the cheapness of machine-made manufactures, what place on earth can be? One remarkable exception to this rule of exclusion must be mentioned. Umbrellas with the touching guarantee "waterproof" pasted inside the peak are fairly common at Lhasa, whither they must have come from India, where their use is widely spread. But except for these occasional adoptions, the race of men who dwell in Lhasa remains in thought and word and deed unchanged and, perhaps, unchangeable from that which listened to Tsong-kapa's passionate appeal for reform, or, before his day, to the deep learning of Atisha, or, earlier still, to the blasphemies of the apostate Lang-darma in the dawn of Tibetan history. Lhasa never changes.

IN THE GROUNDS OF THE LHA-LU HOUSE, THE HEADQUARTERS OF THE MISSION IN LHASA

The gardens of Lha-lu are, as I have said, almost a swamp. On the only really dry portion of them two buildings have been erected, one half summer-house, half temple, the other a glazed greenhouse; these are not of any great interest, though the former is of considerable age, and underneath the dirt collected on the frescoes the exquisite finish of the painting can still be distinguished. To make a circuit of these beautiful grounds one leaves the summer-house and strikes across to the west, picking one's way along the higher and drier "bunds" beneath the willow trees and among swarms of dragon-flies, as fearless and as thick as midges in England. Mr. White and I went for a photographic excursion one morning, and he made some excellent plates. Few, I think, will prove as beautiful as those of the water-meadows of Lha-lu. You can roam about among them at the back of the house for half a mile, and then you will strike a little wooded track, for all the world like a hazel-canopied lane in Devonshire. Kitchen gardens adjoin Lha-lu house to the east, and the little hovels in which the gardeners live are pressed up against the walls of the lane which divides the house from these grounds, but in every other direction there is a water-sodden stretch of plain or plantation across which artificial roads alone give one a dry-shod passage.

Sera Monastery lies due north of the town and De-bung, not three miles distant, lies west-north-west. There was an interesting morning spent outside the latter place. The monks who had undertaken to supply us with tsamba failed utterly to keep their promise within the given time, and it became necessary to enforce our demands. The little column therefore moved out of camp one day with the guns and made ready to occupy the wide-stretching waste of white monastery. After waiting for two or three hours, however, the monks thought it wiser to comply, and, in the General's opinion, enough was given on the spot as earnest of a future delivery to justify him in abandoning his intentions. On this occasion I made first acquaintance with a temple to which I had previously referred as, of all the buildings of Lhasa, second only in interest to the Jo-kang. This is the exquisite temple and house belonging to the Chief Magician of the country. Half a mile short of De-bung, it lies almost concealed in the lower trees of a deep ravine running up into the hills, the only part of it which is visible from a distance being the golden roof.

Returning on the following day, Mr. Claude White and I made a careful tour of inspection through all the buildings of the place, being received by the monks with the utmost hospitality. In many ways this temple stands on a plane of its own, and is not entirely typical of other similar structures in the country, but it was more interesting therefore to make such close acquaintance with an institution unique in the world. Going among the white-washed houses at the foot of the monastery, I took a photograph which shows the essential difference which distinguishes this little community from that of almost every other district in Tibet. It might almost be part of an Italian town in those very Marches of Ancona from which the Capuchin community of Lhasa was drawn. In the early days of the eighteenth century, some fleeting memory of far-distant Macerata may well have home-sickened for a moment Costantino or Beligatti as the pair turned in from the wide, flat Plain of Milk toward the wooded little temple of the chief wizard.

The temple itself may be reached either from the left, or more directly up the sharp flight of steps which faces the reader in the picture here. To the main entrance, that to the left, the visitor makes his way circuitously, passing beside a luxuriant little plantation of deep grass, where rambling shrubs and trees grow so thickly that they almost make a twilight round their stems. As I was passing this on one occasion there was a sound from the hidden depths of the wood which was like nothing in the world so much as the subterranean roar which heralds Fafnir's unwieldy entrance. I suppose that really some of the younger monks were being taught to blow a sixteen-foot trumpet, but the sound was one which added the last note of mystery to the scene. Fifty yards further, we arrive opposite the main entrance on the right.

I am not sure that this temple is not, the Cathedral always apart, the most interesting thing in Tibet. It is small, entirely complete in itself, finished *ad unguem,* daintily clean, and had evidently received more money and attention than any other gompa on our road. The well-wooded ascending track of the valley beside which it is built continues upward after it has debouched into the courtyard, which here, as everywhere, divides the main gateways of the temple from the usual row of cloistered frescoes opposite. The scene here is of unusual beauty and interest; it is very seldom in Tibet that the contrast of luxuriant foliage and vivid temple color is obtained. There is a peculiar color harmony which distinguishes the Na-chung Chos-kyong. Green there is in the background, green of more shades than a camera can detect, and the deep, claret brown of the temple buildings is handsomely accentuated above by golden roofs, and harmonizes well below with the plain gray ocher of the courtyard stones, and the interminable strings of gauzy fluttering prayer-flags of every tint between the two. To his left are the vivid colors of an appalling fresco of flayed human bodies, skulls full of blood, and in general those gory heaps of human vitals which seem peculiarly attractive to the pious Tibetan mind. On his right the flight of steps will take him into the temple itself. He enters at the side of the great cloistered courtyard and passes through a double-pillared corridor ornamented with armor and weapons of strange make, out and again into the sunlight of the quadrangle. In the middle of the court, in front of him now, as he turns to the left, are the main entrances of the temple behind the many-pillared arcade; they are screened by heavy yak-hair curtains through which one can catch a glimpse of a gaudy wealth of color on wall and pillar and ceiling, and of the five or six great doors, scarlet and cardinal and flesh color. In the middle of the courtyard, immediately in front of him, is a little tree growing in a perforated square-stone lattice, within which, all around its stem, is a proud bank of English hollyhocks and a few vivid nasturtiums tumbling carelessly through the lower interstices of the trellis. Beside it is a pillar about eight feet high, with a tiny roof of gold atop. Just over the edge of the temple entrance appears, high up against the blue, the great golden roof, and standing guard by it many gyan-tsen, gilded and fluttering with overlapping flounces of silk, salmon and olive and rose-madder.

The presiding deity of this temple has long fled away with his master, the Dalai Lama, but the services go on and the temple is lovingly cared for in his absence. So far as one may make a guess at the character of a man from his house, it is easy to see that the Chief Magician of Lhasa is of an unusually refined and dainty taste; the care which is visible in every corner of this temple we had not found even suggested in any other building in the country. It looked as though a housemaid had been round with a duster an hour before our arrival. The abbot of the monastery received us very courteously and was interested and amused by Mr. White's large camera.[1] While he was taking a series of views in the pillared arcade outside the doors of the shrine, I sat down and hastily recorded a suggestion of the coloring of this arcade. I can claim with pride that the attractions of Mr. White paled in a second beside the interest which a four or five deep ring of monks took, not so much in my painting as in my paint-box. Some one—he presumably was the artist of the community—was hurriedly sent for, and when he came, must have severely taxed

[1] It was an unfailing source of mystification to the Tibetans to be allowed to look at the reversed picture in the ground glass under the black velvet. The curious thing is that, so far as we could find out from their exclamations, they did not often recognize the reversed picture as that of the scene in front of the lens. It was for them merely a beautiful pattern of varying colors seen in a singularly effective manner.

A STREET SCENE IN THE WIZARD COMMUNITY OF THE NA-CHUNG CHOS-KYONG AT LHASA

The roofs of the houses are made of golden plates

his own ingenuity in his gesticulating and fluent account of such mysteries as a block of Whatman's "hot pressed" and a typewriter eraser. No one in Tibet ever draws anything in front of him, so it was, perhaps, a lenient crowd of critics that watched my rapid daubs of color as I sketched the temple. The colors were blinding in their vividness and juxtaposition, and the whole of this arcaded temple-front was painted from end to end in the same gorgeous manner. Not a corner of the roof has escaped the brush of the painter or the hand of the gilder; the pillars, reported more nobly tinted still, were wound round and round from top to bottom with crimson cloth, so carefully sewn that we had not the face to ask the monks to uncover one; nothing, however, could have added much to the incredible play of gaudy hues.

Soon afterward the great doors, each bearing a monstrous representation of a flayed human skin, were opened for us and we went inside into the temple itself. This, too, was clean and as bright in color as the portico, though the mellowed light which filtered through awnings and screens from above took off somewhat from the painful edge of contrast and crudity.

The ornamentation throughout this temple was of its own kind. It differed in many ways from that which is usually in vogue in Tibet; every doorway has a beading of human skulls or decapitated heads cut roughly out of wood and painted minutely; long hangings of black satin, from the lower edge of which the same heads, with long black tresses of silk, hang helplessly, frieze the walls, and a curious and ghastly *pot-pourri* of skulls, entrails, eyeballs, brains, torn-out tongues, and human beings suffering every conceivable mutilation and torture which man has ever devised, adorn the walls below. Underneath this again was a dado of souls burning in hell-fire. But it says much for the ability of man to adapt himself to his surroundings that, after a moment, even these sights were not entirely disagreeable, and one could soon see beneath these horrible representations the same spirit of devotion which moved the pen of a Dante or the brush of a fourteenth-century Benedictine.

At the far end of the temple, opposite the doors, is the sanctuary, a wide and deep inner chapel. Here a striking departure from the customary arrangement is to be seen; in the central and advanced position, elsewhere invariably occupied by the largest image of Buddha that the foundation possesses, was the empty seat of the Magician himself; on it were heaped his ceremonial robes, his sword of office, and a small, circular shield of exquisite workmanship, ornamented with a golden "Hum" in the center. Into the top of the shield was inlet an irregular lump which may have been merely colored glass, but which looked extraordinarily like one of those guava-jelly-like lumps of polished but uncut spinel ruby which are not infrequently found among the treasures of Indian rajahs. Behind this silver-gilt throne was an embossed silver proscenium, framing in the dispossessed Buddha. To the right of it hung the state crown of the Magician, which is a beautiful piece of work, charmingly finished ivory skulls alternating with florets of silver heavily powdered with imitation diamonds; round the circlet itself were several large imitation sapphires, relieved here and there by some really good turquoise lumps.[1] All round this chapel were cupboards and recesses of which the orifice was in every case entirely concealed by knotted katags. Pushing them aside, one could discover dimly in the darkness beautifully finished brass images, half life-size, either of some repulsive god-monster, or of some one of those groups which, go where you will in Tibet, are accepted as necessary and inevitable symbols of a worship which, in its essence, is purity itself. In one place or another were lying about here the Oracle's gorget, mask, bow,

[1] It was a little difficult to examine this crown, from the darkness of the chapel; but this is, so far as I can remember it, a fair description of the jewel.

and divining-glass, and though he had been gone for four weeks or more, he might have stepped back that evening and found his shrine ready and to the last detail arranged for service. Mr. Claude White was lucky enough to persuade the monks to sell to him the little circular shield I have described. They said they could easily replace it, and I am inclined to think that they made more than a trifle out of the transaction.

We descended the two or three steps of this dais, down on to the chunam floor of the outer temple.[1] On either side of the main aisle were twelve huge drums, and thick heavy cushions lay out in an avenue toward the great doors. On the right, as one came down the sanctuary steps, was a very large silver chorten against the far wall, studded in profusion with lumps of raw amber, as big as, and not much unlike, golden pippins. We came out again into the sunshine of the court and the shade of the portico. Our kindly hosts had provided us with tea and boiled eggs and we sat down on piled-up cushions for luncheon. It did not take us long to realize that it was as well that we had brought some sandwiches with us, for we made the distressing discovery, egg after egg, that Tibetan tastes in this matter are a mean, but not a happy one, between those of Europe and of China. An egg absolutely black with age is not unpleasant to the taste, but these eggs which were only just beginning to qualify for a Chinese menu were something terrible, and we felt confused at having to seem unappreciative of the kindness of our friendly wizards.

A crow had built its nest over the big blue board which surmounts the main door and craked apprehensively from time to time. The orange and blue swallows dipped and wheeled in the sun outside, and the just-seen tree tops beyond the cloister

[1] This chunam floor is a fine banket of minute pebbles and cement which receives a high polish, and though it is nowhere here brought to such perfection as at Agra or Delhi, it makes a very permanent and even handsome flooring and is much used in Tibet.

roof helped to make snugger still the brilliant little home of meditation and of magic. Immediately beyond the trees the dull, unclad rock half inclosed this jewel of a temple, and the faint rustle of the little stream was hushed. We finished our meal and went down again into the courtyard between the two painted lions which guard the five steps. That on the dexter is blue, his sinister companion is green. Nothing seems to have escaped the brush of the painter here. A tour of inspection round the galleries of the cloisters revealed a little plate armor—which is a somewhat remarkable thing—and a large number of shao horns heavily whitewashed, in some cases trophied with dorje-handled swords. Then we were invited to look at the other rooms of the gompa, and we went up the usual slippery ladders to an upper portico as beautifully painted as every other part of the building, and so up again on to the topmost story protected by the great golden roof.

This was the first golden Lhasan roof I had an opportunity of studying carefully. It is always claimed that one at least of the golden canopies of the Jo-kang is really made of plates of gold—and after a close examination I am half inclined to think that the central one is actually made throughout of the precious metal, extraordinary though it seems—but in general the gold is coated heavily upon sheets of copper, after the copper has been embossed or cast, or repousséed, as the fancy of the artist suggests. It is, I believe, laid on in an amalgam of mercury, but of this I could not get any very certain information. These golden roofs are unquestionably the most striking ornaments of Lhasa. One can see them for miles, for, in this light clean air, no distance will dim the burning tongue of white flame that stabs like a heliograph from the upper line of a far misty outline of palace or temple, and there is no doubt that the last and greatest impression of Lhasa, still vivid when nearly all else has been forgotten with age, will be that of the first sight of "the Golden Roofs of Potala." All that that romantic phrase suggested beforehand was realized to the full, and just as to the opium-sodden imagination of De Quincey the words "Consul Romanus" summed up the grandeur of Rome, so perhaps these five words will longest recall to those who saw them the image of that ancient and mysterious faith which has found its last and fullest expression beneath the golden canopies of Lhasa.

Returning to the ground, we passed again through the courtyard and out down the steps. Thence we turned up toward the trees which, from the upper slope, overhang Na-chung Chos-kyong. It was a pretty little spot, cool and sequestered, and if we had not been specially invited to do so, we should never have dreamed of going farther to where a few plain whitewashed walls seemed to indicate one of the monks' dormitories. Somewhat uninterested, we allowed ourselves, however, to be taken forward by a monk, and after avoiding the teeth of a particularly large watchdog, we turned to the left into one of the prettiest and best-protected little gardens I have ever seen. I leave it to botanists to explain how it is that we found here, 13,000 feet above the sea, a tall, flourishing hedge of bamboos, twenty-five feet high, shielding from the only exposed quarter the little garden and the little house of the Magician himself. Even from the little green shaded garden we could see clearly enough that this was no ordinary residence; a tiny stream of running water passed underneath the plain sloping walls of the wizard's abode, separating from its clean and well sun-blinded architecture the mallows and nasturtiums, the trailing roses and the potted stocks which might almost have been collected into that little space together to give the same twinge of memory to an English visitor that the whitened houses three hundred yards away must have conveyed to men of Italy. A large maple tree overhangs the entrance to the house.

The interior of this little residence is of a dainty perfection that you could hardly match in Japan, and instinctively one felt that one should take off one's boots before treading on these exquisite inlaid wooden floors. Every part of the surface of the walls is covered with minute miniature-like frescoes; the private chapel, though stripped of every ornament, remained a gem, and in the wizard's own private room the perforated screens of gilt and painted wood were marvels of intricate and delicate design. We remained here no long time, and soon after made our way back to Lhasa, well pleased indeed with our day's entertainment.

I do not know whether I have been successful in conveying, in even one particular, the aspect of Lhasa in its plain. Perhaps it is impossible to do more than to set out a string of descriptive facts with all the fullness that is possible, and then let the reader reconstruct, with photographs and his imagination, what after all is more essential than anything else, the atmosphere which enshrouds the least interesting thing upon the Plain of Milk.

Every traveler will know at once what I mean when I say that the character of the country is as distinct and peculiar to itself as is that of every other Eastern land, and that the very smell of incense and burning butter, frowziness and never-washed humanity, which is inseparable from the smallest object inside a Tibetan temple, is as different from the clean perfume of Japan, or from the heavy, almost visibly dirty air and stinks of a Chinese temple, as both of these differ from the tawdry gorgeousness and cold make-believe of an Indian shrine. There is only one place that I know in the world which at all recalls the scent of Tibet, and that is the inner chambers of the underground temple in the fort of Allahabad, places which ladies are rarely invited to inspect. Here the undecaying Akshai Bar, sacred to Buddha under the name of Breguman, is probably the only center of Buddhist worship where there has been no break in the continuity of worship from the days of Huien Tsang, the Chinese traveler of the seventh century, to our own. I do not suppose that in this original identity of creed there is anything more than a coincidence—certainly the Hindus have no intention of honoring Gautama here—but in the dark underground chamber of this temple there is the taste of a gompa. There, and there alone, so far as I know, is that greasy warm stench of mingled sweetness and putridity which one comes very soon to associate with the very sound of the letters which spell Tibet.

The Sen-dé-gye-sum or Three Great Monasteries lie round Lhasa, north, west, and east. De-bung lies two and a half to three miles west-north-west; Sera is two miles due north, and Gaden is about twenty-two miles east as the crow flies, but is nearly thirty by road. There is a strong similarity between these three foundations; they are in every case built in closely connected tiers of white houses, rising one above another at the foot of a mountain spur. From a distance they look clean, prosperous, and not unpicturesque; one ribald member of the Mission suggested that they looked like glorified Riviera hotels. The simile is not altogether unfair, though even the wildest dreams of M. Ritz can hardly include a caravansary for eight thousand guests. All three were founded by Tsong-kapa, who is reported, on almost worthless evidence, to have been born in 1357 and to have died in 1419. It seems clear, however, that these foundations date from the extreme end of the fourteenth century to the end of the first quarter of the fifteenth. The central gompa may in each case still be, or at least include, the original work of Tsong-kapa, but the endless series of whitewashed tenements built of mud which surround them in closely packed crowds must often have been replaced since his day. Few indeed are made of granite. De-bung is the senior monastery of the three in point of importance; its name means the "rice heap," and it is spelled in the Tibetan language "abras-spungs." Here nearly

8,000 monks occupy themselves daily in saying their offices, basking in the sun, and intriguing in political affairs. Dorjieff, it will be remembered, was one of this body, and it was commonly reported to us in Lhasa that the influence of De-bung had for a long time been paramount in the Tsong-du. Luckily, perhaps, for others, the hostility between Sera and De-bung is very marked, and it is even asserted by some that the name Sera, which lies just out of sight of De-bung, round a projecting spur of the northern hills, was chosen in order to symbolize the harm which "ser" hail does to rice heaps. But it seems likely that the original name was derived from "ser" gold. Sera[1] is the community in closest religious connection with the Dalai Lama, and it must be remembered that anything which belongs to his Holiness is never mentioned without the prefix "ser." If it were necessary to set on record the fact, the chronicler of great Potala would have to describe an operation uncommon in Tibet, as the blowing of his Holiness' golden nose with his golden handkerchief, or more probably, if strict truth had to be maintained, with his golden fingers. Everything about him is golden in the eye of the Tibetan, his clothes, his food, his chair, his decrees, his prayers, all are golden, and it is more than likely that the derivation from hail was a happy thought of some quick-witted monk who wished to crystallize into a phrase the permanent hostility that exists between these two monasteries.

The distinguishing characteristic of this monastery of De-bung lies in its supernatural and oracular attainments. Sera, on the other hand, is chiefly famous for its relics, and Gaden, which is far removed from the immediate strife and intrigues of Lhasa, retains its reputation for mere piety. At Sera is kept the original dorje of Buddha. I do not know that any European visitor, even Desideri, has ever been permitted to see the imple-

[1] The traditional date of Sera is 1417.

ment, but there is no doubt that its possession, or perhaps its reputed possession, is a source of great superstitious strength to this community. Here there are 5,500 monks, and its nearness and visibility to Lhasa is no doubt a source of considerable strength. The internal jurisdiction of all these monasteries is not unlike that enjoyed by an Oxford college, though more serious offenses have to be submitted to the council of state. "The idols here," reports Nain Singh, "differ in size and hideousness, but the lower parts of the figures are generally those of men." The Abbé Huc allows himself some liberty of description; he records the presence of hollies and cypresses and notes that the monastery buildings stand out upon the green base of the hill. It is necessary to record the fact that Sera is less wooded than any other part of the Lhasa plain, as it stands back against a rocky mountain cliff bare of all vegetation until a small shelf, 800 feet above the monastery, affords root hold for a plantation of hardy poplars only. Beside it, on the plain, are a few more trees of the same species, but the golden roof of Sera must still be counted its chief external attraction. The General pitched the camp of the escort about a mile away from this monastery, and the continual friendliness shown by the good monks of Sera may be attributable partly to this fact, but even more perhaps to the delight with which they saw their hated sister of De-bung compelled to disgorge many hundreds of thousands of pounds of flour and grain.

Gaden is chiefly famous because it contains the tomb of Tsong-kapa himself. The following account of the monastery is taken from the Survey Reports of the Government of India by Sandberg:

"It (the tomb of Tsong-kapa) is a lofty mausoleum-like structure of marble and malachite with a gilded roof; inside this outer shell is to be seen a beautiful chorten shrine of cube, pyramid, and surmounting cone, all said to be of solid gold. Within this golden casket, wrapped in fine cloths, inscribed in sacred Dharani syllables, are the embalmed remains of the great reformer, disposed in a sitting attitude. Another notable object here is a magnificent representation of Champo, the Buddha to come, seated European fashion on a throne. Beside him stands a life-size image of Tsong-kapa in his character of Jan-pal Nin-po, which is supposed to be his name in the Gaden heavens. A rock-hewn wall with impress of hands and feet is also shown as Tsong-kapa's. A very old statue of Shinje, the lord of death, is much reverenced here, every visitor presenting gifts and doing it infinite obeisance. The floor of the large central chamber appears to be covered with brilliant enameled tiles, whilst another shrine holds an effigy of Tsong-kapa with images of his five disciples standing round him. The library contains manuscript copies of the saint's work in his own handwriting."

The last regent of Tibet was Abbot of Gaden, a fact which did not save him from, and perhaps even accelerated, his assassination.

While we were making these investigations and using every moment of our time in the forbidden precincts, negotiations were faring but ill. The Tibetans were trying their usual tactics; they were only anxious to delay negotiations on every possible excuse. It must be remembered that ever since the present Dalai Lama ousted, imprisoned and ultimately put to death the regent in whose hands the entire political control of Tibetan affairs had rested, His Holiness has ruled his ministers with a rod of iron. The state, in a sense far more exact than that in which Louis XIV used the phrase, was himself, and we found a terrified unwillingness on the part of any other official, however high his rank, to accept the responsibility of making any arrangement whatever. It may be suggested that the Tsong-du remained, and that it, as the power behind the throne, was qualified to carry on negotiations; but it must be remembered that the Tsong-du is essentially a deliberative, not an executive body; it is as impossible to make a treaty with the Tsong-du as to make one with the House of Commons, and this disability was one which was readily perceived and turned to use by the Tibetans themselves. Secure by their anomalous composition and acephalous nature, the Tsong-du, which now sat in continual session from morning to night, only rendered the action of the remaining dignitaries of Lhasa the more difficult. The Dalai Lama, whose presence in Lhasa would have simplified matters for us exceedingly, had gone away, ostensibly on a pilgrimage connected with the religious meditation in which he had now been immersed since the first mention of the approach of an English Mission. It is true that, as we have seen, his seclusion was one which His Holiness was ready to suspend at any moment at which he thought that he could deliver an effective stroke in the political arena, but in the eyes of Tibetans it perhaps justified his flight from his capital—an act of prudence which strangely resembled Mr. Kruger's in 1900. It may be that, as in this other case of a people bigotedly superstitious, sensitive to foreign intrusion in any form, and in their origin formed by a distinctly religious exodus, the head of the state may have felt that his absence, by interposing even a few months' delay, allowed time for the operations of Providence. More probably the flight of the Dalai Lama was also commended to him by the fact that in the future he would be able, at his leisure, to deal with the situation which had been created in his absence. That the Chinese would ever actively interfere must have been the last thing he expected, and knowing the climate of his country well, he must have realized a cogent reason for our early withdrawal.

Perhaps he builded better than he knew, but the coping-stone has still to be set upon his policy; we do not even now, in January, 1905, know the real results in Lhasa itself of the expedition, and, though the matter will be touched upon in greater detail hereafter, it may be said that upon the action of this unknown factor in Central Asian politics the future almost entirely depends. When he fled from Lhasa he left the great seal in the charge of the Tipa (or Ti) Rimpoche, but, as the latter plaintively remarked, he had been given no specific authority to use it.

Immediately before our arrival in Lhasa we made the important discovery that the 1890–93 Convention, which was denounced by the Dalai Lama as having been made without the co-operation or consent of Tibet, had, as a matter of fact, been duly discussed and formally approved by the Tsong-du in special session, and this information did not suggest any considerable trustworthiness in any promises the Tibetans might now make. I remember writing to the *Times* a letter dealing with the political situation in which optimism struggled with a recognition of the obvious disadvantages under which the Commissioner labored; on the following day, the 12th of August, the disheartening news arrived that the Tsong-du had actually drafted a letter in answer to our demands of an impertinent and almost defiant nature. The communication was not sent directly to us. The Amban, to whom it had been intrusted, consulted Mr. Wilton privately before officially sending it on. Mr. Wilton's advice was that, unless the Tibetans were looking out for serious trouble, the letter had better be withdrawn at once. This was done, but it was impossible to avoid the conclusion that the Amban himself would have been perfectly willing to deliver the letter unless some such vigorous protest had been made. It was, in fact, a *ballon d'essai* to which he should not have lent the sanction of his position. How far throughout the negotiations Yu-tai was playing a double game no one at present knows, but this first suggestion of his double dealing was afterward unfairly remembered in London when the news that he had ultimately refused to sign the treaty was telegraphed home. He had no authority to sign without the consent of the Wai-wu-pu. To us he presented a never-failing front of sympathy and apparent good-feeling, he never made a speech or wrote a letter without referring to the pig-headed stupidity of the people intrusted to his care, he was enthusiastic in his praise of Colonel Younghusband's moderation in all respects, and to judge from his words one might have thought that by our advance a miniature millennium had been inaugurated for the down-trodden people of Tibet. That there was some ground for these statements is suggested by the complaint of the Dalai Lama himself that by honest and even excessive payment throughout our march we had seduced the affections of his people.

There can be no doubt of our popularity with the laity. The market outside the town, which was formed in spite of the publicly expressed disapproval of the Council, was from the first crowded by hundreds of eager sellers, and it could have been small satisfaction to the monks looking out from the high walls of Potala to see the densely crowded acre of chaffering peddlers and careless or generous purchasers which daily took up a position on some convenient dry patch just outside the camp limits. In this market articles of food naturally predominated; meat and flour were supplied from the De-bung store cellars, so that condiments and other luxuries formed the staple commodities. It was an odd scene. By eight o'clock in the morning a roaring trade was being done in curry powder, turnips, walnuts—they would have been dear in Piccadilly—sugar in yellow and white balls, cigarettes—of the ubiquitous Pedro brand—apples, small russets with a tart flavor, sealing-wax—one of the best products of Lhasa, good transparent brown stuff, of which I secured a large store, chupattis, acid green peaches, native candles—looking like short, squat fireworks, and molded upon a piece of bamboo—lengths of cloth done up in soundly sewn wrappings, cabbages, red pots full of curds, Tibetan shoes, celery, and condensed milk in tins, carrots, onions, eggs in thousands, and milk in big unglazed red ware. It was pleasant to watch the big Sikhs and Pathans cheerily haggling for some coveted sugar plum, sitting down on their heels for half-an-hour to cheapen it an anna, and then, after they had made their bargain, looking in a bewildered way at the little irregularly shaped scraps of silver which a voluble young Tibetaness had given them in change. For in Lhasa a "tanka" has a hole gouged in the middle, has its corners filed off, and is then cut across the middle without ceasing to be legal tender.

The official rate of exchange was three tankas to a rupee, but this, though inevitable for reasons of convenience, represented an enormous profit to the Tibetans, for the intrinsic value of a tanka is about four and a fifth pennies. The first principles of the theory of exchange were grasped at once by the inhabitants, who would go up and down the bazaar holding out tankas in threes and badgering every one they met for a Queen's headed rupee[1] in exchange, with the pertinacity and importunity of a stall holder at a fashionable bazaar. By noon the bazaar dwindled away, and after tiffin there was really no one left on the ground.

To return to the political situation. The assistance and the power of Russia were no longer believed in, and, on the other hand, the capability of the Indian Government to reach Lhasa whenever they might wish to do so had been demonstrated beyond dispute. Other things had no less weight in our favor; the resistance of the Tibetans had been blown away before us like leaves in autumn, and there was not a man in the country who did not realize that our care of their wounded afterward was as thorough as the punishment we inflicted at the moment. Trade and credit

[1] The new rupee with the King's head was looked upon at first with suspicion. The old one is called the "Lama" rupee, from a belief that the Queen's veiled head represents a famous teacher.

are proverbially plants of slow growth, and slower in the East than anywhere else. We may not see much result for years, but the leaven of respect for our strength and confidence in our honesty may safely be allowed in Tibet to work upward from the bottom to the top.

In purely political matters, one name separates itself from that of the common crowd, and it was a name we had not heard before we reached the capital. There is in Lhasa a young monk who apparently to some extent organizes the action of the Tsong-du. The "Loseling Kempo" is a man upon whom the eye of the Indian Government may well be kept. He is strong enough not to desire outward recognition of his strength, and working, as he does, through the Tsong-du, the double intangibility enjoyed by string-pullers and corporations alike makes it ten times more difficult for us to lay our fingers upon this ultimate arbiter whose influence seems likely at no distant date to exceed that of the Dalai Lama himself. That he is actively opposed to us I do not exactly know; he probably represents the sullen and bitter resentment against our intrusion which naturally enough is felt by the official priestly caste, but when the Tibetans have had time quietly to review the whole situation it may be found, even by the Lamaic hierarchy itself, that we have been no enemies to their independence and self-respect, and at that moment, if the good offices of the Loseling Kempo can be unostentatiously secured, our future relations with this hermit kingdom may be facilitated in a manner that ten treaties might fail to achieve.

Meanwhile, in spite of the successful signing of the treaty and in spite of his exile and formal deposition by the Chinese, the dominating factor in the situation is beyond question the Illustrious and Most Holy Dalai Lama, Ngak-wang-lo-zang-tub-dan-gya-tso, Defender and Protector of the Buddhist faith.

CHAPTER XIX

THE POTALA AND THE CATHEDRAL

FOR many days the Mission waited for the Tibetans to arrange their internal affairs and come to the work of negotiation. The first camp near Norbu-ling was abandoned by the expeditionary force, and the Mission, with a guard of one battalion of Pathans, moved across the swampy plain to Lha-lu, which, as we have seen, had been put at the disposal of Colonel Younghusband by the four Councilors. Formal visits were again and again paid within the precincts of Lhasa; the country round was visited and surveyed with care, one party going as far as the plain beyond the Pembu la to the north-east. They reported the existence of a plain even more luxuriant in vegetation than that of Lhasa, but it was admitted by the Tibetans that this was nearly the last of their really fertile tracts of land in a northerly direction. General Macdonald moved the remainder of the force to a comparatively dry patch on the plain about a mile nor'-nor'-east of the Potala, and except for the commissariat officers, whose work on an expedition is never done, there was a quiet time for the men composing the Commissioner's escort. For many of the officers, too, there was not very much to do during the day; fishing was the favorite occupation, and an unexpected number of hooks and lines was discovered in the force. Fly-fishing was soon abandoned for minnows and spoons. Some of the natives obtained excellent sport with tsamba paste. Major Iggulden was beyond question the most successful angler of the expedition, and from time to time he reported catches of over 60 and 70 as the

A CLOSE VIEW OF THE POTALA

Its size can be estimated from the yak-hair curtain hanging from the roof in the middle of the building: it is eighty feet long

result of a short afternoon's sport. A race meeting was organized, and the entries comprised almost every beast of private (and a large number of those of public) ownership in the lines. The view of Lhasa from Lha-lu house is merely that of Chagpo-ri and the back view of the Potala, as the high sand embankments of the Kaling chu [1] effectually prevent any sight of the city itself from the level of the plain. This is a curious thing, and enters considerably into one's conception of the place. The two hills to the west entirely shut off a view of the town as one comes in from De-bung, and looking from Sera on the north, these high, white sand-banks diverging across the plain still conceal the greenery and gold of the city. Only the Potala stands up majestic and defiant.

Ma Shao yün, in his Tibetan itinerary, refers with admiration to the "gorgeous green and dazzling yellow colors which at Potala fascinate the eye." Ta Ching-i-tung chih—who asserts that the height above ground of the golden finials is 436 feet 10 inches—describes it with greater fidelity to nature as a "wondrous peak of green with its halls perched on the summit, resplendent with vermilion and combining natural beauty with architectural charm." It is a pity that this magnificent building should have proved to be so disappointing inside. We discovered that the outside of the Potala and the inside of the Jo-kang are by far the most interesting things in Lhasa. But it is curious, also, that while the interior of the Potala is indistinguishable from the interiors of a score of other large Tibetan lamaseries, the Jo-kang has actually no outside at all. To this latter building I shall return later. There are passages and halls by miles and scores. Here and there in a chapel burns a grimy butter lamp before a tarnished and dirty image. Here and there the passage widens as

[1] From a note in the Wei Tsang t'u chih by Ma Shao yün I am inclined to think that these embankments bury the granite blocks which before the days of Karpi formed the city walls of Lhasa.

a flight of stairs breaks the monotony of grimy walls. The sleeping cells of the monks are cold, bare, and dirty. The actual room in which the Treaty was signed was of fair size—six hundred were easily accommodated in it—and hangings and screens made a brave show for the moment, but for the rest, the Potala is a never-ending labyrinth of corridors and courts and walls as unkempt as those of the Palkhor choide, Jang-kor-yang-tse, or Ta-ka-re. Some of the audience halls are magnificent and well painted, but there is nothing, with one exception, which calls for any particular note from one end of the huge building to the other, so far, at least, as any member of the expedition discovered. For the credit of the Dalai Lama it is to be hoped that the chief ornaments had been removed or buried. Mr. Claude White and Mr. Wilton, who made the examination of the palace their special care, investigated a very large number of the rooms of the Potala, but eventually retreated in disappointment from a task which seemed to possess neither interest nor end. The gilded tombs of a few previous incarnations form the exception to which I have referred, but even these seemed inadequate and out of proportion to the gigantic casket in which they lie. It must be confessed, though the words are written with considerable reluctance, that cheap and tawdry are the only possible adjectives which can be applied to the interior decoration of this great palace temple. Part of it is fine in design, most of it commonplace, all of it dirty. Madame de Chatelain would have smiled to see the disappointment of the Mission, for—though there are no lovely women in Lhasa who play the fiddle, and one doubts whether much enchantment would follow if they did—the effect produced by the first sight of this imposing palace, splendid as the figment of the wildest dream, was as overwhelming and attractive as that which Gilbert saw, and our disillusionment was afterward as great as his.

The first palace on this spot was built by Srong-tsan-gambo,

THE MISSION ENTERING LHASA

but destroyed by the Chinese after a brief existence in 670. It was known as Yumbu Lagang. Different buildings were subsequently erected without regard to any consistent scheme. I confess that I find it difficult to reconcile the present pile with the description or sketch by Grueber. This traveler was in Lhasa in 1661, nineteen years after the reputed completion of the present building, but his picture of it is utterly unlike the reality. There must have been enormous additions in the eighteenth century, and even later, for Manning's note as to the lack of balance and plan in its architecture is surely unjust.

The zigzag stairs, protected by échelon balustrades, lead downward into the great square court at the foot of the Marpo-ri, guarded by seven square bastion-like guard-houses, used as prisons. The rest of the court is used for the accommodation of a few soldiers and a great many beasts of burden; outside it is a squalid little hamlet.

Of the Dalai Lama himself of course we saw nothing. The following description of a reception by the Grand Lama within the Potala palace is taken from the pages of Chandra Das' journal, but it is, I think, only right to point out that in the opinion of many well qualified to judge, to some extent, at least, the writer may have been dependent upon the information of others.

"Arriving at the eastern gateway of Potala, we dismounted and walked through a long hall, on either side of which were rows of prayer wheels, which every passer-by put in motion. Then, ascending three long flights of stone steps, we left our ponies in care of a bystander—for no one may ride further—and proceeded toward the palace under the guidance of a young monk. We had to climb up five ladders before we reached the ground floor of Phodang-marpo, or 'the Red palace,' thus called from the exterior walls being of a dark-red color. Then we had half-a-dozen more ladders to climb up, and we found ourselves at the top of

Potala (there are nine stories to this building), where we saw a number of monks awaiting an audience. The view from here was beautiful beyond compare; the broad valley of the Kyi chu, in the center of which stands the great city surrounded by green groves; the gilt spires of the Jo-kang and the other temples of Lhasa, and farther away the great monasteries of Sera and De-bung,[1] behind which rose the dark-blue mountains.

"After a while three lamas appeared, and said that the Dalai Lama would presently conduct a memorial service for the benefit of the late Meru Ta Lama (Great Lama of Meru gomba), and that we were allowed to be present at it. Walking very softly, we came to the middle of the reception hall, the roof of which is supported by three rows of pillars, four in each row, and where light is admitted by a skylight. The furniture was that generally seen in lamaseries, but the hangings were of the richest brocades and cloths of gold; the church utensils were of gold, and the frescoing on the walls of exquisite fineness. Behind the throne were beautiful tapestries and satin hangings forming a great *gyal-tsan,* or canopy. The floor was beautifully smooth and glossy, but the doors and windows, which were painted red, were of the rough description common throughout the country.

"A Donyer approached, who took our presentation *khatag,* but I held back, at the suggestion of Chola Kusho, the present I had for the Grand Lama; and when I approached him I placed in his lap, much to the surprise of all present, a piece of gold weighing a *tola.* We then took our seats on rugs, of which there were eight rows; ours were in the third, and about ten feet from the Grand Lama's throne, and a little to his left.

"The Grand Lama is a child of eight, with a bright and fair complexion and rosy cheeks. His eyes are large and penetrating, the shape of his face remarkably Aryan, though somewhat

[1] As a matter of fact, De-bung cannot be seen from the Potala.

THE POTALA, THE HOME OF THE GRAND LAMA

One of the wonders of the world

marred by the obliquity of his eyes. The thinness of his person was probably due to the fatigue of the Court ceremonies and to the religious duties and ascetic observances of his estate. A yellow mantle draped his person, and he sat cross-legged with joined palms. The throne on which he sat was supported by carved lions, and covered with silk scarfs. It was about four feet high, six feet long, and four feet broad. The State officers moved about with becoming gravity; there was the Kuchar Khanpo, with a bowl of holy water, colored yellow with saffron; the Censer-carrier, with a golden censer with three chains; the Solpon chenpo, with a golden tea-pot; and other household officials. Two gold lamps, made in the shape of flower vases, burned on either side of the throne.

"When all had been blessed and taken seats, the Solpon chenpo poured tea in his Holiness's golden cup, and four assistants served the people present. Then grace was said, beginning with *Om, Ah, Hum,* thrice repeated, and followed by, 'Never losing sight even for a moment of the Three Holies, making reverence even to the Three Precious Ones. Let the blessing of the Three Konchog be upon us,' etc. Then we silently raised our cups and drank the tea, which was most deliciously perfumed. In this manner we drank three cupfuls, and then put our bowls back in the bosoms of our gowns.

"After this the Solpon chenpo put a golden dish full of rice before the Dalai Lama, and he touched it, and then it was divided among those present; then grace was again said, and his Holiness, in a low, indistinct tone, chanted a hymn, which was repeated by the assembled lamas in deep grave tones. When this was over, a venerable man rose from the first row of seats and made a short address, reciting the many acts of mercy the Dalai Lamas had vouchsafed Tibet, at the conclusion of which he presented to his Holiness a number of valuable things; then he made three prostrations and withdrew, followed by all of us.

"As I was leaving, one of the Donyer chenpo's (or chamberlain) assistants gave me two packets of blessed pills, and another tied a scrap of red silk round my neck—these are the usual return presents the Grand Lama makes to pilgrims."

This is probably the best extant description of a reception at the Potala, and for that reason I have inserted it. It will probably be many years before a white man has the chance of verifying even an incident described in it. Huc, the last European before ourselves to see it, gives an extraordinary description of the palace. It is so strangely beside the truth that one is obliged to wonder what pains he took to verify other statements he made in his book of travels. Here it is:

"Le palais du Talé Lama mérite à tous égards la célébrité dont il jouit dans le monde entier. Vers la partie septentrionale de la ville et tout au plus à un quart d'heure de distance, il existe une montagne rocheuse, peu élevée, et de forme conique. Elle s'éleve au milieu de cette large vallée, comme un ilot isolé au-dessus d'un immense lac.

"Cette montagne porte le nom de Bouddha-La, c'est-à-dire montagne de Bouddha, montagne divine; c'est sur ce socle grandiose, préparé par la nature, que les adorateurs du Talé Lama ont édifié un palais magnifique où réside en chair et en os leur divinité vivante.

"Ce palais est un réunion de plusieurs temples, de grandeur et de beauté différentes; celui qui occupe le centre est élevé de quatre étages, et domine tous les autres; il est terminé par un dôme entièrement recouvert de lames d'or, et entouré d'un grand peristyle dont les colonnes sont également dorées."

Such a description as this is puzzling. Nothing is more characteristic and striking at the Potala than the long, almost un-

THE POTALA AT LHASA, AN ARCHITECTURAL MARVEL

broken front of granite wall, reaching almost from one end to the other of the hill-crest, supporting a homogeneous and closely welded series of buildings. The truth is that very little used to be accurately noted by Asian travelers before the middle of the last century. It is not unlikely that the possibility of having the lie direct given to a verbal description by a later visitor's camera may have helped to bring this about.

Of the other great features of Lhasa, the Jo-kang and the Do-ring remain pre-eminent. The latter, as was said at the beginning of this book, is the oldest existing document in Tibetan history; it records a treaty made in 783 between King Ral-pa-chan of Tibet and his neighbor, and late enemy, the Chinese Emperor. It is a well quarried slab of granite, about six inches in thickness and eight feet in height, set in a granite frame. It immediately fronts the entrance to the Cathedral, from which it is distant only thirty paces across the yard. Immediately over it is the great willow tree which springs from a hair of Buddha buried among its roots—a splendid tree, and one which, perhaps, has been able to grow to greater perfection from the protection of the wall built round its diverging trunk. This inclosure fills the western side of the little courtyard opposite the west door of the Cathedral. Between it and the projecting wings of the Government offices, which here, as elsewhere, crowd all round upon the walls of the Jo-kang, there is a space on either side, and the Do-ring stands in the direct line between them. The design of the pediment surmounting the stone is strong and undoubtedly of the original date of the monument. It represents two dragons, simply designed in somewhat deep relief, of which the edges have been severely treated by the weather of many centuries. Whether the stone itself is or is not the original granite slab is a matter somewhat more difficult to decide. At first I was convinced that it must have been renewed once at least. This appeared to me to be probable for more than one reason; the first was the clean-cut surface of the stone where the quarry-man had originally "flatted" it for the inscription, combined with the recent appearance of the lettering, so far as it can now be seen; and, secondly, the rapidity with which the Tibetans have ground into it the cup-marks with which the whole Chinese or eastern face of the stone is now disfigured. Some twenty years ago the writing was, we are assured by Chandra Das, still distinctly legible; the merest glance at it shows how far this is from being the case to-day. If all this damage has been done in so short a time, it seems impossible this can be the original stone, for the process of cup-marking is one of the oldest in the world, and at this rate would long ago have destroyed the surface of the slab over and over again.

On the other hand, it must be confessed that the inaccuracy of Chandra Das in many places in his book is notorious; if in his time the inscription was totally illegible, if, in fact, as seems more likely, these cup-marks are really the products of half-centuries instead of years, there is no reason, Mr. Hayden tells me, why the granite slab with its inscription, although exposed to the weather of a thousand years and more, should not be the original. He said that the friable appearance of the granite hill slopes we had passed on the way up was deceptive, and that a new piece cut from the living rock was of an exceedingly hard and good character. The western face of the Do-ring, which is turned inward toward the willow, is free from cup-marks, but it is covered with a blackish, mildewed growth which conceals the inscription to a great extent. This is a gritty crust which can be partially removed by the finger-nail, but it seems to have affected the surface of the stone deeply, and this side is scarcely more legible than the other.

This inscription, taken from a translation in the Asiatic Society's journal of the copy still kept as a record in the Amban's Residency, is as follows:

"The learned, warlike, filial and virtuous Emperor of the Great Tang, and the divine and all-wise Tsanpu of the Great Fan, two sovereigns allied as father and son-in-law, having consulted to unite the gods of the land and grain, have concluded a sworn treaty of grand alliance, which shall never be lost nor changed. Gods and men have been called as witnesses, and in order that all ages and generations may resound in praise the sworn text, section by section, has been engraved on a stone monument.

"The learned, warlike, filial and virtuous Emperor, and the divine and all-wise Tsanpu, Te-chih-li-tsan, their all-wise majesties, with intuitive wisdom reaching far, and knowing both present and future, good and evil, with feelings of benevolent pity and imperial grace overspreading all, without distinction of native and foreign, have negotiated an alliance, and resolved to give to the myriad families peace and prosperity, and with like thought have completed a long, lasting and good deed. They have re-connected the bonds of affectionate kinship, strengthened anew the right policy of neighbourly friendship, and made this great peace.

"The two countries Fan and Han keeping the lands and boundaries which they now rule: all to the east shall be within the borders of the great Tang, all to the west shall be the territory of the great Fan. Neither the one nor the other shall slaughter or fight; they shall not move weapons or armour, nor shall they plot to encroach on each other's territory. Should any men be liable to suspicion, they shall be taken alive and their business enquired into, after which they shall be given clothes and food and sent back to their own country.

"Now the gods of the land and of grain have been united to make this great peace, yet to keep up the good relationship of the father and son-in-law there must be constant communication. The one shall rely on the other, and constantly send envoys to and fro. Both Fan and Han shall change horses at the Chiang-chun Pass, and to the east of the Suiyung Barrier the great Tang shall provide for the mission, while to the west of the City of Chingshui the great Fan shall entertain them. They shall both be treated with due ceremony, according to the near relationship of the Imperial father and son-in-law, so that within the two borders neither smoke nor dust shall rise, no word of invasion or plunder shall be heard, and there shall be no longer anxious fear and trembling. The frontier guards shall be dismissed, and the land shall have perfect quiet in consequence of this joyful event. Their grace shall be handed down to ten thousand generations, and sounds of grateful praise shall extend to wherever the sun and the moon shine. The Fan shall be at peace in the Fan country; the Han also shall be joyful in the Han country, and this is truly a great deed of good augury. They shall keep their sworn oath, and there shall never be any change.

"They have looked up to the three Precious ones, to all the holy saints, to the sun, moon, stars and planets, and begged them to be their witnesses. A sworn treaty like this each one has severally written and exposed, having sacrificed the victims for the sworn ceremony and ratified this text. Should they not keep these oaths, and either Fan or Han disregard the treaty and break the sworn agreement, may there come to him misfortune and calamity. Provided only that the work of rebels against the state, or secret plotters, shall not be included as a breach of the sworn ceremony.

"The Fan and Han sovereigns and ministers have all bowed down and solemnly made oath and carefully drawn up the written documents. The witnesses of the two sovereigns, the officers who ascended to the altar, have reverently written their names below, and the sworn treaty, of which this is a true copy, has been deposited in the royal treasury."

As to other misconceptions, it may be said at once that there are no "old willows whose aged trunks are bent and twisted like writhing dragons on either side," nor can the monument, from any point of view, be called a pillar. There is no flag-pole in this courtyard at all. The Jo itself is not anywhere near the propylon.

The Do-ring witnessed one of the famous assassinations of the world. King Lang-darma, who reigned at the close of the ninth century, was the Julian of Lamaism. With a ruthless hand he attempted to extirpate Buddhism and restore the earlier and simpler devil worship of the country. A monk, disguised as a Shamanist or Black Hat devil dancer, approached Lang-darma as he was halting outside the western entrance of the Jo-kang one day in the year 900. Gamboling and capering, now advancing, now withdrawing, he eventually approached the monarch, whose attention he had gained probably by his disguise, near enough to inflict one terrific blow which smashed in Lang-darma's forehead. The apostate fell dead where he stood. This audacious act, which laid the foundation of Lamaic supremacy, is annually recorded by a mystery play, on the spot of Lang-darma's assassination. But in the description of it, vividly written in his book on Lamaism, Colonel Waddell suggests that neither in its origin nor in its realistic details is the play based upon the facts we have mentioned. It has been slightly adapted so as to record the crime, but as a matter of origin it is of a far greater antiquity.

There remains yet to be described the sacred heart and center, not of Lhasa alone, but of Central Asia, and I have been asked to reprint as it stands the description of the Jo-kang which appeared in the *Times* of the 24th of September. Though somewhat doubtful I have therefore, writing months afterward, not cared to make alterations, even when some inducement, such as an added detail or the better turn of a sentence, might increase the literary value of the description. Such additions as are necessary I have added as distinct interpolations. There is to me an intense pleasure in looking back over the pages of my note-book to see the scrawled sketches and illegibly jotted notes which I was careful to make during an experience which, for sheer interest, I suppose will rarely, if ever, be repeated. I almost think, if I may say so in no spirit of boasting, that perhaps no traveler will ever have the chance exactly to feel as much again, however far his travels, however dangerous his pilgrimage. Unexpectedly there rose up, through no deliberate effort of my own, an opportunity of seeing that, without which a visit to Lhasa would have been after all but a half-achieved success, without which there would have been left still the crown and key-stone of all the edifice of Buddhism for another and a later traveler to see for the first time. Three of us were to be the first white men to look upon the great golden idol of Lhasa.

. . . .

"It is not always realized that it is in the Cathedral of Lhasa, not in the palace outside, that the spiritual life of Tibet and of the countless millions of Northern Buddhism is wholly centred. The policy of isolation which has for so long been the chief characteristic of the faith finds its fullest expression in the fanatical jealousy with which this temple, the heart and focus of Lamaism, has been safeguarded against the stranger's intrusion. What Tibet is to the rest of the world, what Lhasa is to Tibet, that the Jo-kang is to Lhasa, and it is not entirely clear, in spite of more than one so-called description of the interior, that any European, or even native spy, has ever before ventured inside. There has, perhaps, been reason enough for this. It is possible that pardon for having visited the city of Lhasa, or the Potala Palace—which is in comparison almost a place of resort—might have been obtained on terms, but there could

THE EXTERIOR OF THE JO-KANG TEMPLE, THE HOLY OF HOLIES OF ALL ASIA

Within is the most sacred shrine in Lhasa

hardly have been a reprieve for the luckless intruder once discovered inside these darkened and windowless quadrangles. Certainly neither the ground plan published by Giorgi in the 18th century nor any of the detailed accounts published more recently suggested that their authors had any first-hand acquaintance with the place.

"As I have noticed in a former letter, the exterior is devoid of either beauty or dignity. The interior, on the other hand, is unquestionably the most important and interesting thing in Central Asia. It is the treasure-house and kaabah, not of the country only, but of the faith, and it is curious that, while the magnificent Potala is a casket containing nothing either ancient or specially venerated, the priceless gems of the Jo-kang should be housed in a building which literally has no outside walls at all. All round the Cathedral the dirty and insignificant council chambers and offices, in which the affairs of Tibet are debated and administered, lean like parasites against it for support, huddled together and obscuring the sacred structure, to which they owe their stability, in a way that seems mischievously significant of the whole state of Tibet.

"From Chagpori the five great gilded roofs are indeed to be seen blazing in the sun through the tree-tops hard by the Yutok Bridge, but even this suggestion of importance vanishes as one treads a way through the filth of the narrow streets to the western entrance. So crowded upon is the Jo-kang that this is actually the only part of the structure which is visible from the street which surrounds it.

"It is not strangers only against whom the great doors of the Jo-kang have been barred. Exclusion from its sacred precincts is officially pronounced against those also who have incurred the suspicion, or displeasure, of the ruling hierarchy of Lhasa, and it is a curious proof of the autocratic power which is exercised with regard to this Cathedral, as well as of the insignificance of the suzerainty, that on August 11, in this year, the Viceroy himself, going in state to the Jo-kang to offer prayer on the occasion of the Chinese Emperor's birthday, had the doors shut in his face. To this insult the opportunity I have enjoyed of examining the temple with a fulness that would otherwise have been impossible was due. Anxious to retaliate, the Amban—who was on a subsequent day grudgingly permitted to visit the ground floor only of the building—used our presence in Lhasa to teach the keepers of the Cathedral a lesson in manners. At any rate, to our surprise, a definite invitation was one day extended to one or two of the members of the Mission to make a morning visit into Lhasa for the purpose of examining the treasures of the innermost sanctuary of Buddhism. It was accepted. A Chinese guard of the Residency, armed with tridents, halberds, and scythe-headed lances, provided our escort, and immediately upon our arrival the great doors, half hidden in the shadow under the many-pillared propylon, were opened and at once barred again behind us.

"Just in front, seen through a forest of pillars, was an open and verandahed court-yard. Its great age was at once apparent. The paintings on the walls were barely distinguishable through a heavy cloak of dirt and grease, and it was difficult to imagine the colours with which the capitals of the pillars, and the raftered roof overhead, had originally been painted. The court is open to the sky and is surrounded by none of the small chapels which are the chief feature of the inner quadrangles of the Jo-kang. The architecture is of the kind invariable in religious buildings in Tibet—a double row of pillars carry the half-roof overhead, each supporting on a small capital a large bracketed abacus, voluted and curved on both sides and charged in the centre with a panel of archaic carving. The wooden doors which secure both entrances of the first court are of immense size, heavily barred, and embossed with filigree ring plates of great age.

THE JO-KANG, WITH THE MOST GORGEOUS INTERIOR OF ALL THE TIBETAN TEMPLES, HAS PRACTICALLY NO EXTERIOR

"At the opposite end of the court an open door communicates with the second court, revealing a bright mass of hollyhocks, snapdragon, and stocks, vivid in the sun. The sanctity of the temple obviously increased as we ventured into the inner court. Its sides are honeycombed by small dark chambers, apparently built in the thickness of the enormous wall. Each is an idol-crowned sanctuary. Into these obscure shrines one stumbles, bent almost double to avoid the dirt of the low greasy lintel. Once inside, the eye requires some time to distinguish anything more than the dim outlines of an altar in the middle of the chamber. On it stand one or two copper or brass bowls filled high with butter, each bearing on its half-congealed surface a dimly burning wick in a little pool of self-thawed oil. These dim beads of yellow light provide all the illumination of the cave, and after a little, one can just distinguish the solemn images squatting round the walls, betrayed by points and rims of light, reflected here and there from the projections and edges of golden draperies or features. The smell is abominable. The air is exhausted and charged with rancid vapours. Everything one touches drips with grease. The fumes of burning butter have in the course of many generations filmed over the surfaces and clogged the carving of doors and walls alike. The floor underfoot is slippery as glass. Upon this receptive foundation, the grime and reek of centuries have steadily descended with results that may be imagined. Except that the images themselves apparently receive from time to time a perfunctory wipe with the greasy rag which is generally to be found in a conspicuous place beside a Tibetan altar, there is not in one of these numerous chapels the slightest sign of consideration, respect, or care.

"One comes out again into the open air with relief, only to find, three or four yards on, the entrance to another of these catacomb-like chapels. They entirely surround the walls of this interior court, and to the eye of the stranger hardly differ one from another. Indeed, the monks themselves when questioned seem to find some difficulty in distinguishing the identity of the images in the successive chapels. In front of some of these recesses hangs a curtain of a curious kind, peculiar, so far as I know, to this temple. Horses' bits, of steel and of a plain pattern, are linked together ring to ring by short lengths of twisted iron, the whole forming an original and effective screen. This is secured to the left-hand jamb by a long bolt and staple, and the whole is fastened by one of the gigantic locks which are adopted from China, and are perhaps the most ingenious product of the country.

"The centre of the court is taken up by an inner sanctuary formed on three sides by low shelves, covered with small brass Buddhas backed by larger images arranged between the pillars supporting the roof of the half-roof, and on the fourth side by a plain trellis or iron pierced by a similar plain gateway. From inside, therefore, none of the chapels or the statues ranged along the walls of the court are visible, and the darkness thereby caused under the portico is greatly increased by the half-drawn awnings, of which the ropes slant downwards across the opening, and form perches for a special colony of orange and purple swallows, whose nests cling up to the overhanging eaves.

"In this central court two statues sit, one—that to the left—is about life size, the other is of gigantic proportions. Both of them present the same peculiarity—one which cannot fail to arrest the eye at once. Each is seated upon a throne in European fashion, and this identifies them at once. Of all the Bodisats, heroes, or teachers which fill the calendars of Lamaism, only the image of the coming Buddha is thus represented. How this tradition arose the lamas themselves are unable to explain, but it is of great antiquity, and it is to Europe that the eyes of Buddhism are turned for the appearance of the next reincarnation of the Great Master. As will be remembered, the Tzar of Russia was recently recognized as a reincarnate Bodisat,[1] and it is not impossible that this legend paved the way considerably for his acceptance. Crowned with a huge circlet set with innumerable turquoises, Maitreya sits here with one hand raised in benediction, the other resting upon his knee. On his breast lies a tangled mass of jewelled chains and necklaces, and vast 'roundles' of gold, set with concentric rings of turquoises, half hide his huge shoulders. We caught only a hurried glimpse as we passed on; for the order in which the sights of a Buddhist temple may be visited is invariable, and we took care not to offend the susceptibilities of the lamas by deviating from the orthodox left-to-right course which forms part of their religious observances. The 'way of the wine' is a custom which would need no explanation to a Buddhist.

"Once under the eastern end of the Jo-kang, one finds the darkness deepen fast. There is no light but such as can find its way under the wide half-roofs and through the trellises, screens, and awnings which almost entirely close in the central court. In the gloom one passes by ancient chapel after chapel, where the dim half-light barely reveals the existence of the dark recess guarded by its iron screen. The archaic walls share with the smooth worn pillars the burden of the warped rafters overhead. The stone slabs underfoot are worn into a channel, and the grime of a thousand years has utterly hidden the pictures —if there ever were any—on the walls. At last one turns to the right, passing close beneath the uplifted figure of the great Tsong-kapa, the Luther of Central Asia. It is a contemporary likeness, and one could wish that there were more light by which to see it than is afforded by the dim radiance of the butter-lamp before his knees. But his very posture is significant; for, instead

[1] Kawaguchi, the Japanese traveler, says that he has been identified as "Ze Zongawa." This, in O'Connor's opinion, is merely a misreading of Tsong-kapa.

of having his back to the wall behind him, Tsong-kapa faces south, and this is the first indication that we are at last drawing near to the Holy of Holies.

"We have now reached the eastern end of the Cathedral, and are passing behind the trellis-work of the inner court; in the twilight it is difficult to distinguish the half-seen figures which people the recesses and line the sides of the path along which we grope our way. Ten paces more and the Jo itself is before us.

"The first sight of what is beyond question the most famous idol in the world is uncannily impressive. In the darkness it is at first difficult to follow the lines of the shrine which holds the god. One only realizes a high pillared sanctuary in which the gloom is almost absolute, and therein, thrown into strange relief against the obscurity, the soft gleam of the golden idol which sits enthroned in the centre. Before him are rows and rows of great butter-lamps of solid gold, each shaped in curious resemblance to the pre-Reformation chalices of the English Church. Lighted by the tender radiance of these twenty or thirty beads of light, the great glowing mass of the Buddha softly looms out, ghostlike and shadowless, in the murky recess.

"It is not the magnificence of the statue that is first perceived, and certainly it is not that which makes the deepest and most lasting impression. For this is no ordinary presentation of the Master. The features are smooth and almost childish; beautiful they are not, but there is no need of beauty here. Here is no trace of that inscrutable smile which, from Mukden to Ceylon, is inseparable from our conceptions of the features of the Great Teacher. Here there is nothing of the saddened smile of the Melancholia who has known too much and has renounced it all as vanity. Here, instead, is the quiet happiness and the quick capacity for pleasure of the boy who had never yet known either pain, or disease, or death. It is Gautama as a pure and eager prince, without a thought for the morrow, or a care for to-day.

No doubt the surroundings, which are effective almost to the verge of theatricality, account for much, but this beautiful statue is the sum and climax of Tibet, and as one gazes one knows it and respects the jealousy of its guardians. The legendary history of this idol is worth retelling. It is believed that the likeness was made from Gautama himself, in the happier days of his innocence and seclusion in Kapali-vastu. It was made by Visvakarma—no man, but the constructive force of the universe—and is of gold, alloyed with the four other elemental metals, silver, copper, zinc, and iron, symbolical of this world, and it is adorned with diamonds, rubies, lapis-lazuli, emeralds, and the unidentified Indranila, which modern dictionaries prosaically explain as sapphire. This priceless image was given by the King of Magadha to the Chinese Emperor for his timely assistance when the Yavanas were over-running the plains of India. From Peking it was brought as her dowry by Princess Konjo in the seventh century. The crown was undoubtedly given by Tsongkapa himself in the early part of the fifteenth century, and the innumerable golden ornaments which heap the khil-kor before the image are the presents of pious Buddhists from the earliest days to the present time. Among them are twenty-two large butter-lamps, eight of a somewhat smaller size, twelve bowls, two 'Precious Wheels of the Law,' and a multitude of smaller articles, all of the same metal.

"These are arranged on the three shelves of the khil-kor, and the taller articles conceal the whole of the image from his shoulders downwards. To this fact may perhaps be due the common, but mistaken, description of the Jo as a standing figure. Across and across his breast are innumerable necklaces of gold, set with turquoises, pearls, and coral. The throne on which he sits has overhead a canopy supported by two exquisitely designed dragons of silver-gilt, each about ten feet in height. Behind him is the panel of conventional wooden foliage, and the 'Kyung,' or

Garuda Bird, overhead can just be seen in the darkness. Closer examination shows that almost every part of the canopy and seat is gilded, gold, or jewelled. The crown is perhaps the most interesting jewel. It is a deep coronet of gold, set round and round with turquoise, and heightened by five conventional leaves, each enclosing a golden image of Buddha, and encrusted with precious stones. In the centre, below the middle leaf, is a flawless turquoise six inches long and three inches wide, the largest in the world. Behind the throne are dimly seen in the darkness huge figures standing back against the wall of the shrine all round. Rough-hewn, barbarous, and unadorned they are, but nothing else could have so well supplied the background for this treasure of treasures as the Egyptian solemnity of these dark Atlantides, standing shoulder to shoulder on altar stones, where no lamps are ever lighted and no flowers are ever strewn. Before the entrance, protecting the treasures of the shrine, is the usual curtain of horses' bits. This was unfastened at our request, and we were allowed to make a careful examination of the image. The gems are not, perhaps, up to the standard of a European market; so far as one could see, the emeralds were large, but flawed, and, as is of course inevitable, the pearls, though of considerable size, were lustreless; but it would be difficult to surpass the exquisite workmanship of everything connected with this amazing image, and a closer inspection did but increase the impression of opulence." Nothing was more striking than the persistent use of pearls, and amber and coral. As one looked, there was almost the very sound of the far distant and unknown sea in among these murky caverns of granite darkness and dirt.

"The altar below the khil-kor is of silver, ornamented with conventional figures of birds in *repoussé* work, and one smiled to see in the most conspicuous place of all, thrown carelessly in a cleft between two of the supports, the usual greasy rag, with which the sacred image was daily rubbed. Two long katags

THE GREAT BUDDHA IN THE HOLY OF HOLIES AT LHASA

The turquoise in the idol's crown is the largest in the world

descend from the crown one from either side above the ears. Between the two dragons and the image itself are two square pillars of silver heavily ornamented. The edge of the canopy above is crisped. One could not see in that light how it was finished above.

"Outside, the maroon-robed monks sat and droned their never-ending chant. We pass by them, and, after a glance at the Maitreya at nearer range, we were taken upstairs to the first floor, which runs only along the inner court, passing on our way the famous representation of Chagna Dorje. This, in one account of the Jo-kang, is said to be the statue round the neck of which a rope was once tied by order of the apostate, King Langdarma, to drag it from its place; thereupon the miscreant was, of course, promptly and miraculously destroyed. As a matter of fact it is an image cut in low relief upon the wall itself of the Jo-kang, gilded and coloured, and honoured always with rows of copper lamps. I made a rapid sketch of it. The right hand is raised and holds something which looks like a sword or a sceptre. All of it is crude and rough to the last degree. This is but another example of the inaccuracy which characterizes all the extant descriptions of the Cathedral of Lhasa. It would be easy to multiply similar cases; in fact, hardly anything has been properly noted. On the first floor there are chapels maintained by the devotion of special races of the Buddhist faith. Among them the Nepalese chapel was pointed out. The story that there is here the image of Buddha brought by the Nepalese wife of Srong-tsan-gambo, is without foundation. This image, or one claiming to be it, is at the monastery of Ki-long or Ki-rong, near the Nepalese frontier.

"Above, on the second floor, is an image which, after the Jo itself, is the most important treasure that the Jo-kang contains. In the south-eastern corner of this storey is the armoury, where the walls and pillars alike are loaded with ancient and grotesque instruments of war. From this room a low, narrow passage leads down half-a-dozen stone steps into a small dungeon, where the statue of the guardian goddess, Palden-Lhamo, is worshipped. This is a most amazing figure. The three-eyed goddess, crowned with skulls, grins affably with mother-of-pearl teeth from her altar; upon her head and breast are jewels which the Jo himself might condescend to wear. Eight large, square charm-boxes of gold and gems, two pairs of gold-set turquoise earrings, each half a foot in length, and a diamond-studded fillet on the brow beneath the crown are perhaps the most conspicuous ornaments. Her breast-plate of turquoise and corals is almost hidden by necklaces, and a huge irregular pearl, strongly resembling the 'Dudley' jewel in shape, is at last distinguishable in the centre leaf of her crown. Before her burn butter-lamps, and brown mice swarm fearlessly over walls and floor and altar, so tame that they did not resent being stroked on the lap of the goddess herself.

"With this famous image of the guardian deity—who, as every Tibetan knows, from the Dalai Lama to the peasant in the field, was reincarnated during the last century as Queen Victoria—the list of treasures in the Jo-kang of a special interest to Europeans is perhaps concluded. But for the Buddhist scholar there is an unexplored wealth which it may be many years before any second visitor will have the privilege of inspecting, or the knowledge to appreciate. The great eleven-faced Shen-re-zig, the 'precious' image of Tsong-kapa, the innumerable figures of divine teachers, each symbolically representing the spiritual powers with which he was endowed, the great series of the disciples of Buddha, the statue of the Guru Rimpoche, the usual 'chamber of horrors,' and hundreds of other objects, each worthy of the great Pantheon of Lamaism—all these must for the moment remain unnoticed. But the longer one stays within these strange and sacred courts, the more amazing does the contrast appear between the priceless riches and historic sanctity of their contents and the squalid exterior of the most sacred structure in all the vast domain of Buddhism. Yet the face of the Buddha remains the dominant impression of the whole."

As we left the Cathedral a significant thing occurred. I do not suggest for a moment that the Chinese deliberately let us in for the hostile demonstration which we now encountered, but the fact that they had used the presence of our troops outside to inflict upon the Jo-kang what the lamas and perhaps the people of Lhasa also regarded as a slight, may have incensed the people. Our horses had been left outside the western gates, and the fact of our being inside the building was therefore patent to every passer-by. We emerged from the dark inclosures of the Cathedral into the blazing sunlight to find half the population of Lhasa waiting for us in a dense, growling crowd. They were pressing upon our horses and men, and they had filled the entire courtyard right up to the Do-ring.

I am not perfectly certain who gave the order, but I am inclined to think that it was the Viceroy's first secretary, who accompanied us on our tour of inspection round the temple; immediately, a great, powerfully built lama with a weighted eight-foot whip of what looked like rhinoceros hide ran forward and struck out right and left, inflicting appalling blows on the packed crowd. It sullenly gave way before him, and an avenue was left through the courtyard, to the road leading out toward the town door and the Yutok Sampa. I had walked forward a few paces to look again at the Do-ring, not entirely realizing the position, while the others mounted their horses and slowly rode out. The first stone came with a crash against the Do-ring itself, missing Mr. White's head by a few inches. It was the signal for a hundred more. Great jagged pieces of granite, weighing two or three pounds, kicked out of the walls or pulled up from the road, crashed from the house-tops and the street upon our little party, and it was interesting to notice that the stones were directed obviously against our Chinese escort rather than against ourselves. We had, of course, our revolvers in our pockets, but even a single shot over their heads under such circumstances, though it would without question instantly have brought the Tibetans to reason, might, in the long run, have complicated the negotiations, so we rode out slowly, trying to look as dignified as we could. But it was probably a relief to all concerned when we reached the little door in the city wall which leads out to the central park.

The real significance of this incident must not be mistaken; in itself it was of no very great moment, but as indicating the utter contempt felt by the Tibetans for the suzerain power of Tibet, it is something which we cannot entirely ignore. The more we acquit the actual guardians of the temple from all complicity in it, the more spontaneous and popular does this outburst of indignation against the normal overlords of Tibet become. Even when their suzerainty was supposed to be supported by the presence of our troops outside, it was possible that this could occur in the heart of Lhasa, and it is in itself a convincing proof that no action of the Chinese with regard to Tibet will, in the future, have any real importance, or be regarded by the Tibetans as binding upon themselves in any way.

This was my last sight of the interior of Lhasa, and I am not sorry that it should have been so—after this, anything and everything would have been but an anti-climax. On the following day before dawn I set off on my long ride back to India, carrying despatches both to the Viceroy and to the Home Government.

CHAPTER XX

THE RIDE FROM LHASA TO INDIA

I LEFT Lhasa just before the dawn on the morning of the 15th of August, passing out toward the western end of the plain, then still enshrouded in darkness, but spanned by the most beautiful rainbow I have ever seen in my life. The Potala, rising straight in front of me as I left the Lha-lu house, was distinct enough against the growing amber of the south-eastern sky. There had been snow in the night, and a white pall came far down the mountain-sides all round. The greenery had not yet begun to detach itself from the darkness, but the road was clear enough, and after gaining the main road by the causeway across the marsh, I turned to the right and set off with the escort.

It is a curious thing that, on the whole, I have found almost more interest taken in this lonely return journey of mine than in anything else that occurred during the seven months of my stay in Tibet; yet the story is simple enough. There were two reasons why I went as fast as possible. The first was that I was carrying despatches both to the Viceroy at Simla and to the Home Government. Another was that there was a certain practical value in knowing exactly how fast mounted men, not unduly pressing their horses, could, with kit, travel from Darjeeling to Lhasa or from Lhasa to Darjeeling. The distance, if a perfectly straight course can be kept, is 390 miles, but, from one reason or another, the total amount that I had to cover was about 400 miles. For example, four miles were lost over the crossing of the Tsang-po alone. The military authorities in India had issued instructions that I was to be assisted in every possible way. Had it not been, in fact, for the kindly co-operation and help which I found at every stage, it would have been impossible for me to do the journey in anything like the time I actually took.

The first stage was a long one. The sun rose about the time that I passed De-bung Monastery, and I was glad of its warmth. Hitherto the road had passed the plantations and thickets, swamps and fields that I had again and again revisited. Henceforward it was to go over an old track indeed, but throughout from a different point of view, which counted for much, and with a rapidity which afforded one a far better proportional view of the whole road between Lhasa and India than the toilsome daily movement of a force can ever give.

Near De-bung I passed many little companies of Tibetans, both men and women, going into Lhasa with ponies laden with goods for market. A light rain blew in their faces as we came along, and, head to wind, they were often almost upon me before they knew of my coming. But there was always the same kindly smile and some unintelligible remark smothered in a fold of their robe. After sunrise the rain ceased. I followed the road through the cultivated patches that lead on from one clump of white houses to another, all nameless so far as I could ascertain. Sooner than I had expected the road raised itself a little and by a stone causeway reached up to Tölung Bridge. The river beneath me was in a different state from that which we had previously known. Sullen floods of brownish water banked themselves against the retaining walls, and swooped down with concentrated viciousness upon the long sterlings of the bridge. A Sepoy sentry on either side roused himself as I passed. On the bridge I turned to look at the Potala, just then reflecting the first rays from its golden roofs. It was strangely clear, and I could hardly believe that it had seemed so far away when we had seen it on our arrival at this point. The clouds seemed driven upward along the whole line of mountains which contained the plain. They formed a pearl-gray canopy, of which the lower edge was cut, as before, with knife-like sharpness. The greenery of the plain ran riot. From Tölung we went on past isolated farmsteads, keeping our right shoulders forward, till at last the tall heap of stones and the chorten, to which I have before referred, crawled slowly up toward us.

When it came to the point, it was no easy thing to see the last of Lhasa. But I knew that when that heap was reached, the last of Lhasa was just about to fade behind the spur which runs out from the southern hills. It needed no pile of stones to tell me that. I had been watching, with concentration and almost sadness, the slowly dwindling palace of the forbidden town. I would have given a good deal then to go back. But the thing was settled, and it had to be done. I went on till I reached the stones, and there halted to look at the two small pyramids of gray which rose far away in the distance just beyond the end of the jagged spur. There the great structure stood, careless, impassive, and eternal as the pyramids. The lines of terrace and descent could still be traced. The dark, red mass—red only because one knew that it was red, not red because at that distance any color could be certainly seen—sat enthroned in its white chair. Its whole intent was cast away from me, away too from the tented camping-ground, and the Lha-lu house which I had left; but every window pre-supposed a greater thing, that thrice-sacred shrine in central Lhasa which is the center of all the life and all the fascination of Buddhism, that golden idol which I should never see again. A spit of gray rain slanted across the hill above Sera. I went on. But I can assure the reader that for twenty yards the Potala is still to be seen.

The road now humps itself over a little stream by a stone-built curve. As you descend on the western side of this small culvert, and not before, the last vestige of the Potala is hidden from your view forever. The road goes on, but for many miles the warmth had gone out of the sun, the light was missing from the distant slopes.

Still sturdily trotting forward, one saw again the landmarks of our advance, and one halted to look at the gigantic Buddha in his stone recess, not only perhaps in curiosity; perhaps also to stave off for thirty seconds the last sight one will ever have of the plain in which Lhasa lies. But there is a long journey still before us, and I went on, something depressed at heart.

At Netang the first halt was made. I thought that, as we had done twelve miles, it was but fair to give both men and beasts a rest and food, so we dismounted on a grassy patch by the roadside, not very far on from where a running stream runs a moat-like course between the white mud-walls of a substantial farm. We went on again in twenty minutes. The road was good enough, but already the coming weariness of this long trek was borne in upon me. There is, perhaps, something suggestive of keen pleasure and quickened appreciation in the idea of traveling fast over mountainous passes and the highest plateau on earth, day after day, day after day. But though I am glad to have done this journey, it was no cheery matter in the doing. I suppose that the knowledge that you may not stop, whatever your need, whatever your weariness, helps, to a certain extent, to tire you in advance. The day's program must be carried through; there is no help for it. To such and such a place you must reach before nightfall; if you do not, you must go on through the night until you do reach it. Morning after morning you must rise at five o'clock or even before five, and you must press on with your strange escort till the next change of horses gives you ten minutes' rest. If you stay to rest, if you slacken your pace for two miles to see some specially beautiful view, you pay for it—not then, when you could well afford to pay for it, but at the end of your day, when you are content to drag yourself into the post you have watched slowly increasing through the gloom with eyes so tired that they have ceased to care much whether they see anything more or not that day. And the knowledge of what is before you every day helps to take away the poetry of such a ride. If, under these circumstances, you want to see the unrivaled beauty and the exquisite attraction of such a journey you must bring a stout heart with you. The fourth day sees you an utterly sore and wearied man, already skinned by the bitter wind, wondering quietly whether the next day can really be done or not. It is not the distance that you have to traverse. This first day we did about forty-seven miles; in all, the average stage was hardly more than thirty-five miles, but it was thirty-five miles covered at an altitude which is felt most heavily in this continual work. One could do seventy miles a day more easily in England.

At 10.37 we reached Nam, where we had another halt. By this time we had caught up the convoy which had left Lhasa on the previous day. It just so happens that the road here winds round by a trang which forbids one to pass a string of laden mules. So there was every excuse for going slowly and resting thereby. The Kyi chu ran sullenly in a swollen flood, and the deep echoes of the water beneath the overhanging cliffs were like the grumblings of the sea at Tintagel. At last the road freed itself from the intruding hills; we set off at a canter across the flat plain and speedily distanced the slowly pacing train. We reached Jang, where the willow trees clog themselves and dam a small lake below the scarp of the granite hill. It is a pretty place, and we had stopped there on our way up. But now there is no time. Chak-sam is a long way ahead, and Chak-sam must be reached that day. So on we go, and at last, after many miles, we reached Chusul.

The barley fields round Chusul were ripening fast. Otherwise there is little change since we passed up by this road a month ago. Round the corner, however, we reach the Tsang-po, and here is a difference indeed. The brown flood water from bank to bank slides by with desperate intention. There is no haste, there is no foam, but there is a long journey to go and the waters of the Tsang-po are losing no time. The road is under water. Again and again I had to climb the cliff-side where the new depth threatened to sweep my pony off his feet, or hid the edge of safety underneath its tarnished flood. The willow trees, which before stood high and dry above the stream, were now waterlogged, and filtered the flotsam of the surface through their reluctant leaves. Then, when this became too heavy a burden to be borne, branch and all cracked and splintered heavily down the stream, which was nearly a mile wide at this point. Beside it the road, sometimes submerged, sometimes not, struck on till the valley opened, and through a picturesque little hamlet where the poplars grew thickly together beneath the level of the road, making a shade in which no grass would grow, the track made onward still toward the low-lying lines of vegetation which mark Pome-tse. Over forty miles from Lhasa our northern picket stood, and one dismounts with utter relief. But all was not over thus. The river has yet to be crossed, and for this one has to plod a mile up-stream, then embark in a kwor—a frail yak-skin boat, distended upon bamboos—and go whirling down-stream, making an almost invisible progress through the brown flood. The land sweeps upstream with amazing velocity as we go. To cross 700 yards we travel two miles. Part of that 700 yards is still water, a small portion is even a gentle back-flow in the way we wish to go. We lose two clear miles in 400 yards. Soon we are swept round just beyond the spur of rock from which the ferry started. Straight across the whirlpools where poor Bretherton died, our frail craft is carried creaking, twisted, awry, as the strain comes alternately on one side and the other. At last, however, just as it seems that we shall be swept down beneath the chains of Chak-sam gompa, the backwater is reached, and we come gently to rest, nosing the bank exactly to a foot where a little ghât had been prepared for us. For sheer skill in watermanship it would be hard to beat the thick-skulled grinning boatmen of Chak-sam ferry. There was never a moment's hesitation, there was never a moment's recovery. The course was as plain to these caramel-eyed barbarians as if we had swung across on an aërial wire. Another mile had to be covered before I reached my camp that night. I dined with Wigram and Davys, good, competent men. The latter, with unheard-of daring, succeeded in saving for Candler the use of his terribly maimed right hand, tying up the tendons with complete and successful disregard of the working drawings of his Creator. The former, after many weary months in unthanked solitude, still spent his own money to save his company of yaks from dying of starvation by decree of the commissariat.

On the next morning I rode on easily to Kamba-partsi, where the road turns abruptly up the high mountain which separates the Yam-dok tso from the waters of the Brahmaputra, 3,000 feet below. We had milk at the house beside which the willow grows which is twisted into a figure of eight. Then we climbed, climbed steadily and wearily, thankful for nothing except that we always kept just ahead of a rainstorm clouding the valley 500 feet below us. We rose and rose until at last, after many halts, we saw the side trail which runs along the river bank to Shigatse join us from the western slope. Then there was not much more to do. We passed the chortens which mark the summit of the pass, and, giving my horse to a Sikh, I thankfully went on my own feet down the long descent which, after giving again and again alternate views of the great blue lake, lands one at last beside its steady unruffled ring of water. Then we went on again round the spurs containing the northern shore still blue with larkspur, here dipping far into the recesses where some stream deposited its scanty waters in the lake, there saving half a mile by taking the lake-shore down where the nettles could no longer grow. Hour after hour passed, and at last Pe-di jong, which we had had in sight for six or seven miles, began to grow in size. Arrived there, I made the best of my way with Lieutenant Dalmahoy to his eyrie high above the lake in one of the few rooms in the castle which was still fit for use. Next day was the most merciful of all the eleven days I rode. Owing to the necessity of exchanging mails at Ra-lung, there was no use in going farther that day than Nagartse jong. This was easy indeed; and quite slowly we made our way round the north-western corner of the lake, over the causeway of Good Luck, and round the arm of the lake to the western shore. It was a short day, and I reached Nagartse before one o'clock.

Here Moody told me that among the duties unexpectedly thrown upon him was that of supplying the bare necessities of life to the neighboring villages which had been mercilessly sacked by the followers of the Tongsa Penlop. In every case we had left in each house sufficient to last it through the winter, but these Bhutanese brigands had swooped down upon the luckless villagers in our rear and had deprived them even of the last pound of grain or meal.

On the 18th I left Nagartse at seven o'clock, and arrived at the scene of the fight on the Karo la four hours later. It was an interesting ride. All the way up the valley the flowers thicken. It would have been impossible for any one, as we came down, to guess how carpeted the desolate valley would be in a month's time. Now there were sheets of blue larkspur below, and above it purple and pink blossoms in myriads. Young green brushes of wormwood, the tall cool green pipes of hemlock, the insistent orange of the marigold, and the yellow of dandelions blended in confusion with the long feathery bents of windlestraws. In every crevice up the rock little ferns clung, vetches and strange violet primulas grew on the very face of the rock itself, and the gray-green and gray-purple pyramids of the monkshood stood amongst all this luxuriant beauty like devils in heaven.

The road was easy enough. I passed the camping-ground below Dzara in good time, and after crossing the stream which had been so black before, turned the sharp corner which gives one the first sight of the position held by the enemy in May and July. By the side of the road, almost within arm's length, there were two enormous Himalayan eagles fastened upon some piece of carrion. One heavily flapped away; the other held his ground, and I was able to examine him closely. They were huge birds, probably of the condor species, and the general effect is heightened by the very untidiness of their plumage. In color black, shot with deep Prussian blues, toning off here and there into grays, but never enough to lighten the somberness of the whole; a beak like a pick-ax, eyes, head, crest, and breast all dark alike.[1] Pushing on past the place where the walls still lay in confusion, I reached the pass at noon, and descended into the Plain of Milk. This was now a shifting, soaked mass of snow and sleet, and one hugged the path by the cliff. At last the narrow gorge down into Gom-tang was passed, and the wide, rolling plain stretched before me to the entering in of Ra-lung. Here I found Lieutenant Arundell, cheerful in spite of the long isolation from which he saw no escape for many weeks to come. He had discovered—what the Chinese mail runners had failed to find—wood in the wilderness, and a great heap of firewood taken from a neighboring nullah helped to make Ra-lung a very different place from what it had been on the three other occasions on which I had passed through it.

On the next day, the 19th, the road was gay with flowers, but the grim severity of the spurs and clefts of granite was only intensified by this thin film of gaiety. At Gobshi, where I arrived shortly before eleven o'clock, crops again appeared—crops, that is, which actually promised ripeness and grain. I made no stay at the village, passing on beside the roughly-piled walls of quartzite, coral pink, sienna, and white through which the feathery nettles

[1] I could not find in the Natural History Museum any bird resembling these, so I cannot give them a name.

stabbed, and over which the clematis sprawled behind a rank growth of larkspur and forget-me-not. I halted for half an hour at the end of the cultivation, and then pressed on over the remaining fifteen miles to Gyantse. There is nothing to record, nothing different, nothing significant; but the weariness of the journey was just then telling heavily upon me, and I was glad, indeed, when at last I made my way in through the Gurkha gate to the post I knew so well. Colonel Hogge received me with the utmost hospitality. Two companies were occupying the jong, and I turned in that night with the comfortable assurance that I should not be disturbed by the raucous war-cry which we had heard so often during our investment. The next day I went on again over the hardest journey of the road.

I rode out with Shuttleworth in the earliest dawn. We had two mounted infantry men with us, but, by this time, it was almost unnecessary to take precaution. We went along aimlessly in the clear morning air. He was only going to Sau-gang, and I trusted to putting on speed afterward to make up for a pleasant and lazy march of thirteen miles. At Sau-gang we had breakfast, but our host, the commandant, was in bed nursing his own quinsy. It seemed a strange thing that so important a post should have not even a hospital assistant to look after it. From Sau-gang I moved on by myself with an escort of four men. The scene of the Red Idol fight was very different from what it was when I had last seen it. The vegetation grew rankly in between the boulders, the eyots in the stream were covered with thick, short, vivid grass, and there seemed to be ten times as many trees as one had expected to find. It is a long and wearying journey, and is, as a matter of exact length, understated in the official estimates. So at least I was assured by the officers at both ends of the stretch, so I was willing enough to believe.

At last the blood-stained altar rock on the hill at the entrance to the gorge was passed, and I came out into the more open ground through which the river ran evenly. But there was still a long pull, and it was not till past one o'clock that I reached the Hot Springs. Forty minutes later I rode into the temple which we had fortified and were using as a post on the road. It was this post which had been attacked by the Tibetans when Colonel Younghusband made his hurried descent upon the Chumbi Valley in the early days of June. I had luncheon there, and inspected the great idol-houses down below on the ground floor. The painting on the walls here is different from that in other temples. It is of a much more archaic type, and approximates rather to Indian than to Chinese art. The place had been kept blocked up, and though it was in the usual confusion which marks Tibetan temples at all times, not much had been taken away. After a halt of three quarters of an hour, I set out again for the stage of the day. I had already covered 31 miles and there remained before me 14. This, I think, was on the whole the most wearisome part of all the ride. People at home are rarely very tired, or if they are, they are generally tired in company; but there is something about the last few miles of a day's journey like that which I was now making, which almost defies description for sheer weariness. One has long ceased to take the slightest interest in the scenery or anything else. One barely raises one's eyes: riding or leading one's horse, one has eyes only for the ground immediately at one's feet. Unless an object comes within the ten-foot radius of your gaze, you do not care to lift your head to see it. The most perfect glow of crimson evening upon the distant ice-fields of the Himalayas is not so interesting as a rare level ten-yards' stretch of good road. Slowly, very slowly, the ribbon of the track unwinds itself and crawls beneath you. The shape of the stones, the wetness of the gray sand between them, the tilt of the sharp outcrop, the stability of a pebble, the little casual weeds and plants that sometimes grow beside the bigger boulders, a leaf thrown down here and there, a piece of wood, every now and then the stepping-stones by which, if you are on your feet, you cross a little angry torrent—all these have a real interest for you. On other days one's attention is chained to the slowly sliding roadway, not from weariness only, but because it is positively dangerous to lift your eyes one moment from the stones on which your next foot was to be placed.

There is an expression used by Sophocles in his "Œdipus Tyrannus" which scholars who sit in arm-chairs have sometimes failed to understand:

> *ἡ ποικιλῳδος Σφιγξ τὸ προς ποσὶ σκοπεῖν*
> *μεθέντας ἡμᾶς τἀφανῆ προσήγετο*

All that Sophocles intended was that the presence of the sphinx made men care little for anything but what lay immediately before them. But only a nation of travelers in a land of mountains could have understood to the full the meaning of the phrase. "What lies at one's feet," that is, indeed, the only thing which chains the attention of wanderers in a land like this. Often one does not lift one's eyes from the road for miles at a time. To look around you perhaps means that you have to halt, and you never forget that you pay for a five minutes' halt in the cool of the afternoon by five minutes' stumbling over sharp and dangerous rocks after night has fallen. There is not much interest or excitement about this work. You go on, and it seems to you that you have been going on for months. The prospect of arriving at your journey's end becomes something in the future so remote that it is hardly worth while troubling yourself about it; only you still go on—on—on. On—though your beast may be too tired to trot, on—though you may yourself be so footsore that each step is pain, on—although you may be dropping with fatigue, on you still have to go. Many people I have met have thought that there was some strange romance about this rapid passage over the very ridge-poles of the world. There was none. What you were doing to-day you would have to do to-morrow, and the day after, and you instinctively shrank from the weariness of anticipating day after day of this tedious tramp. It is true that it was only toward the evening that this depression assailed you. The heat of the day was comfortable compared to this. Then you had at least the contented knowledge that you had hours in front of you; probably, also, you had had, or were going to have, your mid-day meal. It might rain perhaps, or you might have a stinging wind blowing down the funnel of the valley straight into your teeth, but such things make no difference. You may be drenched through, but it is just as easy to go on. One almost ceases to be a free agent on these occasions. If you had had a companion with you, you would not have spoken for five or ten miles—you would have resented his sanest remark as unnecessary and tiresome. And yet the loneliness of my own journey!

I got into camp that evening, luckily finding three men from Kala tso who had made it their first halting place on the road to Gyantse. They gave me the best of dinners, and I rolled myself up in my blankets as soon as the last mouthful had been eaten. Next morning I went on to Kala tso, and there changed horses. Every arrangement had been made for me throughout the journey with the greatest care, and after passing by Chalu and coming out once more by the waters of the Bam tso, I found another relay waiting for me. Here I left all the mounted infantry behind, except one man to lead the pack-horse. However, he was foolish enough to let his own horse go, and as I could not waste the time to catch it again, I led my own beast all the way into Dochen. Riding on again, I set my head for the first time against the bitter wind of the Tang la, and though an ekka was at my disposal, I preferred to ride up over the slope of the spur behind Tuna rather than prolong the tiresome struggle against the ceaseless undeviating cold stress of air against which clothing seemed to be of no use. I came down into the post which the Mission had occupied for so long, and was warmly welcomed by Captain Rice. The usual bunch of telegrams was sent, and I slept on the floor of the little mess-room underneath the pictures cut out from illustrated papers which will remain for a hundred years as a mystery peculiar to the houses along our route. Next morning I reached the Tang la in as good weather as one ever has over this detestable barrier. I dropped down on the farther side to the posting-station, and came on to Phari, where Captain Rawlings met me.

Phari had suffered severely since I had seen it last. Large gaps had broken away from the wall of the jong, and it had been worth no one's while to repair them. They betrayed the shoddiness of the building. It is only a skin of stone, filled in with rubble, and for purposes of defense, it would be better if the whole of the keep were leveled with the ground. Except for this damage the scene was almost unchanged since the 28th of March.

Raw blue-gray shafts and terraces of pointed rock rise rarely from among the unclothed curves of treeless and shrubless brown down-land bosoming and sweeping as far as the eye can see. Here and there on a northern slope the white snow for a few hours after dawn streaks the side of the hills in a tangle of lacework crossed horizontally with burhel or yak tracks. For the rest, the snow that falls at night is, as a rule, thawed and gone by ten or eleven on the following morning, and looking south one saw again the dusty hillsides, rounded from end to end, except where a dry watercourse distinguishes with dirty ocher the dirtier drab which clothes the whole visible field of sight. A painter might force himself to call the dun waste of the ringing hills green, but only in so far as distance veils with a bluish haze the buff-soiled earth at his feet. It is all the same. Above these nearer eminences rose the pointed terraces of snowy mountain ranges—Chumiumo and Pahamri to the west and Ma-song Chungdong to the south glittering at midday with jagged bastions of white and gray, and the curtains of rock which are seen connecting the heights one with another, if they are high enough to top the rounded hills, betray their steepness by the scanty snow that can find a resting-place. I saw Chumolhari again with a feeling of reverence.

Of all the hills which the expedition saw from the Jelep to Phembu-ri, Chumolhari is queen. One cannot wonder at the invention which has clothed this extraordinary peak with a sacred character.

Phari is at its foot, and one watches it from hour to hour with a touch of the respect which has for the Tibetans filled its wind-swept clefts and ravines with baffled demons and glorified its summit with the presence of the Goddess herself. Like very impressive mountains all the world over, in surroundings and in shape, it somewhat resembles the Matterhorn. The great central pyramid rises from a platform—three miles in length and some 5,000 feet below the summit—of which the western mile is composed of four parallel serrated ridges of gray-toothed peaks, so sharp that little snow can rest on them. To the east the main mass rises 2,000 feet, into a great, snowy, right-angled ridge, which makes up with the central pyramid no very fanciful resemblance to the high-peaked, high-cantled Mexican saddle. Twenty-four thousand feet high, the peak itself is still curiously free from clouds. In the evening a periwinkle-colored haze may throw a veil of the thinnest gauze before it, and all the afternoon the great bellying argent clouds crawl helplessly inward from the south and west, powerless to resist the gravitational force of this vast upheaval of rock. But all day and all night she stands out cloudless and unveiled. She holds the sunset long after the plain is in darkness at her feet, and at one moment in the dying red light looks not unlike a westward-facing lioness couching proudly, with the hollows of her huge thigh-bones emphasized by the shadow cast on the cantle of the rock. Siniol chu and the Matterhorn, Chumolhari and Teneriffe have each something in common, each also their own attraction, but the Peak of the Sacred Goddess makes the deepest impression of them all.

I went on over the plain toward Kamparab, and I was sorry enough to turn the last corner and lose forever the sight of the great Tibetan stronghold.[1] At Kamparab the real beauty of the Chumbi Valley begins. It is true that here and there the plain around Phari had been so blue with forget-me-nots that the illusion of still pools of clear water was absolutely irresistible. The barley-fields near the jong were just giving up the attempt to produce a harvest. The weather had been milder than usual, and the bearded ears were all there, but in a whole field there would not have been found an egg-cupful of grain. At Kamparab the converging slopes of the valley were standing thick with colored flowers. I am a poor botanist and I could get very little information from any one during the entire expedition, but I believe that collections were made by native collectors sent up by the director of the Botanic Gardens in Calcutta, but these men were, in themselves, of no use at any time for my purpose. But the result of their labors ought to provide as interesting an herbarium as could be made in any district in the world, though the best collection of pressed flowers is a mere mockery. The sheets of gold and mauve and red which swathed the steep sides of the valley were doubly welcome after one's remembrance of the bleak barrenness of earlier days. Nothing grows very high here except a curious form of dock with wide

[1] The Chinese route-books describe Phari—of which the original name was Namgye Karpo—as a place where neither barley nor rice will grow. It is, they say, the southern frontier of Tibet, and quote the curious Tibetan legend that Phari is protected to the south by a wall of water, and therefore does not need many soldiers. Here the actual numbers of Bhutanese and Sikkimese envoys are counted and recounted when they leave the country again, that no man should remain.

green leaves and a cluster of yellow trumpet-shaped flowers. All else is but a span in height, but the flowers seem to have received the glory which has been denied to the foliage.

At last, after riding steadily for four hours, I dropped down to Dota, where I found the famous frozen waterfall thawed away, and a foolish trickle of water was all that reminded one of what had been there, and what would again begin to form in two months' time. The next day I went on down the rocky and broken path beside the stream, made better, indeed, but still leaving much to be desired, to Gautso, and through the tangled green jungle beside the tumbling waters of the Ammo chu, down, always down, till the waste marsh land of Lingmatang spread out in front of me. I went on till Galin-ka and Chorten-karpo too had been gained and passed, and at last the slowly rising roofs of Bakcham promised a rest. I halted here for luncheon, and set out on the last stage of my travels in Tibet.

Here, for the first time, I began to realize what the phrase "the rains" means in Sikkim. To an English visitor the rain anywhere in India is a somewhat striking experience when met for the first time; but Assam alone can compete with Sikkim for a sheer deluge of water, daily, consistent, never hurrying, and never slackening in volume or rapidity. Beneath it the road, which was my first consideration, had long gone to pieces; only the iron-bound stone trail remained, more stairs than track, which heaves itself up to the top of the Natu la, and thence drops like the side of one of the Pyramids to the lower river levels. The corduroy of the road enabled us to get along, slowly and with many slips, to and, on the next day, from the warmth and welcome of Champitang and Captain H. O. Parr. Beyond the corduroy the road was a sucking mass of black mud, steadied only by unexpected slopes and slants of hard rock, upon which, as one's pony's hoof encountered it, one was as likely to slide as stay. There was no help for it. I got off and walked. There were ten miles of walking in front of us, and as I have already described the road, it will not be necessary to do more than say that they are about the cruellest ten miles over which man ever dragged his unwilling feet. But the day was bright, and there was one great landmark at least by which to reckon our progress. Crossing the Natu la was the snapping of the last link with all that lay behind me. I had again crossed into English territory.

There was not very much more vegetation here than there had been in the earlier part of the year, but there was enough to mark the distinction of the season. It is not until Changu is reached that one dips suddenly below the lake into the trees and luxury of true Sikkim. Captain Drake Brockman, whom I found at Changu, rowed me over the lake, and I set out over the remaining twenty miles of the day's journey about half-past twelve.

There is, perhaps, not much to say about the rest of my journey. The road was bad beyond description, and to those who knew it well, nothing could be more descriptive than the simple truth that the road between the tenth mile and the thirteenth mile was actually the best part of all the journey. Karponang was reached and passed, and then a native Havildar set out with me to lantern me through the dying day to Chumbi. This was the sorest disappointment so far as roads went, for what had, when I went over it first, been a well-metaled good bridle-path developing near Chumbi into a real cart-road, had turned under the downpour into a nubbly sequence of projecting stones, ankle deep in white slush. It was, of course, raining by this time, but that was not of very great account. In any case one would not have been able to do more than about two and a quarter miles an hour. As a matter of fact, it took me four and a half hours to cover the nine and three-quarter miles that lay before me, and long after dark I arrived at the bungalow where dinner was awaiting me. Then I climbed up to the Residency, where I spent the night.

The next day I continued the descent, dropping down through the sizzing grindstones of the cicadæ into the lower valleys of the Tista and the Rang-po, burdened every additional mile with a heavier blanket of air. When I reached Rang-po, the oppression was almost enough to make me faint. My heart was going like a sledge-hammer, my lungs seemed to have no grip upon the air, and I was nearly deaf. These were all the results of coming down too fast from a seven months' residence at an altitude of thirteen thousand feet. In twenty-four hours I descended from 14,500 to 600 feet. Going up was nothing in comparison, and, though the movements of the returning force were far more leisurely, I fancy the descent tried the hearts of some of the men far more than the climb. From Rang-po I still went on down the river to the Tista Bridge, where Mr. Lister's relays were waiting for me, and I climbed up again, to my intense relief, nearly five thousand feet to the welcome shelter of his bungalow among the tea-fields, through the great cactus hedges, skeined with the gossamer of "Mary's hair." Next day I went on early, and reached Ghoom Station, the end of my long ride, at a quarter to nine, having come from Lhasa in eleven days and three hours.

I have done. If it shall seem to some reader that I have brought into the course of the narrative even a flash from that aurora of fascination which haloed every step we took in this strange country, which danced will-o'-the-wisp like along our road before us, which at the end sat like St. Elmo's fire within the shrine of the great golden idol in the heart of Lhasa—then I shall have done more than now seems possible to me as I make an end of writing, and turn back the pages of this volume.

The wide field which the exploration—I had almost said in this case the discovery—of a new country always offers, I have

APPENDICES

APPENDIX A

NOTES ON THE NATURAL HISTORY OF SOUTHERN TIBET

By Captain H. J. Walton

Indian Medical Service, lately Medical Officer and Naturalist to the Tibet Frontier Commission, 1903–4

The following sketch of the Natural History of Southern Tibet is not intended to be, in any sense, an exhaustive list of the fauna of that area; it is merely a brief account of some of the more striking animals that were met with in the districts visited by the Tibet Frontier Commission. While I do not think that much of popular interest is omitted, I would point out that, during the months when Natural History observations would have been of the greatest interest, indulgence in such pursuits for those members of the Commission who were at Gyantse—amongst them myself—was strictly discouraged by the Tibetans, who emphasized their disapproval of the wandering naturalist by forcible protests from the famous "jingals from the Jong."

MAMMALS

Of the larger mammals, that with which we became most familiar was the kiang (*Equus hemionus*). Both at Kamba-jong and at Tuna there were large numbers of these wild asses. They went about, as a rule, in troops of ten to thirty, though, if alarmed, several herds would unite temporarily. There is nothing horse-like about the kiang, but from his size and fine carriage he resembles a large mule, rather than an ass. The reddish chestnut color of the upper parts is well shown off by the white belly and legs. The mane is of a darker color, and this color is continued as a narrow stripe along the middle of the back, and for some distance down the tail.

As the kiang is not harassed by the Tibetans, those we saw were fairly tame, and would allow one to approach to within about sixty yards of them. Then the herd would show signs of uneasiness, and would move off for a hundred yards or so. On several occasions I tried to get at closer quarters with them. I rode slowly toward a herd and the moment the animals became in the least alarmed, I galloped toward them as fast as possible; but the kiangs outdistanced me without an effort; indeed, I never succeeded in getting them to do more than make off at an easy canter. It is true that my Tibetan pony was not particularly speedy, but a greyhound that belonged to one of the officers of the Commission escort was almost equally unsuccessful in the chase of these fleet-footed animals. At Lhasa there were three semi-tame kiangs; all were mares. Even these, however, although one could approach to within twenty yards of them, resented attempts at closer intimacy. The kiang must be a very hardy animal. Those at Tuna seemed none the worse for the very low temperatures experienced there, though their only food consisted of coarse grasses, to reach which they often had to scratch away the snow.

According to Blanford and other authorities, the kiang is merely a variety of the Asiatic wild ass, another variety of which (*E. onager, v. indicus*) occurs in Western India and Baluchistan. It is strange that an animal should be found in the bare desert tracts, west of the Indus, exposed to quite the other extreme of temperature to that to which its near ally is subjected in Tibet.

A few specimens of the Great Tibetan sheep (*Ovis hodgsoni*) were obtained at high elevations, on the slopes of the mountains near Kamba-jong. A fine male is said to measure four feet at the shoulder and bears a pair of massive horns, which differ from those of *Ovis poli* by their curve not forming a complete circle. The Tibetan sheep is closely allied to *Ovis ammon.*

Bharal (*Ovis nahura*) were very common on all the lower mountain ranges. The females and young, which keep together, were constantly seen and were surprisingly tame, but the old males with good heads required careful stalking. The Tibetans used to shoot a good many about Kamba-jong. The bharal is a wonderful climber; even quite young ones negotiate the most formidable-looking precipices with apparent ease. Bharal mutton, except that of old males, is very well flavored, though it is not to be compared, as an article of food, with the Tibetan gazelle.

This Tibetan gazelle or goa (*Gazella picticaudata*) was one of the commonest animals that we encountered. It occurred in large herds on all the open plains and downs. The horns of the male are closely ringed and much curved back, being commonly from twelve to fourteen inches in length. The female is without horns. Gazelle shooting is about the easiest sport to be obtained in South Tibet. The meat is excellent for the table. Except in places where they had been much worried by us, the gazelles were, as a rule, by no means shy. During the day they scatter about grazing over the plains. When alarmed, the individuals generally unite into a herd and make off at a rapid pace at first, but by using ordinary caution one could generally approach within range of them again.

I have been much puzzled by a statement made by Sir Joseph Hooker, in his "Himalayan Journals." He mentions antelopes ("Chiru," *Pantholops hodgsoni*) occurring near the Cholamu Lake. Whatever may have been the case in Hooker's time, I am almost certain that there are no antelopes in this part of Tibet at the present day. The furriers at Lhasa had no skins, nor did I see any horns offered for sale. I made inquiries of several educated Tibetans, and they all asserted that the animal occurred considerably to the west of the country visited by the Tibet Frontier Commission.

Of the carnivora of South Tibet, the snow leopard (*Felis uncia*) is the largest. Though rarely seen by us—I myself only saw one during the fourteen months that I spent in Tibet—it appears to be fairly common, judging by the numerous skins that were offered for sale by the Tibetans.

The lynx (*F. lynx*) also is tolerably common. This animal is by some authors considered to be a distinct species (*F. isabellina*) from the European lynx, but the distinction appears to rest mainly on the fact that the Tibean lynx is paler in color than the other.

On two occasions, near Gyantse, I saw a small light-colored cat. This was probably Pallas's cat (*F. manul*); but as I did not succeed in shooting one, and as the Lhasa furriers had no skins that I recognized as belonging to this species, I am uncertain about their identification.

Wolves (*Canis laniger*) were shot occasionally during the winter. The ordinary Tibetan wolf appears to be considerably paler in color than the European animal, but Dr. Blanford considers that the two belong to the same species. A black variety of the wolf is said to occur in Tibet, but I saw none.

Otters were seen on several occasions in the vicinity of Phari jong. It is much to be regretted that no specimens were obtained.

We shot examples of two species of foxes. At Kamba-jong, *Vulpes alopex, var. flavescens,* is common. It closely resembles the common fox of Europe, of which it is considered a variety, differing, like so many Tibetan animals, in being paler in color. It carries a magnificent brush. The length from nose to tip of tail of one that I procured—an adult male—was 44½ inches, and the height at the shoulder 14¾ inches.

The other fox (*V. ferrilatus*) is a smaller animal, with a relatively much shorter tail. It occurs from the neighborhood of Gyantse to Lhasa. A fine male, shot near the Karo la Pass, measured thirty-six inches in length.

A light-colored weasel (*Putorius alpinus*) was tolerably common at Gyantse. Its habits are very similar to those of the European weasel, and it feeds largely on birds.

The woolly hare (*Lepus oiostolus*) is universally distributed. The most obvious distinction from the British hare is afforded by the large patch of gray fur over the rump of the Tibetan species. This characteristic patch is well marked even in quite young leverets. The woolly hare is singular in its custom of habitually squatting among bare stones on the hillsides in preference to the grassy plains. It was particularly numerous at Kamba-jong, where on one occasion three guns shot fifty-four in about three hours.

The Tibetan marmot (*Arctomys himalayanus*) occurred very locally throughout the country. It was nowhere very numerous, and its whistling call was heard more often than the animal itself was seen. The places affected by this beast were all at very high elevations. The burrows, the entrances to which resemble those of the common rabbit, are frequently made under rocks. The marmots appear to hibernate from about the middle of October to the beginning of April. This is quite a large animal, the body being as much as two feet in length.

A much smaller marmot than the preceding species, specimens of which I saw but did not shoot near Phari jong, in the Chumbi Valley, was probably *Arctomys hodgsoni.* If so, this species would appear not to hibernate as strictly as its larger relative, as it was in January that I saw it.

One of the commonest rodents in South Tibet is Hodgson's mouse-hare (*Lagomys curzoniæ*). Wherever the country is tolerably level the ground is tunneled in all directions by its burrows. This species is highly gregarious, and does not hibernate at all. Even during the severest cold of the winter the little mouse-hares could be seen sitting at the mouths of their runs, sunning themselves. Although they are essentially social animals, large numbers living in close proximity to one another, as a rule their burrows are quite distinct one from another; and although in case of a sudden alarm a mouse-hare will take refuge temporarily in the nearest burrow, I noticed on several occasions the presumably rightful owner of the burrow driving the intruder away. The mouse-hare is a little, tailless beast with small rounded ears. It is in shape rather like a guinea-pig, and is of about the size of a large rat. The friendly terms on which it lives with a small bird—the brown ground-chough (*Podoces humilis*) —recall the somewhat similar association between the "prairie-dog" (*Cynomys sp.*) and the ground-owl (*Speotyto cunicularis*), though in the latter case a rattlesnake is said to form a third member of the "happy family."

Both field-mice and house-mice occur in South Tibet, but the species have not yet been identified. A newspaper correspondent, in an account he gave of a visit to the Jo-kang in Lhasa, speaks of white mice living in one of the shrines of this cathedral. This is an error. The mice in this shrine, which are surprisingly tame, belong to the species of the ordinary house-mouse of Tibet. This is larger than *Mus musculus,* and considerably paler in color.

Although I was constantly on the lookout for them, I did not see a single bat in Tibet. I was informed by an officer of the escort that he had seen some very small bats flying round the jong at Gyantse. I went to the place mentioned on many evenings, but no bats appeared, and I think it probable that the officer mistook for small bats the crag-martins which abounded about the rocks.

At all low elevations musk-deer (*Moschus moschiferus*) were common, and nowhere more so than at Lhasa. Considering its abundance, I was amused at the impudence of some Tibetans who wished to sell me a live specimen for thirty-five pounds! The musk, which is obtained from a gland on the belly of the male, is, as usual, much in demand among the Tibetans for medicinal purposes. The chief characteristics of the animal are the large movable lateral hoofs, the long canine teeth, and the peculiar brittleness and wiry texture of the fur.

I was much disappointed at having no opportunity of becoming acquainted with the shao (*Cervus affinis*). This somewhat mysterious stag—mysterious, at least, as far as its geographical distribution is concerned—must be, to judge from its antlers, one of the finest of the Asiatic *Cervidæ*. I took a great deal of trouble in endeavoring to ascertain from the Tibetans something definite about the area it inhabited. The antlers were common in many monasteries throughout the country we visited, and in the shops at Lhasa, but beyond saying that the shao inhabited a tract of country to the south of Lhasa, my informants were all exceedingly vague in their statements. Two specimens (one of which, a female, was captured alive, but which unfortunately died) were obtained by officers in the Chumbi Valley.[1] These evidently came into the valley from Bhutan, but I obtained no reliable evidence as to how far to the East this species ranges. I was told that the reason so many shao antlers are for sale at Lhasa, is that they are in great demand by Chinese merchants, who export them to China to be used medicinally. It is a great pity that the antlers are considered to be most valuable when "in velvet," as this naturally necessitates killing the animal.

The wild yak (*Bos grunniens*) does not inhabit the parts of Tibet visited by the Tibet Frontier Commission, but domesticated animals are used everywhere for purposes of transport. All tame cattle are phlegmatic creatures, but the palm must certainly be awarded to the yak for the highest form of philosophical imperturbability. It appears to be perfectly indifferent to the weather, provided only that it is cold enough; it forages for itself, and requires no grooming, stabling, or other attention. At night the Tibetans secure their yaks in a row by tying thin yak-hair cords to the beasts' horns and to a thicker pegged-out rope. One would think that the yaks had only to shake their heads in order to free themselves, but it never seems to occur to them how easy it would be to escape. Yak drivers, on the march, encourage the yaks to step out by shrill whistles; if more drastic measures are required they hurl rocks, with unerring aim, or sling stones, with equal skill, at the unfortunate animals. For agricultural work, especially for plowing, the Tibetans generally use hybrids between the yak and ordinary cattle, as these are more docile and easier to manage than the pure-bred yak. A peculiarity of the yak, that I have not seen referred to anywhere, is the color of the tongue. In some yaks this is quite black, while in others it is of the usual red color. In connection with this fact it is interesting to remember that several of the domestic dogs of Eastern Asia (for instance, the chow-chow) have black tongues; but if, as I believe is the case, the Polar bear and occasionally the Newfoundland dog also have tongues of this color, it seems impossible to imagine any rea-

[1] Another small and immature specimen was bought by Brigadier-General Macdonald at Lhasa, but this also died.—P. L.

son for this peculiarity. Possibly it is confined to animals living in cold countries, but this suggestion does not explain why only about half the yaks are black-tongued. More information is required on this subject.

With the exception of the dogs, there is nothing of special interest about the other domestic animals of South Tibet. Excellent wool and well-flavored mutton are provided by the sheep, and the common goat of the country is a small long-haired animal, resembling the goat of Kashmir.

Although, as a rule, not much trouble is taken by the Tibetans in breeding their dogs, these animals are much prized by the people. Apart from the swarms of cross-bred mongrels, it is possible to recognize at least four well-characterized breeds. Of these, the finest is the so-called Tibetan mastiff. This is a great shaggy creature, with a very massive head. It is usually black-and-tan in color, and has a very thick, rough coat. Its eyes show some " haw " like a bloodhound, and it has the pendulous lips of that breed. No monastery of any pretensions in Southern Tibet is without at least a pair of these fierce dogs chained up on either side of the entrance.

The commonest dog is very like a badly bred collie, but lacks the magnificent frill and brush of the latter.

The Lhasa terrier is an entirely distinct breed. It is very similar to a drop-eared Skye terrier, but carries its tail, which is densely feathered, tucked up tightly over its back. It is extremely common at Lhasa, but most of the dogs there are too long in the leg, and I had much trouble in procuring a really good specimen.

The other distinctive breed is the Tibetan spaniel. This is a small black dog—sometimes black-and-white—rather like a Pekinese spaniel. Good specimens of this dog are even more scarce than Lhasa terriers. The dogs that are prized most by the better-class Tibetans are small Chinese lap-dogs, of various kinds, that are brought as presents from Peking by the merchants.

The Dalai Lama has an elephant at Lhasa. This was sent to him, I believe, either from Nepal or Bhutan. It is a small male with slender tusks, and has lived in perfect health at Lhasa for some years.

BIRDS

Among the resident Tibetan birds, two—the lämmergeier (*Gypaëtus barbatus*) and the raven (*Corvus corax*)—are of particular interest. Both species are almost ubiquitous throughout Southern Tibet;

they appear to be quite impervious to the rigors of the climate, and keep fat and lively under conditions that would be fatal to other birds of their great bulk. The powers of flight of the lämmergeier are truly superb, and it is a magnificent sight to see one circling, without an effort, around some precipitous mountain-peak, an occasional flap of the wide wings sufficing to impart all the impetus required. The old stories of lämmergeiers carrying off babies from Alpine villages are pretty well discredited nowadays; certainly the Tibetan bird appears to feed entirely on carrion, associating with griffon vultures around the carcasses of yaks, sheep and other animals. On one occasion I put up a hare, which ran for a hundred yards or more along a bare hillside, a few yards below a lämmergeier that was sailing along close to the ground. The latter took absolutely no notice of the hare, which it might easily have seized. No doubt a lämmergeier *may* occasionally take a living animal, but I fancy that it would only do this if the beast were sickly or very young. There were hundreds of lämmergeiers about the camps of the Commission at Kamba-jong and Tuna, and I had daily opportunities of studying their habits, but I never saw them eating anything but offal or dead animals. The length of the lämmergeier's wings prevents the bird from rising at once from the ground; when it wishes to fly, it is obliged to hop forward for some yards, in order to get up a little "way," and it then presents rather a grotesque appearance. The weak, querulous cry also seems very inappropriate to such a noble-looking bird. During the summer months the lämmergeier retires to the higher mountains, where it makes its large nest on some rocky ledge; but, even then, it comes down to the plains at times, especially in the evening. Thus, both at Gyantse and Lhasa, these birds were always to be seen. The wedge-shaped tail and peculiar flight enable one to recognize a lämmergeier immediately, even at a great distance.

The raven (*Corvus corax*) is an even more familiar bird in Tibet than the lämmergeier. Although the Tibetan bird is the same species as the European raven, it differs from the latter in being usually larger. Ravens occurred at all the camps of the Tibet Frontier Commission, and where these were more or less permanent, the birds literally swarmed, disputing with mongrel dogs for the possession of offal. My own previous acquaintance with wild ravens was mostly acquired in Iceland. In that country ravens are tolerably common, but they are so shy and wild that most of one's observations have to be made through the medium of field-glasses. It was, therefore, a pleasant surprise to me to find the Tibetan raven so utterly devoid of fear that one could stand within five yards of a bird, who, quite undisconcerted by such a close scrutiny, would confine his protest at the most to a croak or two, and resume his unsavory repast with undiminished appetite. In spite, however, of the Tibetan ravens' tameness, they still retain the wariness common to all the *Corvidæ;* although in a land where firearms are rarely carried and where ravens are not molested, they cannot possibly associate the sight of a gun with danger to themselves. I found them apparently fully alive to my fell designs whenever I went after them "on business." As usual with this species, ravens in Tibet are early breeders. I found a nest containing young birds on the 6th of April, at an elevation of about 15,000 feet. The inhabitants of Lhasa keep several species of birds in captivity; considering what excellent pets ravens make, I was rather surprised to see no tame ones there.

The Himalayan griffon vulture (*Gyps himalayensis*) is another common bird occurring up to the greatest altitudes. The wonderful rapidity with which numerous vultures appear about a dead animal (although a few minutes before its death no more may have been visible than a solitary bird soaring high up in the firmament) is a familiar fact, but it nevertheless impresses one afresh each time that one witnesses it; especially is this the case among the bare mountains of Tibet, where such a large tract of country must be required to provide sufficient food for each bird.

Pallas's sea-eagle (*Haliaetus leucoryphus*), a large fulvous-color bird, with a whitish forehead and a broad white band across the tail, was also somewhat numerous, and, in the plains of Gyantse and Lhasa, the black-eared kite (*Milvus melanotis*) abounds. A pair of these kites built their untidy nest on a tree standing in the garden of the house in which the Commission was living at Gyantse. This house was under a daily bombardment from the guns of Gyantse jong for over two months, and the kites' nest was directly in the line of fire. Although jingal balls were whistling through the leaves, or striking the branches, of the tree for many hours on almost every day, they scarcely disturbed the kites in the least, and the latter successfully reared their young.

Of the smaller *Falconidæ*, sparrowhawks (*Accipiter nisus*), hobbies (*Falco subbuteo*) and kestrels (*F. tinnunculus*) were all fairly common; a few kestrels spent the winter at Tuna, but their numbers were largely reinforced by migrants in the spring. Three species of owls occurred, among them, the large eagle-owl (*Bubo ignavus*), which is rather common at Lhasa. In the spring hosts of migratory birds appeared. Thrushes were represented by the red-throated ouzel (*Merula ruficollis*), on its way to breeding grounds in higher latitudes, but most of the following birds remained with us until the cold weather set in: Redstarts (*Ruticilla rufiventris* and *R. hodgsoni*) were particularly numerous, as were also hoopoes (*Upupa epops*), willow-warblers (*Phylloscopus affinis*), rose-finches (*Propasser pulcherrimus* and *Carpodacus severtzovi*), cinnamon sparrows (*Passer cinnamomeus*), and several species of wagtails. The resident sparrow of Southern Tibet is the common European tree-sparrow (*Passer montanus*). This bird abounds even in places which, from the total absence of trees, would apparently prove quite unsuitable; however, the bird accommodates itself to circumstances and occurs in all the Tibetan villages.

The horned lark (*Otocorys elwesi*) is another common resident species, but is only met with in the bare, treeless tracts of country, and retires to the mountains and higher passes to breed. The same applies to the large calandra lark (*Melanocorypha maxima*), whose melodious call-note became very familiar to us.

Skylarks (*Alauda arvensis*) abound from Gyantse to Lhasa; swifts (*Cypselus apus*) and sand-martins (*Cotile riparia*) occur along the well-watered valleys, and swallows (*Hirundo rufula, subsp.*) and crag-martins (*Ptyonoprogne rupestris*) everywhere.

Flocks of red-billed choughs (*Pyrrhocorax graculus*) frequented the whole of the country that we visited. This is the same bird as the Cornish chough, but it differs from the British species in being of a larger size. As they do not feed on carrion, it is difficult to imagine what food such large numbers find in winter in the bare frozen country round Tuna. Magpies (*Pica bottanensis*) are very common at Gyantse and Lhasa. They very closely resemble the British magpie (*P. rustica*), but are distinguishable from the latter by having the rump entirely black; they are also somewhat larger birds.

As might be expected, snow-finches (mountain-finches) are well represented in Tibet. Three species (*Montifringilla blanfordi, M. ruficollis* and *M. adamsi*) spent the winter with us at Tuna. Though there was literally nothing for them to eat there, except the scanty seeds of coarse grasses, they kept in excellent condition, even during the severest weather.

The Tibetan twite (*Acanthis brevirostris*) is also very common and very similar in appearance and habits to the European bird.

No cuckoos were met with; this is rather strange since several species, including the familiar *Cuculus canorus,* are common in summer up to high altitudes in the Himalayas. The wryneck (*Iÿnx torquilla*), known in many parts of England as the "cuckoo's mate," occurred in small numbers at Lhasa, early in September. It was no doubt migrating then, as it is a regular winter visitor to the plains of India.

The blue-hill pigeon (*Columba rupestris*), the differences between which and our own blue rock (*C. livia*) are very trivial, is the common pigeon of South Tibet. Although the Tibetans are not pigeon fanciers, this bird lives in a semi-domesticated state in all the villages. Oddly enough, the "snow" pigeon (*C. leuconota*), a handsome pied bird, was only seen at comparatively low altitudes in the Chumbi Valley.

There is a good stock of game birds. In the Chumbi Valley monals (*Lophophorus refulgens*) and blood pheasants (*Ithagenes cruentus*) were very numerous, and on the mountains and high tablelands the fine Tibetan snow cock (*Tetraogallus tibetanus*) was almost equally common. Snow partridges (*Lerwa nivicola*) were decidedly local in their distribution, but the Tibetan partridge (*Perdix hodgsoniæ*) was plentiful almost everywhere. It is an excellent bird for the table, but is too confirmed a "runner" to afford much sport. From the sportsman's point of view, one of the best birds is the sand-grouse (*Syrrhaptes tibetanus*), which also occurred in considerable numbers.

The Hram or Bam tso and Kala tso, lakes on the road between Tuna and Gyantse, were covered in the spring with innumerable geese and ducks, resting, for the most part, on their way to their breeding grounds. The only goose shot and positively identified was the bar-headed goose (*Anser indicus*). This bird breeds on a lake near Kamba-jong, on the Kala tso, and probably on several others of the larger lakes in Southern Tibet. Indeed, at Lhasa, wild goose's eggs were offered for sale in the bazaar, but only in small numbers. The ruddy sheldrake, or Brahminy duck (*Casarca rutila*), breeds all over the country, making its nest in any sort of hole or hollow in the vicinity of some small stream. This bird, owing to its extreme wariness, is a perfect curse to the sportsman in India who is in quest of wild-fowl. While worthless itself for the table, and consequently seldom shot at, it alarms all the better ducks by its loud call, and by being the first to take to flight. It was therefore quite novel to note how tame the Brahminy was in Tibet. There, when nesting, or about to nest, it scarcely took any notice of one, merely waddling off a few yards if approached too closely. Another duck, which breeds certainly at Lhasa and probably elsewhere, is the white-eyed pochard (*Nyroca ferruginea*). "Flappers," still unable to fly, were shot at Lhasa at the end of August. The other ducks that were met with in Tibet were the mallard (*Anas boscas*), the pintail (*Dafila acuta*), shoveler (*Spatula clypeata*), common teal (*Nettium crecca*), Garganey teal (*Querquedula circia*) and tufted pochard (*Nyroca fuligula*). Goosanders (*Mergus castor*) were also common from the Chumbi Valley to Gyantse.

Two species of snipes, the large solitary snipe (*Gallinago solitaria*) and the pintail snipe (*G. stenura*), were obtained; the latter only at Lhasa, where it was very scarce. At Lhasa also redshanks (*Totanus calidris*), moorhens (*Gallinula chloropus*) and coots (*Fulica atra*) occurred in large numbers.

The Tibetans are apparently not very observant people. I asked an official of high rank at Lhasa, who had held appointments at several places in Tibet, how many species of birds he had seen. He was silent and thoughtful for a minute or two, while he counted off on his fingers those that he knew. He then replied that he knew of twelve kinds of birds, and had heard of, but had not seen, two others!

On the other hand, a few of the Tibetan names of birds imply some little observation of their appearance, size or habits. Thus the tree-sparrow is called "Kang-che-go-mar," or "the little house-bird with the red head"; "Pang-che," or "the little bird (that lives) on grassy hillsides," is Severtzoff's warbler (*Leptopœcile sophiæ*), and "Chi-u-teb-tok," or "the little bird as small as the top of one's thumb," is a willow-warbler (*Phylloscopus affinis*). The following names are very good onomatopœic renderings of the birds' notes:—"Pu-pu-pu-shu" is the hoopoe (*Upupa epops*), and "Di-di-ku-ku" is the turtle dove (*Turtur orientalis*).

At Lhasa many birds are kept in captivity, the favorite cage-birds being larks, rose-finches and turtle doves.

FISH

The streams and lakes of Southern Tibet are well supplied with fish. During the summer fishermen from Gyantse and Lhasa go as far as the Kala tso lake for the purposes of their trade. The fish that they catch vary in weight from about half to two pounds or more. They are split in two, like haddocks, and dried in the sun.

I collected several species, but they are at present awaiting identification. One fish, which furnished a good deal of sport to the anglers of the Commission and escort, is quite like a trout in color and general appearance, but differs in wanting the small "adipose" fin. It was as good for the table as for sport.

Another fish of which we caught large numbers up to four pounds in weight in the Tsang-po and in the streams at Lhasa, is an ugly, slimy brute, with a flattened head and four long feelers hanging from the sides of the mouth. In spite of its repulsive appearance, it was a very excellent and welcome article of food.

REPTILES

Of the reptiles, snakes (non-venomous) are said by the Tibetans to occur in the vicinity of the numerous hot springs, but I was not fortunate enough to come across any.

I collected several species of lizards: the most interesting was a large dark-colored animal, which was often to be seen sunning itself on the rocky hillsides near Lhasa. Its body is remarkably flattened from above downward, and is of a dark stone-gray color, thickly marked with black, and a few large white spots. The largest that I secured measured sixteen inches in length.

AMPHIBIA

I was requested by a distinguished Russian naturalist to keep a sharp lookout for newts, as little or nothing was known of these amphibians. I spent many hours in searching for them, in the most likely places, but I found none. Toads, also, seem to be quite wanting in Southern Tibet, but frogs of two or three species are very common. Owing, presumably, to the brevity of the Tibetan summer, the frogs are only just about able to get through their metamorphoses before the winter sets in, and tadpoles were still common in all the ditches and ponds at Lhasa at the end of August.

INSECTS

To any one possessing an acquaintance with British insects, the Tibetan ones seem quite familiar. The common butterflies at once recall our "whites," "blues," "tortoiseshells," and "fritillaries," and various beetles, crickets, grasshoppers, ants, bees, and dragonflies are strongly suggestive of our own.

Mosquitoes, of savage propensities, were very common at Lhasa, though they were not at all troublesome elsewhere. The extensive swamps and marshes around the city were, doubtless, responsible for these unpleasant creatures.

MISCELLANEOUS

Hunting spiders were common everywhere in summer, but I saw no web-spinning ones. Scarlet "velvet mites" also abounded. A species of centipede, about an inch and a half in length, was obtained in the Brahmaputra valley.

The Tibetans carry about on their persons a particularly luxuriant parasite fauna of the familiar types. As the lower classes of the inhabitants of Tibet do not appear to possess even the most rudimentary ideas on the subject of bodily cleanliness, this is by no means to be wondered at. Earthworms seemed to be very local in their distribution.

The general similarity, referred to above as existing between Tibetan and British insects, was noticeable too in the case of the common mollusks, which closely resemble the fresh-water snails of an English pond.

APPENDIX B

Sir Edward Maunde Thompson has drawn my attention to the following extract from the Warren Hastings papers [British Museum. Additional MS. 29,233, f. 388]. It is a note by George Bogle upon the attitude he assumed toward the Tibetans and Bhutanese, and is not without interest as showing the kind of man Warren Hastings selected for his important commission to Tibet.

. . . . "I sometimes considered that the Character not only of the English, but of all the People of Europe depended upon me. This Idea, of being shown as a Specimen of my Countrymen has often given me a world of Uneasiness, and I dont know that I ever wished so heartily to have been a tall personable Man, as upon this Occasion. It was some Comfort to have Mr. Hamilton with me, and I left it entirely to him to give a good Impression of the Persons of Fringies. But from a national and perhaps excusable vanity, I was anxious also to give the People whom I visited, a favourable opinion of the dispositions of the English. The Hostilities in Cooch Beyhar had shewn them, to the Inhabitants of Bootan and Thibet, as a nation brave and warlike. My Business among them was meek and peaceful. In order to fulfill the Purpose of my Commission I had to gain Confidence and to conciliate Goodwill. With this View I assumed the Dress of the Country, endeavoured to acquire a little of the language & Manners, drank a Deluge of Tea with Salt and Butter, eat Beetle in Bootan, took Snuff and smoked Tobacco in Thibet, & would never allow myself to be out of Humour. If with this view also I have sometimes given presents which a parsimonious Economy might have saved, and have thereby enhanced my Expences a few Thousand Rupees, the propriety or Impropriety of my Conduct may be easily appreciated, by weighing the Object that I aimed at against the Money which it cost me.

"Indeed the whole of my Expences (Servants wages excepted) are in a Manner formed of Presents. Even the Charge of travelling may be included under this Head. An order of Government supplied me with Coolies Horses and Accommodations. The best House in every Village was allotted me for my Quarters, and the best provisions which the Country afforded, were prepared for my supper. During the five Months that I lived in the Lama's Palace, I had Rice, Tea, Sugar, preserved Fruits, Bread, and dried Sheeps' Carcases in Abundance, and the whole Expence of living, for myself and Mr. Hamilton, during that Time, amounts but to about forty Rupees. The Presents, I gave to the Bootieas, were principally made in Money. Those to the Inhabitants of Thibet, in Coral, Broad Cloth, and other Articles. The different Genius of the two Nations required this distinction. The Ideas of the high Class of People in Thibet are more refined, and they with difficulty accepted even of those presents from a Stranger. The Bootieas are of a more sordid Disposition, and receive, with little Ceremony, whatever is offered to them. In return I received in Bootan, besides some Pieces of Silk, Blankets, and other woolen Manufactures, Fruits, Rice, Butter in such quantities that I could have set up as a Tallow Chandler, and a parcell of unmatched Tanyan Horses—which have almost ruined me. In Thibet I received Gold Dust and Talents of Silver, from the Lama and his Officers, for all which, except some small Bulses[1] which I gave away in the same Manner as I got them, I have given Credit in my Accounts.

"I have stated my Charges fairly. The Money which I expended was for the Honour of the Company, and to facilitate the Object which I aimed at, and thus I submit the Accounts to your Judgement."

[1] *Bulse*—package of diamonds or gold dust (Oxford Dictionary).

APPENDIX C

THE PRESENT CONDITION AND GOVERNMENT OF TIBET

By Captain W. F. T. O'Connor, C.I.E.

Secretary and Interpreter to the Tibet Mission, now acting as British Agent at Gyantse

Mr. Landon has asked me to write as an appendix to his book a note on Tibetan affairs, and I have consequently much pleasure in putting together such scraps of information as I have been able to collect—if only as a memento of the many pleasant days we spent together, at Gyantse and at Lhasa, in riding abroad together through the weird landscapes of this strange country.

I would, however, premise that as yet we have only scratched the surface of Tibet and things Tibetan. Every day in the country, every individual one meets, and every manuscript one reads, all reveal some new trait, some bizarre superstition, something unsuspected before. We can only hope that in a few years' time patient study may reveal some of the secrets now hidden and give us a wider comprehension of facts as yet only partially understood.

The first thing that strikes a student of Tibetan administration and affairs in general is the marked resemblance in many points between Tibet at the present time and Europe as it must have been during the Middle Ages or up to the time of the Reformation. Apart from the actual government by absolute monarchs the two most prominent characteristics in the interior economy of Europe of, say, the fourteenth century, were the systems of Feudalism and Monasticism. It was these two institutions which at this period spread far and wide over the whole of Central, Western and Southern Europe, and stifled by the mere fact of their existence all initiative, knowledge, and spirit among the lower orders; and gave learning and power exclusively into the hands of a comparatively small minority of nobles and priests. If one opens any history of Europe relating to the time in question one finds numerous passages which might be quoted almost verbatim as applying to Tibet as we find the country to-day: "Amongst the various evils which oppressed and degraded the people . . . . may be mentioned two of especial prevalence and most baneful influence—the Feudal and Papal despotisms." Again: "The plebeian peasant was still a plebeian by birth, and few circumstances could take away the sting which aggravated his inferior condition . . . . only in the church could he rise to his proper rank or feel his true dignity as a man."

Such remarks and many others of similar import might be used to-day to describe the conditions under which the Tibetan peasant now labors. Practically all the high offices of State are monopolized by men of two classes—either by a most jealous and narrow clique of hereditary nobles, or by dignitaries of the Yellow-Cap or Reformed School of the Buddhist Church. Of these hereditary nobles there are altogether only some twenty or thirty families, but in a small country like Tibet even these furnish, with their numerous connections and hangers-on, sufficient individuals to occupy all lucrative government posts from the highest almost to the lowest. The bulk of these great families have been ennobled by virtue of the blessing of having at one time or another given birth to a Dalai Lama or a Penchen Rinpoche. This inestimable privilege at once *ipso facto* raises the head of the fortunate family to the highest rank of the Tibetan peerage; that is to say, the father or the eldest brother, as the case may be, immediately becomes a "king" or duke, and, in the latter case, the rank is hereditary, passing in direct succession from father to son, while large grants of land are made to support the dignity of the rank. In this way most of the great families have originated. They all possess large estates scattered about in various parts of the country, but the male members almost invariably hold office and reside in or near Lhasa. The younger members may be either monks or laymen, but in any case are entitled to some small office, beginning generally low down on the scale as Jong-pens[1] or clerks in government offices, and rising finally to be Sha-pes, treasurers, etc.

The ecclesiastical or monk officials are selected in two ways. In

[1] Captain O'Connor spells this word with a modified o (ö). I have, for purposes of uniformity, kept to the spelling in the text. The difference is immaterial.

the first place there is a school at Lhasa for the education of young ecclesiastics who desire government employment. These young men, as remarked above, are generally but not necessarily scions of the great families. They are educated as boys in the conduct of official correspondence, the keeping of accounts, etc., and when duly qualified are given some small office from which they may gradually rise to power. They are not monks in the true sense of the word, and although nominally entered at one of the big monasteries as an *In-chung* or novice, they do not as a rule join their monasteries at all, but live at home and attend school in the city. The other class of ecclesiastical official is composed of monks proper, who by dint of force of character and intellect have risen above their compeers in the monastery and are selected for office owing to their proved capacity. They are in a very small minority. In the case of the lay officials each office is accompanied by a gift of land in lieu of salary. In the case of the monks, who are not supposed to value or desire earthly possessions, a small salary is given for their support. Thus it will be seen that as far as the actual administration of the country is concerned the governing body is solely composed of members of the nobility and of a few monks who have risen by force of character. With the latter exception men of low origin, or even of respectable birth, are altogether debarred from office or power. As a natural result of this we find that throughout the country there are two classes—the great landowners and the priests—which exercise each in its own dominion a despotic power from which there is no appeal.

The peasant on an estate is in almost every sense a serf. He is bound to furnish the greater part of his agricultural produce for the use of his landlord, keeping only enough for the bare support of himself and family. He cannot without his lord's permission leave the soil or the country, and he is compelled to furnish free transport and supplies to all official travelers or visitors—Chinese or Tibetan. But in spite of this state of affairs, it need not be supposed that, administratively, the Tibetan peasant is crushed and ground beneath a tyrannical yoke. In spite of the arbitrary rule of the nobles and officials, the country on the whole is well governed and the people well treated. They are not, it is true, allowed to take any liberties or to infringe the orders of their superiors, but as long as they confine themselves to their legitimate sphere of action, and, above all, abstain from political offenses, their lives are lived simply and happily enough under a sort of patriarchal sway. The common people are cheerful, happy-go-lucky creatures, absurdly like the Irish in their ways, and sometimes even in their features. They are always anxious to please and thoroughly understand the art of blarney; they are quarrelsome but good-natured. Discipline of any description is entirely remote from their conception of life, and if employed on any labor, they will only work as long as some European eye is upon them. They sing cheerily and display a deal of vigor while watched, but the moment they are left to themselves they gather under the lee of the nearest wall and spend the time in gossip and drinking buttered tea, for a teapot and the necessary ingredients invariably accompany every party of workmen, and even individuals when detached by themselves. They are, in fact, great children, very ignorant, very simple, and devoid of all idea of moral responsibility.

The regular artificers—carpenters, painters, masons, smiths—are of a better and more intelligent class. They are in their way excellent and conscientious workmen. Brought up to their trade from childhood they thoroughly understand it, and will work away all day without any supervision whatever. Their ideas of art, furniture, etc., are peculiar. They are partly Chinese, partly Indian, and partly the product of their own bizarre imaginations. Everything in Tibet, in fact—dresses, houses, furniture, paintings, ornaments, jewelry, whatever it may be—bears the impress of a country unlike any other country in the world. Every Tibetan, high and low, is a curiosity who ought to be in a museum. His salutations, gestures, clothing, and general *tout ensemble,* stamp him as something apart from the rest of the inhabitants of the globe. Yet with all this they are a highly civilized race. A mere savage would never excite so much interest. But the civilization of Tibet, although derived originally from two such well-known countries as China and India, has been, so to speak, forced into a mold congenial to Tibetan ideas, and during the centuries which have elapsed since its introduction no outside influences have been permitted to modify or modernize the original conceptions as to what was right and proper. The ancient Mexicans and Peruvians no doubt exhibited to the Spaniards a somewhat similar state of affairs. They, too, were the inheritors of a unique civilization, totally uninfluenced by any known form of European culture, which had existed among them for centuries, and had retained throughout the ages all the original peculiarities and superstitions.

But in Tibet, besides the manners and customs peculiar to the country to which allusion has been made, we are confronted by the extraordinary spectacle of a simple agricultural people, superstitious indeed to the last degree, but devoid of any deep-rooted religious convictions or heart-searchings, oppressed by the most monstrous growth of monasticism and priest-craft which the world has ever seen. Here again comparison is invited to Europe of the Middle Ages: a vast number of superfluous ministers of religion were supported in idleness and pomp. There were continual additions made to the various orders of monks, who, pretending to superior sanctity, consumed the revenues of the people. They forged innumerable weapons of servitude, invented degrading legends, and stimulated a spirit of superstition. So it is in Tibet at this moment. A very large proportion (estimated by some at one-fifth) of the male population, having embraced the monastic life, is lost to all intents and purposes as a practical factor in the well-being of the nation. Vast as was the number of superfluous monks in medieval Europe, their sum in Tibet is, in proportion, vaster still. Monasteries abound in profusion all over the whole face of the country. Every valley, however small, owns one at least; one or two are seen on nearly every hill-side. They are found in the immediate neighborhood of the larger towns, and are buried away in the most remote and inaccessible fastnesses. Some are huge collegiate institutions, like the monasteries of Lhasa, Shigatse, and Gyantse, numbering on their rolls 3,000 to 10,000 inmates; others are mere hermitages affording shelter to half a dozen of the ruling caste. But all are run upon much the same lines. To every monastery certain lands have been apportioned by the State, upon the produce of which the monks are to a great extent supported. These estates are occupied and farmed by ordinary peasants, who are in effect the serfs or servants of the monks, and are managed, as a rule, by lay stewards. After harvest the great bulk of the crop is set aside for the monastery, and the cultivators are allowed just enough to support themselves and their families until the next autumn. Very exact records are kept. Every measure of grain and every bundle of straw is noted and has to be accounted for. During this last harvest I have often watched these stewards or agents at their work. While the active operations of threshing and winnowing are in progress the steward will sit all day long beside the threshing-floor keeping a watch upon the laborers. The grain is weighed daily in his presence and the straw put in sacks and duly recorded, and the whole locked up in some convenient storehouse and seals placed upon the openings.

As can easily be imagined, the allotment of estates sufficiently extensive to afford sustenance to the entire corporate body of monks implies the sequestration for this purpose of no inconsiderable portion of the cultivable area of Tibet. Rentals which might otherwise be employed in enhancing the meager revenues of the State or in furnishing a livelihood to more useful members of the community, are now swallowed up in the thankless office of maintaining in idleness a host of ignorant, pretentious sluggards. But besides this more legitimate source of livelihood the monks obtain yearly large sums both in cash and kind in return for their religious offices at births, deaths, marriages, and festivals. The extent of these squeezes is only limited by the degree of the priestly rapacity and the poverty of the victim.

To comprehend in some degree the extent to which the monasteries bleed the country it is only necessary to enter any one of the larger lamaseries, and to mark the extraordinary contrast at once presented by its huge, solid buildings and rich trappings as compared with the houses of even well-to-do people in the neighborhood. These latter, though generally comfortable and well built, are of an extreme simplicity—square, mud-walled, two-storied structures, furnished within with the plainest of household goods, and, with the one exception of the domestic chapel, devoid of ornament or luxury. The monastery presents a remarkable contrast. Here we find massive stone buildings, their roofs often topped with gilded pinnacles and finials, surrounded by great flagged courtyards and a towering outer wall. Inside the temples are hung with silken banners and scrolls, and among the monastic treasures are to be found books and images, *cloisonné* enamels, china and ornaments of gold, silver, and ivory. There are, of course, monasteries of various degrees of riches. In Tashi-lhunpo, for instance, there is an overwhelming display of wealth. The fine tombs of the five previous Tashi Lamas are most richly ornamented, and contain numbers of beautiful specimens of Chinese and Tibetan art, including some finely chased golden cups and bowls. Even the smallest monasteries have one or two temples containing brass images of Buddhist gods and saints and a variety of ornaments, silk scrolls, illuminated missals, etc. When the capital outlay on these treasures is added to the yearly sum necessary to support the vast monk population, to keep the monasteries in repair, and to decorate the chapels, it will be apparent that the people of Tibet pay no light price for the privilege of being included in the fold of the Buddhist Church.

But in pointing out the evils which necessarily follow in the train of two such abuses as feudalism and monasticism, I would nevertheless emphasize the fact that the Tibetan peasant is far from being a depressed or degraded type of mankind. Conditions which in modern Europe would be considered intolerable are the natural heritage of the Tibetan, and he accepts them not only complacently but with remarkable good humor. And taking it all round, he really has not much to complain of. Except at the very highest elevations and in the bleakest and most exposed parts of the Tibetan uplands the soil is of a wonderful fertility. The valley from Gyantse to Shigatse (sixty miles by four or five), that of the Tsang-po, and the whole neighborhood of Lhasa, are all in summer a solid mass of beautiful crops. Wheat, barley, peas, mustard, are the staples, and the yield is in many cases fifty to sixty fold. The soil, which is alluvial, requires but little special nursing. Portions are allowed to lie fallow in rotation once every five years, and this precaution, combined with a copious supply of manure, seems to preclude the danger of exhaustion. The seasons are regular, and except for occasional hailstorms (for which a sure preventative is provided in the shape of professional wizards), little is to be feared from the elements. The agriculturist has consequently an easy time and little anxiety as compared with his brother in the United Kingdom. The standard of comfort among the very poorest is high, and indeed luxurious as compared with that of an Irish cotter. It is no exaggeration to say that the average Tibetan farmer's condition of life is beyond comparison better than that of the average Irish peasant. Their houses are larger, cleaner, and better built. Their household and agricultural implements are superior and more plentiful. They are better dressed and better fed. Naturally a placid and law-abiding people, they chafe not at all at any partiality displayed by the laws of the country, or on account of their lack of political privileges. As to learning it is enough for them that the numerous monks should study the scriptures and expound the dark passages of their religion. But in respect to ordinary education, it is surprising to find how many of the commonalty can read and write—far more certainly than was the case with our own lower orders one hundred or even fifty years ago. In every village not only the headmen but one or two members of nearly every family are tolerably well educated, and can read and write the Tibetan running hand fluently enough.[1] This is no doubt due to a great extent to the diffusion of education by the monks and the teaching faculties of the larger monasteries; so much at least may be attributed unto them for righteousness.

[1] No mean feat. I think O'Connor here also stands alone among white men.

Tibet, in short, with some natural limitations, is a land ripe for enlightenment. Given some reforms in the administration of justice, less partiality in the selection of officials, with more supervision on the part of the central government, a curtailment of the powers and numbers of the monks, the abolition of some of the privileges of the feudal aristocracy, and popular liberty: Tibet will then want for little. The beginnings of free trade and the introduction of European ideas have been effected by the recent mission to Lhasa, and will be continued under the terms of the resulting treaty. All that now remains is for a Tibetan Luther to appear upon the scene; and in a land so fruitful of religious reformers there would appear to be no good reason why a new and up-to-date reformer should not effect great changes, both moral and material, in his native land.

The above notes will serve to give some sort of idea of the present-day conditions of life of the average Tibetan peasant. But, as already noticed, the governing class forms a caste apart—high offices passing from father to son in each of the great families, and the subordinate members or poor relations between them monopolize every single post in the gift of the government. A brief sketch of the principal features of the Tibetan administration may be of interest.

The center of all authority in Tibet is situated at Lhasa, where reside the Dalai Lama, the four Sha-pes or ministers, and the bulk of the administrative officials. The head of the State is the Dalai Lama, known to the Tibetans as the Gyal-wa Rinpoche or Kyap-gon Rinpoche, meaning Precious Majesty or Protector. This personage is believed by the Tibetans to be the incarnation of Padma Pani (Avalokita[1] in Sanskrit, Chen-re-sik in Tibetan), as well as the inheritor of the spirit of the reformer Tsong-kapa. The first Grand Lama was Gedun-tubpa, the nephew of Tsong-kapa, who succeeded his uncle as head of the new Geluk-pa, or Yellow-cap Church, in the year 1419. He was the first of those spiritual reflexes or incarnations, who are now so numerous throughout Tibet, and who play so important a part in the government and general interior economy of the country. The name of the present Dalai Lama is Ngak-wang lo-sang Tub-den gya-tso. He is the thirteenth incarnation, and is now thirty-one years of age. It would be tedious to attempt to trace the history of his predecessors. Some have been men of energetic character and high ambitions, and have exercised great powers. One at least has been dissolute and was removed by order of the

[1] Or Avalokiteswara. The word is equally common in either form.

Chinese Emperor. But the majority of the Dalai Lamas have been mere semi-divine figureheads at the mercy of ambitious and unscrupulous lay ministers; and the natural result has followed that a large proportion of them have been removed from the sphere of earthly grandeur before they could arrive at years of discretion and take into their own hands the reins of temporal power.

The present Dalai Lama, however, showed himself early in his career to be of a very different mettle from the bulk of his ill-fated predecessors. From all accounts he is a man of pronounced traits of character, violent temper, and stormy passions, and when quite a youth evinced uncomfortable symptoms of an intention to have his own way. Shortly after he attained his majority the then Regent—an incarnate abbot of one of the four Lhasa "Lings," or monasteries—was accused of practising witchcraft against the sacred person of the "Protector," and was seized and thrown into prison. It was then conclusively proved that this arch scoundrel had concocted a spell, committed it to paper, and actually sewn the incriminating document into the sole of one of the Dalai Lama's new boots. So heinous an offense could not pass unpunished. The culprit, with several of his relations and his political faction, was interned in a dungeon, where he expired in less than a twelvemonth. The young Dalai Lama now found himself free to act in accordance with the dictates of his own untrammeled will. No person or party of the State dared for a moment to oppose him. His brief rule was signalized by numerous proscriptions, banishments, imprisonings, and torturings. Neither life nor property was safe for a moment. His friends were raised to high honors in the State; his enemies or political opponents were banished and deprived of property and place. Among these last victims were personages no less highly placed than the four Sha-pes or executive ministers of the Tibetan Government. Cases had been known before of single ministers being arraigned for offenses and disgraced. Such precedents in fact were far from uncommon, and the overthrow of any one councilor would have excited little surprise or even unfavorable comment. But to eradicate at one fell swoop the whole executive authority of the country was a measure rendered possible not only by a considerable amount of audacity, but by an authority supported upon a divine as well as a temporal basis.

The above facts have been adduced merely to emphasize the almost unassailable position of one of these incarnate lamas in the queer, topsy-turvy polity of Tibet. These incarnations are, of course, merely conventional, just as the symbols of Buddhist worship scattered broadcast throughout the country are conventions. But it is a conventionality which exercises an extraordinary power over the minds and imaginations of the simple Tibetan folk. During a recent visit to Shigatse I had the opportunity of visiting the second great incarnate Lama of Tibet (the Penchen Rinpoche of Tashi-lhunpo), and I was astonished to see the very real reverence with which he is treated not only by pilgrims from outside but by his own servants and immediate entourage. But it had been different at Lhasa, and even an earthly manifestation of Avalokiteswara may carry things too far. Scandals and ill-feeling, however carefully repressed, will at length find a vent: and it was no doubt partly the storm-clouds which the young ruler felt to be gathering about him no less than the imminent approach of a British army which caused that hasty flight at midnight from the Potala. At Lhasa, under the shadow of the walls of the Palace, people spoke little and with bated breath. But at Tashi-lhunpo and Shigatse, far from the intrigues of Lhasa and the overwhelming influence of the three great monasteries, there was less reticence, and many tales were told of the overbearing ways and cruel acts of the absent Dalai Lama.

Far different in character and general disposition is the Penchen Rinpoche (or, as generally called by us, the Tashi Lama) of the great monastery of Tashi-lhunpo near Shigatse. This prelate, as being the earthly manifestation of Amitabha, the spiritual father of Avalokita now represented by the Dalai Lama, should actually rank in the Buddhist world as the holier and higher of the two—and so he is considered by no small portion of his worshipers. At one time, in fact for some centuries, the Grand Lamas of Tashi-lhunpo not only enjoyed a high spiritual renown, but possessed in addition a full share of temporal power. The greater part of the large province of Tsang (which includes Shigatse, Gyantse, and many other large and flourishing towns) was under his sway, and his jurisdiction extended north beyond the Tsang-po and eastward to Lake Yam-dok. But the grasping and jealous policy of Lhasa has gradually deprived Tashi-lhunpo of almost all remnants of authority, and the provincial government consists now of but three small jongs. Confiscation of property for political offenses is a favorite punishment in Tibet, and the central government does not hesitate to apply the principle here in the case of a person so highly placed as the Penchen Rinpoche. But small as his kingdom is, the Lama still holds his court at Shigatse. Here, as at Lhasa, the Grand

Lama has his winter and his summer residences, his prime minister, his treasurers, and his chamberlain, and maintains all the etiquette of royalty itself. Nor is the divinity which hedges royalty a matter of any doubt. In the case of the present Lama, at any rate, his immediate worshipers regard him with a devotion as real as it is touching. In the ordinary course of his frequent audiences the Lama, in bestowing his blessing upon a supplicant, will but touch with a tassel or wand the scarf extended as an offering; but in the case of holy men or high officials he will touch the uncovered head with his fingers. This is a mark of special honor, and is also much esteemed as a means of grace. On the occasion of my farewell visit to His Holiness numerous poor women and humble persons accompanied my Tibetan servants in the hope that on so propitious an occasion they also would receive the Sacred Touch. Nor were they disappointed, for the Lama graciously accorded to one and all the hoped-for blessing, and they departed happy.

But the character of the young Lama (he is only two-and-twenty), as in the case of nearly all his predecessors, apart from the sacred nature of his person, is such as to inspire his followers with confidence and affection. He is universally beloved and esteemed. His kindness, charity, good sense, and learning are everywhere acknowledged, and I feel impelled to repeat Bogle's oft-quoted words regarding his predecessor, the third Lama: "I endeavored to find out, in his character, those defects which are inseparable from humanity, but he is so universally beloved that I had no success, and not a man could find it in his heart to speak ill of him."

These two Lamas, then, the Dalai Lama and the Penchen Rinpoche, are the two highest spiritual authorities in Tibet. But they are far from being the only ones. There are, besides, the Sakya hierarch, head of a sect of the Reformed Church, which differs but little from the Unreformed or Ancient School, and a vast number of other incarnate Lamas of greater or lesser degree. Some by their own genius or piety rise to the exercise of great spiritual authority, while many are practically unknown except to the inmates of some secluded monastery, where they pass their quiet days encompassed by a perpetual atmosphere of homage and devotion. Their influence in politics is small.

The person next in consideration to the two great Lamas of Lhasa and Shigatse is the Regent, or, as he is generally called by the Tibetans, the King. A Regent is appointed during the period while each Dalai Lama is reaching his majority (generally eighteen years), when the Tibetans are naturally deprived of the offices of their proper ruler. He is invariably an ecclesiastic and has usually been selected from among the higher lamas of the various small monasteries scattered about in the city of Lhasa and its environs. These selections have not always been successful. No human being values or covets political authority more than the Tibetan, and most of the Regents have found themselves so reluctant to relinquish the reins of power that they have actually proceeded to the extremity of quietly doing away with their sacred ward before he arrived at years of discretion. Grave suspicions, amounting in one case to a certainty, have been aroused in previous instances. In fact, the present Dalai Lama is the only one for a hundred years who has reached his majority, and he took the precaution of anticipating any foul play on the part of the Regent by the vigorous measures alluded to above.

But this same ruler, when quitting his capital lately *en route* for a foreign land, made a most excellent selection of a temporary Regent to officiate during his absence. The monk chosen is known as the Gaden Ti Rinpoche. This is really the title of an office, the holder of which occupies what may be described as a sort of "Divinity Chair" in the great monastery of Gaden lying some twenty miles east of Lhasa. The post is won by pure merit, the incumbent being elected by his fellows from among a number of the most learned professors of the Yellow-cap School of Tibetan Buddhism, and the holder is regarded with the greatest respect—amounting to veneration—by all Tibetans, monks and laymen alike. On the Ti Rinpoche entering a room, all, from the highest to the lowest, rise and uncover, and it is an honor to bow and to receive his hand in benediction upon the head. It is curious and almost touching, in this land of self-seeking and scheming politicians, to see how much consideration is attached to an individual who has risen solely through his learning and personal character, and who owes his position to no favoritism or family influence.

The present holder of the Divinity Chair is one of the most charming men it would be possible to meet in any country. He is an elderly man of over sixty years of age, of a perfect simplicity and modesty of character. That his attainments are great and his character above reproach is testified not only by the position he holds, but by the very real affection and respect displayed toward him by all, from the most highly-placed officials to the beggars in the streets. The existence of such a man is in itself a justification of the Buddhist Church in Tibet, and strengthens the hope of a possible Reformer in the near future.

The executive powers of the Tibetan Government are vested in four ministers, known in the vernacular as Sha-pes, of whom three are generally laymen and the fourth an ecclesiastic. Of these the three laymen belong almost invariably to some of the great families, while the monk is often a self-made man. In ordinary circumstances the four Sha-pes are practically, as far as the internal administration is concerned, the rulers of Tibet. They reside, generally speaking, all four in Lhasa, and meet daily in a little office near the Jo-kang or cathedral. Hence they issue all orders to the minor executive officials throughout the country. The collection of the revenue, the posting and changing of officials, the general administration of justice, the levying of troops, transport, and supplies—orders on all these and many other matters emanate from the Council and are stamped with their square seal, well known to all throughout the length and breadth of Tibet.

Occasionally one or other of the Sha-pes will make a tour of inspection to Shigatse or Dingri, or some important frontier post, attended by a body of minor satellites, and received everywhere with all possible marks of respect. But by far the greater portion of their time is spent at Lhasa, where they find themselves sufficiently busy not only in the transaction of their own duties but in circumventing the ceaseless plots of their rivals. I went one day while at Lhasa to visit their office and some of the other public offices and chambers. These are all situated in a range of buildings which, while forming a portion of the main cathedral structure, incloses the actual temple on three sides. Among these offices are found those of the Lhasa magistrates, the financial secretaries, the treasurers, the Sha-pes, and the National Assembly. They are, generally speaking, small, untidy, ill-lighted rooms, furnished with a few cushions, whereon the officials themselves sit while transacting business, and with long files of papers fastened by strings in festoons across the low roofs. The Sha-pes' room, or council chamber, is rather better than the others. There are four fat cushions disposed at the upper end for the four ministers and smaller ones near the door for the clerks, while in addition to the numerous papers there is a small altar on one side with a few little images and the usual Buddhist paraphernalia. But the meeting-hall of the National Assembly (of which more below), where all questions of high policy are discussed, is the worst and untidiest den of all. This is a low-roofed, gloomy room, some thirty feet square, perhaps, lighted by a single window looking out on to the streets of Lhasa, devoid of furniture, fittings, or decorations of any kind—if one may except a few long ragged and very filthy looking cushions set out in parallel rows, whereon sit the members of the Assembly during their deliberations; at one end, facing the window, stands a sort of raised chair or throne for the president—who just now is the Ti Rinpoche. Adjoining the main hall is a small room screened off, where the Sha-pes sit during a momentous debate. They are not permitted by the laws of the Tibetan Constitution actually to attend the meetings of the Deliberative Assembly, but they may listen from behind the screen to what is going on.

Immediately below the four Sha-pes, and forming a part of the Central Administration at Lhasa, come a host of lay and ecclesiastical officials of varying degrees of importance. There are chief secretaries, treasurers, accounting officers (or secretaries to Government in the financial department), judges, paymasters, under-secretaries, and clerks; and among these should be included the De-pens or generals, who, although nominally military officers, have in reality almost no military duties as a rule, but occupy a high rank and important place in the political world. Thus there are a large number of officials resident at Lhasa, who constitute the central government of Tibet. Every question of the slightest importance must be referred sooner or later to Lhasa, and hence issue all orders to the provincial executive authorities, the jong-pens, or district prefects. These latter are distributed all over the country in the various district headquarters or jongs, where they administer justice, collect the revenue, and are responsible to Lhasa for the state of their district. Many of these jongs are picturesque old edifices perched on crags or low rocky hillocks, and are often the remnants of strongholds belonging to independent chieftains or brigands in the old days, before Tibet was united under a single administration. Some of these jongs at Shigatse, Gyantse, Kamba, and elsewhere, are really fine, imposing structures, towering several hundred feet above the plain and villages below; but nowadays they are all falling into a state of more or less decay owing to want of proper attention and repair. Even so as defenses they can give a good account of themselves, as was proved in the case of Gyantse. Each jong-pen has a number of subordinates—such as tax-gatherers, clerks, and understrappers of sorts—through whom his orders are conveyed to the surrounding peasants. Like the majority of Tibetan officials the jong-pen gets little or no pay, but his perquisites are by no means inconsiderable. At the same time, be it understood, the average Tibetan strongly objects to parting with a farthing more than he is obliged to, and while conforming cheerfully to the usages of long-established custom, he will protest most volubly should the jong-pen or any other official push things too far.

Besides the regular government officers at Lhasa there are a large number of purely monkish officials, who are in attendance on the Dalai Lama, and are intrusted with various duties of a ceremonial or religious character. Such, for instance, are the Lord Chamberlain and his assistants, the private secretary, cup-bearer, master of the horse, and numerous others of a similar personal character. These monks, though not properly government servants, exercise nevertheless a considerable amount of influence in the State, and as the confidential advisers of the Dalai Lama may often direct the course of political events.

But there is one institution of high importance in the Tibetan constitution which has not yet been described. This is the Tsong-du, or National Assembly as we might call it, though it is far from being a representative or popular assembly according to European ideas. Allusion had frequently been made to this assembly in reports and correspondence dealing with Tibet, but it is only within the last two years that its real consequence as a factor in the Tibetan government has been properly estimated. The Assembly is of two kinds—the Greater and the Lesser Assembly. The Greater Assembly is composed of all government officials, lay and ecclesiastical, who may wish to attend, representatives from any monastery throughout Tibet, and members of any good family irrespective of office. The Lesser Assembly, which sits constantly when matters of importance are on the tapis, is composed of delegates from the three great Lhasa monasteries—Debung, Sera, and Gaden—and a certain number of the higher officials and noblemen resident in Lhasa. The Sha-pes, as being the direct executive instruments of the State, do not sit in the Tsong-du, but, as noted above, are accommodated with a small room adjoining the Assembly Hall, where they can listen to, but not share in, the proceedings.

The duty of the Tsong-du is to deal with any matters of national importance, and with all questions, however trifling, relating to foreign policy. The Greater Assembly is summoned only when some broad guiding principle has to be decided or some momentous step (such, for instance, as a declaration of war) taken. The

Lesser Assembly may be, and often is, in constant session. It was in this state during the whole period of our stay at Lhasa, and no doubt since the Mission first crossed the frontier at Kamba-jong. Its decisions are final all over Tibet. In minor matters of internal administration the Sha-pes have a fairly free hand; but in any question even remotely connected with the outside world the Tsong-du alone can dictate the policy to be pursued. Its leading lights are the abbots of the three great monasteries, and, as might be expected from a congregation so led, its tendencies are narrow in the extreme, and any liberal or forward movement meets with instant disapproval if not persecution. The monkish element all over the world has always been intolerant, narrow-minded, and at times cruel; the Tibetan monks are no exception to the rule. A national assembly guided by such stiff-necked priests will naturally counsel exclusion of foreign influence, and will look with horror upon the introduction of enlightenment or moral progress before which their authority will inevitably decline. Hitherto they have had their own way and the results are only too apparent. Tibet in remaining a closed land has never advanced a foot beyond the position she assumed one thousand years ago on the first introduction of Buddhism and letters from Chinese and Indian sources. Like China, she is still the slave of worn-out customs and long-exploded ideas. In spite of the intelligence and natural abilities of the people in general, modern science and knowledge are a sealed book to them all, and the wisest and most revered lamas spend their time and waste their brains in poring over aged metaphysics and infantile legends translated into almost incomprehensible Tibetan from old Sanskrit works. Trade, invention, progress, learning, and freedom have alike been stifled by this plethora of priests; and it is typical of the amazing ignorance even of the best-informed and highest-placed officials that the Tibetan government should have deliberately made preparations to declare war upon the greatest Power of the modern world with no better means of manufacturing arms than a hand-power wheel and a forge for an arsenal, under the superintendence of one Mohammedan blacksmith.

There was to my mind something almost pathetic in the stubborn resistance made by these brave, simple peasants with their antiquated muzzle-loaders, swords, and magic spells, without leaders, organization, training, or aptitude for war, in order to defend their fatherland against what they were told was the greedy advance of an unscrupulous enemy, eager to seize and ravage their country.

That phase of our Mission into Tibet has now passed away. A treaty has been made and friendly relations established, and it remains to be seen what the effect will be of a few years of trade and intercourse with a civilized and sympathetic neighbor.

W. F. T. O'Connor,
Capt. R.A.

Gyantse, 8th Dec., 1904.

APPENDIX D

RETURN OF THE EXPEDITIONARY FORCE

After a stay of a few weeks, marked by no incident excepting an attempted "a-mok" run by a fanatic monk in the camp, the expedition left Lhasa on the 23rd of September, and after an uneventful journey returned to the Chumbi Valley and India. Colonel Younghusband, Mr. White, Mr. Wilton and Captain O'Connor rode on ahead of the main body, which was ferried across the Tsang-po most expeditiously by Captain Sheppard. He selected a point about ten miles higher up the river, and the Nabso la was used to conduct the force over the brim of the basin of the Yam-dok tso. No incident occurred during the retirement of the force except a blizzard on the Tang la which caused a good deal of temporary snow-blindness.

Three other return expeditions were planned:—Mr. Wilton proposed to go back through Ta-chien-lu to China; Captain Ryder planned a descent into Assam by the banks of the hitherto unexplored Tsang-po; and eventually Captains Ryder, Rawlings and Wood, and Lieutenant Bailey were detailed for a surveying excursion to Gartok, far along the road to Leh, one of the places at which a trade market was to be established.

For different reasons the third was the only expedition which was actually carried out. I take the following brief account of their journey from the *Times*. Captain O'Connor also makes some reference in his "Political Notes" to the Tashi Lama, with whom he had repeated conversations. He did not accompany Captain Ryder beyond Tashi-lhunpo.

"The Gartok party, consisting of Captain Rawlings and his companions, and accompanied by Captain O'Connor, whose researches in Tibet during the past few years have been so frequently described in the Blue-book, left Gyantse on October 10th, and arrived at Shigatse in three days, after what is described as a delightful journey through richly cultivated and highly irrigated valleys. Villages lay dotted thickly over the slopes, every house and hamlet being surrounded with trees. The harvest had been very good and was being got in, and affairs looked prosperous in this part of Tibet. On nearing Shigatse the British officers were met by a deputation of lamas and laymen, who extended to them a cordial welcome and entertained them with refreshments laid out in tents by the roadside. The streets of the town were filled with large crowds, who gazed with much surprise at the first Europeans seen at Shigatse since Turner's visit 120 years ago. The Tibetan Government, on receiving notice of the setting out of the Mission, had relays of ponies and mules and also coolies, prepared at all the towns and post-stations along the road from the Ladak frontier to Lhasa.

"The reception of the Englishmen was of a pleasing character. The officials could not have been more courteous or hospitable and the populace were most friendly. The two parties were lodged in a nobleman's garden, and Captain Steen, of the Indian Medical Service, was called upon to minister, from morning till late at night, to the sick of Shigatse and the surrounding parts. Rich and poor are said to have sought his good offices, the fame of Captain Walton's skill at Lhasa having spread far and wide. The British officers describe the monastery of Tashi-lhunpo as far finer than anything at Lhasa, its circumference being two miles. Turner says it is a large monastery consisting of three or four hundred houses, the habitations of the Gylongs, besides temples, mausolea, and the palace of the Sovereign Pontiff, in which is comprised also the residence of the Regent and of all the subordinate officers, both ecclesiastical and civil. Its buildings are all of stone, none less than two storeys high, flat-roofed, and crowned with parapets.

"On October 16th Captain O'Connor, accompanied by all the Europeans, paid an official visit to the Tashi Lama, who is at present, by virtue of the decree of the Emperor of China, the head of all the Churches owning the supremacy of the Dalai Lama. The Tashi Lama is a young man of twenty-three years of age, with a pleasing address and owning the reputation of being both pious and able. He received the Englishmen with respect and regard, and impressed his visitors most favourably. On the night of their arrival the lamasery was brilliantly illuminated in memory of some great Lama of the past, and, curiously enough, this date coincided with the date of Captain Turner's arrival, October 13th, 1783, a fact considered by the Lamas to be especially propitious. The monastery contained some wonderful tombs and was far more richly decorated than any of those of Lhasa. Here Captain O'Connor separated from his friends and returned to Gyantse, while Captains Ryder, Wood, and Rawlings, and Lieutenant Bailey continued their long and interesting journey to Gartok."

The last news of the party is that after a pleasant but monotonous journey beside the Tsang-po to Gartok, its members returned in the first week of this year to Simla, having crossed from Tibet to India over the Shipki pass.

APPENDIX E

THE following is, I believe, a complete list of the officers, civil and military, of the Mission who actually reached Lhasa. I am indebted to Major Iggulden for it.

THE MISSION

Colonel Francis E. Younghusband, C.I.E.
Mr. J. Claude White, Political Officer of Sikkim (Deputy-Commissioner).
Mr. E. C. Wilton, Chinese Consular Service (Deputy-Commissioner).
Capt. W. F. T. O'Connor (Secretary and Interpreter).
Capt. H. J. Walton, I.M.S. (Medical Officer and Naturalist).
Mr. H. H. Hayden (Geologist).
Mr. Vernon Magniac (Private Secretary to the Commissioner).

THE ESCORT STAFF

Brig.-General J. R. L. Macdonald, C.B., R.E.
Major H. A. Iggulden, Chief Staff Officer.
Lieut.-Col. L. A. Waddell, C.I.E., P.M.O.
Major W. G. L. Beynon, D.S.O.
Major A. Mullaly.
Major McC. Ray (Intelligence branch).
Capt. J. O'B. Minogue.
Capt. C. A. Elliott, R.E.
Lieut. B. H. Bignell.
Lieut.-Col. E. H. Cooper, D.S.O., Royal Fusiliers.
" " F. Campbell, D.S.O., 40th Pathans.
" " M. A. Kerr, 8th Gurkhas.
" " H. R. Brander, 32nd Pioneers.

Major R. W. Fuller, R.G.A.
" A. R. Row, 8th Gurkhas.
" F. Murray, 8th Gurkhas.
" F. H. Peterson, D.S.O., 32nd Pioneers.
" A. Wallace Dunlop, 23rd Pioneers.

Capt. S. F. Legge, Royal Fusiliers.
" C. V. Johnson, Royal Fusiliers.
" C. H. Peterson, 46th Punjabis (M.I.).
" J. B. Bell, 32nd Pioneers.
" F. A. Easton, R.G.A.
" J. R. Maclachlan, 40th Pathans.
" S. H. Sheppard, D.S.O., R.E.
" L. H. Baldwin, 8th Gurkhas.
" G. J. S. Ward, 8th Gurkhas.
" F. E. Coningham, 12th Pathans, att. 40th Pathans.
" G. A. Preston, 40th Pathans.
" C. Bliss, 8th Gurkhas.
" H. F. Cooke, 32nd Pioneers.
" W. J. Ottley, 23rd Pioneers (M.I).
" H. M. Souter, 14th B.L. (M.I.).
" J. L. Fisher, Royal Fusiliers.
" C. A. H. Palairet, Royal Fusiliers.
" D. W. H. Humphreys, 8th Gurkhas.

Lieut. H. V. L. Rybot, att. 23rd Pioneers.
" G. C. Hodgson, 32nd Pioneers.
" L. A. Hadow, Norfolk Regiment.
" R. N. Macpherson, 40th Pathans.
" J. D. Grant, 8th Gurkhas.
" L. G. Hart, 8th Gurkhas.
" E. H. Lynch, 8th Gurkhas (Treasure Chest Officer).
" W. G. T. Currie, 40th Pathans.
" G. A. Yates, R.G.A.
" C. C. Marindin, R.G.A.
" A. C. S. Chichester, Royal Fusiliers.
" L. A. Bethell, 8th Gurkhas.
" A. D. Walker, R.E.

Lieut. W. A. B. Daniell, Royal Fusiliers.
" W. P. Bennett, R.G.A.
" F. Skipwith, 24th Punjabis (M.I.).
" F. E. Spencer, R.G.A.
" H. G. Boone, R.G.A.
" J. F. S. D. Coleridge, 8th Gurkhas.
" T. de B. Carey, Royal Fusiliers.
" H. St. G. H. Harvey Kelly, 32nd Pioneers.
" E. Marsden, 32nd Pioneers.
" F. M. Bailey, 32nd Pioneers (M.I.).
" J. C. Bourn Colthurst, Royal Irish Rifles.
" H. F. Collingridge, 9th Gurkhas.

MEDICAL CORPS

Major C. N. C. Wimberley, I.M.S.
Capt. C. W. Mainprise, R.A.M.C.
" W. H. Ogilvie, I.M.S.
" E. P. Conolly, R.A.M.C.
" T. B. Kelly, I.M.S.
" W. H. Leonard, I.M.S.
" A. Cook-Young, I.M.S.
Lieut. G. D. Franklin, I.M.S.
" G. J. Davys, I.M.S.

SURVEY

Capt. C. H. D. Ryder, R.E. } Officers in charge of the
Capt. H. M. Cowie, R.E. } Survey.

"S" AND "T" CORPS

Capt. C. H. G. Moore.
" R. C. Moore, A.V.D.
" A. P. D. C. Stuart.
" J. B. Pollock Morris.
" F. T. T. Moore.

Capt. F. G. Ross.
" M. Synge.
" O. St. J. Skeene.

CORRESPONDENTS

Times, Mr. Perceval Landon.
Daily Telegraph and *Pioneer*, Mr. C. B. Bayley.
Daily Mail, Mr. Edmund Candler.
"Reuter," Mr. Henry Newman.

The force which moved to Lhasa from Gyantse was composed as follows:

Head-quarters Staff.
Six guns of the 7th M.B. (10-pr.).
Two guns of the 30th M.B. (7-pr.).
½ company, 3rd Sappers.
Mounted Infantry (2 cos.).
Royal Fusiliers, H.Q. and 4 cos.
32nd Pioneers, H.Q. and 4 cos.
40th Pathans, H.Q. and 6 cos.
8th Gurkhas, H.Q. and 6 cos.
Section British Field Hospital.
2½ Sections Native F.H.
Transport taken from the 7th, 9th, 10th and 12th Mule Corps.

The 23rd Pioneers were left behind at Gyantse, greatly to the regret of the members of the Mission, with which they had been connected for so long.

TOTALS

British Officers	91
British Warrant Officers	11
British N.C.O. and men	521

Native Officers	32
Native Warrant Officers	5

Native N.C.O. and men	1,961
Followers	1,450
Mules and ponies	3,451

APPENDIX F

THE FOLK-LORE OF TIBET

THE three following tales are characteristic of Tibetan folk-lore, and it is interesting to note how similar they are to those of Europe. It is difficult, however, to see how any external influence can have been brought to bear upon them, as there are almost no Chinese or other foreign women in the country:

I

THE TALE OF THE MONKEY AND THE LIZARDS

Once upon a time a Lizard and his family lived in a lake by the side of a great forest in Tibet. Now there was not much to eat in the lake, and after a while Mrs. Lizard said to her husband: "I see on the shore a tree with beautiful fruits upon it; if you really cared about me and the children, you would go ashore and climb the tree and bring us back some of the beautiful fruits, that we may not all starve."

And the Lizard said: "My dear, you know that I cannot climb a tree, so why should I go ashore to try to do that which you know is impossible?"

But Mrs. Lizard kept on day after day saying that he did not really care about her and the children, or he would go ashore and climb the tree and bring back the beautiful fruits for her and the little Lizards.

So at last the Lizard was weary of what his wife said to him day after day, and swam ashore and tried to climb the tree.

Now you know a Lizard cannot climb a tree.[1]

But there was up in the branches of the tree a Monkey, and to

[1] This is the Tibetan story: I should have thought that there was nothing on earth that the big Tibetan lizards could not climb.

him the climbing of a tree is the easiest thing in the world. And he was a clever Monkey, and having made the Lizard very grateful to him, by picking for him the beautiful fruits on the tree, he struck up a friendship with the Lizard and persuaded him to leave his wife and come and live with him in a cave. So there they lived, and the Lizard forgot all about Mrs. Lizard and the children, and remained in the cave eating the beautiful fruits of the tree.

Now after a while Mrs. Lizard began to think that something had happened to the Lizard, and at last, after long hesitation, she sent one of her little children to see what had happened to father Lizard. So the little Lizard went ashore, and spied out to see what had happened to father Lizard who had been away for such a long time. And for a long time he could see nothing of any one, but toward evening he saw father Lizard come out of the cave with the Monkey and go to the tree. And then the Monkey ran up the tree and picked the beautiful fruits and threw them down, and the Lizard carried them into the cave, and that was all he saw.

So he swam back to his mother and told her, and she was very angry, for there was nothing to eat for herself and the children, and now she knew that her husband was living in a cave in the forest and eating plentifully with a Monkey, and forgetting all about his wife and children.

So she sent the little Lizard once again, and she said to him:

"Go to the cave from which you saw your father come out and call to him, and when he comes out to you, take him aside, and say to him, 'Mother Lizard is sick unto death.' And say no more then. And when he says to you, 'What is the matter? How can she be cured?' then say to him, 'Only one remedy there is.' And then say no more to him. And when he shall say to you, 'What is the remedy?' then you shall say, 'There is only one thing which can cure her, and that is a piece of a monkey's heart.'"

So the little Lizard did as he was told, and went on shore, and called out for his father, and said to him as his mother had told him; and he said: "There is only one thing which can cure her, and that is a piece of a monkey's heart."

When he heard that he was sorely frightened, and remembered all about his wife and the children, and he did not know what to do. But at last when he had again and again asked his son, and his son had again and again answered, "There is only one thing which can cure her, and that is a piece of a monkey's heart," he determined to do as his wife asked.

So he went back to the cave, and asked the Monkey to come with him to his own home in the lake, and he offered to carry him on his back. And the Monkey said that he would come and pay a visit to the Lizard's home, and because he could not swim he said he would be very glad to be carried on the Lizard's back.

So they started, and the Lizard was carrying the Monkey across the lake on his back. And the Monkey asked about Mrs. Lizard, and the children, and how she was. And the Lizard, who was not very clever, told him all that his son had said, and even that Mrs. Lizard could only be cured by a piece of a monkey's heart.

Now when he heard this the Monkey was very much frightened, and he wondered what he ought to do, for he said: "There is no doubt that the Lizards are going to kill me and take my heart to cure Mrs. Lizard with." So he said to the Lizard: "I know all about this cure. You are quite right, a monkey's heart is the only thing that can cure Mrs. Lizard, and, indeed, if we cannot get the remedy, she will surely die. But if she is very ill, one monkey's heart is not enough; she must have two monkey's hearts, or she will surely die."

Now in order to bring her husband back to her, Mrs. Lizard had told her son to say that she was very ill indeed, and the Lizard stopped swimming in the middle of the water, and said: "What ought we to do?"

Then the Monkey said: "I have a capital plan. I know where I can get for Mrs. Lizard two monkey's hearts, and then we will bring them back to her and she will recover. Put me on shore again, and I will get them for you at once." So the Lizard, who was not a very clever Lizard, believed all that the Monkey told him, and carried the Monkey back to shore on his back.

Then the Monkey climbed very quickly up into the tree, and said to the Lizard: "Lizard, what a foolish Lizard, even for a Lizard you must be. Did you really think that I was going to find you another monkey for you to kill as well as myself, in order that your ugly wife might recover? It would be a good thing if she were to die—ugly thing. Truly, you must be a very foolish Lizard."

Then the Lizard saw that he had been outwitted, and he became very angry, and determined to kill the Monkey after all. But he could not reach up to the Monkey, and he could not climb a tree. So the Monkey continued to revile the Lizard, who had repaid his kindness so unkindly, and it became night.

And the Lizard, when it became night, said to himself: "I will go away, as if I were going back to the lake, but I will really go to the cave, and when the Monkey comes down and goes back to his cave, I will spring upon him and kill him." And so the Lizard went back to the cave and thought that he was doing a very clever thing.

But the Monkey was a clever Monkey, and when at last it was quite dark, and he could see nothing, he came down from the tree, and cautiously went to his cave. Now he did not know anything about what the Lizard had done, but he suspected that he might be planning some treachery; so when he came about ten yards from the mouth of the cave he stopped, and called aloud:

"Oh, Great Cave! Oh, Great Cave!" And then he listened for awhile, and said out very loud: "It is very strange, there must be some one in the cave, for there is no echo to-night." Now there never was really any echo at all.

And the Lizard heard what he said, and after a while, when the Monkey called out aloud again, "Oh, Great Cave! Oh, Great Cave!" the Lizard answered him: "Oh, Great Cave! Oh, Great Cave!" So the Monkey knew that the Lizard was laying a trap for him, and he ran away jeering at the silly Lizard.

So the Lizard returned to Mrs. Lizard in the lake.

II

THE STONE LION

Once upon a time there was in Tibet a poor woman and she had two sons, and one of them was proud and the other one was humble. And the proud son took unto himself a wife, and he said to his mother: "There is no more room for you in the house, you must go away and get another shelter. I will have you no longer." And to his brother he said the same thing, so the mother and the humble son were driven forth and lived as best they could while the proud brother and his wife lived in comfort and luxury.

And after a long time it came to pass that the humble brother went a-gathering sticks over the hillside, for it was very cold and the old mother needed a fire. And as he went along he found a few sticks here and there, and at last he came to a Stone Lion sitting on the hillside.

And the Lion said to him: "Do not be afraid, but go fetch a bucket, and bring it here." And he brought a bucket, and the Lion said to him: "Hold it beneath my mouth"; and the man did so. And the Lion said: "Take care that not a piece of gold fall to the ground," and as he spoke he let fall from his mouth a stream of pieces of gold until the bucket was nearly full.

So the humble brother went away thankfully to his mother, and they two lived in peace and contentment for a long time.

But at last the proud brother began to hear of the comfort of his mother and brother, and was exceedingly jealous. So he went to where they were living and found that it was true, and his jealousy knew no bounds. And he said to his brother: "Brother, how came you by all these riches? Tell me, that I also may receive much money." And the younger brother told him at once, saying, "On such a hill you will find a Lion made of stone. Be not afraid, but go to him and ask him to fill a bucket with gold pieces for you also, and he will do so."

So the proud brother hasted and took the largest bucket that was in his house, and went as fast as the wind to the place that his brother had told him. And he found the Stone Lion, and the Lion, though unwilling, said to him just what he had said to the other brother, and the heart of the proud brother was exceeding glad, and he hasted and set underneath the great bucket, and the gold pieces dropped from the Lion's mouth even as his brother had said. And he said to himself: "I was a wise man to bring a great bucket, and I will see that it is well filled indeed." So he let the Lion drop gold into the great bucket until it rose in a heap in the middle over and above the brim. And then there fell just one gold piece too many, and it slipped upon the heap and ran over on to the ground. And the proud brother looked up, and saw that the finest and greatest lump of the whole was stuck in the jaws of the Lion, and he put out his hand into the Lion's jaws, and tried to take it, but the Lion's jaws shut tight upon his arm, and he remained caught; and he cried out a great deal, but no one could help him to get free.

And there he remained for many years, while at home his wife and children became very poor and everything in the house was spoiled or stolen. Still the proud brother could not get his arm out of the mouth of the Stone Lion.

Then, after many years, his wife came weeping to the Stone Lion and told him how all the house was ruined because her husband was still being held by the arm, and the Lion laughed to himself as he heard. And the wife went on with her sad tale, and the Lion was more and more glad, until at last he could not help opening his mouth and chuckling. And at once the proud brother pulled his arm away out of the Stone Lion's mouth and became free again.

But he had lost all his money, and from that day he was only able to beg his livelihood at the street corners, while his mother and his brother lived in comfort and luxury in their own house.

III

THE DEFORMED BOY

Once upon a time there was a Boy with a deformed head, and as soon as he was born, his father said that he was so ugly that he would never get any one to marry him, and so it happened. For no one would speak to him, and at last he went away by himself sadly, and kept cattle, and never saw the face of a man or a woman for a long time. Then there happened to him a strange thing. One day he was tending his herds by the side of a great lake, and a white drake came down from the sky toward him and settled upon the surface of the lake. And the bird swam three times all round the lake to the right, and three times all round the lake to the left, and after that the Boy caught the drake.

And the bird struggled to get away, but the Boy held him fast, and at last the drake told the Boy who he really was. Now the drake was no other than the King of the Fairies, and he promised to give the Boy any one of his three daughters to wife if only he would release him. And the Boy consented, and chose the daughter that was neither the eldest nor the youngest, but the middle one. So the drake flew away.

Then after a little time, the middle daughter of the Fairy King appeared, most beautifully dressed, and in her hand she carried jewels of priceless value. So the two were married, though the Fairy King's daughter foretold to her husband that she would be able to remain with him only nine years.

So for nine years everything went as happily as it could, and everything that the Boy wished to have was at once there ready for him, palaces and cattle and servants and silks and jewels. And he almost forgot that there had once been a time when no one would speak to him for his very ugliness.

But at the end of the nine years, the fairy princess vanished without warning, and with her vanished also all the palaces and cattle and servants and silks and jewels. So the Boy was heartbroken, and he went out to search throughout all the land for the princess, but he found her nowhere. Still he went on searching, and as he wandered he came one day to the side of a great lake, and it was the place where he had first seen the drake and won his bride nine years before.

And as he stayed to look he saw a huge nest in the rushes by the side of the lake, and he knew at once what it was. For there is nothing like the nest of a Gryphon in the world. Luckily for the Boy the big birds were away and only the young ones were in the nest, for the Gryphon eats a man at a single meal. And as he looked in terror lest the parent birds should return, there came up out of the lake a Dragon, and he crawled toward the nest to eat up the young Gryphons. Then the Boy ran toward the nest and fought with the Dragon, and at last toward night he killed it; and just then the parent Gryphons came home; and they saw the nest and the dead Dragon, and they could not thank the Boy enough who had saved their young ones from the Dragon.

Then the Boy told them all his sad story, and asked the Gryphons if they would help him, and they said that they would. So the Boy sat upon the back of the male Gryphon, and the Gryphon flew away with him up into the air for a long, long way until at last they reached the kingdom of the fairies. And they went into the kingdom.

Now if there is one thing which the fairies and the gods cannot abide it is the sight of a mortal in their kingdom, so they all called out to him that he must go. But he said: "I will not go except my wife come with me." And they all called out upon his boldness and foolhardiness, and told him that he was but a mortal and might never again mate with a fairy. But he held his ground and said, again and again, "I will not go except my wife come with me." And the fairies and the gods wearied themselves in crying out against him, but always he said the same thing and retreated not an inch.

So at last, in despair, the King of the Fairies (for he found that his middle daughter after all was glad at the thought that she would go back again and be the Boy's wife, although he was so ugly) said to her: "Go, then, with him, and never again show yourself here." And blithely then she went away with the Boy on the back of the Gryphon, and returned to the Boy's country, and there they lived happily ever afterwards.

APPENDIX G

MISCELLANEA

1. The origin of the name Tibet is phonetically curious. The inhabitants of the country spell its name "Bod." This, in accordance with the recognized rules of Tibetan pronunciation, they pronounce "Peu" (as in French, but with a phantom "d"). "Upper" in Tibetan is "Stod," which, for similar reasons, is pronounced "Teu." "Upper Tibet" as opposed to the lower districts to the north, east and west of Lhasa, is about conterminous with what we regard as Central Tibet. The pronunciation of "Teu-peu(d)" was crisped on the Darjeeling frontier into "Tibet," and thus became known to Europeans in this form.

The Chinese name for Lhasa is "Tsang." The two provinces of U (Lhasa) and Tsang (Tashi-lhunpo) are distinguished by them as Chien-tsang and Hou-tsang respectively.

2. Lhasa lies in N. latitude 29° 39′ 16″, and in E. longitude (Greenwich) 90° 57′ 13″. Its height above the sea is approximately 12,900 in feet.

3. I cannot refrain from inserting the following remark of a Chinese historian named Masu. In the I-shih, a work upon the Chinese empire in 160 books, he says, in reference to the fauna and flora of this country, "There is in Tibet a plant which flies. It resembles a dog in shape, its color is like tortoise-shell, and it is very tame. If lions or elephants see it they are frightened: hence it is the king of beasts." If there is really anything in the theory of the transmigration of souls, it is clear that Miss Sybil Corbet must have inherited that of Masu.

4. One of the earliest kings of Lhasa, it is interesting to note, was a practical socialist. Muni-tsanpo three times redistributed the

wealth of the country among its inhabitants, and three times he found it useless. The rich became richer, the poor even poorer, so he abandoned the scheme.

5. The names of MM. Tsybikoff and Norzunoff deserve to be mentioned in connection with Russia's policy of expansion in Tibet. The former is a Buriat of Trans-Baikalia who has visited Lhasa as the personal friend of Dorjieff. He took a series of good photographic views which have been published by the Russian Geographical Society. The latter is chiefly known for an unsuccessful attempt to join his colleague Dorjieff by crossing the frontier from Darjeeling. Neither of these men is of much political importance.

6. As illustrative of the influence which the Dalai Lama has over his present asylum, Urga, it is worth while to draw attention to the following story told by Sven Hedin. Some monk there had offended the Grand Lama of Lhasa, and twice the wretched man was compelled to make the journey from Urga to Lhasa—a three months' posting journey at the quickest—*upon his knees*. Then he was again compelled to perform the same penance only to find the Dalai Lama unrelenting, and the doors of the Sacred City shut upon him.

7. I append a rough translation of the extract from the Odyssey, which I have placed on the title-page. The coincidence is worth quoting:

> "Over the tides of Ocean on they pressed,
> On past the great White Rock beside the stream,
> On, till through God's high bastions east and west,
> They reached the plains with pale-starred iris dressed,
> And found at last the folk of whom men dream."

The Arabian Sea, Ta-karpo, the Himalayas, Gyantse, and the Lhasans seem prophesied here clearly enough.

8. In a blacksmith's shop in Phari, I found a man-trap very similar in construction to those but recently obsolete in England. The jaws were armed with the teeth of some huge fish, and the spring was provided by a strong yak-hair rope. The punishments inflicted by the Tibetans are abominably cruel. The wretched men attached to the Mission who were caught in Gyantse on the night of the 4th of May, were cut to pieces slowly in the "alternate" method,

and during the stay of the Mission at Kamba-jong an unhappy woman, convicted or suspected of adultery, had her nose and lips slit, and was afterward flogged to death. In a country where morality is of the loosest, this was simply inhuman. It is a Tibetan, not a Chinese custom. The "alternate" mutilation is of course Chinese also.

9. On the 16th of February I went for a two-day excursion with Major Ray down the valley of the Ammo chu. After a difficult climb through the rhododendron jungle nine or ten miles below Rinchengong we encamped across the Bhutanese frontier—which is here delimited by the clearly defined line of bamboo growth—in a "dmo" accouchement clearing in the bamboos, named Bolka. Unfortunately, in returning for the mules which were unable to climb further, Ray slipped in the darkness, and fell down the khud. He hurt his arm severely, and on the next day when we moved to the precipitous cliff of the Dé chu, he was not able to climb down, and we yielded to the protests of our servants. The head of the gorge lay immediately to the south of us, and from where we were we could see the extreme difficulty which would attend any attempt to carry the road from India through this locality at the level of the Ammo chu.

10. The Aryan foot is high in the instep, and the big toe projects from the others. The Tibetan foot is flat on the ground from end to end, and has three equally projecting toes which give a foot-print that is unmistakable. It is as square cornered as a brick, except that the heel is narrow.

11. The coldest temperatures we experienced were in January and February near the Tang la. At Chu-gya the thermometer was once observed to go down to 27° below zero (Fahrenheit), but there can be no doubt that had there been the means of taking regular records at this spot, this depth would often have been exceeded. The average temperature nightly at Phari was about —10° during January. The bitter wind over the Tang la of course made the sufferings of the troops infinitely greater, though the dryness of the air no doubt saved us from feeling the full effects of the frost.

12. The rarefaction of the air caused several curious phenomena. The sighting of our rifles on the back-sight was of course entirely

thrown out. A 1,350 range was correctly sighted at 1,050 during our stay at Gyantse (13,000 feet). At 15,000 feet the fusee springs of the Maxim had to be reduced from a seven and a half pound "pull" to four or even three and three-quarters. I have in the book referred to the action of the time fuses of shells at 17,000 feet. The Maxim water-jacket was of course merely a source of trouble until some one hit upon the device of filling it with a mixture of rum and water. Lubrication was also a trouble. The only safe course was found to be a thorough cleaning away of every speck of oil, and a substitution of black-lead.

In other directions also there was difficulty. Water boiled at about 180°, and as a result only Mussoor dal (lentils) would cook properly. Arhar, Moong or Chenna dal was alike useless. Wounds or scratches took an abnormal time to heal, owing to the oxygenless state of the air. Colonel Waddell did indeed try to obtain cylinders of oxygen for certain medical purposes, but they were found to be impossible of transport. Incidentally it may be remarked that for the same reason "instras"—of which the force took up a large number—failed to keep alight, to our great disappointment.

13. Heaven, to the Tibetan, is a vast structure composed of precious stones laid vertically, not horizontally, as in the Revelation. The north is gold, the east, white crystal, the south, Indranila, the west, Pemaraga or ruby. The colors therefore differ somewhat from the recognized Hindu distribution of colors to the quarters, of which the P. and O. houseflag is the best illustration.

14. The medical profession in Tibet is based exclusively upon Chinese practice. This is one of the puzzles of the East. It is naturally a matter of superstition and tradition alone, neither research nor the first requirements of cleanliness are used by the profession. The medicines they employ are in many cases grotesque, powdered lizards, dragon's blood, dry yellow dust, professing to be the remains of the Guru Rinpoche or some other distinguished teacher, the tiny powdered scrapings from a cup-mark, scraps of Daphne paper with charms printed upon them; all these are taken internally. Captain Walton, the surgeon of the Mission, tells me that the Tibetans responded willingly and gratefully to his invitations, and as he expressed it himself, if the expedition has done nothing else it has certainly improved the looks of no small number of the good people of Tibet; six or seven hundred cases in all of

harelip or cataract must have been treated by him alone.[1] The Amchi, or doctor, is a man greatly respected in Tibet. It was in this disguise that Manning was able to enter Lhasa, and the records of the Capuchins betray the fact that their services were in vastly greater request as physicians of the body than of the soul.

15. The brilliancy of the moonlight in Tibet was beyond all conception.

16. There is some little difficulty about the wording of the inscription on the Do-ring. In the journal of the Royal Asiatic Society, Vol. XII. N.S., a rubbing and a translation are given by Dr. Bushell, of which I have incorporated the latter in the text.

It is at once clear that the rubbing was not made from the Do-ring. The proportionate width of the rubbing to the length is about as 6 to 25. That of the Do-ring is about 2 to 3. Further, in the rubbing, the Tibetan and the Chinese versions are side by side in vertical columns. On the Do-ring the Chinese version fills the eastern face, the Tibetan the western. It is possible that the rubbing is taken from the duplicate copy of the lettering on the Do-ring which exists in the Amban's residence. In that case it is difficult to see how the four cup-marks on it have been caused, but the fact seems probable.

It is clear from the wording of the treaty in the rubbing that it was made at a time when "Te-chih-li-tsan" was reigning in Tibet, not "Koli-kotsu." Now Chilitsan (the "Te" is merely an official prefix—see Ti Rinpoche), or "Ralpachan," was reigning in 783 and "Koli-kotsu" or "Yi-tai" reigning in 822. It is therefore clear that this particular treaty dates from 783, not—as Dr. Bushell surmises—from 822.

But I have no doubt that there were at one time *two* treaties recorded on slabs outside the Jo-kang. Masu—who may be more accurate in archæology than he is in natural history—definitely states that there were two, both of the Tang period—one called Té-tsang, the other called Mu-tsang. These are the names, and this statement tallies with the dates, of the two emperors who in 783 and 822 made two distinct treaties with Tibet. Masu goes on to say that Mu-tsang is gone and only Té-tsang remains. If this be so, the Do-ring dates from 783 and the rubbing of Dr. Bushell must

[1] I remember his grimly speculating one day, during our bombardment in Gyantse, as to what his late patients must be doing who ran away from under his charge before the stitches had been taken out.

have been taken from some authentic copy, probably that kept at the Chinese Residency, for it is clear that the text of the rubbing refers to 783.

17. Further examination of the case of Moorcroft merely increases the mystery. It seems that every foreigner connected with the matter was put away. It is difficult to suppose that Moorcroft himself, Trebeck, Guthrie—a native assistant of Moorcroft's—and Mir Izzat Allah, a confidential servant, all died within a year by a mere series of coincidences. No one was with Moorcroft when he was reported to be killed. Trebeck never saw the body which was interred at Balkh; it was probably frightfully decomposed by this time.

The story I have referred to in the first volume was corroborated and given to Huc in a more detailed form by Nisan himself, Moorcroft's servant, in Lhasa, eight years after it had occurred, and he there added a fact which seems to destroy the only obvious reconciliation of the opposing versions of Moorcroft's death. It will at once occur to any one who studies the matter that Moorcroft's papers and effects might have been looted by a Kashmiri traveling to Lhasa, and that the whole story may have arisen from a discovery of this loot in the Kashmiri's kit when he was himself murdered on his return journey.

But Nisan's statement was direct that Moorcroft, before leaving Lhasa, gave him a "chit" or letter of recommendation to some one unknown in Calcutta. The letter was written in English characters, and, as he gave it to Nisan, Moorcroft remarked that if he ever found himself in Calcutta the note would serve him in good stead.

I might suggest to any one who may have the opportunity of doing so that an exhumation of the corpse buried at Balkh as Moorcroft's would settle the matter at once. It might also be a good thing to remove altogether the remains of an Englishman from a place where they have for so long been treated with disrespect. If the skull is that of a European the body is Moorcroft's. If it is that of a native, there will arise a strong probability that the story Huc tells had at least some basis of fact. I should add that so great was the anger in Lhasa over the discovery of Moorcroft's notes and maps, that Nisan destroyed the "chit" lest in some way it should incriminate him.

18. I had not properly read my Marco Polo ("Yule's" latest edition), when I wrote that I could not understand the reference

to the "flesh-licking" yak. The emperor, Humaion himself, told the Turkish admiral, Sidi Ali, that when a yak had knocked a man down, it skinned him from head to heels by licking him with his tongue.

19. I have not drawn sufficient attention in these pages to the danger with which any decrease of our prestige in Lhasa threatens our best recruiting ground—Nepal. The Gurkhas, who are the mainstay of all our hill operations in the North-West, would be the first object of any foreign hostility in Lhasa which still exercises considerable spiritual ascendancy over their races. The excellent work of the 8th Gurkhas, who had been brought almost to perfection by Major Row, and the opportunity of active service, demands mention in this record, though in general I have avoided singling out officers or men for especial comment.

20. In Tibet, only the members of the family are carried out to burial through the door. Others dying in the house are put through a window. In the Chumbi Valley the dead are cremated in a sitting posture. Some important persons in Tibet are cast after death into the Yam-dok tso, others—especially lamas—are reduced to a mere cuticle and enshrined in chortens. The enormous majority are hacked in pieces and given to the pigs, dogs, and vultures.

APPENDIX H

RIDE FROM LHASA

The following bare record of the times of a ride from Lhasa to Darjeeling may, perhaps, be of some small interest. As I have said, the question of the real nearness to India of Lhasa in point of time was one which the authorities were anxious to decide. With a led horse apiece, and with very small kit, a well-found body of men would occupy about the time that I took myself in coming down from Lhasa to Darjeeling. The distances given are those by the shortest route. This was not always available for myself.

	MILES.	
First day:—		
Left Lhasa, 5.36 a.m.		
Arrived Tölung Bridge, 6.55.		
Last view Chorten, 7.22.		
Great Buddha, 8.............		Stayed twenty minutes at Nethang.
First spur, 9.15.		
Spy Hole Rock, 10.12.		
Nam, 10.37.		
Chusul, 2.15 p.m..............		Stayed half-an-hour.
Pome-tse, 3.40.		
Chak-sam Ferry, 4.40.	42	River in flood; an average crossing would be about 20 men per hour.
Second day:—		
Left Chak-sam, 6.45 a.m.		
Arrived Kamba-partsi, 8.35....		Stayed twenty-five minutes.
Top of Kamba la, 11.56.		
Pe-di jong, 4.10 p.m.	27	
Third day:—		
Left Pe-di jong, 8.50 a.m.		
Arrived Kal-sang Sampa, 9.57.		
Arrived Nagartse, 12.40 p.m.	17	

	MILES.	
Fourth day:—		
Left Nagartse, 7.7 a.m.		
Arrived at the Tibetan Wall, 11.0.		
Arrived Karo la, 12 noon.....		Stayed half-an-hour.
Arrived, Ra-lung, 4.19 p.m.	27	
Fifth day:—		
Left Ra-lung, 6.20 a.m.		
Arrived Long-ma, 8.40.		
Arrived Gobshi, 10.50........		Stayed half-an-hour.
Arrived Gyantse, 4.7 p.m.	33	
Sixth day:—		
Left Gyantse, 5.35 a.m.		
Arrived Saugang, 9.20........		Stayed an hour.
Arrived Kang-ma, 2.20 p.m...		Stayed three-quarters of an hour.
Arrived Menza Pass, 7.16.	44	
Seventh day:—		
Left Menza, 5.20 a.m.		
Arrived Kala tso, 8.7.........		Stayed an hour and a quarter.
Arrived Dochen, 12.40 p.m....		Stayed forty minutes.
Arrived Tuna, 5.5.	42	
Eighth day:—		
Left Tuna, 7.5 a.m.		
Arrived Tang la Post, 10.2.....		Stayed eighteen minutes.
Arrived Phari, 11.32...........		Stayed an hour and twenty minutes.
Arrived Dota, 4.35 p.m.	35	
Ninth day:—		
Left Dota, 7.20 a.m.		
Arrived Gau tso, 9.20........		Stayed fifty minutes. Met large convoy on road, which delayed pace considerably.
Arrived Chumbi, 1.45 p.m.....		Stayed an hour and a half.
Arrived Chumbi-tang, 7.15.	31	
Tenth day:—		
Left Chumbi-tang, 6.50 a.m.		
Arrived Natu la, 8.36...........		Nine days five hours to frontier.
Arrived Changu, 11.45..........		Stayed fifty minutes. Raining till I reached Gangtok.
Arrived Karponang, 4.15 p.m....		Stayed half-an-hour.
Arrived Gangtok, 9.12.	32	

	MILES.	
Eleventh day:—		
Left Gangtok, 7.10 a.m.		
Arrived Bridge, 8.30.		
Arrived Rang-po, 1 p.m........		Stayed an hour.
Arrived Tista Bridge, 4.50......		Raining.
Arrived Pashok, 6.5.	41	
Last day:—		
Left Pashok, 5.50 a.m..........		Raining.
Arrived railway station, Ghoom, 8.46.	15	Eleven days three hours and ten minutes from Lhasa.

I reached the hotel at Darjeeling at 10. I may add that I reached Simla at 4.15 on the afternoon of the fifteenth day, and London on the evening of the thirty-fifth day.

APPENDIX I

THE following honors and promotions were awarded in recognition of services in connection with the Tibet Mission:

To be K.C.I.E.

Major Francis Edward Younghusband, C.I.E., British Commissioner.

Major and Brevet Colonel James Ronald Leslie Macdonald, C.B., R.E., in command of the Escort.

To be C.I.E.

John Claude White, Esq., Assistant to British Commissioner.

Captain William Frederick Travers O'Connor, R.A., Secretary to British Commissioner.

Lionel Truninger, Esq., Chief Telegraph Officer.

To be C.M.G.

Ernest Colville Collins Wilton, Esq., His Majesty's Vice-Consul at Chungking.

To be C.B.

Lieutenant-Colonel and Brevet Colonel Hastings Read, Indian Army.

Lieutenant-Colonel Lawrence Augustine Waddell, M.B., C.I.E., Indian Medical Service.

Lieutenant-Colonel Edward Joshua Cooper, D.S.O., Royal Fusiliers.

Lieutenant-Colonel Arthur Fountaine Hogge, Indian Army.

Lieutenant-Colonel Mark Ancrum Kerr, Indian Army.

Lieutenant-Colonel Herbert Ralph Brander, Indian Army.

To be D.S.O.

Major Alexander Mullaly, Indian Army.
Major Frank Murray, Indian Army.
Major Robert Cobb Lye, Indian Army.
Major MacCarthy Reagh Emmet Ray, Indian Army.
Captain Charles Hesketh Grant Moore, Indian Army.
Captain Thomas Mawe Luke, Royal Artillery.
Captain Julian Lawrence Fisher, Royal Fusiliers.
Captain Dashwood William Harrington Humphreys, Indian Army.
Lieutenant George Cecil Hodgson, Indian Army.

Brevet

To be Colonel

Lieutenant-Colonel Frederick Campbell, D.S.O., Indian Army.

To be Lieutenant-Colonels

Captain and Brevet Major William George Lawrence Beynon, D.S.O., Indian Army.
Major Richard Woodfield Fuller, Royal Artillery.
Major Herbert Augustus Iggulden, the Sherwood Foresters (Nottinghamshire and Derbyshire Regiment).

To be Majors

Captain Seymour Hulbert Sheppard, D.S.O., Royal Engineers.
Captain William John Ottley, Indian Army.

The following officers had been brought to notice by Brigadier-General J. R. L. Macdonald, C.B., as deserving of special approval for their services with the military forces attached to the Tibet Mission:

Staff.—Colonel H. Read, Indian Army, commanding Line of Communications; Major H. A. Iggulden, Nottinghamshire and Derbyshire Regiment, D.A.A.G.; Brevet Major W. G. L. Beynon, D.S.O., 2nd Batt. 3rd Gurkhas, D.A.Q.M.G.; Major J. M. Stewart, 2nd Batt. 5th Gurkhas, Special Service Officer Line of Communications; Major M. R. E. Ray, 7th Rajputs, D.A.Q.M.G.; Major J. O'B. Minogue, West Yorkshire Regiment, D.A.A.G.; and Lieutenant B. H. Bignell, 117th Mahrattas.

Royal Artillery.—Major R. W. Fuller, No. 7 Mountain Battery R.G.A.; Captain F. A. Easton, No. 7 Mountain Battery R.G.A.; and Captain T. M. Luke, No. 73 Company R.G.A.

Royal Engineers.—Major C. H. Heycock, 2nd Company Sappers and Miners; Captain C. H. D. Ryder, Survey Officer; Captain S. H. Sheppard, D.S.O., 1st Company Sappers; Captain C. Elliott, Field Engineer; and Lieutenant J. A. McEnery, Assistant Field Engineer.

The Queen's Royal West Surrey Regiment.—Captain G. H. Neale, Transport Officer.

Royal Fusiliers.—Colonel E. J. Cooper, D.S.O., Captain J. L. Fisher, and Captain C. A. H. Palairet.

Norfolk Regiment.—Lieutenant A. L. Hadow, commanding Machine Gun Section.

Royal Highlanders.—Captain J. B. Pollock Morris, Transport Officer.

14th Murray's Jat Lancers.—Captain H. M. W. Souter, Transport Officer.

19th Punjabis.—Major L. N. Herbert.

23rd Sikh Pioneers.—Lieutenant-Colonel A. F. Hogge, Major R. C. Lye, Captain H. F. A. Pearson, and Captain W. J. Ottley (commanding Mounted Infantry Company).

32nd Sikh Pioneers.—Lieutenant-Colonel H. R. Brander, Major F. H. Peterson, D.S.O., Captain E. H. S. Cullen, and Lieutenant G. C. Hodgson.

40th Pathans.—Lieutenant-Colonel F. Campbell, D.S.O., Captain T. R. Maclachlan, and Captain G. A. Preston.

46th Punjabis.—Captain C. H. Peterson (commanding Mounted Infantry Company).

2nd Batt. 2nd Gurkhas.—Captain F. G. C. Ross, Transport Officer.

8th Gurkha Rifles.—Lieutenant-Colonel M. A. Kerr, Major F. Murray, Captains C. Bliss and D. W. H. Humphreys, and Lieutenant J. D. Grant.

Supply and Transport Corps.—Major A. Mullaly, Captains C. H. G. Moore and H. H. Roddy, and Lieutenant W. Dunlop.

Royal Army Medical Corps.—Major A. R. Aldridge.

Indian Medical Corps.—Lieutenant-Colonel L. A. Waddell, C.I.E., Major C. N. C. Wimberly, and Captain T. B. Kelly.

Army Veterinary Department.—Captain R. C. Moore.

Volunteer Nursing Sister A. Taylor.

APPENDIX K

THE POLITICAL RESULTS OF THE MISSION

I HAVE waited till the last moment to sum up the results of the Mission in order to include the latest possible phase. At the moment of the publication of this book there still remains much to be done, if the full benefit of the expedition is to be reaped; but already matters have arranged themselves in a more satisfactory manner than at one time seemed likely, and though the ultimate action of the Dalai Lama is an unknown factor of the highest importance, it is now possible to forecast with some certainty the effect which any action of his or of the Chinese will have upon our own position in the country.

After tedious and prolonged discussion during the month of August, Colonel Younghusband determined to bring matters to a head, the more so as General Macdonald was pressing him to retire from Lhasa. The first serious hint of his determination to delay no longer was enough, and with the assistance of the Amban himself, the Nepalese Resident, and the Tongsa Penlop, the representatives of Tibet agreed to sign, and actually did sign, on the seventh of September the long-demanded Treaty. The ceremony of affixing the seals of the Dalai Lama, of the Sen-dé-gye-sum and of the Tsong-du, took place with all possible solemnity in the hall of the Potala Palace, in the presence of a large gathering of all the more important officers and officials on either side. In form the Treaty corresponded closely with that which I have already sketched out on pages 224 and 225. One important clause there was, however, to which special attention must be drawn. The indemnity demanded by the British Commissioner—this question having been left entirely to him—was adjusted so that the Tibetans should pay about one-half of the expense to which the Indian Government had been put in its effort to come to a final and amicable arrangement with its Tibetan neighbors. This sum was, as at first arranged with the Chinese Resident—who thought it an entirely inadequate demand—to be paid within a period of three years, but at the dismayed protest of the Tibetans, Colonel Younghusband at last consented to adopt their own suggestion and accept payment in seventy-five annual instalments. In return for this, they willingly consented that the Indian Government should hold the Chumbi Valley as a security till the debt was paid off.

This, it must be remembered, was the Tibetans' own suggestion, and it is not surprising that they looked upon this occupation with unconcern. The Chumbi Valley is of no importance to Tibet; it was wrested by them from what is now an Indian Native State, and from the point of view of value, agricultural, mineral, or otherwise, the valley is an insignificant property. Its whole value lies in the fact that it is the Lobby joining the two great Houses of India and Tibet. There was, therefore, no difficulty in making this arrangement, so far at least as our late opponents were concerned. But there was violent opposition at home. As I have said before, the Home Government had repeated their assurances to Russia that we had no intention of annexing Tibetan territory. In June, this pledge was not regarded by the Cabinet as interfering with any mortgage to us of the Chumbi Valley, even if we admitted that the soil of it properly belonged to them at all. But a certain deference to the susceptibilities of Russia—it is hard to pick the right words to describe the attitude of ministers at this time—now intervened, and the fact that by the Tibetans' own deliberate action a state of war between them and ourselves had taken the place of the previous peaceful relations to which the assurances had referred, was not regarded as affecting the status of these voluntary undertakings. They were even construed with greater rigidity than before.

The agreement, therefore, to which the Commissioner has signed his name has now to be modified lest Russia should resent what she might regard in us, if not as a positive act of bad faith, at least as a want of delicacy of conscience in ultra-Asian affairs. There is no doubt much to be said from this somewhat cynical point of view, and the fact that it received the support of our representatives in St. Petersburg lends to it considerable weight. The Treaty, therefore, is still awaiting ratification so far as the suzerain power is concerned, but it cannot be too widely remembered that, as against the Tibetans themselves, the Treaty, in the form in which they themselves agreed to its terms, is a valid document, and if China should attempt to evade its formal ratification—subject of course to such acts of remission in the terms as we may and, no doubt, shall think it advisable to grant—her action must inevitably be construed as a *pro tanto* renunciation of her rights of suzerainty over Tibet. This, however, is not really to be feared. We have acted throughout with the cordial assent and advice of the Wai-wu-pu, and China has already reaped no small advantage from our vigorous action. In addition, she has committed herself to support of our policy by no less significant an action than the deposition of the Dalai Lama from his temporal authority by proclamation of the Amban in Lhasa on September 11th.

This action deserves some notice. It is by no means the first time that the Celestial Government has found itself obliged to interfere with even the sacrosanct position of the Tibetan pontiff. In 1706 Lo zang rin-chen tsang-yang gya-tso was beheaded at Dam, and his successor was degraded and exiled by the Chinese conquerors for fourteen years. Whether it was the latter's private or public demoralization which offended his new suzerains, it is clear that no protest was ever raised by the people of Tibet, either then or eight years later, when His Holiness was again cast into prison for the murder of the Chinese "Regent."

But Tubdan gyatso is no ordinary man. He is fully aware of the almost irresistible influence which his incarnate self possesses over a country trained in the narrow school of Lamaism, and if he does not choose to accept his demission, he may find strong support, especially among the outlying portions of his spiritual kingdom. In Lhasa itself his absence will probably be little regretted, and should he again put himself within the grasp of the hierarchy which he has so deeply offended, the chance of his escaping the poison which always lies handy to secure the devolution of Avalokiteswara's spirit is small indeed.

In the event of his assassination or continued exile, the results of the Mission will have been indirectly achieved, for Tubdan gyatso is the only man of his own way of thinking among the greater dignities of Tibet. If, on the other hand, he can force his way single-handed back to power and reinstate Dorjieff, the Russophile tendencies of Tibetan politics will of course be redoubled, and we may again have to intervene to put things again upon a proper footing. But Russian influence in Eastern Asia has naturally waned, and the Grand Lama has gone to the very place where the real lesson of the Japanese war will have been perceived and assimilated more perhaps than anywhere else in the dominions of China, and the recent foolish Russian restrictions upon the Baikalia will have had time to bring about a different estimate also of Russia's real sympathy with the faith of which he is the divine head. Kiakhta, which is said to be his present residence, is on the Siberian frontier less than a hundred miles from Missovaia on Lake Baikal and the railway.

The temporary, almost nominal, Government which we helped the Chinese to set up in Lhasa may almost be dismissed from consideration, except in so far as the Three Monasteries are concerned. The Tashi Lama—for whom we secured the temporary ascendancy in things spiritual and, provisionally, in things temporal also—has had no intention even of leaving his secure retreat at Tashi-lhunpo to risk the unpopularity, impotence, and personal danger which he would surely meet with in Lhasa. The jealousy between the two capitals still plays a most important part in Tibetan politics, and this deliberate challenge on our part was intended rather to set the Tibetans thinking than to achieve any immediate re-devolution to Tashi-lhunpo of the power of which, as we have seen, she was deprived by Lhasa in the seventeenth century. The Chinese Amban may also be omitted from our estimates. He is powerless to vindicate his Emperor's suzerainty or influence Tibetan counsels in any way. His very life is insecure.

In the hands of the Three Monasteries, therefore, lies all the power at this moment, and their bitter hostility to foreign influence of any kind is the strongest guarantee we have that no further philanderings with Russia will be allowed to go on. This, after all, is our chief aim. All other considerations are of insignificant importance, and we are willing on our part to co-operate with the Tibetans on our side of the frontier to keep unauthorized persons from visiting Tibet, provided of course that an equally strict isolation is enforced on all other frontiers.

We have not made ourselves beloved by the Lamaic hierarchy, but their grudging respect we have won, and that for an understanding with an Eastern oligarchy is a better basis than love. How important that understanding is for India I have before in these pages attempted to show, and at the approaching conference in Calcutta with Tang—the Chinese special envoy sent to discuss the terms of the Tibetan Treaty—Lord Curzon may be trusted to safeguard the advantages we have now fairly gained.

I have just said that in dealing with an Eastern political oligarchy affection counts for little. But I should be sorry to lay down my pen without re-stating in this connection that in almost every other department of Oriental life it counts for much indeed, and herein—in the slowly spreading influence which the first acquaintance with Englishmen must have among the mass of the Tibetan people—in their memory of our fair dealing—in their gratitude for sick tended and wounded made whole—perhaps even in return for the blow we have unintentionally struck at the spiritual fetters which bind them down—in these we may perhaps find in the end a greater advantage to that vast Asian Empire for which we have made ourselves responsible, than any secured by the mere letter of the Treaty as it will eventually be interpreted and modified.